Professionalization of Foreign Policy

Michael Haas

Professionalization of Foreign Policy

Transformation of Operational Code Analysis

Foreword and Afterword by David O. Wilkinson

Michael Haas
Emeritus Professor of Political Science
Los Angeles, CA, USA

ISBN 978-3-031-37151-6   ISBN 978-3-031-37152-3   (eBook)
https://doi.org/10.1007/978-3-031-37152-3

© The Editor(s) (if applicable) and The Author(s), under exclusive license to Springer Nature Switzerland AG 2023

This work is subject to copyright. All rights are solely and exclusively licensed by the Publisher, whether the whole or part of the material is concerned, specifically the rights of translation, reprinting, reuse of illustrations, recitation, broadcasting, reproduction on microfilms or in any other physical way, and transmission or information storage and retrieval, electronic adaptation, computer software, or by similar or dissimilar methodology now known or hereafter developed.
The use of general descriptive names, registered names, trademarks, service marks, etc. in this publication does not imply, even in the absence of a specific statement, that such names are exempt from the relevant protective laws and regulations and therefore free for general use.
The publisher, the authors, and the editors are safe to assume that the advice and information in this book are believed to be true and accurate at the date of publication. Neither the publisher nor the authors or the editors give a warranty, expressed or implied, with respect to the material contained herein or for any errors or omissions that may have been made. The publisher remains neutral with regard to jurisdictional claims in published maps and institutional affiliations.

Cover credit: @Ali Kahfi

This Palgrave Macmillan imprint is published by the registered company Springer Nature Switzerland AG
The registered company address is: Gewerbestrasse 11, 6330 Cham, Switzerland

Foreword

Michael Haas has written an excellent and challenging book on the professionalization of foreign policy. But why should we want to professionalize foreign policy decision-making? How can this be done? Who needs this, and who can supply it? And is foreign policy not in any case professionalized already?

Haas contends that American foreign policy has long been characterized by high-level blundering. Recent memories of the U.S. failures in reforming and in abandoning Afghanistan, misunderstanding and mismanaging Iraq under and after Saddam Hussein, and disbelieving in and underpreparing against Russian president Putin's determination to extend and deepen his 2014 war against Ukraine, need to be enlarged by looking backward over more than a generation; and Michael Haas has begun this needed work.

Professionalization in a society valuing democracy, for Haas, requires some form of democratic, i.e., public, participation in foreign policy decision-making. But how?

Haas elects to employ the tool of "Options Analysis." Full Disclosure: I delivered a paper in which I developed this subject, rather a long while ago, and I find its use—and its significant extension—by Michael Haas to be more than I then hoped for or could hope for.

As a historical footnote: I was supported in the development of Options Analysis by UCLA's short-lived (1969–c. 1974) "Center for Computer-based Behavioral Studies," under the aegis of Gerald Shure.

vi FOREWORD

Shure's vision of a future of interactive inter-human online computing has been so well realized as to have become routinized and perhaps even obsolescent; we may now look forward to a world that may delegate analytic and even diplomatic tasks to artificial intellects.

For the nonce, however, we may permit ourselves to monopolize both analysis and diplomacy. Haas sees particular value for decentralized use of Options Analysis to minimize "groupthink" in foreign policy decision-making. Groupthink has been notably studied by William H. Whyte Jr. (1952), Irving Janis (1971, 1972), and many others since 1972, but despite recognition, diagnosis, and therapeutic proposals, groupthink in high places continues unabated, as witness the cited us foreign policy failures in Iraq, Afghanistan, and Ukraine.

Perhaps the democratization of Options Analysis can serve as an organizational corrective to high-level collective delusionality in foreign policy decision-making. Michael Haas believes so; I would like to do the same. But the keys are not held alone by Haas or by me. They are widely distributed; you, the reader, also hold them. Are you persuaded? Read and judge!

Political Scientist, University of
California, Los Angeles, USA

David O. Wilkinson

References

Janis, Irving. 1971. Groupthink. *Psychology Today* 43 (6): 74–76.

Janis, Irving. 1972. *Victims of Groupthink: A Psychological Study of Foreign Policy Decisions and Fiascoes*. Boston: Houghton Mifflin.

Whyte, William H., Jr. 1952. Groupthink. *Fortune*, March, pp. 114–117, 142, 146.

PREFACE

The most professional foreign policy decision ever made occurred after the Cold War, when pressure existed to cut the budget of the U.S. Department of Defense: Staff members then compiled a matrix consisting of a list of criteria to apply in the left column and an enumeration of all military bases as options for possible closure in the right columns. Using the Decision Pad program, they were able to rank each base from least to most important on the criteria and shut down several bases as a result (USGAO 1993). I did not know about the decision when I used the same methodology in studying why the United States funded the Khmer Rouge during the 1980s (Haas 1991). I only found out by a Google search of "Decision Pad" while writing the present volume, which proposes the same professionalization, known as Options Analysis, for all foreign policy decisions in the future.

In order to make the case for Options Analysis, the present book culminates a very long historiography. For a century, scholars have lamented that key foreign policy decisions are generally made by government leaders with little input from the public (Lerche 1967: 44–57; Miller and Stokes 1963; Rosenberg 1965; Miller 1967; Holsti 2006: PtII). Important facts in policy deliberations are withheld from the people due to "national security" secrecy, so leaders often consider the public as manipulable and label critics of their decisions as uniformed. The public, nevertheless, is likely to react when policies are viewed as incorrect for many reasons—but unfortunately after the decisions have been made.

vii

viii PREFACE

In the case of the atom bomb dropped on Hiroshima, for example, a simple media mistranslation of *mokusatsu* has been blamed for the use of a weapon that now haunts the world (Zanettin 2016; cf. Naimushin 2021).

Foreign policy analysis began after World War I within international relations, a subfield of political science, because scholars believed that foreign policy decisions should be made democratically (Bryce 1921). However, the public has made little progress in holding foreign policy decision-makers accountable, and scholarship has made little impact on the foreign policy process. Mass protests against the American intrusion into the civil war in Vietnam proved to be the only way the public could demand a president to stop an ill-conceived decision.

Throughout my career I have identified American foreign policy mistakes, seeking to understand why they were made and what could be done to avoid them. In my research on the Cambodian peace process, for example (Haas 1991, 2020a), I learned that the administrations of Jimmy Carter and Ronald Reagan diplomatically supported and financially bankrolled the Khmer Rouge after Vietnam liberated the people of Cambodia from genocide—and Washington refused to allow the Security Council to answer Hanoi's plea for the United Nations to bring peace to the country. Later, I discovered that North Korea leaders developed nuclear weapons despite their repeated efforts to achieve peace that have been rebuffed by almost every administration in Washington (Haas 2018). Even today, media reports characterize North Korean missile tests as "provocative," even though they are in fact responses to aggressive military exercises involving Japan, South Korea, and the United States that simulate conquest over North Korea (Klingner 2022; Al Jazeera 2022).

Analyses of foreign policy decisions have multiplied over the years, with many scholars adding important incremental insights. Textbooks have presented alternative perspectives as a maze leading nowhere. But one of the most interesting and practical essays is an unpublished paper by David Wilkinson (1977), which inspired me herein to undertake Options Analysis. He also deserves credit for making helpful suggestions that are incorporated in the volume.

The present volume has the aim of professionalizing foreign policy decision-making, not just for scholars but also for those who make policies at the highest levels of government. Too many blunders and mistakes have been made, so the process needs improvement. The proposal presented

PREFACE   ix

herein will definitely be successful in improving how foreign policy decisions are made because what is proposed is to undertake foreign policy analysis in a more thorough manner than has ever before been attempted.

The first part of the book is a review of earlier approaches to foreign policy analysis, beginning with the familiar dichotomy between emotional and rational ways in which foreign policy decisions are made. Next, structural theory and perfectibility theory are examined, followed by a discussion of nineteenth-century approaches, including theories developed during the Industrial Revolution, and the impact of World War I, a conflict that almost every analysis agrees could have been prevented. In Chapter 2, the focus is on efforts to utilize social science approaches to the study of foreign policy decision-making after World War II, including "pre-theory" that developed conceptual schemes but lacked a well-developed theoretical approach. Chapter 3 then places the various concepts into a 4x4 framework, which identifies four ways of defining a situation (affective, cognitive, evaluative, structural) at each of the four phases of the decision-making cycle (prestimulus, stimulus, information-processing, and outcome). Then, each of 32 well-documented decisions is scored on the basis of the 16 conceptual nodes, with the outcome "decision for war" as the main dependent variable. The scores for each decision are then subjected to factor analysis, yielding several decision-making clusters. Variables on the most important clusters are then regressed against the "decision for war" factor in three causal frameworks. The result is a conclusion that decisions of one country to go to war with another country are primarily due to cultural dissimilarity between the two countries.

Part II then unpacks the importance of cultural dissimilarity by identifying the concept of operational code, which was originally developed by Nathan Leites (1951, 1953) to explain why the perspectives of the Soviet Union were so different from those of Western countries; his aim was to improve how decision-makers in Washington would interpret actions and words coming from Moscow. Nevertheless, research on operational codes floundered in subsequent decades. The main problem was an inability to discern the meaning of the word "code" in anthropological terms. A critique of several alternative formulations is presented, pointing out that various scholars tried to construct structural codes for decision-makers rather than developing a methodology to improve foreign policy decisions that would operationalize cultural elements.

x PREFACE

Part III then develops Options Analysis by showing how operational codes can be defined as the relative importance that decision-makers place on various foreign policy criteria. The result transforms operational code analysis.

For decades during the Cold War, such foreign policy scholars as Henry Kissinger and Zbigniew Brzezinski preferred "realist" criteria over "idealist" criteria, with the resulting foolish entry into the civil war in Vietnam and siding with the Khmer Rouge. But the Cold War is over. Writing after the end of the Cold War, I once argued that such a contrast was outdated by considerations of such matters as democracy, the economy, the environment, and human rights (Haas 1997).

The four main considerations in any foreign policy decision, as I first indicated in my writings about Cambodia, are whether a decision will enhance a country's power, wealth, or prestige, and whether the execution of a decision is feasible (Haas 1991). I later linked subcriteria for the four considerations to major paradigms in social science research (Haas 2020b).

Options Analysis focuses on the tendency for leaders to choose limited criteria pointing to peculiar courses of action, often failing to consider more sensible options. The key to providing a more professional form of Options Analysis for foreign policy decision-makers is to determine how well each of several foreign policy options accomplish the four criteria and subcriteria. The computer program Decision Pad is designed to find the ranking of options after weights are assigned to the subcriteria and each option is appraised by the extent to which each option satisfies the subcriteria. To illustrate how Options Analysis can be conducted, three studies are provided. One is to determine why the United States funded the Khmer Rouge in the 1980s. The second example evaluates why a decision was made that in effect allowed North Korea to develop nuclear weapons. The third case study is an evaluation of options chosen by President Joe Biden, Jr., in connection with the Russian attack on Ukraine.

The final chapter concludes that Options Analysis enables decision-makers to professionalize how they choose among various alternative politics. What emerges will also enable scholars to make valuable contributions to ongoing challenges of foreign policy decision-makers.

Those familiar with my previous work will note that I am merging portions of three previous studies into one compact volume. Although rewritten, much of Part I previously appeared within Part II of my book *International Conflict* (1974). Part II herein rewrites my essay entitled

"Operational Codes in Foreign Policy: A Deconstruction," which was published in 2020 on the online website of the *Oxford Research Encyclopedia in International Studies*. Part III relies on the initial formulation of Options Analysis and the application to American policy toward the Khmer Rouge, which appeared in Chapter 5 of my *Cambodia, Pol Pot, and the United States: The Faustian Pact* (1991; 2nd edition, 2020a). I also use material from my *United States Diplomacy with North Korea and Vietnam: Explaining Failure and Success* (2018) and brand new material about the Ukraine War that erupted in 2022. To reprint some of the material, I am grateful to Macmillan, Oxford University Press, and ABC-CLIO Praeger.

The purpose of the present book is to inform both scholars and practitioners that there is a way to avoid groupthink and other traps that lead to foreign policy blunders. The remedy is to assess how multiple options achieve various goals of foreign policy. Scholars can do so by teaming together to make recommendations. Practitioners can learn how different members of a group can get together, make independent assessments, and then join together in group discussions to reach consensus before providing recommendations to the current secretary of state and president of the United States and their counterparts abroad. Such professionalization should ensure that very few further blunders will occur in future foreign policy decisions.

Political Scientist, Los Angeles,   Michael Haas
USA

References

Al Jazeera. 2022. N Korea Warns of 'All-Out' Nuclear Response to US 'Aggression'. November 19. https://www.aljazeera.com/news/2022/11/19/north-korea-warns-of-all-out-nuclear-response-to-us-provocation.

Bryce, James. 1921. *Modern Democracies*. London: Macmillan.

Haas, Michael. 1974. *International Conflict*. Indianapolis: Bobbs-Merrill.

Haas, Michael. 1991. *Cambodia, Pol Pot, and the United States: The Faustian Pact*. New York: Praeger.

Haas, Michael. 1997. International Communitarianism: The New Agenda of World Politics. In *Deconstructing International Relations Theory*, ed. Michael Haas, 102–126. New York: Norton.

Haas, Michael. 2018. *United States Diplomacy with North Korea and Vietnam: Explaining Failure and Success*. New York: Peter Lang.

Haas, Michael. 2020a. *Cambodia, Pol Pot, and the United States: The Faustian Pact*, 2nd ed. Los Angeles: Publishing house for Scholars.

Haas, Michael. 2020b. Operational Codes in Foreign Policy: A Deconstruction. *Oxford Research Encyclopedia in International Studies*. June. https://doi.org/10.1093/acrefore/9780190846626.013.5.

Holsti, Ole R. 2006. *Making American Foreign Policy*. New York: Routledge.

Klingner, Bruce. 2022. The Troubling New Changes to North Korea's Nuclear Doctrine. October 17. https://www.heritage.org/asia/report/the-troubling-new-changes-north-koreas-nuclear-doctrine.

Leites, Nathan. 1951. *The Operational Code of the Politburo*. New York: McGraw Hill.

Leites, Nathan. 1953. *A Study of Bolshevism*. Glencoe, IL: Free Press.

Lerche, Charles O., Jr. 1967. *Foreign Policy of the American People*, 3rd ed. Englewood Cliffs, NJ: Prentice-Hall.

Miller, Warren E. 1967. Voting and Foreign Policy. In *Domestic Sources of Foreign Policy*, ed. James N. Rosenau, 213–230. New York: Free Press.

Miller, Warren E., and Donald Stokes. 1963. Constituency Influence in Congress. *American Political Science Review* 57 (1): 45–56.

Naimushin, Boris. 2021. Hiroshima, Mokusatsu and Alleged Mistranslations. *English Studies at New Bulgarian University* 7 (1): 87–96.

Rosenberg, Milton J. 1965. Images in Relations to the Policy Process: American Public Opinion on Cold War Issues. In *International Behavior*, ed. Herbert C. Kelman, 278–334. New York: Holt, Rinehart, Winston.

United States, General Accounting Office. 1993. Analysis of DOD's Recommendations and Selection Process for Closures and Realignments. April 15. https://www.gao.gov/assets/nsiad-93-173.pdf.

Wilkinson, David O. 1977. Options Analysis: A Technique for the Analysis of Conflict-and-Bargaining Interactions. Paper presented at the annual conference of International Studies Association, Western Branch.

Zanettin, Federico. 2016. 'The Deadliest Error': Translation, International Relations and the News Media. *The Translator* 22 (3): 303–318.

CONTENTS

Part I   Approaches to the Study of Foreign Policy

1   Early Approaches to the Study of Foreign Policy   5
Early Philosophical Approaches   6
   Dualistic Approach: Emotion and Reason   6
   Augustinian Approach   7
   Structural Theory   7
   Perfectibility Theory   8
Nineteenth-Century Thinking   9
Second Industrial Revolution (1870–1914)   13
Impact of World War I   14
Conclusion   18
References   19

2   Pre-Theories of Decision-Making   23
Approaches During World War II   23
Response to the Cold War   24
Birth of Behavioral Foreign Policy Analysis   25
Anti-Behavioral Attack   35
Post-Cold War Foreign Policy Analysis   36
Twenty-First Century Developments   38
Conclusion   39
References   40

xiii

xiv CONTENTS

3 Quantifying Alternative Pre-Theories   51
Concepts   51
   Prestimulus Concepts   52
   Stimulus Concepts   53
   Information-Processing Concepts   55
   Outcome Concepts   58
Database   60
Factor Analysis   60
Causal Analysis   71
Conclusion   73
Appendix: Decision-Making Cases   73
References   77

Part II Operational Code Analysis

4 Omnipresence of Codes   85
Defining "Operational Code"   85
Leites' Operational Code of the Soviet Union   89
J. David Singer's Approach: Basic Issues   91
Ole Holsti's Approach: Belief System   92
Alexander George's Revival of the Operational Code   95
Myth Systems   100
Geopolitical Codes   102
Lucian Pye's Approach   103
*Epistemic Communities and the Liberal International
Order (LIO)*   103
Further Development of the Concept of Operational Code   105
References   105

**5 Developments and Problems in Operational Code
Research**   111
Psychological and Sociological Focus   112
Role Theory   115
Methodological Problems   116
Theoretical Confusion   120
Conclusion   123
References   123

CONTENTS   xv

Part III Professionalization Through Options Analysis

6	**Parameters of Decision-Making and Options Analysis**	135
	Basic Criteria	135
	Transformation of Operational Codes	142
	Computerization of Options Analysis	145
	Conclusion	147
	References	147
7	**American Policies Toward Cambodia**	151
	Cambodia, Vietnam, and the United States	151
	American Policy Options Toward Cambodia, 1981–1988	153
	Operational Codes	153
	Options Analysis	158
	Cambodian Peace Agreement	162
	Current Relations with the United States	163
	Appendix: American Policy Options for Cambodia, 1981–1988	163
	References	169
8	**American Policies Toward North Korea**	171
	North Korea, South Korea, and the United States	171
	Operational Codes	175
	Options Analysis	179
	Current Relations	182
	Conclusion	185
	Appendix: American Policy Options for North Korea, 2009–2018	185
	References	188
9	**American Policies Toward Ukraine**	193
	Ukraine as an Independent Country	193
	Vladimir Putin's Operational Code	195
	Operational Code of Volodymyr Zelensky	198
	Biden's Operational Code	200
	American Response to Russia's Threatened Invasion	203
	Russia Attacks Ukraine	206
	Phase One	206
	Phase Two	208
	Phase Three	210
	Phase Four	212

xvi CONTENTS

	Phase Five	214
	Phase Six	216
	Phase Seven	219
	Options Assessment	220
	Conclusion	225
	Appendix: American Policy Options for Ukraine	226
	References	230
10	**Implications for Foreign Policy Research**	247
	Options Analysis	248
	Decision-Making Implications	251
	References	252

Afterword	255
Index	259

LIST OF FIGURES

Figure 3.1	Crisis Model of Violent Decision-Making	72
Figure 3.2	Irrationality Model of Violent Decision-Making	72
Figure 3.3	Cultural Exchange Model of Violent Decision-Making	72
Figure 4.1	Ole Holsti's Decision-Making Map (*Source* Holsti 1962: 245, 250)	92
Figure 4.2	Alexander George's Decision-Making Map (*Note* Subjective considerations are italicized in contrast with objective considerations. *Source* George 1969)	97
Figure 5.1	Socialization Paradigm of Operational Code Formation (*Source* Walker 1983)	112
Figure 5.2	Cognitive Decision-Making Map of Walker, Schafer, and Young (*Source* Walker et al. 2003)	115

xvii

LIST OF TABLES

Table 3.1	A Decision-Making Schema	52
Table 3.2	Reliability Coefficients of Conceptual Variables	61
Table 3.3	*R*-Factor Analysis of Decision-Making Conceptual Variables	64
Table 3.4	Predictions and Degree of Fit for Decision-Making Models	73
Table 4.1	Ole Holsti's Categorization of Operational Codes	93
Table 4.2	Alexander George's Parameters for Operational Code Analysis of Decision-Makers (DMs)	98
Table 6.1	Parameters of Decision-Making	136
Table 6.2	Basic Criteria of Decision-Making	136
Table 6.3	Basic Criteria and Subcriteria of Decision-Making for Options Analysis	143
Table 6.4	Foreign Policy Decision-Making Subcriteria Guidelines	144
Table 6.5	Scoring and Ranking of Subcriteria of Decision-Making for Options Analysis	146
Table 7.1	United States Funding of the Khmer Rouge, 1980–1986 (in 2021 dollars)	153
Table 7.2	Operational Code of Phạm Văn Đ`ông	156
Table 7.3	Operational Code of the Reagan Administration Toward the Khmer Rouge	156
Table 7.4	Policy Options of the United States Toward Cambodia and Pol Pot, 1981–1988	158
Table 7.5	Matrix of Subcriteria of Cambodia Decision-Making with Options Assessments	160
Table 8.1	Operational Code of Kim Jong-Il	176

xix

xx   LIST OF TABLES

Table 8.2	Operational Code of Barack Obama	179
Table 8.3	Policy Options of the United States Toward North Korea, 2009–2016	181
Table 8.4	Matrix of Subcriteria of North Korea Decision-Making with Options	183
Table 9.1	Operational Code of Vladimir Putin	195
Table 9.2	Operational Code of Volodymyr Zelensky	199
Table 9.3	Operational Code of Joe Biden	201
Table 9.4	Policy Options of the United States Toward Ukraine in 2023	221
Table 9.5	Matrix of Criteria and Subcriteria of Ukraine Decision-Making with Options Assessments	223

PART I

Approaches to the Study of Foreign Policy

Analyses of foreign policy decisions have multiplied over the years, but blunders still haunt the landscape. Textbooks now present alternative perspectives on foreign policy analysis as a maze leading nowhere. Meanwhile, some practitioners have come to the conclusion that those involved in government agencies relating to foreign policy need revitalization (Zeya and Finer 2020). What is clearly needed is professionalization of foreign policy decision-making.

Currently, there is a lack of clarity in the field of foreign policy analysis. The earliest efforts merely recorded what happened and speculated why (Knutsen 1992). After World War II, there was a quest for scientific analysis, presenting efforts to construct empirical theories of foreign policy at a middle (empirical) level amid the three main types of scientific inquiry—theoretical science, empirical science, and applied science.

For centuries, scholars described foreign policy as a contest between emotion and reason. The empirical science of foreign policy analysis that developed during the early period of the Cold War, sometimes called the behavioral approach, involved concepts and theories consisting of hypotheses about how the concepts are linked. Many studies were guided by a single mid-level empirical theory, but very little knowledge was accumulated. The idea of cross-testing empirical theories was largely absent—that is, scholars failed to use the same database to test predictions of several alternative empirical theories in order to determine whether any are to be discarded, corrected, or broadened. In short, scholars have been

2   PART I: APPROACHES TO THE STUDY OF FOREIGN POLICY

pushing their own mid-level theoretical agendas with little concern for the larger landscape of how they all might fit together.

Theoretical science focuses on paradigms. A paradigm is a theory that applies at several levels of analysis—global, national, regional, subgroups, and even at the level of family. That is, a paradigm has applicability not just to foreign policy but will be applicable to similar problems at several levels of analysis.

For most behavioral scholars in the 1950s, more empirical knowledge had to be assembled before a theoretical science could be developed around a paradigm. Nevertheless, the ultimate aim of the behavioral approach was to craft an applied theory—one that could be applied successfully by those making foreign policy decisions. The aim was to generate empirical knowledge as a basis for an applied science of foreign policy decision-making. But that goal thus far remains unfulfilled. Indeed, theory development has languished.

One reason for an abrupt end to theory development was that the American intervention in Vietnam was extremely unpopular. A revolt against the behavioral approach resulted because empirical theorists were viewed as naïvely developing concepts, databases, and theories while ignoring an ongoing policy disaster. Nevertheless, as late as 1990, one of the finest textbooks on international relations provided a catalog of behavioral (empirical) theories (Doughetry, Pfaltzgraff, Devetak 1990).

Today, all international relations theory textbooks in the field but one (Haas 2017) survey isms—that is, ideologies whose adherents accept various dogmas without bothering to determine whether evidence proves that they have empirical validity. What has happened is that scholars have lost concern for empirical analysis of how and why foreign policies are formulated. The present volume, accordingly, serves as a corrective to the tendency to view foreign policy as a matter of ideology.

In general, the field of foreign policy analysis focuses on five stages. The first stage is recognition of a problem to be addressed. Stage 2 involves setting goals to be achieved in addressing the problem; the goals involve determining how much emphasis to place on a country's power, economy, and prestige as well as ensuring that the decision chosen is feasible. Stage 3 consists of an identification of all possible policy options to address the problem. Stage 4 is the determination of which options best achieve the goals. Stage 5 is implementation of the options chosen. Whereas stage 1 is unique in any foreign policy research study, and Stage 5 deals with such

PART I: APPROACHES TO THE STUDY OF FOREIGN POLICY 3

matters as logistics and resources, the present volume focuses on stages 2, 3, and 4.

Part I attempts to review empirical theories of foreign policy. Chapter 1 discusses the earliest commentaries—from Thucydides to E.H. Carr. Chapter 2 brings the analysis up to the present by focusing on behavioral empirical concepts and theories, which have unfortunately failed to advance for several decades because they have lingered, still focusing on mid-level theory without a desire to advance knowledge accumulation. Chapter 3 presents an empirical test of several alternative empirical theories, concluding that the key explanation for foreign policy blunders, especially those involving violence, is whether two opposing countries are culturally dissimilar.

Part II reviews the concept of "operational code," which hitherto has focused on bureaucratic operations more than cultural codes. The narrative explains how insights from operational code theorizing can be redirected into the need to improve how best to choose options to deal with foreign policy problems.

Part III redefines "operational code" as a means to enable decision-makers to choose policy options based on their policy codes. The aim is to improve how decision-makers choose options presented to them by their advisers. Three decisions are chosen in American foreign policy— the decision to support the Khmer Rouge during the 1980s, the ongoing decision to refuse negotiations with North Korea, and the present focus on Ukraine. The first two illustrate serious blunders that continue to demonstrate the consequences of unprofessional decision-making. The latter example, however, has been remarkably professional.

The book concludes that foreign policy analysis, whether by practitioners or scholars, can become far more professionalized. Accordingly, no new empirical or ethical theory is advanced. Instead, the aim is to broaden the consideration of goals so that the options chosen will avoid blunders. Instead of the current stalemate in foreign policy analysis, the overall impact of the volume should be to transform the agenda into constructive new directions.

REFERENCES

Dougherty, James E., Robert F. Pfaltzgraff, and Richard Devetak. 1990. *Contending Theories of International Relations: A Comprehensive Survey*, 3rd ed. New York: Harper & Row.

4   PART I: APPROACHES TO THE STUDY OF FOREIGN POLICY

Haas, Michael. 2017. *International Relations Theory: Comparing Empirical Paradigms*. Lanham, MD: Lexington.

Knutsen, Torbjörn L. 1992. *A History of International Relations Theory*. Manchester, UK: Manchester University Press.

Zeya, Uzra S., and Jon Finer. 2020. *Revitalizing the State Department and American Diplomacy*: Council Special Report 89. New York: Council on Foreign Relations.

CHAPTER 1

Early Approaches to the Study of Foreign Policy

Studying foreign policy involves understanding who makes key decisions and why. The earliest analyses of foreign policy decision-makers tended to focus on two aspects of human nature—calculations and emotion. Decision-makers are often viewed as rational beings who make calculations as well as miscalculations because they are swayed by emotion. The relative weight of the two factors has been the subject of much dispute. Decision-makers are also constrained by the type of country and political system that they lead as well as how their country interacts with other countries within the international system. The purpose of the present chapter is to trace how foreign policy analysis was conducted in several periods of time before the rise of more scientific approaches after World War II; the latter are identified in the following chapter.

Many early thinkers believed that educated upper classes are calculators, whereas uneducated lower classes are emotional. Another view was that decisions are made cognitively but under conditions of uncertainty, taking into account pressures from citizens and international constraints. A third view is that the sources of decisions lie within the human psyche, embedded in the very organization of a personality and its mechanisms of tension management, with cognitive processes only a superstructure tailored to fit the demands of basic personality needs. The various approaches bear closer examination:

© The Author(s), under exclusive license to Springer Nature
Switzerland AG 2023
M. Haas, *Professionalization of Foreign Policy*,
https://doi.org/10.1007/978-3-031-37152-3_1

Early Philosophical Approaches

The first detailed foreign policy analysis, *The History of the Peloponnesian War* by Thucydides (431 BCE), provided a factual account of the contest between Athens and Sparta for nearly 30 years. In addition to quoting speeches of the leaders that transparently revealed aspects of their psychological profiles, he cited the role of the political culture of a country and the structure of the Greek international system in the thinking of leaders of the two adversaries. Although many contemporary scholars have sought to classify his narrative in various ways (Bloxham 2011), the impact of his account was to inspire at least three approaches in the following centuries:

Dualistic Approach: Emotion and Reason

Plato and Aristotle drew their own interpretations based on their view of the psychological needs within members of various social classes. Plato (375 BCE), while observing aristocracies, democracies, and monarchies within fifth century BCE Greece, delineated a continuum in human drives from desire to reason. He came to the conclusion that foreign policies of controlling elites were specific to the social classes dominating various forms of government. Populist democracies determined policies on basic, even violent, desires because demagogues can easily sway the public. Middle-class rulers calculated economic gains and losses, using reason to satisfy greedy desires. Monarchs calculated how to expand or maintain power based on how their desires or fortunes might fluctuate. Humans behave better when they live in a good political system; they misbehave in corrupt polities (cf. Waltz 1959: 5; Waltz 1964; Dougherty, Pfaltzgraff, Tevetak 2000; van Kersbergen and Vis 2003).

Because the early training of a child seems to dictate whether desires or reason will guide conduct as an adult, Plato urged his students to contemplate what would happen in an ideal peaceful republic where a select few would be so well educated that reason in the interest of the good would prevail (Plato 360 BCE). However, he realized that rule by his intellectual gentry would never emerge.

For Aristotle (350 BCE), the middle classes seek gain rather than folly. Accordingly, rule by a commercial class would be more rational than mass-based democracy or self-serving monarchs.

Augustinian Approach

Writing just after the sacking of Rome by one of the many migratory bands, Augustine (426) presented the view that passions always dominate reason (cf. Wright 1931). Self-preservation was a fundamental motive. As the bishop of Hippo, a seaport in what is now Algeria, he sought to provide the Christian view that humans bit the apple in the Garden of Eden and therefore are inherently sinful. Scoffing at some Greeks who believed that a Golden Age would emerge in the future, he viewed humans as progressing toward the day of final judgment with more capacity for an emotional than a rational life. Thus, he believed that rational calculation only occurs to serve human passions. Decisions for war can be traced to the lust of conquest and other sinful behavior that accounts for anarchy. Because all humans are socialized to love sin, he argued, all forms of government and social classes favor destructive behavior. A strong central state will keep order by establishing firm restraints on individuals, though the rulers of that state will be unrestrained.

Augustine's analysis was echoed by Thomas Hobbes and Baruch Spinoza (Waltz 1959: 3). Even David Hume (1739) concurred with the view that reason is the slave of passions, a fundamental tenet of conservative political ideologies. Others subscribing to the Augustinian view include the urbane Edmund Burke (1791) as well as the jingoistic Friedrich Nietzsche (1901).

Structural Theory

Unlike Augustine and Hobbes, most later democratic conservative thinkers wanted to avoid the temptation to welcome an absolute ruler, who inevitably would be tyrannical. They sought a form of government in which those with different prejudices could veto one another. The checks-and-balances system advocated by John Locke (1690) and James Madison (1788) was grounded in the view that political existence will be less capricious when no one group is able to control political decision-making. Major foreign policy decisions, according to their logic, would have to involve convergence among the self-interest of many groups. Decisions for war would have to be made only after wide agreement to commit considerable resources to a conflict. Decisions with disastrous economic consequences could then never be made. Madison, therefore,

8   M. HAAS

crafted three branches of government, each of which can be checked by the other two.

Perfectibility Theory

Although Augustine believed that no utopia is in the cards for the human race, his pessimism was rejected by many philosophers, who felt that humans can be guided by moral absolutes. Accordingly, reason can be used to engineer polities and societies to better days. Seeking to negate Augustinian pessimism, Thomas Aquinas (1485) was a notable precursor to the thinkers of the Enlightenment (Becker 1932). Aquinas developed the concept of "just war," namely, that decisions are just if a legitimate authority with an upright intention pursues a just cause (Reichberg 2017).

The Enlightenment view of the eighteenth century was that humans can become more rational through better education and orderly social conditions. Adam Smith (1776) argued the case of capitalism as the best pathway to stable progress by an "invisible hand" that would facilitate fair competition.

Jean-Jacques Rousseau (1762), an Enlightenment theorist, warned that socialization processes determine human behavior, favorably or otherwise. But Marquis de Condorcet (1795), Denis Diderot (1746), Claude Helvétius (1758), and Immanuel Kant (1795) were more optimistic, believing that human existence will be more meaningful and rewarding when society as a whole is reconstructed in a rational manner. In particular, Enlightenment thinkers wanted to supplant imperial régimes with rulers who felt free to embark upon frivolous wars to satisfy personal ambitions and dynastic pride. Their wider goals for the human race were unrealized until governments and philanthropists, particularly in the nineteenth century, supported the Baconian penchant for trying to harness political and social reality to serve noble purposes through the development of science at universities (Kuhn 2014; cf. Bacon 1620).

Jeremy Bentham (1780) was the first perfectibility theorist to provide a metric for decision-making. His utilitarianism involved a cost–benefit analysis in which any decision must produce more favorable than unfavorable outcomes—"the greatest good for the greatest number" (ibid.: ch4–5). Clearly, he believed that humans are driven by desires, so the goal of government is to satisfy as much of their needs as possible. For those concerned that such a majoritarian approach would leave out minorities, Bentham's proposed reforms were based on the concept of individual rights—abolition of slavery, right to abortion, animal rights, children's rights, freedom of expression, end to capital punishment, gay rights, separation of church and state, and women's rights. Although most rights would be secure if individuals were free from government control, he clearly opened the pathway to the welfare state.

Assuming that human nature is plastic, and therefore perfectible, perfectibility theorists hoped ultimately to explain under what conditions a decision-maker might behave emotionally or miscalculate in one situation, while at other times calculations would be accurate and emotions would be under control. Perfectibility theories agreed that the main evil is the pursuit of hedonistic goals and the consequent eclipse of rational impulses. A society that brings leisure to its citizens by redistributing wealth would provide the opportunity for humans to transfer their attention to more meaningful matters, such as how to make decisions most consonant with an effective attainment of goals.

Other theories have also been authored by scholars in ancient China, India, Islam, and Israel, though they focus more on justifications for war and principles of war avoidance rather than the decision-making process (Knutsen 1992; Dougherty and Pfaltzgraff, Tevetak 2000: ch5). Although the concept of *jihad* was once claimed as obsolete in Islamic thinking (ibid.: 193), the concept refers to the existence of a constant war between Islamic peoples and the rest of the world.

NINETEENTH-CENTURY THINKING

Some ideas of the Enlightenment began to be realized as the American and French revolutions proved that institutions of representative government could ensure that foreign policy decisions would take into account rising international trade by middle class entrepreneurs that brought new wealth to enterprising states.

When the French Revolution became chaotic, however, Napoléon Bonaparte took control of France and tried to establish hegemony in Europe by military conquest, seeking to defeat empires and replace them with vassal democracies. When several major European countries joined forces to defeat Napoléon by 1814, a conference known as the Congress of Vienna was convened to construct a more peaceful order in Europe. According to the view of Austrian statesman Klemens von Metternich, powers of states should be in enough balance that international disputes would be settled by face-to-face negotiations known as diplomacy, something that had developed in the days of Athens and Greece but now seemed essential in multistate Europe (May 1946).

Metternich believed that the most stable order would consist of autocratic states with loyal armies and efficient bureaucracies and police. Principles of diplomacy and international law were then to be developed as conflicts arose, leaders negotiated, and Europe derived several decades of peace (Palmer 1972). He viewed the rise of self-centered democratic states as a threat to peace.

One important Metternichian principle of international law derived at the Congress of Vienna was that any government violating an intergovernmental treaty to go to war has committed a war crime. International law was to be based on treaties, with diplomacy the peaceful method for resolving conflicting interpretations of treaty texts. In short, the future of foreign policy was viewed as developing and upholding treaties adopted through diplomatic compromise. Metternich developed a new institution—the Concert of Europe, which would consist of leaders of the major countries of Europe committed to a balance of power between them. Any attempt to disrupt the equilibrium would then be resolved by a meeting of the Concert. Meanwhile, as diplomats got better acquainted with one another, they would develop mutual trust; treaties would then be honored, thereby guaranteeing international order. Building community among diplomats would result in a community of nations.

As the nineteenth century developed, however, the middle class was gradually accumulating more wealth than the gentry and nobles who had long held political power by paying armies to advance and protect their interests. As middle classes demanded representative government to replace imperial rule, they advanced the concept of national identity in which armies could be assembled through governmental appeals of nationalism. As businesses arose with assembly-line production modes, peasants could enrich themselves and send money to their families by moving to cities where factories produced goods sold around the world.

David Ricardo (1817) developed a detailed explanation of how the capitalist economic system could replace feudal economies. He believed that governments should no longer interfere in the economy, such as by adopting Poor Laws to rescue individuals from poverty. Just as businesses should cooperate through contracts enforceable by courts, states should advance capital accumulation worldwide. Self-interest was to dominate emotion. Meanwhile, Bentham's views became increasingly popular in the nineteenth century due to the prominence of later utilitarian John Stuart Mill, who expanded the theory in his book *Utilitarianism* (1863).

Into that societal transformation, sometimes called the First Industrial Revolution, the writing of Karl Marx questioned how foreign policy was conducted. He and his co-author Friedrich Engels (1848) believed that material conditions shaped attitudes. The feudal economy was being replaced by the capitalist economy, and in due course workers would be numerous enough to reject capitalism for a socialist economy in which the state would seek to establish a more just economy up to the point of self-abolition as social cooperation became the preferred method of interaction, with top-down rule abandoned once and for all. The Marxian theory was that as the economic environment changed from competing small businesses to dominant capitalist monopolies, the working class would clearly see that the goods they made with their own hands would be sold at prices far beyond their own contributions, and that "surplus value" would result in massive profits for owners of capitalist enterprises. Such exploitation, which would increasingly be on full display, would galvanize a future proletarian revolution to end capitalist control of the economy, society, and the political system. Workers were alienated because they owned nothing and thus were not a part of the wealth accumulation by capitalists. Marx and Engels drew considerable insight from the working class revolts that swept Europe in 1848. As the revolts were quashed, a basic principle was applied to foreign policy: "It is not the consciousness of men that determines their existence, but, on the contrary, their social existence determines their consciousness" (Marx 1859 [1904]: 437). Pursuit of self-interest was the main explanation for human behavior.

Advances in capitalist innovation were possible because scientific knowledge was increasing. Human behavior, previously considered unpredictable, was now the subject of scientific scrutiny. After Charles Darwin returned from travels to South America in the middle of the nineteenth century, he published *On the Origin of Species* (1859), declaring that there is an inexorable process of biological evolution. Thomas Huxley (1860) then reinterpreted the thesis to mean that evolution is a contest between strong and weak species, with the strong inevitably prevailing over the weak. That view, later called Social Darwinism, then became a rallying cry for Otto von Bismarck and the Prussian state to make war on weaker states in a quest to constitute a single nation of persons speaking the same language, to be known as Germany (Weikert 1993). Although Bismarck adopted elements of Bentham's welfare state, his aim was to outflank the Socialist Party while creating a country of strong, healthy Germans (Steinbergen 2013: 8, 422–444; van Kersbergen and Vis 2003: 38).

Bismarck was clearly influenced by Karl von Clausewitz (1832 [1968]: 103), who famously said that war was "a continuation of politics by other means" in which "one side dictates the law to the other" in a "feeling of passion" that is presumably justified if in the "national interest." Von Clausewitz built on insights from military history in the tradition of Sun Tzu, whose fifth century BCE *The Art of War* was first translated into a European language (French) in 1772.

However, Social Darwinists favoring conquest developed a form of Triumphalist Social Darwinism. Most Social Darwinists were Libertarians, arguing that government should not interfere in economic and social life so that the natural course of evolution would favor the strong over the weak (Spencer 1882, 1898). Libertarians, thus, explained the replacement of feudalism by capitalism as consistent with Social Darwinist principles. Libertarians favored free trade, thus placing capital accumulation as a major basis for foreign policy.

Darwin, however, tried to refute Social Darwinism in his later *The Descent of Man in Relation to Sex* (1871), where he argued that humans differed from all other species because they are motivated by emotion. His best illustration of the principle that emotions can dominate human choice was the observation that men tend to choose beautiful women as their marriage partners.

Meanwhile, the Concert of Europe disbanded as England and France became more democratic, allowing their parliaments to make decisions for the country, including appointing prime ministers as the chief foreign policy decision-makers. The breakup occurred as democracies were arising to replace authoritarian governments. Nevertheless, European countries began to adopt treaties with one another to establish a rules-based cooperative international order. One of the first was the formation of two regional bodies—the Central Commission for the Navigation of the Rhine in 1815 and the European Commission of the Danube in 1856.

In June 1859, Swiss businessman Henry Dunant went to Solferino, Italy, to meet Napoléon III hoping to make business dealings in the French colony of Algeria. Upon arrival, he was shocked to see 40,000 soldiers strewn across the battlefield of a recent skirmish in the Italian War of Independence. Many combatants were wounded on the field without medical help, left to die. When he returned home, he wrote about what he found (Dunant 1862) and began to organize a conference that eventually adopted the Geneva Convention for the Amelioration of the Condition of the Wounded in Armies in the Field, otherwise known as the Red Cross Convention of 1864. The convention came one year after Professor Francis Lieber had assembled numerous past international customs and treaties, including principles developed by Aquinas and the Catholic Church during the Middle Ages (Haas 2014: 182–183), into a war crimes code, known as the Lieber Code (1863).

The quest for a rules-based international order then jumped to the forefront of world politics. International conferences brought together diplomats of many European countries. The Declaration of Paris of 1856 banned privateering and respect for neutrality in time of war. In 1874, the first truly intergovernmental organization was formed—the Universal Postal Union. In 1884/1885, Bismarck organized a conference in Berlin that drew lines in Africa around colonial domains to avoid wars between colonial powers (Adebajo 2011).

Next came the effort to advance the laws of warfare with conferences held at The Hague in 1899 and, eight years later, in 1907. A total of 13 treaties and 3 declarations were adopted at the meetings (Scott 1915). One treaty in 1899 established the Permanent Court of Arbitration in The Hague primarily for economic and political disputes. Consistent with the perfectibility quest, the third Hague Conference was scheduled eight years later for 1915. But the meeting was never held. A world war had broken out.

Second Industrial Revolution (1870–1914)

The Second Industrial Revolution, based on the technological changes involving electricity, had much larger factories involving assembly-line mass production. Many theoretical formulations then emerged.

Émile Durkheim (1893) challenged Marx by turning the concept of alienation into a social psychological concept. Instead of the Marxian notion of "alienation" as living without holding property in society, Durkheim defined "alienation" as a situation of workers who lacked feelings for one another and therefore could not be politically mobilized as Marx had predicted. His analysis of suicide was the first major quantitative analysis in sociology (Durkheim 1897), demonstrating that those finding no interest in continuing their lives lacked ties with other humans.

14   M. HAAS

Max Weber (1894) also contradicted Marx by arguing that ideas are central to human behavior. He believed that rational individuals would pursue economic gain, and government would become more rational through well-organized bureaucracies that could eliminate corruption (Weber 1920).

Normal Angell (1910) argued that war is no longer profitable for industrial powers and their citizens. In so doing, he came to the same conclusion as Herbert Spencer (1898: 568–642). Therefore, the task was to inform the public so that they would resist war as a policy option. But the public played no role in Germany's decision to attack France to begin World War I.

Impact of World War I

In 1914, war broke out when Germany attacked France, greenlighting Japan to take over German colonies in the South Pacific. Numerous theorists tried to determine why the war broke out, but the perspective among many observers was that the international system lacked a single forum and set of principles for resolving disputes before they could escalate into war.

Woodrow Wilson was the most prominent theorist of the day. When World War I began, he initially decided not to involve the United States, and he promised to keep the country out of war while running for re-election in 1916. Nevertheless, the important decision to send American troops on April 6, 1917, followed Germany's announcement of renewed unrestricted submarine warfare and the later sinking of ships with Americans on board as well as the alleged Zimmerman telegram that urged México to become a German ally. In stating that the aim of the United States was to make the world "safe for democracy," he was declaring that principles of the American progressive movement would be applied internationally (Heckscher 1991: 470).

In September 1917, Wilson made foreign policy history by asking Colonel Edward House, his presidential adviser, to assemble a group of academics to determine provisions of the treaty of peace to be written after the war. House then chose ethics philosopher Sidney Mezes to supervise a group of almost 150 persons, including James Truslow Adams, Louis Brandeis, Walter Lippmann, A. Lawrence Lowell, and James Shotwell, who initially met at the New York Public Library on 42nd Street. Experts on various parts of the world involved in the war then were invited to join what was then called The Inquiry (Gelfand 1963). They recommended such measures as the breakup of the Austrian Empire, the League of Nations, mandates, plebiscites, and other measures as new institutions of the international system (Gross 1996). About 20 members were part of the American delegation to the Paris Peace Conference in 1919. Some members of the group formed the nongovernmental Council on Foreign Relations after the war.

On January 5, 1918, British Prime Minister David Lloyd George made a speech about how the peace should be decided after the war after consultation with members of the British Commonwealth of Nations. Although quite similar to Lloyd George's speech, Wilson was far more eloquent when, three days later, he announced his Fourteen Points (Grigg 2002: 383–335): Wilson summarized and stated some of the recommendations from the group of academics—democracy, free trade, open agreements, a reduction in armaments, and the self-determination of peoples—albeit without favoring decolonization of non-White peoples. Instead of just an armistice, he wanted to establish a basis for enduring peace. Among the criteria apparently guiding Wilson's speech were to keep Bolshevik Russia in the war, strengthen the morale of the Allied powers, build support with American public opinion, and undermine German public support for the war. Prime Ministers of Britain, France, and Italy, not consulted before the speech, were initially skeptical (Unger 2007: 561). But they were ultimately persuaded in Paris to go along with many of Wilson's recommendations, provided that Wilson agreed that Germany should pay reparations for the war within the Treaty of Versailles (Hakim 2005: 16–20).

Nevertheless, Wilson failed to gain support from the Republican Party in Congress to ratify the Treaty of Versailles. One result of The Inquiry was the launching of the field of international relations within the discipline of political science (Haas 2017: ch1). Another was the quest among American international relations scholars to build the case for joining the League of Nations and thereby continuing to build a rules-based international order. Analyses of the war and subsequent peace continue to the present.

Among the most important analyses of World War I was one by Vladimir Lenin. He was disappointed that the working class of Germany was "bribed" by higher wages and then encouraged to fight for capitalist overlords (Lenin 1917 [1964]: 154; cf. Wimmer 2019). He concluded that the decision to begin the war was based on a desire of capitalist countries to "seize lands and conquer foreign nations, to ruin competing nations, to pillage their wealth" (Lenin 1914 [1935]: 123). Since capitalism was destined to fail, Lenin believed that the purpose of the war was to eliminate competition from other countries while engaging in superexploitation abroad to compensate falling profits at home. He also developed "diversionary theory," arguing that war is an effort "to diversify the attention of the laboring masses from the domestic political crises" (ibid.: 130). War served "to disunite the workers and fool them with nationalism, to annihilate their vanguards in order to weaken the revolutionary movement of the proletariat" (ibid.: 125). When his Bolshevik Revolution succeeded, he withdrew Russia from World War I and sought to build momentum for a global revolution that would topple capitalism.

Before the war, historians wrote about causes of specific wars, but afterward the focus became how wars in general break out (Howard 1983; Dougherty and Pfaltzgraff, Tevetak 2000: ch5; Knutsen 1992). Similarly, Herbert Kelman (1965: 5–6) found that psychologists in times past tended to focus on human aggressiveness as the sole cause of war, whereas World War I was much more complicated.

The academic field of international relations began in 1919 with the first chair in international relations established at the University of Wales in Aberystwyth. Other universities followed, and the subject became popular (Knutsen 1992: 1995). A major focus was to strengthen international law and the League of Nations system. Three of the earliest textbooks were C. Delisle Burn's *International Politics* (1920), Pitnam Potter's *Introduction to the Study of International Organization* (1922), and Frederick Schuman's *International Politics: An Introduction to the Western State System* (1933). Clyde Eagleton (1932) also made a strong argument for what was later called the democratic "liberal international order," which differed from the rules-based order advocated by imperial leaders. Although all four were later accused of being "idealists," studies of decision-making were embedded in historical accounts of past situations rather than based on analytical frameworks.

Progressive reformer John Dewey (1922), who opposed the Spanish-American War and the American annexation of the independent state of Hawai'i, both in 1898, asserted that war occurs when decision-makers are unable to achieve their desires in political and social arenas because they lack knowledge of the linkage between fundamental cognitive processes. Elites experiencing frustration because of their misperceptions and miscalculations resort to war in an act of desperation, not rationality. His remedy

1 EARLY APPROACHES TO THE STUDY OF FOREIGN POLICY 17

was to increase public input into the policy-making process. Some scholars then wrote about how the public could intervene in the decision-making process (e.g., Lindsay 1917; Wright 1922).

Another person who was disappointed by the peace agreement after World War I was Mohandas Gandhi (1927). Rather than promoting self-determination of peoples, the Wilsonian quest ignored those being suppressed in colonies around the world. Gandhi regarded elite manipulation of the public by deliberate distortion of truth as the source of human hostility toward persons in other countries. He wanted new rulers for India, just as Kant two centuries earlier opposed dynastic states as pointlessly warlike. Because the colonized often lack the economic wherewithal to engage in an American-type revolution, he urged the anti-colonial movement to adopt nonviolent protest. Such efforts would identify the immorality of colonialism, and shaming would force colonial powers to grant independence.

Assembly-line production, according to Sigmund Freud (1930) produced frustration leading to violence. World War I, in his judgment, enabled "primitive" instincts to emerge (Freud 1915 [1964]: 281–282). His remedy for violence was "more truthfulness and upright dealing between humans" to build "emotional ties between humans" (Freud 1933 [1964]: 215). As civilization grew, the impulse for violence would subside (Freud 1930). His writing encouraged later psychoanalytic analyses of leaders to find out what codes operate in their heads while processing information, in particular studies of Woodrow Wilson (Freud and Bulllitt 1957; George and George 1956).

Perhaps the most fascinating sociological contribution to the field of foreign policy analysis after World War I was by Pitirim Sorokin. In the third volume of his *Social and Cultural Dynamics* (1937), he found that changes in cultural patterns—that is, codes of conduct—led to war. He identified three basic cultural patterns—"ideational," "sensate," and "idealistic." The values of ideational cultures are spiritual, either an ascetic desire for detachment to achieve inner peace or an active desire to spread a particular ethic. Sensate cultures seek to derive pleasure from one's five senses of hearing, sight, smell, taste, and touch. Sensate cultures operate in three ways—exploiting the word, changing the world through science, or cynically allowing the end to justify any means. Idealistic cultures try to blend the nobler forms of the other two cultures in various ways. Having traced cyclical changes from ideational to idealistic cultures to sensate cultures in various parts of the world, and back to idealistic cultures, he found that wars are found whenever cultural change creates proponents of one confronting proponents of the next.

In early 1941, with war raging in Europe but before the Japanese attack on Pearl Harbor, sociologist Theodore Abel (1941) examined 25 decisions to go to war. In his qualitative analysis, he found that deliberation among options was quite careful, anticipating consequences. "In no case is the decision precipitated by emotional tensions, sentimentality, crowd behavior, or other irrational emotions" (p. 855).

Perhaps the most important foreign policy scholar of the interwar period was Quincy Wright, whose *A Study of War* was first published in 1942, with a second edition issued in 1965 totaling 1,637 pages. Similar to Sorokin, Wright's theory focused on aspects of human existence that can fall out of balance—technology of armaments, law, social and political institutions, and values upheld by the public. New war technologies, legal impunity, breakdown of social and political institutions, and fundamental value disagreements were traced as causes of war. For Wright, peace requires an equilibrium in all four realms of human reality. When disequilibrium emerges, conflicts between countries will become so fundamental to life that war will be used to resolve imbalance. He hoped that countries could achieve a mutual balance of power that could develop an international or supranational community of peace.

Conclusion

Many other writings could be cited from various time periods (e.g., Knutsen 1992). However, the period between the two world wars has been painted with a single brush as constituting idealism. The most eloquent critic was E.H. Carr, whose *Twenty Years Crisis* (1939) exposed idealists as asleep to the rise of Nazi Germany—as utopian thinking with no concern for power politics.

But Carr agreed with idealists in one important respect, arguing that there is a need to improve the content of decisions rather than the process for determining the content. Only Bentham, Sun Tzu, von Clausewitz, and Weber were concerned about how policy options were appraised to reach objectives. An increased focus on the decision-making process came after World War II, as reviewed in the following chapter.

REFERENCES

Adebajo, Adekeye. 2011. *The Curse of Berlin: Africa After the Cold War.* Capetown: University of Capetown.

Abel, Theodore. 1941. The Element of Decision in the Pattern of War. *American Sociological Review* 6 (6): 853–859.

Angell, Normal. 1910. *The Great Illusion: A Study of the Relation of Military Power to National Advantage.* New York: Putnam.

Aquinas, Thomas. 1485/1947. *Summa Theologica.* New York: Benzinger Brothers.

Aristotle. 350 BCE. *Politics*, trans. Ernest Barker. Oxford, UK: Clarendon, 1961.

Augustine, Bishop of Hippo. 426. *The City of God.* New York: Modern Library, 1950

Bacon, Francis. 1620. *Novum Organum.* Oxford, UK: Clarendon Press, 1878.

Becker, Carl L. 1932. *The Heavenly City of Eighteenth-Century Philosophers.* New Haven, CT: Yale University Press.

Bentham, Jeremy. 1780. *An Introduction to the Principles of Morals and Legislation.* Oxford, UK: Clarendon Press, 1907. See utilitarianism/jeremy-bentham/#4.

Bloxham, John A. 2011. *Thucydides and US Foreign Policy Debates After the Cold War.* Irvine, CA: Universal Publishers.

Burke, Edmund. 1791. *Reflections on the Revolution in France.* Oxford, UK: Oxford University Press, 2009.

Burns, C. Delisle. 1920. *International Politics.* London: Methuen.

Carr, Edward Hallett. 1939. *The Twenty Years Crisis, 1919–1939: An Introduction to the Study of International Relations.* London: Macmillan.

Darwin, Charles. 1859. *On the Origins of Species.* New York: Crown, 2019.

Darwin, Charles. 1871. *The Descent of Man in Relation to Sex.* Princeton, NJ: Princeton University Press, 1981.

de Condorcet, Nicolas. 1795. *Sketch for a Historical Picture of the Progress of the Human Spirit.* London: Weidenfeld and Nicolson, 1975 [University Microfilms].

Dewey, John. 1922. *Human Nature and Conduct.* New York: Holt.

Diderot, Denis. 1746. *Philosophical Thoughts.* Albuquerque, NM. http://tems.umn.edu/pdf/Diderot-Philosophical%20Thoughts.pdf.

Dougherty, James E., Robert L. Pfaltzgraff, Jr., and Richard Devetak. 2000. *Contending Theories of International Relations: A Comprehensive Survey*, 5th ed. Pearson.

Dunant, Henry. 1862. *A Memoir of Solferino.* Geneva: International Committee of the Red Cross, 1986.

Durkheim, Émile. 1893. *The Division of Labor in Society.* New York: Free Press, 1949.

Durkheim, Émile. 1897. *Suicide: A Study in Sociology*. New York: Free Press, 1951.

Eagleton, Clyde. 1932. *International Government*. New York: Ronald Press.

Freud, Sigmund. 1915. Thoughts for the Times on War and Death. In *The Standard Edition of the Complete Psychological Works of Sigmund Freud*, XIV, 275–302. London: Hogarth, 1964.

Freud, Sigmund. 1930. *Civilization and Its Discontents*. London: Penguin, 2002.

Freud, Sigmund. 1933. Why War? In *The Standard Edition of the Complete Psychological Works of Sigmund Freud*, XXII, 199–215. London: Hogarth, 1964.

Freud, Sigmund, and William C. Bullitt. 1957. *Thomas Woodrow Wilson: Twenty-Eighth President of the United States: A Psychological Study*. Boston: Houghton Mifflin, 1967.

Gandhi, Mohandas. 1927. *The Story of My Experiments with Truth*. New York: Dover, 1983.

Gelfand, Lawrence E. 1963. *The Inquiry: American Preparations for Peace, 1917–1919*. New Haven, CT: Yale University Press.

George, Alexander, and Juliette L. George. 1956. *Woodrow Wilson and Colonel House: A Personality Study*. New York: Day.

Grigg, John. 2002. *Lloyd George: War Leader*. London: Allen Lane.

Haas, Michael. 2014. *International Human Rights: A Comprehensive Introduction*, 2nd ed. London: Routledge.

Haas, Michael. 2017. *International Relations Theory: Competing Empirical Paradigms*. Lanham, MD: Lexington.

Hakim, Joy. 2005. *War, Peace, and All That Jazz*. New York: Oxford University Press.

Heckscher, August. 1991. *Woodrow Wilson*. Greenwood, SC: Eaton Press.

Helvétius, Claude Adrien. 1758. *De l'esprit*. Whitefish, MT: Kessinger, 2004.

Howard, Michael. 1983. *The Causes of War and Other Essays*. Cambridge, MA: Harvard University Press.

Hume, David. 1739. *A Treatise of Human Nature: Being an Attempt to Introduce the Experimental Method of Reasoning*. Oxford, UK: Oxford University Press, 2000.

Huxley, Thomas H. 1860. On the Origin of Species. In *Collected Essays: Darwiniana*, 71–79. London: Macmillan.

Kant, Immanuel. 1795. *Perpetual Peace: A Philosophical Sketch*. Las Vegas, NV: FQ Classics, 2007.

Kelman, Herbert C., ed. 1965. *International Behavior: A Social-Psychological Approach*, Chap. 1. New York: Holt, Rinehart, Winston.

Knutsen, Torbjörn. 1992. *A History of International Relations Theory*, 3rd ed. Manchester, UK: Manchester University Press, 2016.

Kuhn, Thomas. 2014. The History of Science. In *Philosophy, Science, and History: A Guide and Reader*, ed. Lydia Patton, Chapter 9. New York: Routledge.

Lenin, Vladimir. 1917. *Imperialism: The Highest Stage of Capitalism*. Beijing: People's Publishing House.

Lieber, Francis. 1863. *Lieber's Code and the Law of War*, ed. Shelley Hartigan. Chicago: Precedent, 1983.

Lindsay, Rogers. 1917. *Popular Control of Foreign Policy*. The Hague: Nijhoff.

Locke, John. 1690. *The Two Treatises of Government*. Cambridge, UK: Cambridge University Press, 1988.

Madison, James. 1788. Federalist Paper #51. In Alexander Hamilton, James Madison, and John Jay, *The Federalist Papers*. New Haven, CT: Yale University Press, 2009.

Marx, Karl. 1859. *A Contribution to the Critique of Political Economy*. New York: International Library, 1904.

Marx and Engels: *Manifesto*. *The Marx-Engels Reader*, ed. Robert C. Tucker, 335–362. New York: Norton, 1972.

May, Arthur J. 1946. *The Age of Metternich, 1814–1848*. New York.

Mill, John Stuart. 1863. *Utilitarianism*. Oxford, UK: Oxford University Press, 1998.

Nietzsche, Friedrich. 1901. *The Will to Power*. New York: Random House, 1968.

Palmer, Alan. 1972. *Metternich*. New York: Harper & Row.

Plato. 360 BCE. *The Laws*, trans. A.E. Taylor. London: Dent, 1934.

Plato. 375 BCE. *The Republic*, trans. Benjamin Jowett, Book IV, §439–448. New York: Modern Library, n.d.

Potter, Pitnam. 1922. *An Introduction to the Study of International Organization*. New York: Appleton.

Reichberg, Gregory M. 2017. *Thomas Aquinas on War and Peace*. Cambridge, UK: Cambridge University Press.

Ricardo, David. 1817. *The Principles of Political Economy and Taxation*. London: Dent, 1911.

Rousseau, Jean-Jacques. 1762. *Émile, or On Education*, trans. Allan Bloom. New York: Basic Books, 1979.

Schuman, Frederick. 1933. *International Politics: An Introduction to the Western State System*. New York: McGraw-Hill.

Scott, James Brown. 1915. *The Hague Conventions and Declarations of 1899 and 1907*. New York: Oxford University Press.

Smith, Adam. 1776. *An Inquiry into the Nature and Causes of the Wealth of Nations*. New York: Modern Library, n.d.

Sorokin, Pitirim. 1937. *Fluctuations of Social Relationships, War, and Revolution*. Volume III of *Social and Cultural Dynamics*. New York: American Book Company.

Spencer, Herbert. 1882. *Political Institutions*. New York: Appleton.

Spencer, Herbert. 1898. *Principles of Sociology*, Vol. II. New York: Appleton.

Steinbergen, Jonathan. 2013. *Bismarck: A Life*. Oxford, UK: Oxford University Press.

Thucydides. 431 BCE. *The History of the Peloponnesian War*, trans. Richard Crawley. New York: Modern Library, 1951.

Tzu, Sun. n.d. *The Art of War*. Minneapolis, MN: Filiquarian, 2007.

Unger, Urwin. 2007. *These United States: The Questions of Our Past*, 4th ed. Upper Saddle River, NJ: Pearson.

van Kersbergen, Kees, and Barbara Vis. 2003. *Comparative Welfare State Politics: Development, Opportunities, and Reform*. Cambridge, UK: Cambridge University Press.

von Clausewitz, Karl. 1832. *On War*. Princeton, NJ: Princeton University Press, 1976.

Waltz, Kenneth. 1959. *Man, the State, and War: A Theoretical Analysis*. New York: Columbia University Press.

Waltz, Kenneth. 1964. Stability of the Bipolar World. *Daedalus* 93 (2): 881–909.

Weber, Max. 1894. *The Protestant Ethic and the Spirit of Capitalism*. New York: Scribner, 1930.

Weber, Max. 1920. *The Theory of Social and Economic Organization*. New York: Free Press, 1997.

Weikart, Richard. 1993. The Origins of Social Darwinism in Germany, 1859–1895. *Journal of the History of Ideas* 54 (3): 469–488.

Wimmer, Andreas. 2019. Why Nationalism Works: And Why It Isn't Going Away. *Foreign Affairs* 98 (2): 27–34.

Wright, Herbert F. 1931. St. Augustine and International Peace. *Fordham University Quarterly* 6 (3): 399–416.

Wright, Quincy. 1922. *The Control of American Foreign Relations*. New York: Macmillan.

Wright, Quincy. 1942. *A Study of War*. Chicago: University of Chicago Press.

Wright, Quincy. 1965. *A Study of War*, 2nd ed. Chicago: University of Chicago Press.

CHAPTER 2

Pre-Theories of Decision-Making

The previous chapter surveyed relatively simple modes of foreign policy analysis before the social sciences adopted scientific methods. The devastation of World War II prompted scholars to develop more complicated approaches, as explained below. Nevertheless, most analysis was pre-theoretical—that is, engaged in concept innovation without constructing causal theories.

APPROACHES DURING WORLD WAR II

E.H. Carr (1939) has been identified as a "realist" in contrast with "idealists" of the period between the two world wars. The latter were trying to convert a rules-based international order into a "liberal international order." For example, "idealist" David Mitrany (1943) believed that a network of intergovernmental technical organizations would ensure peace by intertwining all countries to work for the common good, a proposal later rebranded as "global governance" (Rosenau 1992). Mitrany's "functional" approach was further developed after World War II by Ernst Haas (1958) as neofunctional theory, a variant of the Community Building Paradigm (Haas 2017a: ch6).

During World War II, the most prominent political scientist working for the American government was Harold Lasswell, whose doctoral dissertation was about decoding German propaganda during World War I

© The Author(s), under exclusive license to Springer Nature
Switzerland AG 2023
M. Haas, *Professionalization of Foreign Policy*,
https://doi.org/10.1007/978-3-031-37152-3_2

23

(Lasswell 1927). He was hired in 1942 to assist decision-makers in decoding the intentions of Nazi Germany from government texts by using a methodological approach known as content analysis—analyzing the hidden thematic meaning of words.

RESPONSE TO THE COLD WAR

The Cold War emerged when the army of the Soviet Union captured control of most of Eastern Europe and was cemented by Moscow's first test of an atomic bomb, both achieved by 1949. In 1950, North Korea, backed by Russia, attacked South Korea, which the United States defended, and the war continued until an armistice in 1953. Fear of nuclear war between superpower adversaries became the number one concern.

The first major theoretical advance came from political scientist Hans Morgenthau (1948), who developed the concept of "realism" much more fully. He cited examples from history as far back as Thucydides to back up his maxims of how foreign policy should be conducted strategically, using relative power status as the major criterion for evaluating policy options.

But Morgenthau's cherrypicking examples hardly constituted systematic proof. Echoing sociologist C. Wright Mills (1958), who labeled Morgenthau's approach as "crackpot realism," former Governor Jerry Brown (2022) later attributed the monomaniacal focus on power in the administration of George W. Bush for expensive failures in Afghanistan and Iraq despite the fact that both were considered weaker countries. For Mills, "realists" encourage more spending on the military, enriching what President Dwight Eisenhower in 1961 called the "military industrial complex." Mills and Eisenhower pointed out that decisions regarding the annual military budget are more likely to reflect the pursuit of wealth by weapons manufacturers than interstate power considerations.

In 1954, a group of East Coast scholars, many from the Council on Foreign Relations, held a conference sponsored by the Rockefeller Foundation to determine which approach should be preferred in dealing with the Soviet Union. The outcome was to accept Morgenthau's "realism" and to reject something called "behavioralism," which they assumed was a cover for interwar "idealism" (Guilhot 2008: 299). Close to Washington, they felt that they had to offer guidance to the White House.

But ideologies are guides to policymakers that consist of maxims perceived as self-evident truths. Those subscribing to ideologies remain outside the realm of scientific thinking and cater to their own prejudices regarding preferred criteria for evaluating foreign policy options.

As the Cold War ensued, the fear was that the Soviet and Western blocs might use nuclear weapons to settle their differences. Among the possibilities were misunderstandings that could lead to an escalatory conflict situation and ultimately nuclear war destroying the planet. A major concern was about decisions under a situation of crisis, when a quick decision is needed to respond to a severely threatening stimulus yet the response might be less than rational. The need was to go beyond the model of rational decision-making involving Morgenthauian power calculations.

BIRTH OF BEHAVIORAL FOREIGN POLICY ANALYSIS

In 1958, four years after the Rockefeller conference, the Center for Advanced Study in the Behavioral Sciences was independently established on a hill overlooking Stanford University. Among the first fellows in the Center were Herbert Kelman, Harold Lasswell, Charles Lindblom, and many others. (The Center became a unit of Stanford University in 2008.) The focus was on empirical research instead of ideology.

While serving in government during World War II, Lasswell (1948, 1949) learned that government officials were often starved for information relevant to their decisions. Accordingly, he promoted "policy science" after deconstructing the policy process into seven stages—(1) intelligence, (2) promotion, (3) prescription, (4) invocation, (5) application, (6) termination, and (7) appraisal. To improve the "intelligence" stage, he designed a decision room (including his later classroom at Yale University) filled with charts and graphs relevant to foreign policy options so that those deliberating on policy options would relate to as much information as possible. His vision, as explained in a book with philosopher Abraham Kaplan, *Power and Society* (1950), specified that power was only one of eight sources of political influence within the policymaking process. Next, he co-authored with sociologist Daniel Lerner *The Policy Sciences: Recent Developments in Scope and Method* (1951). And, co-edited with political sociologist Nathan Leites, what emerged was *Language of Politics: Studies in Quantitative Semantics* (1949). The latter pursued content analysis.

Lasswell was one of several scholars promoting the "behavioral approach" to the study of foreign policy. He sought to import perspectives of psychologists who seek explanations for peculiar behavior, sociologists who explore group influences, economists who focus on how entrepreneurs make risky choices, and executives concerned about "cost effectiveness." Whereas much of the traditional foreign policy literature treated states as primary actors on the international stage, behavioralists penetrated inside states to study the deliberations and inner workings of the key makers of decisions.

Hitherto, conventional explanations of Soviet behavior were found in well-respected publications on Russian national culture (Gorer and Rickman 1949). But, based on his analysis of the Politburo, Nathan Leites (1948; Leites et al. 1951) began a thematic content analysis of statements by Vladimir Lenin and Josef Stalin, ultimately resulting in a short book, *The Operational Code of the Politburo* (1951), and a longer volume, *A Study of Bolshevism* (1953). The aim was to unmask the strategy and tactics of Soviet leaders, who went far beyond their adherence to the Marxian Paradigm of the class struggle in pursuing the Cold War (cf. Haas 2017a: ch4).

A similar concern interested anthropologists Jürgen Ruesch and Gregory Bateson (1951). They coined the term "metacommunication" to refer to whether two persons are talking past each other or are on the same page. In other words, the same word might have differing meanings for rival persons or groups, triggering unexpected responses if they represented two different operational codes.

Political scientist Richard Snyder appears to have been the most consequential behavioral foreign policy theorist in many ways. He was the one who coined the terms "decision-making" and "decision-maker." While previous work presumed that decisions occurred in a "black box," unknown to the public, he and his associates pointed out that there is a process of decision-making that stretches out over time (Snyder et al. 1954: 74). Similar to Lasswell, Snyder identified several stages of decision-making—(1) the internal setting and social structure, known as the prestimulus phase, (2) stimulus, (3) information-processing, (4) the decision, a choice among alternative options, (5) implementation, (6) impact on the target of the decision, and (7) feedback of the impact back to the decision-maker. Each stage inside the process, thus, requires separate analysis rather than the assumption in prior research that foreign policies were kneejerk responses to either emotions or rational calculation. Opening the decision-making "black box," in effect, created foreign policy analysis as a distinct empirical field of international relations. Snyder's major contribution was to develop an avalanche of new concepts through which to view decision-making. He and his colleagues classified two types of criteria used to explain decisions (Snyder et al. 1954: 144): "Because of decisions" involve fundamental psychological motivations, unconscious or semiconscious, that account for decisions. "In order to decisions" have objectives and implementation in mind—how X might best accomplish Y. In the field of foreign policy analysis, all roads have led from Snyder. More details of Snyder's conceptual innovations appear in the following chapter.

Further developing the policymaking approach, Harold and Margaret Sprout (1956) distinguished between the "psychomilieu" of images and the "operational environment," since reality to decision-makers is what they perceive within a larger objective reality. Yet what they perceive is also a function of how the state is organized bureaucratically and politically.

In 1958, the same year when the behavioral center was established near Stanford, a group of West Coast scholars founded the International Studies Association (ISA) as an interdisciplinary home for nonideological scholars. Such political scientists as Charles McClelland (1961) and Robert North (1967) rejected ideological isms, instead seeking to go beyond simple approaches by formulating theories, assembling databases, and testing theories systematically. ISA founders also included traditional scholars, who followed a more historical approach. Their joint aim was to counter the East Coast acceptance of "realism," which they believed was dangerous because efforts to assert power to counteract power might inevitably result in war during the new nuclear age.

Next, political scientist Herbert Simon (1958) tried to explain frequent departures from the Rational Choice Paradigm, popular in economics, in terms of what he called "bounded rationality." Instead of maximizing or optimizing, he argued that decision-makers seek to "satisfice." In other words, they choose options that are at least minimally "acceptable," though they may not be able to acquire all the information needed for a truly rational decision.

Economist Charles Lindblom (1959) then argued that decision-makers try to break big decisions into small ones. The aim was to make pragmatically "incremental" decisions so that they can "muddle through" as a situation evolves (cf. Braybrooke and Lindblom 1963).

Whereas the early literature on foreign policy often ascribed decision-making to a particular country or the leader of a state, political scientist Robert Dahl and economist Charles Lindblom (1953) identified a continuum between authoritarian states and polyarchic states. In the latter case, several sources of power can veto a decision. In between the two poles they identified bargaining between a wide variety of options that must fulfill a variety of goals. They had in mind Harold Lasswell's concept of society consisting of eight pillars of influence—power, respect, rectitude, affection, wealth, well-being, skill, and enlightenment—in which autocracies are defined as in agglutinative control of all eight, whereas democracies have independent sources of influence on policymaking (Lasswell and Kaplan 1950).

Political scientist, psychologist, and sociologist Harold Guetzkow (1959, 1962) was concerned that decision-makers often make choices at one point in time without anticipating chessmove responses. Based on game theory, he argued that decision-makers should ponder alternative scenarios through simulations. Over the years, many simulation studies have been conducted within foreign policy analysis, now using computers with artificial intelligence methods, though the theoretical payoff has lagged (Pepinsky 2005). Simulation has also been used as a teaching tool in classrooms. Nevertheless, simulation was used twice recently in connection with how to cope with the outbreak of a pandemic (Haas 2021: 13,161).

Political scientist Charles McClelland (1961), meanwhile, was tracing the trajectory of escalation in events leading to war. He influenced the collection of a database of "events data," which unfortunately was developed without a theory and was later buried as an approach by Maurice East (1987).

Psychologist David McClelland (1961) decided to perform a "mental factor analysis" on the long list of human motivations developed by Henry Murray (1938). He came up with three major motivations—need for affiliation, need for achievement, and need for power. Previously, "irrationality" applied to foreign policy decision-making as a blanket concept referring to the criterion in choosing policy options known as "psychological need." McClelland thus opened the concept to three major types of psychological needs. Later, he applied his trichotomy in the study of alcoholism, economics, leadership, and student development (McClelland 1987).

Next came James Rosenau's proposed five categories of explanatory factors—actions, perceptions, opinion-making, opinion-submitting, and decision-making (Rosenau 1961). He stressed the role of public opinion during several phases of the decision-making process. He later modestly referred to his contribution as "pre-theory" (Rosenau 1966), a term applicable to most of the research thus far because concepts had been advanced without linking them into a complex theoretical pattern.

Political scientist Robert North, seeking to discern causes of World War, contradicted Theodore Abel's analysis of the prevalence of rational considerations in decisions for war. Through a thematic content analysis, he and his associates found that messages between key decision-makers before World War I, particularly those of Kaiser Wilhelm, contained statements of perceived hostility escalating to the point that he sent troops to aid Austria-Hungary's quarrel with Serbia, thereby bringing Russia into the conflict, which in turn prompted Germany to attack France in the hope of avoiding a two-front war (Zinnes et al. 1961). A later study of World War I, however, returned to Abel's thesis that strategic considerations prevailed (Farrar 1992).

In another effort to find causes of World War I, Bruce Russett (1962) utilized the framework for studying automobile accidents by social psychologist Paul Lazarsfeld (1960). After analyzing all participants, he made qualitative judgments about why decisions for war were inevitable whenever there was poor intelligence. Next, Russett (1963) tested the Deterrence Paradigm of Thomas Schelling (1960) after developing a database of 17 decisions from 1935 to 1961. Using nine independent variables, he found qualitatively that deterrence fails when the utility of war exceeds the utility of peace. Even when the probability of victory is slim, larger countries will attack smaller countries, he concluded.

Political scientist Charles Hermann (1963, 1969) then classified foreign policy decisions into routine decisions and crisis decisions. The traditional cognitive approach applies to routine decisions, he argued, but crisis decisions involve high threat, surprise, stress, need for a quick response, and especially outcome uncertainty. Hermann tried to ascertain which aspects of crisis decision-making have the potentiality for escalation of conflict situations. Later, Hermann and political scientist Linda Brady (1972) extracted 311 propositions from the literature worthy of testing under several alternative theories—cost calculation, hostile interaction, individual stress, and organizational response. But no testing occurred despite a large number of concepts included in the propositions.

In 1964, J. David Singer launched the Correlates of War Project, collecting data on war casualties, durations, and other matters, ultimately expanding in the present to include data on alliances, cultural attributes, national and systemic attributes, diplomatic ties, geographic proximity, intergovernmental organizations, territorial changes, and trade flows (Sarkees and Wayman 2010). His main interest was in determining the relative importance of demographic, economic, and military dimensions of power in testing the classic realist theory of whether power preponderance or power balance leads to peace in the international system (Deutsch and Singer 1964). In short, he deconstructed the "power" criterion of decision-making so that foreign policy options could be assessed separately on whether they achieved balance or dominance.

Physicist Herman Kahn (1965) then applied game theory, which been developed by mathematician John von Neumann and economist Oscar Morgenstern (1944) and as the "prisoner's dilemma" by political scientist David Rapoport and his colleagues (Rapoport and Orwant 1962; Rapoport et al. 1965). Kahn's aim was to "think about the unthinkable," developing what became the nuclear strategy of the United States (Kahn 1960, 1962). He argued that rational considerations come to the fore during times of stress rather than irrational impulses (Kahn 1965: 35). He recommended that decision-makers should evaluate alternative scenarios before making decisions, even including the option of nuclear war. The cinematic character Dr. Strangelove was based on his approach (Boyer 1996).

Dean Pruitt (1965), however, found that conditions of low and high stress were more likely to result in blunders compared to intermediate levels of stress. What is crucial is how urgent decision-makers define (later called "frame") the situation that they confront—in other words, whether they assign high or low (rather than mid-level) weights to the criteria that they apply to policy options.

Next, political scientist Ole Holsti discovered that message overload came earlier for aggressors than for countries responding to aggression (Holsti 1965). As war seems imminent, more messaging involved government heads, though the aggressor shuts off communication first. His study with David Brody and Robert North found that aggressors tend to prioritize policy criteria regarding emotions more than on the capabilities needed to win the war; aggressors overperceive adversaries as hostile, aiming to persecute them (Holsti et al. 1965). In contrast, decision-makers avoiding war focus on the criterion of the magnitude of military operations required to enter war.

Quincy Wright (1965) paid particular attention to escalation of disputes across 45 conflicts from 1921 to 1965. He concluded that escalation only occurs when decision-makers consider vital interests at stake, provided that the cost is affordable and forces are immediately available, with hostility perceptions playing no role. Thus, his key criteria were whether national power was in jeopardy, the cost of implementation, military resources, and logistics.

James Robinson and Roger Majak (1967) suggested five concepts to be considered—situation, participants, organization, process, and outcome. All five are relevant to what they called the three main types of decisions—intellectual, social, and routine (semi-mechanical). Craig Lundberg (1962) developed similar concepts for the field of public administration.

Political scientist Robert North and associates also focused on information-processing and feedback, a modified stimulus → response model (Holsti et al. 1968). The S-r-s-R model included stimuli (S) in the external environment only if perceived by decision-makers as inputs to a problem-solving task, whereas (r) constituted reactions (s) toward a target with eventual policy outcomes (R). Although most previous analyses focused on S and R, North unlocked information-processing as the s and r. The aim was to develop concepts about the decision-making process. Political scientist Robert Jervis (1968, 1970, 1976) then proceeded to document many examples of how foreign policy blunders are a function of informational misperceptions and cognitive limits during the input phase.

The next important effort to develop theories about the decision-making process was by political scientist Graham Allison, who wrote "Conceptual Models and the Cuban Missile Crisis" (1969) and *Essence of Decision: Explaining the Cuban Missile Crisis* (1971). Entirely qualitatively, he developed two alternative decision-making theories, which he called the governmental politics model (now known as the bureaucratic politics theory) and the organizational process model. The bureaucratic politics theory focused on the information-processing phase, arguing that decisions emerged from bargaining among presidential advisers, each seeking to advance their roles within the administration—engaging in turf battles. The most powerful and skillful adviser, Allison argued, is

32   M. HAAS

able to prevail, though the result may not necessarily be either a compromise or a rational decision. On the other hand, the organizational process theory, based on Herman Simon's "satisficing" concept, gave priority to how large bureaucracies with parochial priorities and perceptions follow standard operating procedures in processing information about stimuli selectively and then formulate options based on previously established priorities and procedures. Among many commentaries on Allison's contribution, political scientist Barbara Kellerman (1983) added three more models—the role of small groups, the dominant leader, and the cognitive process in shaping decisions. What Allison introduced was the notion that each presidential adviser might push their own policy option based on criteria derived from their roles in the decision-making process.

Social psychologist Kenneth Terhune (1970) argued that "national culture," however difficult to define, impacts not only how decisionmakers are guided in making their decisions but also affects how they attempt to legitimize what they do. In other words, when foreign policy options are debated, one important criterion was whether the public would support the decision. He was writing while protests mounted in opposition to the American intervention in Vietnam.

Psychologist Margaret Hermann (1970, 1978) sought to classify the personality of foreign policy decision-makers. She focused on beliefs, decision styles, interpersonal styles, and motivations to provide more holistic images.

In 1971, meanwhile, James Dougherty and Robert Pfaltzgraff published the first of several editions of *Contending Theories of International Relations*. The book not only reviewed foreign policy research but all other existing theories of international studies, bringing together behavioral and traditional scholarship.

Although President John F. Kennedy's decision-making in the Cuban Missiles Crisis has been universally praised, his legacy also includes the blunder known as the Bay of Pigs. In the latter situation, he accepted advice from the military to allow Cuban expatriates to attack Cuba under the assumption that they would mobilize Cuban support to overthrow Fidel Castro's government without considering the risks involved. After psychologist Irving Janis read an account of the Kennedy Administration by Arthur Schlesinger, Jr. (1965), he applied previous social psychological research (Whyte 1952; Lanzetta 1955) to assess the Bay of Pigs decision as a function of "groupthink"—that is, a search for "we-feeling" among a group of comrades who did not consider alternative options

(Janis 1971, 1972). He also attributed groupthink to President Lyndon Johnson's decision to enter Vietnam's civil war and many other examples. Groupthink, Janis asserted, is more likely under conditions of stress, since members of the decision-making unit will bind together vis-à-vis an adversary. With a feeling of invulnerability, ignoring evidence to the contrary, the result will be a decision involving extreme risks. Groupthink, thus, explained how Allison's bureaucratic process model operated.

According to Alexander George (1972), heads of competing bureaucracies may conspire to limit policy options. George then recommended consideration of as many options as possible by having the key decision-maker encourage "multiple advocacy" and thus competitive deliberation rather than groupthink or bureaucratic bargaining-and-compromise.

Political scientist Francis Rourke (1972: 49–50) stressed that bureaucracies are so vast that bureaucrats prefer inertia—doing things as they have in the past. Implementation, therefore, is frustratingly slow before and after decision-makers make their choices. Bureaucrats are the ones who feed information to those who deliberate among various options, and they assess feasibility of those options before and after decisions are made.

Concepts relating to how pressure groups impact foreign policy emerged from the analysis of political scientist Robert Dahl (1973). Similar studies were conducted on the role of public opinion by political scientist John Mueller (1973).

Contrary to George's "multiple advocacy" recommendation, political scientist John Steinbruner (1974) suggested that humans are not analytic in making decisions; instead, they engage in "cybernetic" responses to stimuli—that is, they respond to stimuli based on past experience by instinctively steering away from confusion and danger. If a decision is simple, then not much attention is required, and the matter is left to a specialist on the subject. As problems are more complicated, more people are drawn into the process, though each one will view how to handle the situation from the standpoint of their power in the bureaucracy, so leaders need to develop an integrated response. Steinbruner then distinguished between three types of thinking by leaders—grooved, uncommitted, and theoretical. "Grooved thinking" involves classifying a problem into a previously well-defined box—framing one problem as similar to a previous dilemma. Leaders engage in "uncommitted thinking" when they have no particular bias on the topic and make decisions that shift back and forth, accepting recommendations from various groups of advisers. "Theoretical thinking," which is much less likely, involves adhering to a particular abstract criterion as the basis for decisions even when conditions are uncertain. Clearly, he prioritized cognitive over analytic and emotional approaches.

Political scientists Glenn Snyder and Paul Diesing (1977) compiled a database of about 50 cases of crisis decision-making to test Allison's bargaining and bureaucratic models along with Simon's bounded rationality model. They found that the models were usually complementary, whereas the factor making the most difference was whether a decision-maker tried to be rational or instead had a rigid agenda.

The next major contribution to decision-making theory came from economist Amos Tversky, who earlier had critiqued expected utility theory as a variant of the Rational Choice Paradigm (Tversky 1975), which enjoys a long tradition from mathematician and physicist Daniel Bernoulli (1738) as developed into subjective expected utility theory by mathematician Leonard Savage (1954). Joined by fellow economist Daniel Kahneman, Tversky sought to explain gambling as a game of enjoying gains to offset the pain of losses. What they found was that in risky or stress situations, gamblers will violate expected utility considerations (Kahneman and Tversky 1979). The innovation was later imported to foreign policy analysis as prospect theory by political scientist Jack Levy (1992): When decision-makers are in a losing situation, he argued, they frame their role as seeking to achieve gains. One example is when President Jimmy Carter planned a mission to rescue Americans trapped in the American embassy in Tehran in 1960—an operation that failed (McDermott 1998).

Political scientist Bruce Bueno de Mesquita demonstrated the importance of expected utility theory in *The War Trap* (1981, 1985), which sought to discover when conflicts are most likely to escalate or be resolved. In so doing, he negated the Morgenthauistic "realist" notion that power distribution between countries is necessarily considered when countries go to war. Later, more scholars have argued the case for a more general game-theoretical approach (Snidal 1985; Brams and Marc Kilgore 1988; Putnam 1988).

Political scientist Richard Ned Lebow (1981), after reviewing several crisis situations, found that decision-makers seeking cognitive consistency and success ignore information contrary to their mindset, committing resources only when vital interests are at stake. He thereby demonstrated flaws in the Deterrence Paradigm. With a larger database, political scientists Michael Brecher, Jonathan Wilkenfeld, and Sheila Moser (1988) found that decision-makers in crises work with a smaller number of advisers than in ordinary situations, contradicting the findings of Steinbruner.

Behavioral research, which included far more scholarship than the summary above, identified criteria for evaluating foreign policy options beyond the extent of power that a state had available to invest and the feasibility of invoking that power in coping with a situation. Economic and prestige considerations mattered little during the Cold War.

Theories become paradigms when they apply at several levels of analysis, and behavioral research on decision-making pertained beyond foreign policy, often because insights were derived from other disciplines. Nevertheless, most scholars were testing very simple propositions, often with only two variables, one hypothesized to cause the other.

Anti-Behavioral Attack

Because the behavioral approach initially appeared to negate traditional international relations scholarship (Bull 1966), a debate ensued between the two approaches. However, the debate appeared to end when an essay urged recognition of both approaches as equally valuable (Haas 1967). After all, behavioral scholarship was only in its infancy.

Meanwhile, in 1965 American troops intervened in the ongoing civil war in Vietnam on the side of South Vietnam. As the count of war dead increased, so did the discontent over the American role in the war. International studies scholars began to claim that behavioral scholars were on a fishing expedition while the discipline needed to unite in opposition to the war. "Realism" regained support in the form of "postbehavioralism," particularly after Morgenthau (1965) argued that participation in the war was contrary to American national interest.

Whereas behavioral research was anti-ideological, opponents tagged them as "positivists." One such person was political scientist Henry Teune, who later reflected on the heyday of behavioral research in international studies, as scholars outside the United States were increasingly contributing to the literature but eschewed quantitative analysis (Teune 1982). From his viewpoint, behavioral research exclusively focused on decisions and decision-makers rather than on macro-trends. Many scholars were turned off as behavioral research became filled with statistical tables contrasting "models" and presented arguments that developed a series of equations described by unclear narratives.

In 1973, public pressure worked, and the United States withdrew military forces from Vietnam. When the Viet Cong marched into Saigon in 1975, the American embassy was evacuated. As a result, financial support for quantitative behavioral research on foreign policy plummeted.

Then in 1974, political scientist Warren Philipps (1974) decried the disappearance of empirical theory. In his essay, he could only identify four theories actively being pursued—arms-race theory, conflict-of-interest theory, field theory, and rank theory. All four were outside the field of foreign policy analysis and have subsequently languished.

The first book with the title *Theory of International Politics* (1979), written by political scientist Kenneth Waltz captured widespread attention and became a textbook. While some of the book belittled behavioral research, his main contribution was to transform "realism" into "neorealism." Thereby ideologies, which are primarily ethical principles, became inappropriately crowned as "theories" (cf. Barkin 2009).

Conflict between the Soviet and Western blocs of nations was still ongoing in the 1980s. But the Cold War ended in 1989 with the destruction of the Berlin Wall and 1991, when the Soviet Union was dissolved. Some critics of behavioral research speciously argued that all prior behavioral theories were wrong because they did not predict the end (cf. Ray and Russett 1996), whereas behavioral approaches were still searching for consensus.

Post-Cold War Foreign Policy Analysis

Quantitative behavioral approaches, adopted within the Cold War context, suddenly seemed irrelevant to many scholars, particularly those who grew up in the field by reading Waltz's *Theory of International Politics* as their bible. His "neorealism," relevant during the Cold War, continued to attract attention even though he prioritized ideology over empirical theory.

One study challenged researchers to determine which among several paradigms serve as the best explanations for international violence and international community (Haas 1992). But instead, the field returned to "pre-theories," developing approaches and concepts for a new era from several perspectives. As critics once stated, theories operationalize concepts with measures and then test relationships that occur in reality, whereas the field of foreign policy analysis then consisted of "models" that only dealt with relationships between concepts (Majeski and Sylvan 1984).

James Rosenau (1990) mused that the end of the well-managed conflict between two power blocs unleashed a world of unpredictable turbulence. One answer to his evident anxiety was to realize that the downplaying of military considerations opened the door to a host of new issues—culture, civil society, environment, human rights, regional cooperation, and the world economy (Haas 1997).

While realism became transformed as neorealism (Mearsheimer 2001) or perhaps as a "new world order" (Nye 1992), liberalism became neoliberalism (Keohane 1990; Baldwin 1993) and advanced into globalization theory (Held and McGrew 1993; Held et al. 1999). Global governance, a phrase popularized by Rosenau (1997), emerged as a fulfillment of the goal of a world engulfed in technical cooperation mechanisms first proposed by David Mitrany (1943).

When Samuel Huntington (1993) predicted the world would be afflicted by *The Clash of Civilizations* (1996), similar to the thinking of Pitirim Sorokin (1937), culture and religion were added to the list of foreign policy concerns (Hudson 1997). Francis Fukuyama (1992) suggested that history had come to an end with the culmination of Western liberal democracy as the only model of the future. Bruce Russett (1993) then began peddling the notion that the gradual spread of democracies would bring world peace, though tests and re-tests of his theory did not validate his "predictive approach" (Haas 2014) as he ultimately admitted (Russett 2005). Nevertheless, "regime type," with democracy in mind, has spawned many studies up to the present.

Instead of an opportunity for a revitalization of empirical theory and theory testing, such as how to improve human rights (Haas 1994), the field became more obscure as critics emerged to question not only each new trend but the foundation of foreign policy analysis itself. Alexander Wendt (1992, 1999) launched constructivism, a view that humans create reality for social purposes as a set of practices that observers often mislabel. Whereas structuralism placed state foreign policy into an uncertain context between world economic forces (Cox 1996), post-structuralism argued that meaning is derived from decoding language, which may be used to construct unreal visions—often, propaganda to

38   M. HAAS

delude (Wæver 1993). For example, "security" had formerly been interpreted to refer to military matters, but the term could also be used for such notions as economic security and social security.

Asking a more practical question about how decision-makers evaluate foreign policy options, political scientist Alex Mintz (1993) launched poliheuristic theory. His approach was an attempt to integrate the Rational Choice Paradigm, which assumes that alternatives are selected to maximize utilities, and the cybernetic approach that assumed decision-makers back options that satifice fundamental utilities—that is, the familiar dichotomy between reason and emotion (Mintz 2003). For Mintz, there is a two-stage process in choosing policies. During the first stage, options are evaluated in terms of feasibility, especially their political survival. In stage two, the options are evaluated in terms of minimizing risks and maximizing benefits. Evidence has been found to support the approach (James and Zhang 2005; Keller and Yang 2008, 2016).

TWENTY-FIRST CENTURY DEVELOPMENTS

The twenty-first century has experienced very little advancement in theory development. Examining issues of the *Foreign Policy Analysis* (FPA) journal, which began in 2006, indicate that the word "theory" rarely appears in titles. Most are descriptive accounts of particular issues with no attempt to theorize beyond the issue considered—a "large tent," according to political scientist Juliet Kaarbo (2015: 191). Even if theories have not been a concerted focus, the field should be praised for expanding the scope of knowledge, often concentrating on particular problems that remain dilemmas in an uncertain international environment.

Nevertheless, a new contribution is role theory, which was highlighted within an entire FPA issue in January 2012. Although the idea had been introduced earlier (Holsti 1970; Walker 1987), such scholars as political scientist Cameron Theis (2012) have argued that sociology's role theory brought into a single framework how decision-makers are socialized by several levels of reality—personal, group, national, and international—whether by coercion, self-interest, or a sense of legitimacy (Wendt 1999: 250)—and thus accommodated the conceptualization of constructivism.

However, role theory is a variant within the Socialization Paradigm, as previously developed by psychologists George Herbert Mead (1934) and Erik Erikson (1980). Some of those previously endorsing operational code theory shifted attention to role theory (Walker and Schafer 2021),

2 PRE-THEORIES OF DECISION-MAKING   39

a matter to be reviewed in Part II below. Several scholars have preferred to rely on the Socialization Paradigm and skip interest in the role theory variant (Checkel 2005; Fritz 2015).

Accordingly, the field of international studies today consists of several "models," not theories: (1) rational actor model, (2) governmental bargaining model, (3) organizational process model, (4) inter-branch process model, (5) self-aggrandizement model, and (6) political process model, including the role of civil society (Wikipedia 2022). Tacked onto the list are two more "approaches": (7) multilevel and multidimensional using major theories, and (8) constructivism, which focuses on "ideas, discourse, and identity." Such formulations are found in almost every textbook on foreign policy analysis (Alden and Aran 2016; Breuning 2007; Gvosdev et al. 2019; Hudson and Day 2019; Jentleson 2013; Morin and Paquin 2018; Smith et al. 2008).

Meanwhile, most textbooks on international relations theory today focus on propagandistic isms, thereby socializing a generation of scholars into accepting some views as established wisdom despite an absence of empirical evidence—and resistance to any effort to challenge such propaganda. While only a couple of early international relations theory textbooks had focused only on isms (Burchill and Linklater 1996; Viotti and Kauppi 1987), since the year 2000 nearly all textbooks on international relations theory have focused entirely on nonscientific ideological isms, with very few exceptions (Kydd 2015; Haas 2017a). The last edition of the textbook by Dougherty, Pfaltzgraff, and Devetak (2000) reviewed both behavioral and nonbehavioral studies, but the chapter on foreign policy analysis mutated into one on "decision-making theory."

During the twenty-first century, the focus on operational codes was also revived. A topic of interest as far back as 1948, the concept was developed more fully by several scholars. That approach is discussed in detail within Part II of the current volume.

CONCLUSION

Behavioral foreign policy analysis has developed many concepts, models, and theories. What is presented above is a brief summary. Scholars now diverge in their emphases, and the result has been a "jigsaw puzzle" of confusion (cf. Sigelman 2006), with graduate students following whatever their mentors prefer, competing for attention with other schools of thought. Yet scholars in the twenty-first century appeared to return

40 M. HAAS

to pre-theories. As David Houghton (2007: 26) once observed, foreign policy analysis has become "a body of microtheories logically unanchored in any extant theory of international relations." More recently, Klaus Brummer (2022) has observed that foreign policy analysis had not yet made a "critical turn," though he has shared "critical insights" that might assist. A recent collection of 34 methods for studying foreign policy remains at the pre-theoretical level (Mello and Ostermann 2022). With the multiplication of international studies journals, many scholars have focused exclusively on essays in the journal *Foreign Policy Analysis* and therefore are unaware of developments in other subfields as well as such other disciplines as economic and sociology.

Theories are developed to explain puzzles. The utility of empirical theories, as identified in the present chapter, is that they can be formulated and tested as possible explanations for particular decisions. However, many scholars today are pushing theories on an agenda that appears to be "theory supremacism"—that is, one scholar or a team of scholars advance one theory as the only theory of value. Yet many alternative theories have been advanced to explain the outbreak of war, how to build international institutions, and similar phenomena (Haas 1992, 2017a).

To his credit, Graham Allison accepted one model and rejected two in explaining decision-making during the Cuban Missiles Crisis, but few studies thus far have tried to cross-test theories (Allison and Halperin 1972; cf. Haas 2017b: ch11). Among other cross-tests of theories, two tried to find how best to build intergovernmental organizations (Haas 2013, 2022), and another was a study to determine why the United States normalized diplomatic relations after losing to Vietnam but failed after an armistice with North Korea—a study that involved three propositions from each of four major paradigms (Haas 2018).

What has been needed all along is an attempt to pool all the concepts, treat them as variables, find out their interrelationships, and test paradigmatic causal models. That is the agenda of the following chapter.

REFERENCES

Alden, Chris, and Ammon Aran. 2016. *Foreign Policy Analysis: New Approaches*. New York: Routledge.

Allison, Graham T. 1969. Conceptual Models and the Cuban Missile Crisis. *American Political Science Review* 63 (3): 689–718.

Allison, Graham T. 1971. *Essence of Decision: Explaining the Cuban Missile Crisis.* Boston: Little, Brown.

Allison, Graham T., and Morton Halperin. 1972. Bureaucratic Politics: A Paradigm and Some Policy Implications. *World Politics* 24 (1): 40–79.

Baldwin, David Allen. 1993. *Neorealism and Neoliberalism: The Contemporary Debate.* New York: Columbia University Press.

Barkin, Samuel. 2009. Realism, Predictions, and Foreign Policy. *Foreign Policy Analysis* 5 (3): 233–246.

Bernoulli, Daniel. 1738. Hydrodynamica. In *Landmark Writings in Western Mathematics 1640–1940*, ed. G.K. Mikhailov, 131–142. Amsterdam: Elsevier.

Boyer, Paul. 1996. Dr. Strangelove. In *Past Imperfect: History According to the Movies*, ed. Mark C. Carnes, 266–269. New York: Holt.

Brams, Steven J., and D. Marc Kilgore. 1988. *Game Theory and National Security.* New York: Basil Blackwell.

Braybrooke, David, and Charles E. Lindblom. 1963. *A Strategy of Decision.* New York: Free Press.

Brecher, Michael, Jonathan Wilkenfeld, and Sheila Moser. 1988. *Crises in the Twentieth Century: A Handbook of International Crises.* Oxford: Pergamon.

Breuning, Marijke. 2007. *Foreign Policy Analysis: A Comparative Introduction*, 2nd ed. New York: Palgrave Macmillan.

Brown, Jerry. 2022. Washington's Crackpot Realism. *New York Review of Books* 69 (5): 12, 14.

Brummer, Klaus. 2022. Toward a (More) Critical FPA. *Foreign Policy Analysis* 18 (1). https://doi.org/10.1093/fpa/orab031.

Bueno de Mesquita, Bruce. 1981. *The War Trap.* New Haven, CT: Yale University Press.

Bueno de Mesquita, Bruce. 1985. The War Trap Revisited: A Revised Expected Utility Model. *American Political Science Review* 79 (1): 156–177.

Bull, Hedley. 1966. International Theory: The Case for a Classical Approach. *World Politics* 10 (3): 361–377.

Burchill, Scott, and Andrew Linklater, eds. 1996. *Theories of International Relations.* New York: St. Martin's Press, 3rd ed., 2005.

Carr, Edward Hallett. 1939. *The Twenty Years Crisis, 1919–1939: An Introduction to the Study of International Relations.* London: Macmillan.

Checkel, Jeffrey T. 2005. International Institutions and Socialization in Europe: Introduction and Framework. *International Organization* 59 (4): 801–826.

Cox, Robert W., ed. 1996. *Approaches to World Order.* Cambridge, UK: Cambridge University Press.

Dahl, Robert A., ed. 1973. *Regimes and Oppositions.* New Haven, CT: Yale University Press.

Dahl, Robert A., and Charles E. Lindblom. 1953. *Politics, Economics, and Welfare.* New York: Harper.

Deutsch, Karl W., and J. David Singer. 1964. Multipolar Power Systems and International Stability. *World Politics* 16 (3): 390–406.

Dougherty, James E., and Robert L. Pfaltzgraff, Jr. 1971. *Contending Theories of International Relations: A Comprehensive Survey*, 1st ed. Philadelphia: Lippincott.

Dougherty, James E., Robert L. Pfaltzgraff, Jr., and Richard Devetak. 2000. *Contending Theories of International Relations: A Comprehensive Survey*, 5th ed. London: Pearson.

East, Maurice A. 1987. The Comparative Study of Foreign Policy: We're Not There Yet, But .... *International Studies Notes* 13 (2): 31–46.

Erikson, Erik H. 1980. *Identity and the Life Cycle*. New York: Norton.

Farrar, Lancelot L., Jr. 1992. Villain or Scapegoat? Nationalism and the Outbreak of World War I. *History of European Ideas* 15 (3): 377–381.

Fritz, Paul. 2015. Imposing Democracy to Ensure the Peace: The Role of Coercive Socialization. *Foreign Policy Analysis* 11 (4): 377–396.

Fukuyama, Francis. 1992. *The End of History and the Last Man*. New York: Free Press.

George, Alexander L. 1969. The 'Operational Code': A Neglected Approach to the Study of Political Leaders and Decision-Making. *International Studies Quarterly* 13 (4): 190–222.

George, Alexander L. 1972. The Case for Multiple Advocacy in Making Foreign Policy. *American Political Science Review* 66 (3): 751–785.

Gorer, Geoffrey, and John Rickman. 1949. *The People of Great Russia: A Psychological Study*. London: Cresset.

Guetzkow, Harold. 1959. A Use of Simulation in the Study of Inter-Nation Relations. *Behavioral Science* 4 (3): 183–191.

Guetzkow, Harold, ed. 1962. *Simulation in Social Science: Readings*. Englewood Cliffs, NJ: Prentice-Hall.

Guilhot, Nicholas. 2008. The Realist Gambit: Postwar American Political Science and the Birth of IR Theory. *International Political Sociology* 2 (4): 281–304.

Gvosdev, Nikolas K., Jessica D. Blankshain, and David A. Cooper. 2019. *Decision-Making in American Foreign Policy: Translating Theory into Practice*. New York: Cambridge University Press.

Haas, Ernst. 1958. *Beyond the Nation State: Functionalism and International Organization*. Stanford, CA: Stanford University Press.

Haas, Michael. 1967. Bridge Building in International Relations: A Neotraditional Plea. *International Studies Quarterly* 11 (4): 320–338.

Haas, Michael. 1992. *Polity and Society: Philosophical Underpinnings of Social Science Paradigms*. New York: Praeger.

Haas, Michael. 1994. *Improving Human Rights*. Westport, CT: Praeger.

Haas, Michael. 1997. International Communitarianism: The New Agenda of World Politics. In *Deconstructing International Relations Theory*, ed. Michael Haas, 102–107. New York: Norton.

Haas, Michael. 2013. *Asian and Pacific Regional Cooperation: Turning Zones of Conflict into Arenas of Peace*. New York: Palgrave Macmillan.

Haas, Michael. 2014. *Deconstructing the 'Democratic Peace': How a Research Agenda Boomeranged*. Los Angeles: Publishinghouse for Scholars.

Haas, Michael. 2017a. *International Relations Theory: Competing Empirical Paradigms*. Lanham, MD: Lexington.

Haas, Michael. 2017b. *Political Science Revitalized: Filling the Jigsaw Puzzle with Metatheory*. Lanham, MD: Lexington.

Haas, Michael. 2018. *United States Diplomacy with North Korea and Vietnam: Explaining Failure and Success*. New York: Peter Lang.

Haas, Michael. 2021. *The Politics of Lockdowns, Masks, and Vaccines: The Trump Administration and the Coronavirus*. New York: Peter Lang.

Haas, Michael. 2022. Building Growth Areas in Asia for Development and Peace. *Jadavpur Journal of International Relations* 26 (1): 1–36.

Held, David, and Anthony McGrew. 1993. Globalization and the Liberal Democratic State. *Government and Opposition* 28 (2): 261–288.

Held, David, David Goldblatt, Anthony McGrew, and Jonathan Perraton. 1999. *Global Transformations: Politics, Economics and Culture*. Stanford, CA: Stanford University Press.

Hermann, Charles F. 1963. Some Consequences of Crisis Which Limit the Viability of Organizations. *Administrative Science Quarterly* 7 (1): 61–82.

Hermann, Charles F. 1969. *Crises in Foreign Policy: A Simulation Analysis*. Indianapolis, IN: Bobbs-Merrill.

Hermann, Charles F., and Linda Brady. 1972. Alternative Models of International Crisis Behavior. In *International Crises: Insights from Behavioral Research*, ed. Charles F. Hermann, 281–303. New York: Free Press.

Hermann, Margaret G. 1970. Explaining Foreign Policy Behavior Using the Personal Characteristics of Political Leaders. *International Studies Quarterly* 24 (1): 7–46.

Hermann, Margaret G. 1978. Effects of Personal Characteristics of Leaders on Foreign Policy. In *Why Nations Act: Theoretical Perspectives for Comparative Foreign Policy Studies*, eds. Maurice A. East, Stephen A. Salmore, and Charles F. Hermann, 49–68. Beverly Hills, CA: Sage.

Holsti, Kalevi J. 1970. National Role Conceptions in the Study of Foreign Policy. *International Studies Quarterly* 14 (3): 233–309.

Holsti, Ole R. 1965. Perceptions of Time and Alternatives as Factors in Crisis Decision-Making. *Peace Research Society Papers* III: 79–120.

Holsti, Ole R., Richard A. Brody, and Robert C. North. 1965. Affect and Action in International Reaction Models. *Journal of Peace Research* 1 (3–4): 170–190.

Holsti, Ole R., Robert C. North, and Richard A. Brody. 1968. Perception and Action in the 1914 Crisis. In *Quantitative International Politics*, ed. J. David Singer, 123–158. New York: Free Press.

Houghton, David Patrick. 2007. Reinvigorating the Study of Foreign Policy Decision-Making: Towards a Constructivist Approach. *Foreign Policy Analysis* 3 (1): 24–45.

Hudson, Valerie M., ed. 1997. *Culture and Foreign Policy*. Boulder, CO: Lynne Reiner.

Hudson, Valerie M., and Benjamin S. Day. 2019. *Foreign Policy Analysis: Classic and Contemporary Theory*, 3rd ed. Lanham, MD: Rowman & Littlefield.

Huntington, Samuel P. 1993. The Clash of Civilizations? *Foreign Affairs* 72 (3): 22–49.

Huntington, Samuel P. 1996. *The Clash of Civilizations and the Remaking of World Order*. New York: Simon & Schuster.

James, Patrick, and Enyu Zhang. 2005. Chinese Choices: A Poliheuristic Analysis of Foreign Policy Crises, 1950–1996. *Foreign Policy Analysis* 1 (1): 31–54.

Janis, Irving. 1971. Groupthink. *Psychology Today* 43 (6): 74–76.

Janis, Irving. 1972. *Victims of Groupthink: A Psychological Study of Foreign Policy Decisions and Fiascoes*. Boston: Houghton Mifflin.

Jentleson, Bruce. 2013. *American Foreign Policy: The Dynamics of Choice in the 21st Century*, 5th ed. New York: Norton.

Jervis, Robert. 1968. Hypotheses on Misperception. *World Politics* 20 (3): 454–479.

Jervis, Robert. 1970. *The Logic of Images in International Relations*. Princeton, NJ: Princeton University Press.

Jervis, Robert. 1976. *Perception and Misperception in International Politics*. Princeton, NJ: Princeton University Press.

Kaarbo, Juliet. 2015. A Foreign Policy Analysis Perspective on the Domestic Politics Turn in IR Theory. *International Studies Review* 17 (2): 189–216.

Kahn, Herman. 1960. *On Thermonuclear War*. Princeton, NJ: Princeton University Press.

Kahn, Herman. 1962. *Thinking About the Unthinkable*. New York: Horizon Press.

Kahn, Herman. 1965. *On Escalation: Metaphors and Scenarios*. New York: Praeger.

Kahneman, Daniel, and Amos Tversky. 1979. Prospect Theory: An Analysis of Decision Under Risk. *Econometrica* 47 (2): 263–292.

Keller, Jonathan W., and Yi Edward Yang. 2008. Leadership Style, Decision Context, and the Poliheuristic Theory of Decision Making: An Experimental Analysis. *Journal of Conflict Resolution* 52 (5): 687–712.

Keller, Jonathan W., and Yi Edward Yang. 2016. Empathy as Strategic Interaction in Crises: A Poliheuristic Approach. *Foreign Policy Analysis* 5 (2): 169–189.

Kellerman, Barbara. 1983. Allison Redux: Three More Decision-Making Models. *Polity* 15 (3): 351–367.

Keohane, Robert O. 1990. Multilateralism: An Agenda for Research. *International Journal* 45 (4): 731–764.

Kydd, Andrew H. 2015. *International Relations Theory: The Game-Theoretical Approach*. New York: Cambridge University Press.

Lanzetta, John T. 1955. Group Behavior Under Stress. *Human Relations* 8 (1): 29–52.

Lasswell, Harold. 1927. *Propaganda Technique in the World War*. London: Kegan Paul, Trench, Trubner.

Lasswell, Harold. 1948. *The Analysis of Political Behavior: An Empirical Approach*. London: Routledge.

Lasswell, Harold, and Abraham Kaplan. 1950. *Power and Society: A Framework for Political Inquiry*. New Haven, CT: Yale University Press.

Lasswell, Harold, and Nathan Leites, eds. 1949. *Language of Politics: Studies in Quantitative Semantics*. New York: Stewart.

Lasswell, Harold, and Daniel Lerner. 1951. *The Policy Sciences: Recent Developments in Scope and Method*. Stanford, CA: Stanford University Press.

Lazarsfeld, Paul F. 1960. Review of 'Delay in the Court.' *Public Opinion Quarterly* 24 (4): 695–700.

Lebow, Richard Ned. 1981. *Between Peace and War: The Nature of International Crisis*. Baltimore: Johns Hopkins Press.

Leites, Nathan. 1948. Psycho-Cultural Hypotheses About Political Acts. *World Politics* 1 (1): 102–119.

Leites, Nathan. 1949. Interaction: The Third International on Its Change of Policy. In *Language of Politics: Studies in Quantitative Semantics*, ed. Harold D. Lasswell and Nathan Leites, Chapter 11. New York: Stewart.

Leites, Nathan. 1951. *The Operational Code of the Politburo*. New York: McGraw Hill.

Leites, Nathan. 1953. *A Study of Bolshevism*. Glencoe, IL: Free Press.

Leites, Nathan, Else Bernaut, and Raymond L. Garthoff. 1951. Politburo Images of Stalin. *World Politics* 3 (3): 317–339.

Levy, Jack S. 1992. Prospect Theory and International Relations: Theoretical Applications and Analytical Problems. *Political Psychology* 13 (2): 283–310.

Lindblom, Charles E. 1959. The Science of Muddling Through. *Public Administration Review* 19 (2): 79–88.

46 M. HAAS

Lundberg, Craig C. 1962. Administrative Decisions: A Scheme for Analysis. *Journal of the Academy of Management* 5 (2): 165–178.

Majeski, Stephen J., and David J. Sylvan. 1984. Simple Choices and Complex Calculations: A Critique of the War Trap. *Journal of Conflict Resolution* 28 (2): 316–340.

McClelland, Charles A. 1961. The Acute International Crisis. *World Politics* 14 (2): 182–204.

McClelland, David C. 1961. *The Achieving Society*. New York: Van Nostrand.

McClelland, David C. 1987. *Human Motivation*. New York: Cambridge University Press.

McDermott, Rose. 1998. *Risk Taking in International Politics: Prospect Theory in Post-War American Foreign Policy*. Ann Arbor: University of Michigan Press.

Mead, George Herbert. 1934. *Mind, Self, and Society*. Chicago: University of Chicago Press.

Mearsheimer, John. 2001. *The Tragedy of Great Power Politics*. New York: Norton.

Mello, Patrick A., and Falk Ostermann, eds. 2022. *Routledge Handbook of Foreign Policy Analysis Methods*. New York: Routledge.

Mills, C. Wright. 1958. *The Causes of World War III*. New York: Simon & Schuster.

Mintz, Alex. 1993. The Decision to Attack Iraq: A Non-Compensatory Theory of Decision Making. *Journal of Conflict Resolution* 37 (4): 595–618.

Mintz, Alex. 2003. *Integrating Cognitive and Rational Theories of Foreign Policy Decision Making: A Poliheuristic Perspective*. New York: Palgrave Macmillan.

Mitrany, David. 1943. *A Working Peace System. An Argument for the Functional Development of International Organization*. London: Royal Institute of International Affairs.

Morgenthau, Hans J. 1948. *Politics Among Nations: The Struggle for Power and Peace*. New York: Knopf.

Morgenthau, Hans J. 1965. Are We Deluding Ourselves in Vietnam? *New York Times*, April 18.

Morin, Jean-Frédéric., and Jonathan Paquin. 2018. *Foreign Policy Analysis: A Toolbook*. New York: Palgrave Macmillan.

Mueller, John E. 1973. *War, Presidents, and Public Opinion*. New York: Wiley.

Murray, Henry. 1938. *Explorations in Personality*. New York: Oxford University Press.

North, Robert C. 1967. The Analytical Prospects of Communication Theory. In *Contemporary Political Analysis*, ed. James C. Charlesworth, 300–316. New York: Free Press.

Nye, Joseph R., Jr. 1992. What New World Order? *Foreign Affairs* 71 (2): 83–96.

Pepinsky, Thomas B. 2005. From Agents to Outcomes: Simulation in International Relations. *European Journal of International Relations* 11 (3): 367–394.

Philipps, Warren. 1974. Where Have All the Theories Gone? *World Politics* 26 (2): 155–188.

Pruitt, Dean G. 1965. Definition of the Situation as a Determinant of International Acts. In *International Behavior: A Social-Psychological Analysis*, ed. Herbert C. Kelman, 391–432. New York: Holt, Rinehart, Winston.

Putnam, Robert D. 1988. Diplomacy and Democratic Politics: The Logic of Two-Level Games. *International Organization* 42 (3): 427–460.

Rapoport, Anatol, Albert M. Chammah, and Carol Orwant. 1965. *Prisoner's Dilemma: A Study in Conflict and Cooperation*. Ann Arbor: University of Michigan Press.

Rapoport, Anatol, and Carol Orwant. 1962. Experimental Games: A Review. *Behavioral Science* 7 (1): 1–37.

Ray, James Lee, and Bruce Russett. 1996. The Future as Arbiter of Theoretical Controversies: Predictions, Explanations and the End of the Cold War. *British Journal of Political Science* 26 (4): 441–470.

Robinson, James A., and R. Roger Majak. 1967. The Theory of Decision Making. In *Contemporary Political Analysis*, ed. James C. Charlesworth, 175–188. New York: Free Press.

Rosenau, James N. 1961. *Public Opinion and Foreign Policy*. New York: Random House.

Rosenau, James N. 1966. Pre-Theories and Theories in Foreign Policy. In *Approaches to Comparative and International Politics*, ed. R. Barry Farrell, 27–92. Evanston, IL: Northwestern University Press.

Rosenau, James N. 1990. *Turbulence in World Politics: A Theory of Change and Continuity*. Princeton, NJ: Princeton University Press.

Rosenau, James N. 1992. Governance, Order and Change in World Politics. In *Governance Without Government: Order and Change in World Politics*, eds. James N. Rosenau and Ernst-Ottawa Czempiel, Chapter 1. New York: Cambridge University Press.

Rosenau, James N. 1997. *Exploring Governance in a Turbulent World*. New York: Cambridge University Press.

Rourke, Francis E. 1972. Review of *Essence of Decision: Explaining the Cuban Missile Crisis* by Graham T. Allison. *Administrative Science Quarterly* 17 (3): 431–443.

Ruesch, Jürgen, and Gregory Bateson. 1951. *Communication: The Social Matrix of Psychiatry*. New York: Norton.

Russett, Bruce M. 1962. Cause, Surprise, and No Escape. *Journal of Politics* 24 (1): 3–22.

48 M. HAAS

Russett, Bruce M. 1963. The Calculus of Deterrence. *Journal of Conflict Resolution* 7 (3): 97–109.

Russett, Bruce M. 1993. *Grasping the Democratic Peace: Principles for a Post-Cold War World*. Princeton, NJ: Princeton University Press.

Russett, Bruce M. 2005. Bushwhacking the Democratic Peace. *International Studies Perspectives* 6 (4): 395–408.

Sarkees, Meredith Reid, and Frank Wayman. 2010. *Resort to War, 1816–2007*. Washington, DC: CQ Press.

Savage, Leonard J. 1954. *The Foundations of Statistics*. New York: Dover.

Schelling, Thomas C. 1960. *The Strategy of Conflict*. Cambridge, MA: Harvard University Press.

Schlesinger, Arthur M., Jr. 1965. *A Thousand Days*. Boston: Houghton Mifflin.

Sigelman, Lee. 2006. The Coevolution of American Political Science and the American Political Science Review. *American Political Science Review* 100 (4): 463–478.

Simon, Herbert A. 1958. *Administrative Behavior*. New York: Macmillan.

Smith, Steve, Amelia Hadfield, and Tim Dunne, eds. 2008. *Foreign Policy: Theories, Actors, Cases*, 3rd ed. New York: Oxford University Press.

Snidal, Duncan. 1985. The Game Theory of International Politics. *World Politics* 38 (1): 25–57.

Snyder, Glenn H., and Paul Diesing. 1977. *Conflict Among Nations: Bargaining, Decision-Making and System Structure in International Crises*. Princeton, NJ: Princeton University Press.

Snyder, Richard C., H.W. Bruck, and Burton Sapin. 1954. *Decision-Making as an Approach, to the Study of International Politics*. Princeton, NJ: Princeton University Press.

Sorokin, Pitirim. 1937. *Fluctuations of Social Relationships, War, and Revolution*. Volume III of *Social and Cultural Dynamics*. New York: American Book Company.

Sprout, Harold, and Margaret Sprout. 1956. *Man-Milieu Relationship Hypotheses in the Context of International Politics*. Princeton, NJ: Center of International Studies, Princeton University.

Steinbruner, John D. 1974. *The Cybernetic Theory of Decision*. Princeton, NJ: Princeton University Press.

Terhune, Kenneth W. 1970. From National Character to National Behavior: A Reformulation. *Journal of Conflict Resolution* 14 (2): 203–263.

Teune, Henry. 1982. The International Studies Association. https://www.isanet.org/Portals/0/Documents/Institutional/Henry_Teune_The_ISA_1982.pdf.

Theis, Cameron G. 2012. International Socialization Processes vs. Israeli National Role Conceptions: Can Role Theory Integrate IR Theory and Foreign Policy Analysis? *Foreign Policy Analysis* 8 (1): 25–46.

2 PRE-THEORIES OF DECISION-MAKING 49

Tversky, Amos. 1975. A Critique of Expected Utility Theory: Descriptive and Normative Considerations. *Erkenntnis* 1: 163–173.

Viotti, Paul R., and Mark V. Kauppi. 1987. *International Relations Theory: Realism, Pluralism, Globalism*. New York: Macmillan.

von Neumann, John, and Oscar Morgenstern. 1944. *Theory of Games and Economic Behavior*. Princeton, NJ: Princeton University Press.

Wæver, Ole. 1993. *Securitization and Desecuritization*. Copenhagen: Centre for Peace and Conflict Research.

Walker, Stephen G. 1987. *Role Theory and Foreign Policy Analysis: An Evaluation*. Durham, NC: University of North Carolina Press.

Walker, Stephen G., and Mark Schafer. 2021. The Interface Between Beliefs and Roles in World Politics. In *Operational Code Analysis and Foreign Policy Roles: Crossing Simon's Bridge*, eds. Mark Schafer and Stephen G. Walker, 3–16. New York: Routledge.

Waltz, Kenneth. 1979. *Theory of International Politics*. New York: McGraw-Hill.

Wendt, Alexander. 1992. Anarchy Is What States Make of It: The Social Construction of Power Politics. *International Organization* 46 (2): 395–421.

Wendt, Alexander. 1999. *Social Theory of International Politics*. New York: Cambridge University Press.

Wikipedia. 2022. Foreign Policy Analysis, March. https://en.wikipedia.org/wiki/Foreign_policy_analysis. Accessed February 10, 2023.

Whyte, William H., Jr. 1952. Groupthink. *Fortune*, March, pp. 114–117, 142, 146.

Wright, Quincy. 1965. The Escalation of International Conflicts. *Journal of Conflict Resolution* 9 (4): 434–449.

Zinnes, Dina A., Robert C. North, and Howard E. Koch. 1961. Capability, Threat, and the Outbreak of War. In *International Politics and Foreign Policy*, ed. James N. Rosenau, 469–482. New York: Free Press.

CHAPTER 3

Quantifying Alternative Pre-Theories

Some foreign policy analysts, as reviewed above (Chapters 1–2), tend to stick to their own idiosyncratic concepts, deliberately ignoring others as if they were magically in possession of the golden truth. If someone were to pool almost all of their concepts into a single study to determine which theory is best at explaining decision-making, then the field might advance. What follows below is such an effort, explaining conceptual variables employed, the source of data, methods utilized, and conclusions drawn. The concepts are drawn from pre-theoretical formulations from the days of Richard Snyder (Snyder et al. 1954) and James Rosenau (1966) to the present. Because the focus is on decision-making, concepts will be applied to international, national, and subnational decisions.

CONCEPTS

The concepts in the foreign policy literature can be standardized into a table of sixteen positions with two metaconcepts (Table 3.1). The phases in the Decision-Making Cycle are familiar—prestimulus, stimulus, information-processing, and outcome (Snyder et al. 1954: 74). What is also important to classify four ways in which the decision-makers define or frame their task—as an affective, cognitive, evaluative, and structural challenge (Holsti 1967). Each box in the table is home to one or more concepts, sixteen in all.

© The Author(s), under exclusive license to Springer Nature Switzerland AG 2023
M. Haas, *Professionalization of Foreign Policy*,
https://doi.org/10.1007/978-3-031-37152-3_3

51

52 M. HAAS

Table 3.1 A Decision-Making Schema

Framing of the Situation	Phases in the Decision-Making Cycle			
	Prestimulus	Stimulus	Information-Processing	Outcome
Affective aspects				
Cognitive aspects				
Evaluative aspect				
Structural aspects				

The *affective* category refers to psychological motivation. When decision-makers frame a task as *cognitive*, they focus on the intellectual task of object appraisal, using communication and information. Weighing alternative means and ends is the *evaluative* element in a situation. The *structural* aspect is the hierarchical level of the agent, stimulus decision-making body, and the target, sometimes known as the "sphere of competence."

Each concept, drawn from studies cited in the previous chapter, is used as an independent variable hypothetically to explain the dependent variable—outbreak of violence. Accordingly, one dependent variable is identified for each phase, as indicated next.

Prestimulus Concepts

Affective Aspects. Emotional attachment to a situation is expressed by two variables: (1) *Prior concern* distinguishes between old and new challenges. Regardless of the degree of previous attention to a problem, decision-makers may (2) *invoke precedent* or treat the situation as de novo. For example, Woodrow Wilson's request for Congress to declare war in 1917 has been called the "great departure" (Smith 1965), whereas nomination of someone to serve as an ambassador traditionally has involved Congressional deference to the president.

Cognitive Aspects. Challenges also differ in terms of the (3) *correctness of intelligence estimates* about the situation and (4) *accuracy of warning signs*. Hitler received excellent intelligence prior to attacking Norway, arriving at the fjords just one day before Britain (Ziemke 1959), whereas the discovery of missile sites in Cuba was a total surprise to the Kennedy Administration (Abel 1966; Schlesinger 1965).

Evaluative Aspects. Prestimulus evaluation is manifested by (5) *prior planning*, such as anticipatory commitments and contingency plans. An apriori evaluation exists on the basis of (6) *alignment status*, such as whether the potential stimulus has been an agent's adversary, ally, or a neutral relationship. Lack of planning before the unexpected Korean War (Paige 1968) contrasts sharply with the set of plans drawn up for dropping an atomic bomb on Japan (Batchelder 1961; Morton 1959a). Baron Kantarō Susuzi's appointment as prime minister of Japan in 1945 by an inner circle of decision-makers (Butow 1954) is easily distinguished from Vladimir Lenin's decision to launch the October Revolution, thereby overthrowing progress achieved by the February Revolution (Shapiro 1955).

Structural Aspects. The concept of (7) *prior cohesion* refers to whether the administrative structure of a decision-making organization is integrated or fragmented. A critical element is (8) *probability of office-holding* by the main decision-maker. High cohesion was present within the Kennedy Administration's actions toward Cuba (Abel 1966; Schlesinger 1965), but was uncertain at the time when negotiations stretched out for more than a year to achieve an armistice to end the Korean War (Vatcher 1958).

Dependent Variable. (9) *Ongoing violence* is the appropriate dependent variable at the prestimulus phase. Decisions should differ considerably when war suddenly emerges as opposed to tactical moves in an ongoing war. President Harry Truman's decision to drop an atomic bomb occurred when war was in progress, but the outbreak of the Korean War was a surprise (Batchelder 1961; Morton 1959a; Paige 1968).

Stimulus Concepts

Affective Aspects. Stimuli can evoke a variety of emotional responses by an agent vis-à-vis a target. One consideration that quickly emerges is (10) *trust*—that is, whether the agent believes that the target is well intentioned. Suzuki's appointment differed considerably from Truman's assessment of Japan's willingness to surrender prior to authorizing the Hiroshima bomb (Butow 1954; Batchelder 1961; Morton 1959a). Decision-makers also perceive their degree of (11) *control over events* and (12) *time pressure*. Adolf Hitler was quite confident that the German army could take over Poland after he negotiated a nonaggression pact with Josef Stalin (Bullock 1964), but Woodrow Wilson was unsure what would

54 M. HAAS

happen after American troops were sent to Siberia on a mission of eventually overthrowing the Bolshevik regime (Unterberger 1956). Senators often take their sweet time in confirming presidential appointments, but the Chicago police acted immediately to clear Haymarket Square as soon as a bomb went off to prevent their entry during 1887 (Zeisler 1956; David 1958).

Cognitive Aspects. When a decision-making task is triggered by a stimulus, an initial intellectual task is to ascertain the scope of the problem, notably whether the issue is a simple one or instead is a *multi-issue* (13) problem. For example, Wilson evaluated Germany from economic, ideological, and military perspectives in 1917, but the German army's takeover of Norway 23 years later was based entirely on military considerations (Smith 1965; Ziemke 1959). Because a stimulus interrupts ongoing activities, another element is the (14) *noise level*—that is, whether the decision-maker can focus intensely or has other issues that may crowd out a recent stimulus. The Bolsheviks were single-minded about seizing power (Shapiro 1955), whereas Congressional actions to pass a law are handled within a mix of multiple activities.

Evaluative Aspects. While decoding a stimulus, decision-makers classify it in several ways. The most obvious is how important the problem is, so (15) *cruciality* is one of the major determinations. The Bolsheviks were concerned with their raison d'être in 1917 (Shapiro 1955), but a governor's commutation of a death sentence does not shake a state to its very foundations (David 1958). Because decision-making occurs at several levels—from inside a family, a city, a province, an entire country, or is of international significance—, a second evaluative concept if (16) *level of analysis*. Decisions to enter wars are at a higher level than police conduct in a town square.

Structural Aspects. The source of the stimulus places the decision-making problem into at least three contexts—(17) *foreign stimulus*, (18) *cultural similarity*, and (19) *power superiority*. Domestic stimuli usually involve civil society and situations where information is easier to collect than something outside a country. Those advising Truman in 1945 applied cultural lenses and thereby misinterpreted the *mokusatsu* comment by a spokesperson for the Japanese prime minister to be an arrogant rejection of the Potsdam Declaration, resulting in the order to bomb Hiroshima (Kawai 1950). But when Truman fired General Douglas MacArthur as commander of American troops during the Korean War, he had the full power to do so (Spanier 1959; Truman 1959).

Dependent Variable. At the stimulus level, (20) *threat of violence* differs considerably from nonviolent intrusions. Positioning military units on three sides of a country deemed hostile and clearly constituted threat of violence against Ukraine in 2022 (Sonne et al., 2022).

Information-Processing Concepts

Affective Aspects. The moods and personal needs of decision-makers are difficult to decipher until a scholar reviews statements and comments by those involved. Three obvious windows into the psychology of decision-makers are (21) *risk propensity*, (22) *tolerance of ambiguity*, and (23) *self-esteem*. Hitler took incredible risks by not ordering German forces surrounded in Stalingrad to retreat; he did not want to hear adverse information about their plight, and he was confident that he always made correct decisions (Zeitzler 1965). Even deeper into the personality of decision-makers is whether they express (24) *needs for achievement*, (25) *needs for power*, or (26) *needs for affiliation*. Bolsheviks had high needs for achievement and power in 1917, and they were not interested in cooperating with the Provisional Government of Alexander Kerensky (Shapiro 1955). Decision-makers also perceive the targets of their deliberations in terms of (27) *perceptions of frustration* and (28) *perceptions of hostility*. American negotiators were both frustrated and hostile toward North Korea during armistice negotiations, which lasted two years at Panmunjom (Vatcher 1958).

Cognitive Aspects. Extensiveness of deliberation can be measured by (29) *decision time*, counting the number of days between the stimulus and the decision. Some laws are formulated and debated for an entire year before passage, whereas the Chicago police made a snap decision to clear Haymarket Square after a bomb went off (Zeisler 1956; David 1958). The amount of information processed can be assessed in two ways— (30) *cognitive complexity* refers to the facets of information consulted, whereas (31) *input load* is the amount of information processed. The American decision in the Cuban Missiles crisis was multifaceted, involving direct and secret diplomacy, aerial reconnaissance, and military leaders in the air force and navy (Allison 1971), whereas MacArthur's deliberate disobedience involving a plan to attack inside China was all the information that Truman needed to fire him (Spanier 1959: ch10–13; Truman 1959). Input load can be classified as overload, underload, or optimum load. Hitler's decision to leave German soldiers in Stalingrad

56   M. HAAS

was based on information underload (Zeitzler 1965), yet negotiators at Panmunjom were overloaded (Vatcher 1958), and the amount was about right for Congress to ratify the Japanese Peace Treaty in 1952 (Jacobs and Gallagher 1967). In addition, (32) *input intensity* refers to the amount of redundant information processed. For example, Hitler stuck by his Stalingrad decision despite frequent warnings from his generals (Zeitzler 1965), whereas Wilson kept seeking as much information as possible before sending American troops to Murmansk, Russia, in 1917 (Strakhovsky 1937). (33) *Input range* is a count of the number of channels used during discussions—oral, written, official, unofficial, and at how many hierarchical levels in the agent as well as the target. Complex decision-making during the Cuban Missiles Crisis stands in stark contrast with President Franklin Roosevelt's decision to force Japanese on the West Coast into internment camps after the Pearl Harbor attack in 1941 (Allison 1971; Conn 1959). The (34) *input/output ratio* is a judgment about how much information was needed before a decision is made. Deliberations at Panmunjom from 1951 to 1953, for example, were "talkathons," with a lot of communications about an agreement to stop troops from fighting and establish normality in Korea (Vatcher 1958). The (35) *metacommunication level* refers to whether communications reach a point of "Aha!" fidelity, when each side explains itself honestly (Ruesch and Bateson 1951). The objectives of the Bolsheviks were clear to everyone in October 1917, whereas the situation at the Vietnamese battlefield of Dienbienphu in 1954 was too obscure for those in Washington to make a definite decision to assist the French (Shapiro 1955; Ziemke 1959). Yet another element is whether there is a (36) *reduction in communications* as deliberation proceeds. Sometimes decision-makers stop asking for information, as when London decided in 1956 to seize control of the Suez Canal rather than continuing to deliberate on a compromise agreement with Washington (Epstein 1964; Robertson 1965). Finally, information-processing can be assessed in terms of the (37) *learning rate* during deliberations. Decision-making bodies that do not correct distortions and misperceptions are unlikely to cope adequately with the situation at hand. Hitler let his troops in Stalingrad starve because he continued to believe that they were invincible (Zeitzler 1965).

Evaluative Aspects. Appropriate alternatives, cues, and values are determined during information-processing. There is a possibility of (38) *stereotypic decoding*, which involves decoding information nonveridically, as when the Kennedy Administration foolishly decided to support a "coalition" government in Laos during 1961 (Hilsman 1967). (39) *Structured evaluation* is characterized by separating the deliberation process into component parts. Truman's decision to fire MacArthur was much clearer than Kennedy's decision to allow the Bay of Pigs operation to proceed (Spanier 1959; Truman 1959; Bullock 1964). A broad or narrow (40) *range of alternatives* can also distinguish how information is processed. Congress, for example, may be asked to declare war or instead to pass a law after first considering one hundred or more amendments. (41) *Intraorganizational consonance* occurs when there is wide agreement on each aspect of deliberation. In 1962, the Kennedy Administration was united in asking the steel industry to rescind a price increase, whereas *contention* plagued negotiations at Panmunjom (McConnell 1963; Vatcher 1958). Some processing proceeds through (42) *hierarchical resolution*, a continuum that runs from one person in charge to polyarchic situations where many exercise veto powers over decisions, such as when the public or civil society had checks on the executive. Dulles, for example, arbitrarily decided not to answer Egypt's request for funding the Aswan Dam without seeking advice from anyone (Finer 1964). Legitimation of the resulting decision can be handled (43) *pragmatically* rather than *ideologically*. Fighting communism was the reason Wilson gave to send troops to Siberia in 1917 (Unterberger 1956).

Structural Aspects. One measure of structural complexity is (44) the *size of the decision-making body*. Legislative bodies are much larger than executives in deliberating. (45) *Decision latitude* refers to how much authority a decision-making unit has. For example, negotiators at truce talks in Panmunjom were restricted by their superiors in Washington on what positions they could take (Vatcher 1958), whereas Hitler refused his general's request to withdraw German troops from Stalingrad, where Russian troops completely surrounded the city (Zeitzler 1965). (46) *Officiality* refers to whether a decision is processed through an established body or instead is made outside normal channels, such as the official Stalingrad and multi-country Panmunjom decisions. (47) *Contraction in authority* often occurs when a number of persons are excluded from deliberation. Lenin decided to have the Central Committee rather than the plenary body of the Bolsheviks consider when to launch the Bolshevik revolution (Shapiro 1955). After a legislative body initiates a law, members can either work together or seek executive input.

58   M. HAAS

Dependent Variable. Information-processing is distinguished by whether there is (48) *consideration of violence* as a possible option. Congress, for example, rarely decides what to do when a stimulus involves violence, leaving the matter for executive action.

Outcome Concepts

Affective Aspects. When an agent and/or a target revises an opinion of the other, (49) *sociometric change* has occurred. Dulles' decision to deny funds to Egypt for the Aswan Dam was entirely unexpected because he previously had a friendly policy toward the Arab world (Finer 1964). Another emotional element occurs when a policy is implemented on a (50) *continuous* rather than half-hearted (intermittent) basis. The decision to move Korean truce talks from Kaeson to Panmunjom had a continuous impact, whereas progress in the talks was intermittent (Vatcher 1958). In addition, decisions might be characterized as (51) *cumulative* rather than sporadic. When Congress passed the Full Employment Act in 1946, not everyone got a job; however, the Congressional decision in 1950 to require men aged 18–26 to register for the military draft had a cumulative effect (Bailey 1950; Jacobs and Gallagher 1967).

Cognitive Aspects. Decisions are more impactful if they produce change, but there are many types of change. A high degree of (52) *guidance* involves a situation in which the agent controls the target like a puppet, as when Roosevelt ordered internment of all Japanese on the West Coast during World War II (Conn 1959). Some decisions, however, can have (53) *revocability*, unlike the impact of atomic bombs dropped on Hiroshima and Nagasaki. Historians are pleased to classify decisions as (54) *turning points* that alter history dramatically, such as Japan's decision to bomb Pearl Harbor (Morton 1959b; Wohlstetter 1962). If a decision accomplishes the objectives sought, the result is regarded as (55) *success*, a concept that should be judged rigorously, such as Hitler's invasion of Poland in 1939 that ended up with Nazi occupation of the country (Bullock 1964). (56) *Implementation speed* focuses on the bureaucratic element of a decision—the time between a decision is made and is carried out. The Chicago police promptly dispersed German language protesters at Haymarket Square in 1877, but the Bolshevik Revolution did not completely control Russia until foreign attacks were defeated (Zeisler 1956; David 1958).

Evaluative Aspects. Decisions are supposed to change a situation, but there are differences in what has been called the "character of change" (Rosenau 1961: 226). One impact is a (57) *stabilizing* decision, as when Hitler did not give an order for German troops to leave Stalingrad (Zeitzler 1965). If a decision involves (58) *goal-restructuring*, sometimes called a "flip" in decision-making, then a new hierarchy of ends and means is created. Voluntary repatriation of prisoners from the Korean War was innovative, since some Americans stayed in Korea due to what was called brainwashing (Vatcher 1958). A (59) *promotive* decision differs from a preventive decision, such as when the U.S. Congress established the International Development Association (Robinson 1960), whereas a presidential veto would have prevented that agency from coming into existence. The familiar distinction between (60) *maximizing* and *satisficing* also is a matter of outcome evaluation.

Structural Aspects. Some outcomes have bigger impacts than others. The (61) *penetration* of a decision refers to a situation when attitudes, behavior, and structures are modified. The Bolshevik Revolution had a monumental impact until the end of the Cold War, whereas nothing much changed when Illinois Governor Richard Oglesby commuted a death sentence of two participants in the Haymarket Riot to life terms (Zeisler 1956; David 1958). The (62) *transience* of a decisional impact refers to how long the decision endures, from momentary to temporary to permanent. Kennedy's "quarantine" of missiles headed from the Soviet to Cuba had a lasting effect from 1962 to 1989, when the Cold War came to an end, but vetoes by executives of laws passed by legislature often ensure that nothing will change. In addition, some outcomes are (63) *procedural* rather than *substantive*; the former occurred when Governor John S. Fine vetoed a bill passed by the Pennsylvania legislature that would have substantively limited loads carried by trucks (Hacker 1962). In addition, an outcome that is written down is (64) *formal*, not *informal*. Statutes are more formal than speeches.

Dependent Variable. The final outcome variable is a decision that results in (64) *violence* rather than avoiding violence, though some foreign policy decisions fall somewhere in between.

DATABASE

Many articles and books have been written about domestic and foreign policy decisions. One in particular, *Command Decisions* (1959) by Kent Roberts Greenfield, provides the nuts and bolts of several decisions within a single volume. More cases are selected herein, with a total of 32 decisions involving domestic and foreign policy in several countries (see Appendix at the end of the chapter). The cases span the years 1887 to 1962 and thus are detached from contemporary bias. Some but not all involve violence.

Most event databases pretend that they are 100 percent correct. But since sources of information can vary in reliability, three more measures are employed: (66) *extent of documentation*, whether the source is (67) *academic* or *journalistic*, and the (68) *length* of description.

Because all cases are to be compared on so many variables, reliability with a large sample might be difficult. Nevertheless, a reliability coefficient was derived for some randomly selected variables (Table 3.2) by making assessments at two different times. The coefficient is constructed as follows: agreements/(agreements + disagreements). Results suggest sufficient reliability to proceed.

FACTOR ANALYSIS

Most foreign policy analyses over the years have been pre-theoretical, seeking to develop concepts within theories but never putting the theories to test. During the Cold War the primary focus was on determining the causes of war and escalation leading to war. The present database has violence as a dependent variable across all four phases of decision-making, so there are 64 conceptual variables.

Each case is next placed on a six-point scale, as determined qualitatively. The six judgmental positions are very high, high, medium–high, medium–low, low, and very low. The appropriate scaling quota will thus be $1 + 5 + 10 + 10 + 5 + 1$. The approach is similar to Glenn Paige (1968), who had two cases for comparison and therefore used one (1) and zero (0) scale positions (cf. Haas 2018). Such a distribution of cases, approximating a normal curve for statistical analysis, is known as the Q-Sort or Q-Technique Method, long used in the social sciences (Stephenson 1953; Block 1961).

3 QUANTIFYING ALTERNATIVE PRE-THEORIES 61

Table 3.2 Reliability Coefficients of Conceptual Variables

Conceptual Variable		Reliability Coefficient
1	Prior concern	
2	Probability of office-holding	0.82
3	Correct intelligence	
4	Warning signs decoded	0.77
5	Prior concern	
6	Precedent invoked	
7	Prior planning	
8	Alignment status	
9	Ongoing violence	
10	Foreign stimulus	0.82
11	Cultural similarity	0.83
12	Power superiority	0.89
13	Multi-issue problem	
14	Noise level	
15	Trust	
16	Control over events	
17	Time pressure	0.82
18	Cruciality	0.83
19	Level of problem	
20	Threat of violence	0.82
21	Decision-making body size	0.55
22	Decision latitude	0.91
23	Officiality	0.76
24	Authority contracted	0.75
25	Decision time	
26	Cognitive complexity	0.76
27	Input load	0.77
28	Input intensity	0.64
29	Input range	0.73
30	Input/output ratio	
31	Metacommunication level	0.77
32	Communication reduction	0.91
33	Learning rate	0.91
34	Risk propensity	0.74
35	Tolerance of ambiguity	
36	Self-esteem	
37	Desires for achievement	
38	Desires for power	
39	Desires for affiliation	
40	Frustration perceptions	

(continued)

Table 3.2 (continued)

Conceptual Variable		Reliability Coefficient
41	Hostility perceptions	
42	Stereotypic decoding	0.82
43	Structuredness	0.77
44	Range of alternatives	0.85
45	Intraorganizational consonance	0.85
46	Hierarchical resolution	0.82
47	Pragmatism	0.77
48	Violent option considered	0.91
49	Penetration	
50	Transcience	0.86
51	Procedurality	0.86
52	Formality	0.91
53	Guidance	0.77
54	Revocability	0.77
55	Turning point	
56	Success	
57	Implementation speed	0.91
58	Sociometric change	
59	Continuousness	0.77
60	Cumulativity	0.82
61	Stabilizing	0.77
62	Goal-restructuring	0.94
63	Promotive	0.86
64	Maximizing	
65	Violent decision	1.00
66	Extent of documentation	
67	Academic source	
68	Length of description	

Because the database is constructed with variables that have normal curves, allowing Pearsonian intercorrelations between the conceptual variables, a factor analysis can be run to determine whether any concepts are closely associated with violence. Factor analysis can also determine whether several conceptual variables are interlinked and provide greater or lesser interrelationships with decision-making involving violence. Rather than starting with a theory to test, factor analysis can end up with a pattern of relationships that suggest theoretical explanations. Factor analysis, thus, can transform pre-theory into an image of theoretical connections.

With 68 variables for 32 cases scaled into normal curves, standard Pearsonian correlations are calculated. Next, factor analysis of the 68×68 correlation matrix can determine not only which variables among various competing theories are closely related but also how many irreducible correlational dimensions are found, eliminating spurious relationships. Accordingly, a total of 35 factors were derived, with eigenvalues over 0.0, whereas 17 factors exceeded 1.0. According to the scree test (Cattell 1966), a possible cutoff would be 11 factors but definitely by 17 factors. Thus, there was considerable heterogeneity in the data. When Kaiser's varimax rotation was run next, results met simple structure criteria. Oblique rotation yielded greatly inflated factor loadings (over 1.0) in the corresponding P-matrices, so the varimax results are accepted instead (Table 3.3).

Factor I, which explains about one-fifth of the variance of all 68 variables, brings together *Crisis* concepts, perhaps no surprise in view of so much attention to the subject in foreign policy decision-making studies with a plethora of definitions (cf. Lentner 1972). The variables with high loadings are cruciality, prior concern, mistrust, desires for power and achievement, frustration, hostility, risk propensity, turning point, low noise level, maximizing, and a destabilizing decision against an enemy rather than an ally. High loads are for affective and evaluative concepts. Consideration of violence as an option has a moderately high loading, as one would expect in a crisis situation.

Innovative decision-making appears to link high loadings on Factor II, with cognitive and structural variables, notably formality, officiality, implementation lag, and lengthy decision process with little time pressure. The cluster on Factor II indicates that innovative decisions can be promotive of something new, implementation is top-down (guidance), and there are no violent elements. With more inputs than outputs, bottlenecked decisions appear to consist of small, specialized tasks yet communications are reduced at some point. Each factor is unrelated to all others, so crisis decisions are quite different from innovative decisions.

Routine decision-making emerges as Factor III because associated factors are power superiority, high control over domestic events, many inputs in a highly structured but low-level problem involving individuals with cultural similarity. No violence is on the radar. The highest loadings tend to be for stimulus situations.

Table 3.3 *R-Factor Analysis of Decision-Making Conceptual Variables*

Conceptual Variable		h^2	Varimax Factors[a]							
			I	II	III	IV	V	VI	VII	VIII
1	Prior concern	0.85	12	−22	−04	06	−16	−00	−46	26
2	Probability of office-holding	0.93	27	06	−13	−29	−32	19	05	**66**
3	Correct intelligence	0.85	−06	31	23	−03	−06	13	00	00
4	Warning signs decoded	0.90	−24	49	23	−21	−20	−11	02	−06
5	Prior concern	0.85	**80**	05	−03	03	−21	−05	−05	02
6	Precedent invoked	0.86	−03	−02	05	09	−06	11	03	−07
7	Prior planning	0.93	24	37	08	−35	25	12	−13	−01
8	Alignment status	0.92	**−63**	13	45	−06	38	20	−10	−09
9	Ongoing violence	0.93	19	−04	−19	−10	22	04	**74**	−19
10	Foreign stimulus	0.94	11	04	−55	01	**−53**	36	05	−11
11	Cultural similarity	0.88	−26	05	**74**	07	16	00	−05	13
12	Power superiority	0.96	−11	−03	62	−33	−07	−02	−13	11
13	Multi-issue problem	0.76	14	17	−14	18	03	07	12	−03
14	Noise level	0.92	**−73**	18	06	−11	−07	05	−19	−09
15	Trust	0.96	**−70**	05	22	13	−03	−19	06	−02
16	Control over events	0.89	−40	08	67	−23	12	25	17	09
17	Time pressure	0.94	**52**	**−50**	03	08	05	08	−07	22
18	Cruciality	0.94	**85**	−16	−09	12	−23	−14	−07	−03
19	Level of problem	0.88	04	30	−52	36	−02	22	−01	**−52**
20	Threat of violence	0.90	46	−18	−57	08	−02	14	01	−02
21	Decision-making body size	0.87	−01	**54**	−07	14	17	−31	08	−02
22	Decision latitude	0.86	−02	−26	−19	00	−36	02	04	02
23	Officiality	0.93	−22	**54**	02	05	03	−06	20	−18
24	Authority contracted	0.83	34	−09	02	−39	**53**	−05	25	26
25	Decision time	0.92	−21	**78**	21	22	−01	−00	−10	01

Conceptual Variable		h^2	Varimax Factors[a]							
			I	II	III	IV	V	VI	VII	VIII
26	Cognitive complexity	0.92	45	**58**	−31	19	03	05	−29	13
27	Input load	0.91	−11	19	**69**	44	03	14	09	−15
28	Input intensity	0.90	03	07	−39	28	−12	13	00	19
29	Input range	0.89	11	41	−16	44	−05	−06	−33	−05
30	Input/output ratio	0.95	−13	**64**	26	32	−04	14	11	−06
31	Metacommunication level	0.93	07	27	**78**	26	−14	−22	−06	04
32	Communication reduction	0.94	20	**50**	26	−68	−18	08	04	00
33	Learning rate	0.88	−12	25	17	**56**	20	15	06	05
34	Risk propensity	0.94	**65**	14	−23	−13	−27	04	10	−12
35	Tolerance of ambiguity	0.88	13	21	−22	**78**	−09	−13	−03	00
36	Self-esteem	0.89	−25	−11	45	−26	00	47	26	11
37	Desires for achievement	0.92	**66**	23	00	17	23	26	−01	33
38	Desires for power	0.95	**78**	−08	−02	−32	01	11	19	13
39	Desires for affiliation	0.91	−03	25	−05	**54**	20	−21	03	−01
40	Frustration perceptions	0.93	**76**	−06	−22	03	37	15	22	−02
41	Hostility perceptions	0.97	**65**	−17	−26	−32	10	−04	03	08
42	Stereotypic decoding	0.89	08	01	−15	**−83**	−22	−05	−00	−16
43	Structuredness	0.90	−14	−13	77	−20	01	19	06	−03
44	Range of alternatives	0.83	10	41	−25	13	40	17	−16	13
45	Intraorganizational consonance	0.91	−04	−40	40	−16	−02	−14	−15	01
46	Hierarchical resolution	0.93	11	−19	−07	−19	**−87**	04	−16	−09
47	Pragmatism	0.82	−11	08	12	19	−01	05	−03	09
48	Violent option considered	0.87	**57**	−01	−16	−14	−22	−05	−05	01
49	Penetration	0.94	38	18	32	06	−14	25	24	29
50	Transcience	0.85	−06	**−66**	00	−19	−14	07	−16	−16
51	Procedurality	0.90	−42	13	11	42	04	−26	−03	06

(continued)

Table 3.3 (continued)

Conceptual Variable		h²	Varimax Factors[a]							
			I	II	III	IV	V	VI	VII	VIII
52	Formality	0.95	04	**91**	03	02	−03	−06	−04	−05
53	Guidance	0.92	30	**52**	11	06	−02	11	25	13
54	Revocability	0.91	−07	−03	−01	34	−14	−26	−06	−36
55	Turning point	0.83	**71**	09	−12	−10	02	05	10	04
56	Success	0.94	19	07	12	35	18	05	09	**84**
57	Implementation speed	0.91	11	**−84**	−06	−15	−18	−11	03	04
58	Sociometric change	0.93	01	−09	−02	13	−02	**86**	−05	08
59	Continuousness	0.91	02	13	22	15	04	−03	**83**	15
60	Cumulativity	0.90	20	−15	−07	−10	−12	−07	**83**	13
61	Stabilizing	85	**−65**	12	07	19	14	03	−07	−04
62	Goal-restructuring	0.93	17	20	02	−24	−01	**78**	−07	02
63	Promotive	0.84	−05	**63**	05	−05	21	12	06	28
64	Maximizing	0.91	**63**	31	21	02	02	18	02	28
65	Violent decision	0.96	48	−07	−35	−11	−17	−03	23	−06
66	Extent of documentation	0.80	14	10	04	10	−08	11	19	−03
67	Academic source	0.90	−20	21	16	37	11	−13	−03	−05
68	Length of description	0.94	14	08	11	14	03	05	−11	01
Eigenvalues[b]			13.3	9.7	6.6	5.0	3.7	3.0	2.7	2.6
Percent total variance										
Percent common variance										
			19.6	14.3	9.1	7.3	5.5	4.5	4.0	3.8
			21.7	15.7	10.7	8.1	6.0	4.9	4.8	4.3

Conceptual Variable		h^2	Varimax Factors[a]								
			IX	X	XI	XII	XIII	XIV	XV	XVI	XVII
1	Prior concern	0.85	20	−04	19	36	22	12	−11	36	−17
2	Probability of office-holding	0.93	10	−06	17	12	08	−04	−25	23	−05
3	Correct intelligence	0.85	−82	−06	00	−01	−06	00	−04	−00	−00
4	Warning signs decoded	0.90	−41	12	05	−27	−15	01	40	07	08
5	Prior concern	0.85	−11	−15	−01	29	−09	−01	14	06	07
6	Precedent invoked	0.86	08	90	01	−01	−05	−02	−04	−05	07
7	Prior planning	0.93	−66	−07	05	22	−01	−11	07	03	07
8	Alignment status	0.92	13	−11	06	12	−08	07	20	−04	−04
9	Ongoing violence	0.93	−28	−21	24	−09	−04	−00	15	03	−04
10	Foreign stimulus	0.94	27	23	09	03	03	07	09	07	−20
11	Cultural similarity	0.88	01	03	12	20	−18	−16	27	11	15
12	Power superiority	0.96	17	26	−01	−13	02	29	−12	36	−28
13	Multi-issue problem	0.76	−04	−06	−04	67	−10	39	00	02	14
14	Noise level	0.92	06	−18	03	−18	41	−15	−06	09	−13
15	Trust	0.96	08	−01	−01	04	−05	−01	55	14	17
16	Control over events	0.89	−09	06	−03	−07	−12	09	−03	06	−28
17	Time pressure	0.94	−06	49	06	−03	−04	−10	30	11	−01
18	Cruciality	0.94	−09	−00	01	−03	09	14	−18	11	−10
19	Level of problem	0.88	−02	19	04	08	11	−06	−01	15	−04
20	Threat of violence	0.90	10	−07	−12	−05	−01	19	−11	41	−23
21	Decision-making body size	0.87	03	−07	02	05	−04	17	62	−06	−02
22	Decision latitude	0.86	07	−05	05	−14	70	−06	−10	09	−30
23	Officiality	0.93	−15	−20	−13	−29	−31	17	−11	−43	14
24	Authority contracted	0.83	−19	10	−12	20	13	−08	02	−11	−04
25	Decision time	0.92	−26	−25	−05	−06	−13	−05	−03	−10	06
26	Cognitive complexity	0.92	07	18	17	08	−14	08	09	10	−17
27	Input load	0.91	−21	04	22	03	−13	03	−17	−07	−04
28	Input intensity	0.90	51	−12	25	17	−00	23	27	32	−06

(continued)

Table 3.3 (continued)

Conceptual Variable		h^2	Varimax Factors[a]								
			IX	X	XI	XII	XIII	XIV	XV	XVI	XVII
29	Input range	0.89	17	28	02	32	−11	32	−09	17	−08
30	Input/output ratio	0.95	−03	10	−33	20	−34	04	−14	−09	12
31	Metacommunication level	0.93	−13	11	−04	−02	−04	04	10	−15	17
32	Communication reduction	0.94	−14	07	−07	12	13	−06	07	11	−04
33	Learning rate	0.88	17	24	28	07	42	−01	01	−08	22
34	Risk propensity	0.94	09	−07	−08	04	**52**	15	−06	04	−02
35	Tolerance of ambiguity	0.88	10	04	05	21	−22	08	11	−06	08
36	Self-esteem	0.89	05	29	−33	−14	13	08	09	−05	03
37	Desires for achievement	0.92	13	02	−20	13	−02	06	21	22	02
38	Desires for power	0.95	25	05	−03	−16	04	09	−04	24	−02
39	Desires for affiliation	0.91	12	42	12	37	−00	34	04	07	−01
40	Frustration perceptions	0.93	−07	11	01	04	−20	−13	02	−11	−08
41	Hostility perceptions	0.97	−22	10	−24	02	12	00	−44	09	−05
42	Stereotypic decoding	0.89	−00	04	−03	02	−19	−12	−11	00	−16
43	Structuredness	0.90	−17	−08	−07	−30	13	16	−04	−13	07
44	Range of alternatives	0.83	01	−33	−30	13	−22	20	15	11	−06
45	Intraorganizational consonance	0.91	44	10	35	14	−23	20	−01	−00	30
46	Hierarchical resolution	0.93	07	−06	02	−04	13	05	−02	16	−07
47	Pragmatism	0.82	03	01	**86**	−01	03	−01	03	−04	−06
48	Violent option considered	0.87	−14	04	27	−16	02	19	−25	44	−16
49	Penetration	0.94	07	34	−11	07	05	40	16	25	20
50	Transcience	0.85	−09	−09	−10	37	−18	−26	19	02	−01
51	Procedurality	0.90	−00	−11	20	−01	−25	−06	−11	**−55**	−04
52	Formality	0.95	−16	09	14	15	01	−02	06	14	03
53	Guidance	0.92	−08	20	11	13	−08	10	03	**59**	15

3 QUANTIFYING ALTERNATIVE PRE-THEORIES 69

Conceptual Variable		h^2	Varimax Factors[a]								
			IX	X	XI	XII	XIII	XIV	XV	XVI	XVII
54	Revocability	0.91	34	**-55**	12	11	-09	-26	06	-19	-07
55	Turning point	0.83	16	-26	-07	19	14	29	13	13	10
56	Success	0.94	-00	06	07	-06	-03	-02	07	-04	-02
57	Implementation speed	0.91	13	06	-09	-13	-15	-06	-23	03	-03
58	Sociometric change	0.93	-29	06	08	04	16	-06	-09	04	-15
59	Continuousness	0.91	18	04	-16	-02	03	13	-10	09	10
60	Cumulativity	0.90	07	16	-01	15	04	-05	-05	09	-13
61	Stabilizing	85	-15	08	04	26	-13	13	14	-16	40
62	Goal-restructuring	0.93	09	13	00	03	-21	30	-09	09	08
63	Promotive	0.84	-17	-02	-11	03	-10	11	26	-08	40
64	Maximizing	0.91	07	16	25	03	-09	02	18	34	-08
65	Violent decision	0.96	03	08	-07	-01	05	-02	-01	**68**	-10
66	Extent of documentation	0.80	-02	-07	16	06	-19	**71**	04	34	09
67	Academic source	0.90	03	-00	-09	04	-21	-02	01	-03	**75**
68	Length of description	0.94	09	07	-12	13	11	**88**	03	-15	-08
	Eigenvalues[b]		2.4	2.2	1.9	1.8	1.5	1.4	1.3	1.2	1.1
	Percent total variance		3.5	3.2	2.7	2.6	2.3	2.0	1.9	1.8	1.6
	Percent common variance		3.8	3.8	3.0	2.9	2.4	2.2	2.1	2.0	1.8

[a]Factor loadings have been multiplied by 100; loadings > 0.50 are in boldface
[b]Based on principal axis factors

70   M. HAAS

Tolerance of ambiguity, desire for affiliation, high learning rate, lack of stereotypic assessment, and no reduction in communications dominate Factor IV. *Rational* decision-making seems the appropriate label.

Nonhierarchical decision-making has the highest loading on Factor V, with some contraction of authority and mainly a domestic focus. The term *Collegial* comes to mind as a way in which a small group works together.

Watershed decisions emerge on Factor VI, which combines goal-restructuring and sociometric change, both of which are outcome concepts. Decisions involving a major reconsideration have moderate loadings for foreign targets and high self-esteem of decision-makers.

Highest loadings on Factor VII are for continuous decisions that have cumulative impacts in response to ongoing violence. What the factor suggests is *Strategic* rather than tactical decisions.

Factor VIII clusters together elements of prospect theory, a factor that could be characterized as *Self-Congratulatory*: Decision-makers confident that they will be re-elected choose low-level decisions that are judged as successes, with the level of risk neither high nor low. There is a definite association with needs for achievement.

About two-thirds of the variance has been explained from Factors I to VIII. Factors IX to XVII tend to be defined by one or two conceptual variables. Factor IX could be called *Unexpected* because the decision at the prestimulus phase is subsequently judged to lack prior planning and have incorrect prior intelligence, whereas during information-processing there is a somewhat deluge of inputs to correct the picture.

Invocation of precedent dominates Factor X, with a moderate loading for unwillingness to change or revoke that precedent. One rendering would regard the factor as *History-Mindedness*, though one might prefer Old Fashioned as the name of the factor.

Factor XI has one high loading—pragmatism. A factor designated *Pragmatism* that stands alone and accounts for little variance across 68 variables is evidence that many cases in the sample, though selected to be dramatic, are quite ordinary. To assert that decision-makers are rarely pragmatic, however, seems a farfetched indictment.

Multi-Issue decisions have highest loading on Factor XII. Decision latitude seems to define Factor XIII but is associated with risky decisions; evidently risk takers are the ones with more authority, so the Factor XII could be described as *Imperious*.

Factor XIV has two high loading variables that deal with *Quality Control*—extent of documentation and length of the description in sources consulted. Factor XVII is defined by *Academic* rather than journalistic source. Fortunately, none of the quality control measures influenced the overall picture.

Factor XV isolates *Bipartisanship*, bringing together large decision-making bodies with a lot of mutual trust and low levels of hostility. Clearly, the factor refers to decisions by Congress when cooperation was once the norm.

Factor XVI is called *Aggressiveness*, with highest loading for the decision for violence. Very moderate loadings associated are threat of violence, prior cohesion among decision-makers, power superiority, input intensity, intraorganizational consonance, top-down legitimation, maximizing metric applied, with substantive (not procedural) decisions made outside normal channels. Even so, the factor explains only 2 percent of the variance across all 68 variables.

Causal Analysis

Based on the factor analysis, causal models can be constructed by choosing variables that have the highest loadings on the most important factors. Cruciality (C) is an obvious choice. Cruciality, an evaluative choice during the stimulus phase, had the highest loading on Factor I in the first factor analysis run. Factor I was also labeled the Crisis factor.

Frustration (F) refers to an affective aspect during the information-processing phase. Perceptions of frustration have a very high loading on Factor I. The variable is selected for the causal model because of the well-respected frustration → aggression theory in psychology (Dollard et al. 1939; Miller 1941; Berkowitz 1962).

Cultural dissimilarity (C) is also found during the stimulus phase as a structural element. Cultural similarity/dissimilarity has the highest loading on Factor III, which was designated with a cluster of either routine or nonroutine decisions.

That leaves information underload (U) as a cognitive information-processing choice. Input load also has a high loading on Factor III. The analysis of the Cuba Missiles Crisis stressed information load as a critical element accounting for nonviolent conflict resolution (Allison 1969, 1971).

Violent aggressiveness (V), an outcome concept, is the dependent variable. At least three possible causal pathways can be constructed with decision for violence as the endpoint (Figures 3.1, 3.2, and 3.3).

Figure 3.1 Crisis Model of Violent Decision-Making

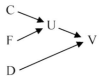

Figure 3.2 Irrationality Model of Violent Decision-Making

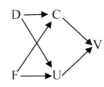

Figure 3.3 Cultural Exchange Model of Violent Decision-Making

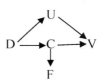

To determine how any of the three models comes close to a causal relationship, Pearsonian correlations are calculated for all five variables. Each pathway is then a prediction based on whether the relationship is a direct or modified correlation (Table 3.4). For example, the C → U path is a direct correlation, whereas the C → U → V relationship involves deriving the direct correlation between C and V when U is held constant.

The Cultural Exchange model is by far the best explanation. The meaning of the model is that two dissimilar countries go to war under two conditions. One is when decision-makers process insufficient information. The other link is that one or both dissimilar countries choose war if the decision-maker considers the matter to be crucial to vital national interests. The more national interests are crucial, the more frustration in deliberating, but frustration has no role in the eventual violent decision. By some coincidence, the same finding was reported in Lewis Richardson's *Statistics of Deadly Quarrels* (1960), which used a different methodology.

3 QUANTIFYING ALTERNATIVE PRE-THEORIES 73

Table 3.4 Predictions and Degree of Fit for Decision-Making Models

Model	Prediction	Observation
I	1. $r_{cf} = 0$	0.45
	2. $r_{cd} = 0$	0.39
	3. $r_{df} = 0$	0.21
	4. $r_{du} = 0$	0.55
	5. $r_{cv} \bullet _{u} = 0$	0.58
	6. $r_{fv} \bullet _{u} = 0$	0.28
II	1. $r_{df} = 0$	0.21
	2. $r_{f v} \bullet _{cu} = 0$	0.04
	3. $r_{dv} \bullet _{cu} = 0$	0.05
	4. $r_{cu} \bullet _{df} = 0$	−0.12
III	1. $r_{dv} \bullet _{cu} = 0$	0.05
	2. $r_{df} \bullet _{c} = 0$	0.04
	3. $r_{fv} \bullet _{c} = 0$	0.08
	4. $r_{cu} \bullet _{d} = 0$	−0.08
	5. $r_{fu} \bullet _{d} = 0$	0.05

CONCLUSION

What has emerged from a pooling of concepts is a finding that more attention should be paid to cultural factors in the minds of decision-makers. Misperceptions of the meaning of foreign policy gestures have indeed been crucially linked to major foreign policy blunders (Jervis 1968, 1970, 1976, 2017). Because cultures follow distinct and unique codes of conduct and resulting behavior, operational code research is a subject reviewed in depth within Part II.

APPENDIX: DECISION-MAKING CASES

1. **Bohlen**. The decision of the Senate of the United States to provide "advice and consent" to President Dwight Eisenhower's nomination of Charles "Chip" Bohlen to become the American ambassador to the Soviet Union is made on March 2, 1953, about a month after the nomination was made (Rosenau 1960).
2. **Quarantine**. The Kennedy Administration decides to impose a naval quarantine on shipments of missiles from the Soviet Union to Cuba on October 21, 1962, one week after aerial reconnaissance photographs showed that missile installations were being

constructed by Soviet technicians in Cuba (Abel 1966; Allison 1969, 1971).

3. **Japan**. The U.S. Senate ratifies the Japanese Peace Treaty on July 4, 1952, about 10 months after the treaty is submitted for ratification by President Harry Truman (Cohen 1957: ch2–13).

4. **Draft**. The Selective Service Act passes Congress on June 19, 1950, thereby compelling young men aged 18–26 to service in the armed forces of the United States. President Harry Truman addressed Congress urging passage three months earlier (Jacobs and Gallagher 1967: ch3).

5. **Korea**. Two days after North Korea attacks South Korea on June 24, 1950, the Truman Administration sends troops to defend South Korea (Paige 1968: ch2–11).

6. **Monroney**. Congress agrees on July 23, 1958, to establish the International Development Association as a body to provide loans to less developed countries on a low-interest, long-term basis. The decision comes five months after Senator Mike Monroney begins hearings on the proposal (Robinson 1960).

7. **Employment**. Congress adopts the Full Employment Act on February 6, 1946, about one year after the bill is introduced by Senator James E. Murray with the aim of full reutilization of all workers after the end of World War II (Bailey 1950).

8. **Hiroshima**. On August 3, 1945, President Harry Truman orders to have an atomic bomb drop on Hiroshima one week after Japanese leaders apparently fail to respond to the Potsdam Declaration (Batchelder 1961: ch5–9; Morton 1959a).

9. **Suzuki**. The Japanese Privy Council selects Baron Kantarō Suzuki as prime minister on August 5, 1945, due to the deadlock the previous day between Co-Premiers Kuniaki Koiso and Mitsumasa Yonai (Butow 1954: ch2–3).

10. **Pearl Harbor**. The government of Hideki Tōjō agrees to attack Pearl Harbor. The order is made on November 30, 1941, five days after peace negotiations break down between Japan and the United States in Washington (Wohlstetter 1962: ch6; Morton 1959b).

11. **Norway**. On April 1, 1940, Hitler's staff orders an attack to take over Norway before Britain, which had hinted a desire to do so about 45 days before (Ziemke 1959).

12. **Vietminh.** On April 24, 1954, one day after France appeals for military assistance against the Vietminh in Vietnam, the Eisenhower Administration declines to intervene (Roberts 1954).
13. **Aswan.** Secretary of State John Foster Dulles turns down Egypt's request for American funds to build a high dam at Aswan on July 19, 1956, coming three days before an Egyptian diplomat is scheduled to arrive in Washington for an answer to the application (Finer 1964: ch1–3).
14. **Suez.** On October 23, 1956, nine days after the United Nations turns down the Anglo-French "compromise" over Egypt's operation of the Suez Canal, the British Cabinet decides to seize the canal militarily (Epstein 1964: ch3, 5; Robertson 1965: ch1–8).
15. **Laos.** On March 21, 1961, two weeks after the Pathet Lao wins a major battle, controlling half the country, the Kennedy Administration decides to back a neutralist government in Laos to end the civil war between left and right factions (Hilsman 1967: ch10–12).
16. **Bay of Pigs.** On April 7, exactly 36 days after Cuban refugees are informed that they can no longer engage in military training within Guatemala, the Kennedy Administration authorizes them to attack Cuba at the Bay of Pigs (Schlesinger 1965: 223–279).
17. **U-Boat.** Germany seeks peace with Britain at the end of 1916, but London does not respond by January 2, 1917. The German High Command then resumes unrestricted submarine warfare on January 9 (May 1963: ch19).
18. **Wilson.** The United States declares war against Germany on April 1, 1917, after a request within an address to Congress by President Woodrow Wilson 37 days after the Zimmermann Note is decoded (Smith 1965: ch1–5).
19. **Murmansk.** American troops are dispatched to Murmansk, Russia, on July 26, 1917, responding to an "invitation" from the Murmansk Soviet three weeks earlier (Strakhovsky 1937: ch4–5).
20. **Siberia.** Eight days after Czech troops seize Vladivostok, the Wilson Administration dispatches American troops to Siberia with the eventual aim of toppling the Russian government of Vladimir Lenin (Unterberger 1956: ch2–4; Smith 1965: ch8).
21. **Poland.** After negotiations for a Nazi-Soviet nonaggression pact is signed on August 23, 1939, Hitler's staff on August 31 agrees to order an attack on Poland (Bullock 1964: ch9)

22. **Stalingrad.** A few hours after the Soviet Army begins an offensive against Nazi Germany on November 20, 1942, Hitler refuses to order a withdrawal of German troops from Stalingrad, thus allowing 250,000 the troops to be encircled by the Soviet Army (Zeitzler 1965: ch4).
23. **Panmunjom.** Although Pyongyang recommends truce talks at Kaeson, a location held by North Korea, the United States objects. Forty-seven days later, the talks begin at Panmunjom—on October 22, 1951 (Vatcher 1958: 59–75).
24. **POWs.** After the Korean War ends, negotiations ensue about repatriation of prisoners of war (POWs) for about six months. On June 8, 1953, there is an agreement on the basis of voluntary repatriation, allowing some soldiers to defect to the other side (Vatcher 1958: ch6–7).
25. **Truckers.** A bill increasing the minimum load haulable by trucks is adopted by the Pennsylvania legislature. On January 21, 1952, Governor John S. Fine vetoes the law after one week of consideration (Hacker 1962).
26. **Steel.** On April 10, 1962, a representative of U.S. Steel Corporation announces that steel prices will be raised. The following day, the Kennedy Administration urges the company to rescind the price increase (McConnell 1963: ch5–6).
27. **Potsdam.** On July 26, 1945, the Potsdam Declaration is issued by the Allied Powers in Europe with a provision for terms of Japan's surrender. When asked to comment, a spokesperson for Prime Minister Baron Kantarō Suzuki issues a statement interpreted in Washington as an arrogant "No comment" remark, though in fact the statement indicates that the Cabinet has not yet decided how to respond (Kawai 1950). In response to the mistranslation, President Harry Truman authorizes dropping a nuclear bomb on Hiroshima.
28. **MacArthur.** President Harry Truman fires General Douglas MacArthur of his command in Korea on April 6, 1951. The decision is made two weeks after MacArthur sends a letter to Joe Martin, Republican House Minority Leader, who reads the letter on the floor of the House of Representatives, suggesting that American troops should go past the border to unite Korea by ousting North Korea and using Taiwan troops to attack the Chinese military supporting North Korea (Spanier 1959: ch10–13; Truman 1959: ch27–28).

29. **Evacuation.** After Pearl Harbor, a report is prepared about the potential danger of Japanese and Japanese Americans living in the United States. On February 19, 1942, some 25 days after the report is completed and released, the Roosevelt Administration issues an order to evacuate all Japanese and Japanese Americans from Pacific Coast states for resettlement in internment camps (Conn 1959).
30. **Haymarket.** English language protests assemble near Chicago's Haymarket Square on May 3, 1887, with no incident. On the following day, police shoot at German protesters in the same location after a bomb explodes near the approaching police (Zeisler 1956: ch1–11; David 1958: ch9).
31. **Oglesby.** Several Haymarket Riot "anarchists" are sentenced to death by a court in Illinois. The U.S. Supreme Court denies a writ of error to review the case on November 1, 1887. Then days later, Governor Richard J. Oglesby commutes two sentences to life terms (Zeisler 1956: ch19–22).
32. **Bolshevik.** The Provisional Government, which is established in Russia after the February 1917 revolution, decides to convene a meeting of the new legislature on September 20, 1917. On October 10, the Bolshevik Central Committee resolves to oust leaders of the Provisional Government, and Russia's second revolution begins (Shapiro 1955: ch3–4).

REFERENCES

Abel, Elie. 1966. *The Missile Crisis.* New York: Bantam.

Allison, Graham T. 1969. Conceptual Models and the Cuban Missile Crisis. *American Political Science Review* 63 (3): 689–718.

Allison, Graham T. 1971. *Essence of Decision: Explaining the Cuban Missile Crisis.* Boston: Little, Brown.

Bailey, Stephen K. 1950. *Congress Makes a Law.* New York: Columbia University Press.

Batchelder, Robert C. 1961. *The Irreversible Decision.* New York: Macmillan.

Berkowitz, Leonard. 1962. *Aggression: A Social Psychological Analysis.* New York: McGraw-Hill.

Block, Jack. 1961. *The Q-Sort Method in Personality Assessment and Psychiatric Research.* Springfield, IL: Thomas.

78 M. HAAS

Bullock, Alan. 1964. *Hitler*. New York: Harper & Row.

Butow, Robert J.C. 1954. *Japan's Decision to Surrender*. Stanford, CA: Stanford University Press.

Cattell, Raymond B. 1966. The Scree Test for the Number of Factors. *Multivariate Behavioral Research* 1 (2): 245–276.

Cohen, Bernard C. 1957. *The Political Process and Foreign Policy*. Princeton, NJ: Princeton University Press.

Conn, Stetson. 1959. The Decision to Evacuate the Japanese from the Pacific Coast. In *Command Decisions*, ed. Kent Roberts Greenfield, 88–109. New York: Harcourt, Brace.

David, Henry. 1958. *The History of the Haymarket Affair*. New York: Russell.

Dollard, John, N.E. Miller, and Leonard W. Doob. 1939. *Frustration and Aggression*. New Haven, CT: Yale University Press.

Epstein, Leon D. 1964. *British Politics in the Suez Crisis*. Urbana: University of Illinois Press.

Finer, Herman. 1964. *Dulles Over Suez*. Chicago: Quadrangle.

Greenfield, Kent Roberts, ed. 1959. *Command Decisions*. New York: Harcourt, Brace.

Hacker, Andrew. 1962. Pressure Politics in Pennsylvania: The Truckers Vs. the Railroad. In *The Uses of Power*, ed. Alan F. Westin, 324–375. New York: Harcourt, Brace, World.

Hilsman, Roger. 1967. *To Move a Nation*. Garden City, NY: Doubleday.

Holsti, Ole R. 1967. Cognitive Dynamics and Images of the Enemy. *Journal of International Affairs* 21 (1): 16–39.

Jacobs, Clyde E., and John F. Gallagher. 1967. *The Selective Service Act*. New York: Dodd, Mead.

Jervis, Robert. 1968. Hypotheses on Misperception. *World Politics* 20 (3): 454–479.

Jervis, Robert. 1970. *The Logic of Images in International Relations*. Princeton, NJ: Princeton University Press.

Jervis, Robert. 1976. *Perception and Misperception in International Politics*. Princeton, NJ: Princeton University Press.

Jervis, Robert. 2017. *Perception and Misperception in International Politics*, New Edition. Princeton, NJ: Princeton University Press.

Kawai, Kazuo. 1950. Mokusatsu, Japan's Response to the Potsdam Declaration. *Pacific Historical Review* 19 (4): 409–414.

Lentner, Howard. 1972. The Concept of Crisis as Viewed by the United States Department of State. In *International Crises: Insights from Behavioral Research*, ed. Charles F. Hermann, 112–135. New York: Free Press.

May, Ernest R. 1963. *The World War and American Isolationism, 1914–1917*. Cambridge, MA: Harvard University Press.

McConnell, Grant. 1963. *Steel and the Presidency*. New York: Norton.

Miller, Neal E. 1941. The Frustration-Aggression Hypothesis. *Psychological Review* 48 (4): 337–442.

Morton, Louis. 1959a. The Decision to Use the Atomic Bomb. In *Command Decisions*, ed. Kent Roberts Greenfield, 388–410. New York: Harcourt, Brace.

Morton, Louis. 1959b. Japan's Decision for War. In *Command Decisions*, ed. Kent Roberts Greenfield, 63–87. New York: Harcourt, Brace.

Paige, Glenn D. 1968. *The Korean Decision (June 24–30, 1950)*. New York: Free Press.

Richardson, Lewis F. 1960. *Statistics of Deadly Quarrels*. Chicago: Quadrangle.

Roberts, Chalmers. 1954. The Day We Didn't Go to War. *Reporter*, 11, September 14, 31–35.

Robertson, Terence. 1965. *Crisis: The Inside Story of the Suez Conspiracy*. New York: Atheneum.

Robinson, James A. 1960. *The Monroney Resolution*. New York: McGraw-Hill.

Rosenau, James N. 1960. *The Nomination of "Chip" Bohlen*. New York: McGraw-Hill.

Rosenau, James N. 1961. *Public Opinion and Foreign Policy: An Operational Formulation*. New York: Random House.

Rosenau, James N. 1966. Pre-Theories and Theories in Foreign Policy. In *Approaches to Comparative and International Politics*, ed. R. Barry Farrell, 27–92. Evanston, IL: Northwestern University Press.

Ruesch, Jürgen, and Gregory Bateson. 1951. *Communication: The Social Matrix of Psychiatry*. New York: Norton.

Schlesinger, Arthur M., Jr. 1965. *A Thousand Days*. Boston: Houghton Mifflin.

Shapiro, Leonard. 1955. *The Origin of the Communist Autocracy*. Cambridge, UK: Cambridge University Press.

Smith, Daniel M. 1965. *The Great Departure*. New York: Wiley.

Snyder, Richard C., H.W. Bruck, and Burton Sapin. 1954. *Decision-Making as an Approach to the Study of International Politics*. Princeton, NJ: Princeton University Press.

Sonne, Paul, Robyn Dixon, and David L. Stern. 2022. Russia Invades Ukraine. *American Journal of International Law* 116 (3): 593–604.

Spanier, John W. 1959. *The Truman-MacArthur Controversy and the Korean War*. Cambridge, MA: Harvard University Press.

Stephenson, William. 1953. *The Study of Behavior: The Q-Technique and Its Methodology*. Chicago: University of Chicago Press.

Strakhovsky, Leonid I. 1937. *The Origins of American Intervention in North Russia (1918)*. Princeton, NJ: Princeton University Press.

Truman, Harry S. 1959. *Memoirs*. Garden City, NY: Doubleday.

Unterberger, Betty Miller. 1956. *America's Siberia Expedition, 1918–1920*. Durham, NC: Duke University Press.

Vatcher, William H., Jr. 1958. *Panmunjom*. New York: Praeger.

80 M. HAAS

Wohlstetter, Roberta. 1962. *Pearl Harbor*. Stanford, CA: Stanford University Press.

Ziemke, Earl P. 1959. The German Decision to Invade Norway and Denmark. In *Command Decisions*, ed. Kent Roberts Greenfield, 39–62. New York: Harcourt, Brace.

Zeisler, Ernest B. 1956. *The Haymarket Riot*. Chicago: Isaacs.

Zeitzler, Kurt. 1965. Stalingrad. In *The Fatal Decisions*, eds. William Richardson and Seymour Freidin, Chapter 4. London: World Distributors.

PART II

Operational Code Analysis

When the various concepts of decision-making were developed by James Rosenau and Richard Snyder, their efforts were called "pre-theory" because the field of foreign policy analysis had not yet risen to the level of theory-building (Snyder, Bruck, Sapin 1954; Rosenau 1966). Consequently, the effort in Chapter 3 to place all their concepts into a statistical analysis was to discover which concepts were highly linked. Empirical theory, of course, involves linking concepts into a causal pathway. The result of the statistical exercise in Chapter 3 was to discover that when cultural backgrounds of two opposing decision-makers are quite diverse, the decision to go to war is more likely.

Ever since the era of pre-theory, foreign policy analysis has been struggling to develop important concepts in mid-level theories. One such effort has been the concept of "operational code" as a way to characterize the complexity of how decision-makers perceive the world. Developed during the Cold War, the aim has been to explore the minds of decision-makers—to get inside the "black box" of how they choose options. Part II is devoted to an explanation and critique of operational code analysis in order to broaden the discussion and ultimately provide a vision in a new direction.

Definitionally, an "operational code" is a set of beliefs on which individuals and groups rely in making decisions. The beliefs are utilized as criteria for evaluating alternative courses of action before decisions are made and operations are conducted.

82 PART II: OPERATIONAL CODE ANALYSIS

While operational code research progressed, theoretical developments in international studies proceeded to develop competing empirical paradigms (Haas 1992; 2017). Each paradigm encompasses several alternative mid-level theories. Operational code analysis thus far has not been connected to paradigms, which is another goal of Part II.

By way of opening the paradigmatic debate, a consensus exists that decision-makers operate rationally or they will lose power (Bueno de Mesquita and Smith 2011). Known as the Rational Actor Paradigm or Rational Choice Paradigm (Haas 2017:ch7), the view is that leaders are usually well informed and intelligent, thus formulating and choosing options that will efficiently accomplish their goals. But when they err, another paradigmatic explanation is needed. Therein lies the main puzzle that operational code research seeks to solve.

Among the alternatives are the Community Building, Mass Society, and Socialization paradigms (Haas 2017). The Community Building Paradigm seeks ways in which a world polity can be constructed into a legal or semilegal order to bring about world peace. The Mass Society Paradigm focuses on how civil society (pressure groups, political parties, media) can direct the will of the people to secure action from government. The Socialization Paradigm posits that individual attitudes and behavior today are a function of prior experience and role positions.

Although many operational code scholars have implicitly sought to build a coherent Cognitive Decision-Making Paradigm, the lack of explicit linkage between empirical paradigms and operational code research has stifled theory-building. Such a connection is pursued in the following chapters.

Chapter 4 explains the meaning of "codes" and how various scholars initially attempted to use operational code in their research. Chapter 5 traces newer approaches to operational codes, which have struggled without theoretical progress. Part III then transforms operational code research into a way to professionalize foreign policy decision-making.

References

Bueno de Mesquita, Bruce, and Alistair Smith. (2011). *The Dictator's Handbook: Why Bad Behavior Is Almost Always Good Politics*. New York: PublicAffairs.
Haas, Michael. (1992). *Polity and Society: Philosophical Underpinnings of Social Science Paradigms*. New York: Praeger.

PART II: OPERATIONAL CODE ANALYSIS 83

Haas, Michael. (2017). *International Relations Theory: Competing Theoretical Paradigms*. Lanham, MD: Lexington.

Rosenau, James N. (1966). Pre-Theories and Theories of Foreign Policy. In *Approaches to Comparative and International Politics*, ed. R. Barry Farrell, 27–92. Evanston, IL: Northwestern University Press.

Snyder, Richard C., H.W. Bruck, and Burton Sapin. (1954). *Decision-Making as an Approach, to the Study of International Politics*. Princeton, NJ: Princeton University Press.

CHAPTER 4

Omnipresence of Codes

During Part I, evidence was presented that war is most likely when two countries have very different cultures. The term "culture" refers to a set of normative beliefs about life, sometimes known as a "code." Persons adhering to a code in one country may not realize the content of the code in another country. Indeed, actions consistent with a code in one country may be viewed as unexpected and incomprehensible to those in other countries. If a foreign policy leader expects that leaders in other countries will behave like themselves, the result can be a serious miscalculation. During the Cold War and beyond, the feared result has been Armageddon.

Accordingly, the aim of the present chapter is to define the concept of "operational code." Because many scholars have embraced different definitions, the present chapter proceeds historiographically. The following chapter explains why operational code research has floundered.

DEFINING "OPERATIONAL CODE"

Inside a country, a code may be difficult to discern for new residents, who often have to learn how to acculturate. They may need psychological and even psychiatric assistance to avoid making deliberate or unintended moves contrary to the code operating in the mainstream. But such interventions are unlikely after someone has become a country's major foreign

© The Author(s), under exclusive license to Springer Nature Switzerland AG 2023
M. Haas, *Professionalization of Foreign Policy*,
https://doi.org/10.1007/978-3-031-37152-3_4

policy decision-maker, who in turn must deal with countries with very different codes.

Decisions of those with key political roles have consequences for millions, so their interpretation of unexpected behavior from leaders in other countries could result in serious collisions and disasters. But how is a leader in one country to determine the code of an adversary?

One conventional method in foreign policy studies is biographical or historical analysis. By studying the lives of leaders in other countries, one may learn their strong and weak points, their codes of behavior and conduct as well as attitudes and norms. History may provide cues of a country's operational code. The utility of biographical and historical analysis, however, is limited. More rigorous approaches exist, as indicated next.

Sociologist Robert K. Merton (1940), in studying the behavior of bureaucrats and bureaucracies, discovered that the ambiguity of their assignments left some latitude for various teams of government officials to implement policies, even when they were personally opposed to the policies. He found that bureaucrats within an agency develop an unwritten "code" of acceptable behavior—that is, a coping guide within a team based on their norms and beliefs. Although Merton is usually credited with inventing the term "operational code," he never coined that term; his use of the word "code" appears on the last page of his frequently cited essay.

Later, George Orwell's 1949 novel *1984* used the term "doublethink" to refer to a situation in which someone is indoctrinated to believe two opposite things, or claims to believe something but does the opposite. Evidently based on that concept, adherence to a single code within a decision-making group has been called "groupthink" (Whyte 1952; Janis 1971, 1972). According to Irving Janis, "mindguards" monitor what is set within a group so that there will be agreement and no deviation from the thinking of a group leader. Janis was trying to explain why advisers are deterred from bringing up contrary facts, opinions, and options before a government leader that might avoid blunders.

Within cultural anthropology, the concept of a code of conduct is fundamental to understanding how a group maintains itself despite environmental challenges, human idiosyncrasies, and actual or potential foreign intrusions (Boas 1940; Malinowski 1944; Geertz 1973). Using participant observation, anthropologists seek to determine an ethnographic "cultural code" of a people. The code is a system of beliefs,

4 OMNIPRESENCE OF CODES   87

expressed nonverbally and verbally, which describe how members of a culture behave, communicate, and otherwise interact so that they will live in a relatively stable community (cf. Hyatt and Simons 1999). However, some parts of a cultural code will remain unknown despite an anthropologist's participant observation; another problem is that cultural codes are often in flux over time. The study of cultural codes is important in studying race relations and other subjects beyond foreign policy analysis within the Community Building Paradigm (Haas 2017: ch6).

As anthropologist Gregory Bateson (1935, 1936: ch13) has noted, cultural groups only maintain solidarity if their norms (embodied in codes) are well understood by members and enforced. A group schism emerges whenever a subgroup recoils from elite domination and follows a heretical code, especially in authoritarian cultures (Haas 2014: ch6). Although some leaders prefer to observe their cultural code religiously, their effectiveness depends upon "dynamic equilibrium"—the term used by Bateson to refer to how well they adapt their thinking and behavior to unexpected situations.

One thing is clear about codes: They exist only if enforced, usually by persons in authority; personal codes only exist if self-enforced. Sociologist Émile Durkheim (1893), for example, noted two forms of group or national solidarity: Noncompetitive pre-industrial societies are held together by ethical norms, which he identified as *mechanical solidarity*. Industrial societies, however, maintain themselves through economic interdependence, which he labeled *organic solidarity*.

Group codes exist everywhere; individuals must learn them to navigate their lives successfully. American novelist Emily Post (1922) wrote the most famous American code, a standard set of rules of etiquette so that everyone can enjoy amiable interactions at home, in public, and at work, especially where individuals from different cultures are present (cf. Meine and Dunn 2013). Motor vehicle codes promote highway safety. Members of police departments, welfare agencies, and private clubs also operate on the basis of codes. Operational codes are common within businesses (Doig and Wilson 1998) and in the sciences (Cournand and Meyer 1976).

There are at least three levels of political codes. *Macro-level* operational codes operate at the national and international levels. Decision-makers usually develop their unique *micro-level* operational codes. Individuals showing loyalty to a subgroup follow a *meso-code*.

In the field of comparative politics, the concept of "political culture" was developed to explain variations in political style from country to country (Almond and Verba 1963; Pye 1991). Political decision-makers are held accountable to the public by behaving in a manner consistent with a "political culture," and a leader who deviates from expectations embedded in the national political culture may face adverse consequences (Pye 1972). Political cultures, thus, consist of macro-level codes.

Bipartisanship in foreign policy was a goal of American foreign policy during the Cold War. However, each successive administration tended to design a different operational code in dealing with the Soviet Union. Foreign policy leaders developed their own micro-codes, called "doctrines," as a guide to whether a decision-maker would use force in response to a particular situation. Because situations change, each new president developed a new doctrine, particularly when dealing with the Soviet Union—the Truman Doctrine, the Eisenhower Doctrine, and so forth.

A decision-maker's operational code consists of beliefs derived from experience that serve as a filter through which a leader perceives, processes, and responds to whatever behavior or information appears to need attention. Operational codes of foreign policy leaders were not recognized as playing a significant role in studies of foreign policy until the Cold War (cf. Grove 2018). The main reason for studying operational codes was how to avoid a catastrophic World War III between the two nuclear powers, the Soviet Union and the United States. Resolving differences between two superpowers clearly required an understanding of otherwise hidden operational codes in Moscow and Washington.

To ascertain the content of operational codes, foreign policy researchers cannot replicate the participant observation approach of anthropologists or sociologists unless they have been co-workers with important political leaders. Instead, they construct theoretical frameworks using political concepts, often invoking social psychological perspectives, along with social science methodological rules (also codes) about how to analyze texts in remarks and speeches by leaders in order to determine the particulars of their codes. The task, in other words, is so challenging that very few scholars have ventured down that path. The intellectual development of the concept of "operational code" has thus far been erratic, as will be described in the rest of the present chapter. Nevertheless, the reason for studying operational codes was to prevent serious foreign policy blunders.

LEITES' OPERATIONAL CODE OF THE SOVIET UNION

The first use of operational code research in foreign policy studies was by political sociologist Nathan Leites. His early innovation was almost forgotten until several scholars, notably Alexander George, later decided to utilize and broaden the concept. Whereas Leites constructed a code shared by a particular decision-making group (a meso-code), later operational code research has mostly focused on micro-codes of individual decision-makers; there has been very little interest in macro-codes of countries or international organizations.

In *The Operational Code of the Politburo*, Leites devoted 20 chapters to identifying principles with no effort to find logical connections between items on the list. Some, he admitted, might seem contradictory (Leites 1951: xii). He defined "operational code" as "rules... for effective political conduct" (p. xi).

His use of "operational code" might be considered consistent with the Rational Choice Paradigm as a way to explain the logic behind decisions that might otherwise seem inexplicable. But when that paradigm made inroads into international studies during the mid-1960s (Petracca 1991), operational codes were viewed as a source of irrational decisions.

Although born in Russia, Leites was an American citizen, not a member of the Politburo. Therefore, he could not utilize insights from participant observation to learn the Politburo Code. Instead, he relied on his understanding of the Russian cultural macro-code. What he uncovered were themes in the writings of Vladimir Lenin and Josef Stalin, utilizing a form of analysis known as *verstehen*. After codifying various themes into principles, he validated what he was proposing by citing how the Soviet Union handled various historical events—a case of both external or outcome validation.

Leites reported that Lenin and Stalin were quite strict in enforcing their code: Those who deviated were often executed. Leites argued that the Bolshevism Code was developed to replace the previous macro-code developed by psychologist Geoffrey Gorer and psychoanalyst John Rickman (1949), which they based on an understanding of Russian political culture. Leites (1951: xv) critiqued their Russian cultural code as unable to predict the Bolshevik revolution.

Leites' next book, *A Study of Bolshevism* (1953), had 102 subchapters stating principles, and thus provided considerably more depth. He explained that he was utilizing a psychological analysis of the emotional

90 M. HAAS

and goal-seeking propensities of Lenin and Stalin to "discover" their principles (p. 15). He also mined his Russian cultural background (p. 21), quoting Russian novelists. Praise for his second effort to construct the code of the Bolshevik subculture came from anthropologist Clyde Kluckholm (1955: 117).

Leites continued to analyze Soviet behavior and broadened his approach in several later publications. Although he acknowledged that there were differences between Lenin and Stalin—and Gregori Malenkov after Stalin's death—, he did not present micro-codes for any specific leader (Leites 1953: Epilogue; 1977: 17, 19). Since macro-codes refer to an entire culture of a nation, he identified Russian political culture as a macro-code (Leites 1977: ch14). In contrast, his Bolshevism Code was a meso-code for members of the ruling elite, superseding micro-codes that might exist for Lenin or Stalin. He also pointed out that the Bolshevism Code was observed by Communist Party members outside the Soviet Union. In a later publication on French political culture, he continued to construct meso-codes for subcultures (Leites 1959; 1977: ch6–7, 16).

Although familiar with quantitative approaches (Lasswell and Leites 1949), Leites' methodology was qualitative thematic content analysis. He did not develop a specific theory, though his contribution was clearly within the traditions of both the Community Building Paradigm (how the Politburo maintained solidarity) and the Rational Choice Paradigm (how the Politburo designed strategy and tactics to achieve objectives). Implicitly, he argued that all political leaders seek to make accomplishments, while ideologies guide strategy and tactics to achieve goals. Leites critiqued the Bolshevism Code as blinding leaders in Moscow to important opportunities to advance Soviet goals (Leites 1953: Prologue).

The Bolshevism Code, consistent with the Marxist lens of viewing events through an ongoing class struggle for dominance, might serve as a model for other ideologically driven political movements. For Karl Marx, the class struggle between the bourgeoisie and the proletariat was inexorable, though Lenin and Stalin believed that a vanguard was essential to accelerate that struggle, using violence whenever necessary (Leites 1953: 429). Thus, Leites showed that Bolsheviks developed a meso-code within the Marxian Paradigm.

However, the meso-level Bolshevism Code may be a misnomer. Leites identified the code in the years before Stalin's death, so he actually identified the micro-level Stalin Code. Stalin might have developed principles to which Lenin would have objected, but Stalin never contradicted Lenin.

Those who praised Leites' approach and wanted to apply his approach to other matters would have had to follow his *verstehen* methodology to make similar scholarly contributions. But no one did for several decades. Lacking methodological and theoretical advances during the era of foreign policy pre-theory, researchers continued as usual to provide biographical accounts of foreign policy decision-makers as guides without identifying their analyses as micro-codes (e.g., Spanier 1959).

When scholars decided to use the term "operational code" decades later, they varied in their approaches, as noted in the next sections of the present chapter. As a result, there is scholarly confusion about what constitutes an "operational code"—a confusion to be cleared up in the following chapter.

J. David Singer's Approach: Basic Issues

The next political scientist to utilize the concept of operational code was J. David Singer (1964: 425), who identified four basic issues of foreign policy for a quantitative comparison:

A. How does each side's foreign policy elite perceive and evaluate the international political system—the environment in which the deterrent relationship must be maintained?
B. What is each foreign policy elite's evaluation of the contemporary and predictable distribution of power?
C. How does each elite evaluate the foreign policy operational code of its adversary?
D. What are the main characteristics of each elite's articulation of its own operational code?

Under each issue, he identified sub-issues, for a total of 31 total components. Based on newspaper accounts, he then compared the Soviet Union and the United States on all 31 dimensions. However, his categorization was not followed by other scholars.

Ole Holsti's Approach: Belief System

Political scientist Ole Holsti was fascinated by the actions of Secretary of State John Foster Dulles during the administration of President Dwight Eisenhower as well as Allen Dulles, head of the Central Intelligence Agency. For Holsti, the Dulleses approached the Cold War in an aggressive, undiplomatic manner during a risky phase in the Cold War. While aware of Leites' scholarship, Holsti (1962) was more influenced by the decision-making approach of Richard Snyder (Snyder et al. 1954). However, Holsti went beyond Snyder and associates by identifying "belief system" (cf. Converse 1964: 207–208) as central to the decision-making process (Figure 4.1). Holsti and Snyder developed concepts but not a coherent theory, so their approach was then known as "pre-theory"—that is, concepts and conceptual maps without testing causal linkages (Rosenau 1966).

Beliefs, according to Holsti, were posited to mediate between events (information inputs) and decisions (action outputs). When cognitive processing prevailed, Holsti postulated that beliefs played an indirect role. If careful information-processing was neglected, beliefs led directly to decisions (and inevitably blunders) through affective considerations. Holsti concluded that the Dulleses were hostile to the Soviet Union and perceived aggressive Kremlin moves as a sign of strength, whereas they considered cooperative Soviet actions as evidence of weakness.

For Holsti, a decision-maker's beliefs filter perceptions of another country, especially a belief with a high score on a hostility/friendliness scale. And filtered perceptions prioritize the strong/weak response option. Therein he could claim to have found an operational code.

To prove that the concept of beliefs is a crucial causal concept, Holsti initially analyzed one decision-maker (John Foster Dulles) whom he

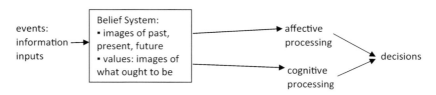

Figure 4.1 Ole Holsti's Decision-Making Map (*Source* Holsti 1962: 245, 250)

considered to have a dominant belief system. However, he did not explicitly set forth a theory or paradigm. Instead, he tried to identify elements in the "black box" of how decision-makers respond to inputs and then determine what decision options to choose (outputs).

Later, Holsti (1967) constructed a table in which six aspects of a target country's power (economic, external support, military, political, popular support, technological) were assessed in terms of four conceptual parameters. The concepts, running from low to high, were as follows: (1) ambiguity of information inputs, (2) consistency of the operational code, (3) diversity of reality perception judgments, and (4) strength of the decision. Presumably, the 24 elements (6 × 4) consisted of the major parameters of operational codes. But he did not undertake correlational or causal analysis.

Ten years later, Holsti (1977b) identified a common pattern within belief systems of public officials based on the intersection of two "master beliefs." In so doing, he adapted the concept of "political belief system," which he equivalenced to operational code (Table 4.1).

One "master belief" was whether decision-makers believe that human political conflict is inevitable or temporary, contrasting the ideologies of realism and liberalism, respectively. His second "master belief" is whether political leaders perceive that the main source of political conflict is at the individual, national, or international level of analysis, referring to the three standard levels of analysis of Kenneth Waltz (1959) and J. David Singer (1960).

His resulting sixfold categorization was identified by letters (A to G) rather than labels (Table 4.1). The title "master beliefs" appeared to refer to micro-codes that guide decision-makers. He developed a "coding manual" to guide research (Holsti 1977a).

Table 4.1 Ole Holsti's Categorization of Operational Codes

Fundamental Nature of the Political University	Fundamental Sources of Conflict		
	Human Nature	Attributes of Nations	International System
Harmonious	A	B	C
Conflictual	D	E	F

Source Holsti (1977b: 158)

94 M. HAAS

Holsti (1977a) then sent questionnaires to authors of previous foreign policy studies. His major finding, consistent with Leites, was that most decision-makers tend to stick to their beliefs (self-enforce), even if their rigid views often distort information-processing.

Based on Holsti's insight, political scientist Douglas Stuart (1979) soon conducted a study of the operational code of President John Kennedy. But he concluded that Holsti's categories were inadequate for his analysis.

Holsti's implicit causal proposition was the tautology that harmonious pairs of decision-makers reach cooperative decisions, but conflict-oriented leaders are constantly frustrated (cf. Cutler 1982: Table 5.2). Although Holsti could have constructed a game-theoretical 2×2 table to accommodate all four possibilities, he did not do so. He came close to developing a causal Decision-Making Paradigm but never advanced down that path.

There are several major differences distinguish between Holsti and Leites. Whereas Leites determined that the Bolshevism Code assigned primacy to inexorable forces in an ongoing class struggle, Holsti's formulation was elitist and assigned little explicit role for public opinion as an influence on decision-making. His early scholarship occurred during a period in the Cold War when Congress was conceding power in foreign policy to the executive branch. But later, public opinion was demanding an end to American intervention in Vietnam, as acknowledged by Holsti (1992).

A second difference between Holsti and Leites was methodological. Leites built his operational code by examining texts, using qualitative content analysis and *verstehen*. Holsti's analysis of Dulles was based on quantitative content analysis—that is, he counted particular types of words in texts and then plotted them over time. The words selected were Dulles' references to the Soviet Union as hostile, strong, frustrating, and negative—as well as their antonyms.

A third difference was ontological. Leites demonstrated how aspects of the Bolshevik Code shaped decisions. Holsti assumed that leaders acted on the basis of their unique perceptions of reality. Leites wrote about Marxists, who assigned priority to material reality, viewing history as the story of an ongoing class struggle that the proletariat will inexorably win, with the vanguard leading the way. In contrast, Holsti assumed that ideas in the heads of decision-makers filtered physical reality entirely based on idiosyncratic belief systems, and he therefore conceived of Dulles and possibly all other world leaders as inherently limited in their perceptions—in other words, lacking in the qualities assumed by the Rational Choice Paradigm.

Both scholars envisioned enforcement mechanisms: Leites was aware that Lenin and Stalin removed deviants from the Politburo Code by force. Beyond his causal map, Holsti (1962: 251) posited that decision-makers with rigid beliefs had "closed" personalities (Rokeach 1960: 50), though later he clarified that individuals seek "cognitive balance" (Holsti 1967; cf. Zajonc 1960). Holsti hypothesized that leaders in undemocratic political systems are more likely to be rigid in their operational codes, whereas leaders in democracies have more "open" personalities. Nevertheless, he found that Dulles was quite rigid (Holsti 1962: 249; 1967: 23–24).

Leites decoded words coming from members of the Politburo into a set of principles to better understand their thinking process and strategic patterns. Holsti tried to do it for a specific person. Leites developed a meso-code for a societal subgroup, though his contribution might perhaps be considered a Stalinist micro-code. Holsti's analysis of Dulles yielded a micro-code. Similar to Leites, Holsti derived 41 beliefs of John Foster Dulles.

Both Holsti and Leites agreed that there was a serious danger of nuclear war, especially when the Soviet Union and the United States had such rigid views of each other that they were unable to achieve a détente. They agreed that analytic methods were needed to assist decision-makers in Washington to have greater understanding of actions and words emerging from the Kremlin. They both employed operational code analysis, albeit in different ways.

ALEXANDER GEORGE'S REVIVAL OF THE OPERATIONAL CODE

Alexander George, who completed a political science doctorate at the University of Chicago, was a student of Nathan Leites. Rather than initially undertake operational code analysis, he was interested in completing a biography of Woodrow Wilson, with secondary attention to his White House adviser Colonel Edward House. Co-authored with his wife (George and George 1964), the research sought a psychological explanation for Wilson's peculiar behavior. A major finding was that Wilson's Irish background, stressing human rights and independence, was in direct conflict with needs for power embedded in his Scottish ancestry.

96   M. HAAS

The analysis focused on the distinction between fundamental beliefs and situational strategic thinking, somewhere halfway in the direction of operational code analysis.

Five years later, George declared that the operational code approach had unfortunately been overlooked but needed revival. One reason for the neglect, he believed, was a misinterpretation of the term "operational code." Whereas many scholars believed that operational code analysis involved a "mechanical" application of principles by decision-makers to their behavior, George (1969: 194) interpreted Leites as having identified how the Bolshevism Code was developed to cope with (and counteract) the psychological mindset embedded in Russian national culture.

Nevertheless, George's research never referred to the meso-level cultural backgrounds of American presidents and their advisers in Washington. He did not treat American political culture as a macro-code that held decision-makers in Washington accountable. And he did not analyze ideological meso-codes within political parties. Instead, he focused entirely on micro-codes.

Similar to Gregory Bateson and other anthropologists, George acknowledged the crucial importance of participant observation to determine operational codes. Since scholars lack direct exposure to the decision-making process, he argued, codes would have to be discerned through the analysis of words, spoken and written by prominent individuals and their immediate subordinates. He then reformulated Leites' concept of "operational code" as an enumeration of decision-oriented principles into "a set of premises and beliefs about politics" (ibid., p. 169). He also suggested the following terms as verbal equivalents of "operational code": "cognitive map," "elite political culture," and "Weltangschauung" (p. 197). At the end of his pathbreaking essay, he even suggested replacing the term "operational code" with "approaches to political calculation" (p. 220).

Leites did not judge whether the Bolshevism Code was rational or irrational, though his formulation of operational code had a logical appearance. In contrast, George (1979b: 99) sought to explain irrational decision-making as a function of bias. Consistent with the Rational Choice Paradigm, George systematized how to construct an operational code, allowing for both objective and subjective considerations. One way of understanding his formulation is by drawing a decision-making map (Figure 4.2). Although there were no specific hypotheses in his formulation, three operationalizable concepts are found in column 3. Similar

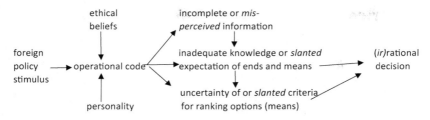

Figure 4.2 Alexander George's Decision-Making Map (*Note* Subjective considerations are italicized in contrast with objective considerations. *Source* George 1969)

to Holsti, George considered most foreign policy decision-makers to be "naïve empiricists" (p. 98).

Whereas Leites developed a code for a group, George and Holsti tried to apply operational code analysis to individuals. But meso- and micro-codes are not the same thing. Growing up in Chicago with Assyrian parents from Persia, Alexander George grew up in the environment of American individualism, which tends to discount the role of culture, even the ever-shifting concept of "American culture." George's focus on individual decision-makers, thus, would inevitably be broadened, since codes of conduct in other national cultures are often communitarian rather than individualistic.

Subjective factors in operational codes, according to George, include ethical beliefs and personality preferences. Leites also took the same factors into consideration, though more of the former than the latter. Later proponents of operational codes have referred to George's formulation as one of "bounded rationality" (rather than "substantive rationality") because they imagine that decisions are made rationally yet within the bounds of incomplete information, cognitive limitations, and time constraints (Walker 1983; cf. March and Simon 1958).

George pointed out that cognitive limitations involved misperceiving and selectively processing information, whereas ethical beliefs are used to guide and choose options for reaching goals. He distinguished between instrumental and ethical (or ideological) elements in operational codes, referring to how choices are made between alternative options in a decision-making situation. He then delineated 10 cognitive parameters that must be present in any operational code (Table 4.2). George's main goal was to provide a how-to-do-it guide for future operational code

98   M. HAAS

Table 4.2   Alexander George's Parameters for Operational Code Analysis of Decision-Makers (DMs)

Philosophical Parameters	Instrumental Parameters
DM's view of the "essential" nature of political life as inherently conflictual or harmonious	DM's selection of goals and perceived character of opponent
DM's optimism or pessimism of goal attainment	DM's selection of possible means
DM's belief that the future can be predicted	DM's risk estimates and responses
DM's confidence that efforts will achieve goals	DM's timing of action to reach goals
DM's view that chance plays a role in history	DM's evaluation of the best means

Source George (1969: 201–216)

analyses in foreign policy case studies. Although he admitted that psychological factors also play a role, they were not explicitly a part of his contrast between instrumental factors and ideological preferences (George 1979a).

As political scientist Akan Malici (2017) has noted, George's 10 parameters then became standard components for many future operational micro-code studies. However, the basis for wide acceptance of such a standard was never justified, theoretically or otherwise. And the 10 components left out the underlying social and psychological forces that impact decision-makers.

Based on his 10 parameters, George then reformulated Leites' Bolshevism Code. Ole Holsti (1970) responded to George by accepting the instrumental and philosophical beliefs to reconceptualize Dulles' "belief system" into the concept of operational code. But there was nothing in the formulations of George and Holsti about democracy, economic goals, environmental concerns, human rights, or even military security. What they designed was for a Cold War that today no longer exists.

An operational code presumably consists of norms with at least minimal coherence and consistency. Enforcement of an operational code by a group requires a strong leader, but that leaves the puzzle of how leaders self-enforce their own codes when unique situations arise.

George posited that conscientious decision-makers will develop a learning curve as they apply their own operational code to situations over time. Accordingly, he attributed modifications (code breaking or refining) by decision-makers either to personality or objective changes (events) in the international system (George 1969: 219–220). Although he included psychological factors within what appeared to be a Cognitive Decision-Making Paradigm (Figure 4.2), they were not included in the 10 cognitive components.

George congratulated one scholar who sought evidence by interviewing participant observers during a particular decision-making crisis (Horelick 1964). Nevertheless, he hoped that the operational code approach would continue to develop along his thematic approach.

In 1979, George (1979b: 98) sought to improve operational code analysis, based on the "cognitive revolution" in research on decision-making (Tetlock 1998). His view was that an operational code is useful as an explanation for how a decision-maker processes information, develops options, and chooses among options (the third column in Figure 4.2). But he conceded that there are likely to be other influences on decision-makers besides operational codes. Decision-makers, he implied, self-enforce their operational codes by unspecified predispositional psychological factors, which otherwise play an indirect role.

To prove the utility of operational codes, which might be congruent (consistent) with decision outcomes without an in-depth analysis of decision-making, he recommended "process tracing" at each stage of decision-making—that is, how the code impacts all three phases in the process of making decisions—a very time-consuming exercise (George and Bennett 2004). George's rigorous "process tracing" methodology for case studies has seldom been followed (cf. Walker 1977: 162–168; Walker and Schafer 2006).

For Leites (1951, 1953) and Holsti (1962: 252), the perilous Cold War necessitated a better understanding of how the United States might deal with the Soviet Union to avoid World War III. George agreed, but he also advised in his essay on coercive diplomacy how the United States might successfully act in the manner of a world bully rather than follow the strict diplomatic code (George 1971; cf. de Callières 1716; Berridge 2010).

Acknowledging the divorce between academia and policymakers, George (1994) identified three types of knowledge especially needed by the former. He encouraged scholars to feed the following into analyses of foreign policy decision-making: (1) models of strategy, such as deterrence, (2) conditions favoring successful use of strategic models, and (3) operational codes of targets of a strategy. By "models of strategy," he could have referred to the Deterrence Paradigm. But he chose the fork in the road toward the apriori thinking of structural realism, abandoning the other fork—empirically oriented proposition testing that might have provided answers based on paradigmatic formulations.

Instead of maintaining Leites' interest in group codes, George encouraged studies of individuals—primarily to explain why decision-makers have made blunders in past foreign policy decisions, contrary to assumptions of the Rational Choice Paradigm. "Blunders" have been identified as options that resulted in unwelcome decision outcomes, which may be a function of miscalculated goal priorities rather than anomalous beliefs. Similar to Holsti and Leites, George ignored the need for democratic control over foreign policy decision-makers.

Yet another problem with George's formulation is that he failed to mention the widely used concept of "foreign policy doctrine"—that is, the basis on which decision-makers are prepared to use force. Also missing is a role for conventional or public diplomacy within operational code analysis.

George developed cognitive operational code components to predict how leaders behaved during the Cold War, aware that blunders could be cataclysmic. But if motivational psychological factors are considered of equal value with cognitive components, the multidimensional "political personality" index of psychologist Margaret Hermann (2005) might be more useful than George's bidimensional typology. Some of her seven components overlap with those of George.

What followed George's effort to advance a research agenda over the next decade or so have been characterized (Walker and Schafer 2010: 5495) as numerous "idiographic-interpretive studies" (e.g., McLellan 1971), lacking comparability and cumulative theory-building payoff. Several scholars deviated entirely from George, Holsti, and Leites in developing the concept of operational code, as reviewed next.

Myth Systems

The term "operational code" has been utilized as relevant to legal aspects of foreign policy. Law professor W. Michael Reisman, without citing George, Holsti, Leites, or Singer, used the same term to refer to how decision-makers operate within legal systems (Reisman 1977). Based on inspiration from the Code of Hammurabi, Reisman's approach mirrored that of Robert Merton (1940).

His term "myth system" refers to the formal legal code of conduct (meso-code) within a political culture (macro-code). His "operational code" refers to actual yet unwritten micro-rules that sometimes violate the legal codes (meso-codes) because of lack of enforcement of the formal code. Legal macro-code violations are often permitted because of group solidarity, which consists of the acceptance of meso-codes and the exercise of political power by leaders, who operate on the basis of their own individual micro-codes. One possible reason for his distinction is that customs of international contact (meso-codes) are viewed as the source of formal international law (macro-codes), thereby given almost equal status as written laws (Meron 1996).

Reisman (1977: 233–234) has paid most attention to higher levels of codes. Nevertheless, he has acknowledged that decision-makers either accept the macro- or the meso-code or deviate from both in constructing their own micro-codes, usually in order to maintain electoral support but often to increase national solidarity. He almost connected his concepts of codes with the Rational Choice or Community Building paradigms.

Reisman wanted to prove that rigid enforcement of legal codes often does not accomplish goals that laws were designed to achieve. Instead, the intended goals often result in secret meso-codes that do so. In short, meso-codes arise from a desire to violate macro-codes so that laws will work for humans, rather than the other way around.

One of the best examples of Reisman's approach applied to the United Nations civil service, which consists of individuals from several countries who may be more loyal to their own country's foreign policy than to the goals of a UN agency. The macro-legal code based on the UN Charter, which applies to all employees, thus may be at variance with micro-codes followed by civil servants from particular countries. Accordingly, UN bureaucrats have developed an informal operational meso-code, just as Robert Merton predicted (cf. Meron 1981).

Another illustration is how the U.S. Supreme Court found new rights (the right of marriage and the right to privacy), which were not written into the Constitution. His explanation is that justices engaged in "judicial activism." Following Reisman, the claim has been made that there are two constitutions—one written and the other unwritten (Miller 1985/1986; 1987). But that means that judicial activism is available to rescind previously granted rights, as occurred when the right to an abortion was canceled by the Supreme Court in *Dobbs v Jackson* (2022). Similarly, China's constitutional code has been argued to transcend the bureaucratic and politburo codes (Backer 2012).

102   M. HAAS

Reisman's "myth system" is equivalent to the content of operational codes constructed by anthropologists to describe cultures and subcultures. Within a particular culture, leaders are the enforcers of the myth (macro-code) but often occupy roles that pragmatically require some deviation from the code. Ideologically supported deviations by political groups are meso-codes. Deviations by decision-makers in particular situations provide evidence of micro-codes. Reisman has indicated that within a given legal code's myth system there might be several subcultures espousing competing meso-codes.

For Reisman (1977: 238–239), "anomie" characterizes members of the public who lack understanding of the myth system and fail to join subcultures that provide an intelligible meso-code. Reisman has thereby demonstrated how operational codes can play a major role within the Mass Society Paradigm, which assigns civil society (pressure groups, political parties, media) to a critical role in translating needs of the mass public to government (cf. Lazarsfeld, Berelson, Gaudet 1944).

Reisman's approach has been applied to several foreign policy issues. For example, he explains why bribery takes place with impunity in certain countries despite clear constitutional norms against bribery (Reisman 1979). Torture has also been justified despite legal codes to the contrary (Benvenisti 1997; Nagan and Atkins 2001). Although constrained by the UN Charter, the use of force has been broadened in international law to allow military action when justified by the ambiguous concept of humanitarian intervention (Gordon 1984/1985).

First Amendment Liberalism has been identified as yet another operational code, one that justifies the formation of an independent global civil society (Kingsbury 2002). National security considerations in the United States have led federal officials to violate the law by opening mail before reaching their destinations, and journalists have sometimes exposed "secrets" in covering the news (Reisman 1977: 241–242). Riesman's applications have covered such topics as global environmental problems, human rights, and international investment and trade (Arsonjani et al. 2010; Land 2013/2014).

Geopolitical Codes

While the Cold War was still in full bloom, military historian John Lewis Gaddis (1982) decided upon an alternative to the concept of operational code, renamed as the "geopolitical code." With a focus on "who" and "how," he urged scholars to ask five basic questions in studying foreign policy decision-making:

1. Who are a country's current and potential allies?
2. Who are a country's current and potential enemies?
3. How can a country maintain allies and nurture potential allies?
4. How can a country counter current enemies and emerging threats?
5. How can the four calculations be justified to the public and the global community?

Gaddis' simplified code is policy-oriented and non-elitist while on the same wavelength as the Realism ideology of Hans Morgenthau (1948). He did not explicitly reject the concept of the operational code, but several British scholars have used his fivefold scheme instead of the operational code in analyzing foreign policies (e.g., Dijkink 1998; Sidaway and Simon 2007; Adhikari et al. 2008; Naji and Jawan 2011).

LUCIAN PYE'S APPROACH

After the end of the Cold War, political scientist Lucian Pye (1993: 440) used the term "operational code" in referring to macro- and micro-cultures. His contrast between Mao Zedong and Deng Xiaoping attributed the latter's deviation from Maoism in terms of the Socialization Paradigm (Haas 2017: 170–173). By "socialization," he referred not just to experiences of youth but also to how domestic experiences and international conferences have served to socialize leaders about the benefits of adopting standards prevailing in the international system.

EPISTEMIC COMMUNITIES AND THE LIBERAL INTERNATIONAL ORDER (LIO)

Yet another potential operational code is called the "liberal international order," which is often defined as a set of norms, rules, and structures governing interstate behavior that aim to promote cooperation rather than conflict between independent states (Lake et al. 2021). Reisman's approach, which posits a code based on both domestic and international custom as well as law, defines a "rules-based international order," whereas the LIO involves intergovernmental organizations that advance and police the political norms and rules, including free trade and other rules of the international economy. Nevertheless, the content of the international norms and rules remains a matter of dispute.

However, the impersonal LIO does not rise to the level of operational code. For an operational code to function, there must be a human element. Accordingly, the term "epistemic community" was advanced by Peter Haas (1992) to refer to a group of experts aligned in a set of beliefs who advance common goals. Whereas the United Nations has political delegates seeking to advance the LIO in diverse directions, the Arctic Council consists of multicountry representatives of indigenous, political, and scientific political circles who, without any enforced legislation measures, have successfully launched and reproduced hundreds of projects on Arctic emergencies, environmental protection, and respect for the rights of indigenous people (Ivanova and Thiers 2023). The technical experts who design and implement Arctic Council projects constitute an epistemic community.

During World War II, David Mitrany (1943) envisaged a set of global institutions at the technical level that might bind the world together after the war, making everyday life so orderly around the world that war would be too disruptive. Later, James Rosenau (1992) made a similar case for the rise of "global governance" by technical intergovernmental organizations that might ultimately spill over into political arenas. What they had in mind built on the success of the Universal Postal Union (UPU), which was formed in 1874 as the first intergovernmental institution, and established a common mail distribution system that exists today. What makes UPU and similar institutions successful is the existence of a common operational code among an epistemic community composed of those who staff and govern the organization as well as mail communities within all countries around the world.

Following the approach of Michael Reisman, an operational code of international law exists among the epistemic community of experts in international law who form a consensus regarding the interpretation treaties and international customs. Similarly, international medical epistemic communities reach consensus on how to cope with worldwide diseases. In short, an epistemic community agrees to a meso-code that might be interpreted as micro-codes within specific countries. Enforcement of the meso-code, thus, is achieved by the consensus within the epistemic community.

Further Development of the Concept of Operational Code

What emerges as a common theme thus far is an attempt to identify a set of opinions as operational codes rather than a set of criteria that decision-makers assess in evaluating alternative options when leaders make policy choices. Contrary to Leites, who is concerned about how leaders decode stimuli in accordance with their values, most early operational code thinking consists of personality assessments. More recently, political scientist Stephen Walker and his associates developed the concept of operational code to an entirely new level. Encompassing methodological, psychological, and sociological aspects, their innovations are discussed in the following chapter.

References

Adhikari, Sudeepto, Akhouri Radha Krishna Sinha, and Mukul Kamle. 2008. India's Changing Geopolitical Code: An Attempt at Analysis. *Geopolitics Quarterly* 3 (4): 4–32.

Almond, Gabriel A., and Sidney Verba. 1963. *The Civic Culture*. Boston: Little, Brown.

Arsonjani, Mahnoush H., Jacob Cogan, Robert Sloane, and Siegfried Wiessner, eds. 2010. *Looking to the Future: Essays on International Law in Honor of W. Michael Reisman*. The Hague: Brill.

Backer, Larry Catá. 2012. Party, People, Government and State: On Constitutional Values and the Legitimacy of the Chinese State-Party Rule of Law System. *Boston University International Law Review* 30 (1): 331–408.

Bateson, Gregory. 1935. Culture Contact and Schismogenesis. *Man* 35 (December): 178–183.

Bateson, Gregory. 1936. *Naven: A Survey of the Problems Suggested by a Composite Picture of the Culture of a New Guinea Tribe Drawn from Three Points of View*. Cambridge: Cambridge University Press.

Benvenisti, Eyal. 1997. The Role of National Courts in Preventing Torture of Suspected Terrorists. *European Journal of International Law* 8 (4): 596–612.

Berridge, G.R. 2010. *Diplomacy: Theory and Practice*, 4th ed. New York: Palgrave Macmillan.

Boas, Frank. 1940. *Race, Language, and Culture*. Chicago: University of Chicago Press.

Converse, Philip E. 1964. The Nature of Belief Systems in Mass Publics. In *Ideology and Discontent*, ed. David E. Apter, 206–261. New York: Free Press.

106   M. HAAS

Cournand, André, and Michael Meyer. 1976. The Scientist's Code. *Minerva* 14 (1): 79–96.

Cutler, Robert M. 1982. Unifying the Cognitive-Map and Operational-Code Approaches: An Integrated Framework with an Illustrative Example. In *Cognitive Dynamics and International Politics*, ed. Christer Jönsson, 91–121. London: Frances Pinter.

de Callières, François. 1716/1994. *The Art of Diplomacy*, ed. H.M.A. Keens-Soper and Karl W. Schweizer. Lanham, NJ: University Press of America.

Dijkink, Gertjan. 1998. Geopolitical Codes and Popular Representations. *GeoJournal* 46 (4): 293–299.

Doig, Alan, and John Wilson. 1998. The Effectiveness of Codes of Conduct. *Business Ethics: A European Review* 7 (3): 140–149.

Durkheim, Émile. 1893/1997. *The Division of Labor in Society*. New York: Free Press.

Gaddis, John Lewis. 1982. *Strategies of Containment: A Critical Appraisal of Postwar American National Security Policy*. New York: Oxford University Press.

Geertz, Clifford. 1973. *The Interpretation of Cultures*. New York: Basic Books.

George, Alexander L. 1969. The 'Operational Code': A Neglected Approach to the Study of Political Leaders and Decision-Making. *International Studies Quarterly* 13 (4): 190–222.

George, Alexander L. 1971. Coercive Diplomacy: Definition and Characteristics. In *The Limits of Coercive Diplomacy: Laos, Cuba, Vietnam*, eds. Alexander L. George, David K. Hall, and William Simons, Chap. 1. Boston: Little, Brown.

George, Alexander L. 1979a. Case Studies and Theory Development: The Method of Structured, Focused Comparison. In *Diplomacy: New Approaches in History, Theory, and Policy*, ed. Paul Gordon Lauren, 191–214. New York: Free Press.

George, Alexander L. 1979b. The Causal Nexus Between Cognitive Beliefs and Decision-Making Behavior: The 'Operational Code'. In *Psychological Models in International Politics*, ed. Lawrence S. Falkowski, 95–124. Boulder, CO: Westview.

George, Alexander L. 1994. The Two Cultures of Academia and Policy-Making: Bridging the Gap. *Political Psychology* 15 (1): 143–172.

George, Alexander L., and Andrew Bennett. 2004. *Case Studies and Theory Development in the Social Sciences*. Cambridge: MIT Press.

George, Alexander L., and Juliette L. George. 1964. *Woodrow Wilson and Colonel House: A Personality Study*. New York: Dover.

Gordon, Edward. 1984/1985. Article 2(4) in Historical Context. *Yale Law Journal* 10: 271–278.

Gorer, Geoffrey, and John Rickman. 1949. *The People of Great Russia: A Psychological Study*. London: Cresset.

Grove, Andrea K. 2018. Culture and Foreign Policy Analysis. In *Oxford Research Encyclopedia of International Studies*, eds. Robert A. Denemark and Renée Marlin-Bennett. New York: Oxford University Press.

Haas, Peter M. 1992. Introduction: Epistemic Communities and International Policy Coordination. *International Organization* 46 (1): 1–35.

Haas, Michael. 2014. *Neobehavioral Political Science: A Profession's Fascinating History, Subfields, Paradigms, Research Agenda, Policy Applications, and Future*. Los Angeles: Publishinghouse for Scholars.

Haas, Michael. 2017. *International Relations Theory: Competing Theoretical Paradigms*. Lanham, MD: Lexington.

Hermann, Margaret G. 2005. Assessing Leadership Style: Trait Analysis. In *The Psychological Assessment of Political Leaders: With Profiles of Saddam Hussein and Bill Clinton*, ed. Jerrold M. Post, Chap. 8. Dearborn: University of Michigan Press.

Holsti, Ole R. 1962. The Belief System and National Images: A Case Study. *Journal of Conflict Resolution* 6 (3): 244–252.

Holsti, Ole R. 1967. Cognitive Dynamics and Images of the Enemy. *Journal of International Affairs* 21 (1): 16–39.

Holsti, Ole R. 1970. The 'Operational Code' Approach to the Study of Political Leaders: John Foster Dulles's Philosophical and Instrumental Beliefs. *Canadian Journal of Political Science* 3 (1): 123–157.

Holsti, Ole R. 1977a. The Operational Code Approach to the Analysis of Belief Systems. Final Report to the National Science Foundation, Grant SOC 75-15368, Duke University, Durham, NC.

Holsti, Ole R. 1977b. A Typology of 'Operational Code' Belief Systems. In *Decision-Making Research: Some Recent Developments*, eds. Daniel Heradstveit and Ove Narvesen, 31–131. Oslo: Norsk Utenrikspolitisk Institutt.

Holsti, Ole R. 1992. Public Opinion and Foreign Policy: Challenges to the Almond-Lippmann Consensus Mershon Series: Research Programs and Debates. *International Studies Quarterly* 36 (4): 439–466.

Horelick, Arnold. 1964. The Cuban Missile Crisis: Analysis of Soviet Calculations and Behavior. *World Politics* 16 (3): 363–389.

Hyatt, Jenny, and Helen Simons. 1999. Cultural Codes—Who Holds the Key? The Concept and Conduct of Evaluation in Central and Eastern Europe. *Evaluation* 5 (1): 23–41.

Ivanova, Anna, and Paul Thiers. 2023. Conflict Disruptions of Epistemic Communities: Initial Lessons from the Impact of the Russian Invasion of Ukraine. Paper presented at the Annual Convention of the Western Political Science Association, San Francisco, April 8.

Janis, Irving L. 1971. Groupthink. *Psychology Today* 43 (6): 43–46, 74–76

Janis, Irving L. 1972. *Victims of Groupthink: A Psychological Study of Foreign-Policy Decisions and Fiascoes*. Boston: Houghton Mifflin.

Kingsbury, Benedict. 2002. First Amendment Liberalism as Global Legal Architecture: Ascriptive Groups and the Problems of the Liberal NGO Model of International Civil Society. *Chicago Journal of International Law* 3 (1): 183–195.

Kluckhohn, Clyde. 1955. Politics, History, and Psychology. *World Politics* 8 (1): 112–123.

Lake, David A., Lisa L. Martin, and Thomas Risse. 2021. Challenges to the Liberal Order: Reflections on International Organization. *International Organization* 75 (2): 225–257.

Land, Molly. 2013/2014. Reflections on the New Haven School. *New York Law School Law Review* 58: 919–928.

Lasswell, Harold, and Nathan Leites, eds. 1949. *Language of Politics: Studies in Quantitative Semantics*. New York: Stewart.

Lazarsfeld, Paul F., Bernard Berelson, and Helen Gaudet. 1944. *The People's Choice: How the Voter Makes Up His Mind in a Presidential Campaign*. New York: Duell, Sloan, Pearce.

Leites, Nathan. 1951. *The Operational Code of the Politburo*. New York: McGraw Hill.

Leites, Nathan. 1953. *A Study of Bolshevism*. Glencoe, IL: Free Press.

Leites, Nathan. 1959. *On the Game of Politics in France*. Stanford, CA: Stanford University Press.

Leites, Nathan. 1977. *Psychopolitical Analysis: Selected Writings of Nathan Leites*. Beverly Hills, CA: Sage.

Malici, Akan. 2017. Foreign Policy Belief Systems and Operational Code Analysis. In *Oxford Research Encyclopedia of World Politics*. New York: Oxford University Press.

Malinowski, Bronislaw K. 1944. *A Scientific Theory of Culture and Others Essays*. Chapel Hill: University of North Carolina Press.

March, James G., and Herbert A. Simon. 1958. *Organizations*. New York: Wiley.

McLellan, David S. 1971. The Operational Code Approach to the Study of Political Leaders: Dean Acheson's Philosophical and Instrumental Beliefs. *Canadian Journal of Political Science* 4 (1): 52–75.

Meine, Manfred F., and Thomas P. Dunn. 2013. The Search for Ethical Competency: Do Ethics Codes Matter? *Public Integrity* 15 (2): 149–166.

Meron, Theodor. 1981. In re Rosescu and the Independence of the International Civil Service. *American Journal of International Law* 75 (4): 910–925.

Meron, Theodor. 1996. The Continuing Role of Custom in the Formation of International Humanitarian Law. *American Journal of International Law* 90 (2): 238–249.

Merton, Robert K. 1940. Bureaucratic Structure and Personality. *Social Forces* 18 (4): 560–568.

Miller, Arthur S. 1985/1986. Pretense and Our Two Constitutions. *George Washington Law Review* 54 (1): 375–403.

Miller, Arthur S. 1987. The President and Faithful Execution of the Laws. *Vanderbilt Law Review* 40 (2): 389–406.

Mitrany, David. 1943. *A Working Peace System: An Argument for the Functional Development of International Organizations*, rev. ed. Chicago: Quadrangle, 1966.

Morgenthau, Hans J. 1948. *Politics Among Nations: The Struggle for Power and Peace.* New York: Knopf.

Nagan, Winston P., and Lucie Atkins. 2001. The International Law of Torture: From Universal Proscription to Effective Application and Enforcement. *Harvard Human Rights Journal* 14: 87–121.

Naji, Saeid, and Jayum Anak Jawan. 2011. The US Geopolitical Codes and Its Influences on the US-Iran Relations: The Case of George W. Bush's Presidency. *Journal of Politics and Law* 4 (1): 231–241.

Orwell, George. 1949. *1984.* London: Secker & Warburg.

Petracca, Mark P. 1991. The Rational Choice Approach to Politics: A Challenge to Democratic Theory. *Review of Politics* 53 (2): 289–319.

Post, Emily. 1922. *Etiquette in Society, in Business, in Politics and at Home.* New York: Funk & Wagnalls.

Pye, Lucian W. 1972. Culture and Political Science: Problems in the Evaluation of the Concept of Political Culture. *Social Science Quarterly* 53 (2): 285–296.

Pye, Lucian W. 1991. Political Culture Revisited. *Political Psychology* 12 (3): 487–508.

Pye, Lucian W. 1993. An Introductory Profile: Deng Xiaoping and China's Political Culture. *China Quarterly* 135 (3): 412–443.

Reisman, W. Michael. 1977. Myth System and Operational Code. *Yale Journal of International Law* 3 (2): 229–249.

Reisman, W. Michael. 1979. *Folded Lies: Bribery, Crusades, and Reform.* New York: Free Press.

Rokeach, Milton. 1960. *The Open and Closed Mind: Investigations into the Nature of Belief Systems and Personality Systems.* New York: Basic Books.

Rosenau, James N. 1966. Pre-Theory and Theories of Foreign of Policy. In *Approaches to Comparative and International Politics*, ed. R. Barry Farrell. Evanston, IL: Northwestern University Press.

Rosenau, James N. 1992. Governance, Order and Change in World Politics. In *Governance Without Government: Order and Change in World Politics*, eds. James N. Rosenau and Ernst-Ottawa Czempiel, Chap. 1. New York: Cambridge University Press.

Sidaway, James D., and David Simon. 2007. Geopolitical Transition and State Formation: The Changing Political Geographies of Angola, Mozambique and Namibia. *Journal of Southern African Studies* 19 (1): 6–28.

110 M. HAAS

Singer, J. David. 1960. International Conflict: Three Levels of Analysis. *World Politics* 12 (3): 453–461.

Singer, J. David. 1964. Content Analysis of Elite Articulations. *Journal of Conflict Resolution* 8 (4): 424–485.

Snyder, Richard C., H.W. Bruck, and Burton Sapin. 1954. *Decision-Making as an Approach to the Study of International Politics*. Princeton, NJ: Princeton University Press.

Spanier, John W. 1959. *The Truman-MacArthur Controversy and the Korean War*. Cambridge, MA: Harvard University Press.

Stuart, Douglas. 1979. The Relative Potency of Leader Beliefs as a Determinant of Foreign Policy: John F. Kennedy's Operational Code. Ph.D. dissertation, University of Southern California, Los Angeles.

Tetlock, Philip E. 1998. Social Psychology and World Politics. In *Handbook of Social Psychology*, eds. Daniel Gilbert, Susan Fisher, and Gardner Lindzey, 869–912. New York: McGraw-Hill.

Walker, Stephen G. 1977. The Interface Between Beliefs and Behavior: Henry Kissinger's Operational Code and the Vietnam War. *Journal of Conflict Resolution* 21 (1): 129–168.

Walker, Stephen G. 1983. The Motivational Foundation of Belief Systems: A Re-Analysis of the Operational Code Construct. *International Studies Quarterly* 27 (1): 179–201.

Walker, Stephen G., and Mark Schafer. 2006. Structural International Relations Theories and the Future of Operational Code Analysis. In *Beliefs and Leadership in World Politics: Methods and Applications of Operational Code Analysis*, eds. Mark Schafer and Stephen G. Walker, Chap. 12. New York: Palgrave Macmillan.

Walker, Stephen G., and Mark Schafer. 2010. Operational Code Theory: Beliefs and Foreign Policy Decisions. In *The International Studies Encyclopedia*, ed. Robert A. Denemark, Vol. VIII, 5942–5514. West Sussex, UK: Wiley Blackwell. Reprinted online in Robert A. Denemark and Renée Marlin-Bennett, eds. 2017. *The International Studies Encyclopedia*. https://www.oxfordreference.com/view/10.1093/acref/978019184 2665.001.0001/acref-9780191842665-e-0291?rskey=hOcAMZ&result=329.

Waltz, Kenneth N. 1959. *Man, the State, and War: A Theoretical Analysis*. New York: Columbia University Press.

Whyte, William H., Jr. 1952. Groupthink. *Fortune*, March: 114–117, 142, 146.

Zajonc, Robert B. 1960. The Concepts of Balance, Congruity, and Dissonance. *Public Opinion Quarterly* 24 (2): 280–296.

CHAPTER 5

Developments and Problems in Operational Code Research

Political scientist Stephen Walker first undertook operational code research in the late 1970s and soon led the field. In an initial study, he discovered that onetime Secretary of State Henry Kissinger, though fixated on an ideological dogma (realism), preferred negotiations in order to achieve incremental progress (Walker 1977). The purpose of the present chapter is to trace how he integrated previous approaches and then proceeded theoretically and quantitatively, resulting in confusion that will be resolved and applied in Part III of the present volume.

Walker's most important initial contribution was to integrate Alexander George's ten parameters with Ole Holsti's sixfold framework (Walker 1983: 182–186). Because he discovered overlaps, he combined Holsti's D, E, and F, though he also overlooked the non-elitist potential in B and E (see Table 4.1). It was Walker's aspiration that operational code research would predict political events (Walker and Murphy 1981). Later, a mystery was discovered about Lyndon Johnson's decision-making, whose operational code was far more consistent than those of his policy advisers (Walker and Schafer 2000).

Walker then steered operational code research into entirely new directions. The present chapter explains and critiques his many innovations.

© The Author(s), under exclusive license to Springer Nature
Switzerland AG 2023
M. Haas, *Professionalization of Foreign Policy*,
https://doi.org/10.1007/978-3-031-37152-3_5

111

Psychological and Sociological Focus

For Walker (1983: 188–191; 1990), foreign policy operational code analysis had to take both cognitive and psychological (motivational) factors into account. Consistent with the earliest foreign policy analyses, he believed that decision-makers had varying codes due to idiosyncratic psychological drives.

For example, the familiar frustration → aggression theory (Dollard et al. 1939) was tested: A qualitative content analysis of the operational codes of two Irish leaders in 1913–1915 revealed that their increased frustration was linked to their advocacy of violence during the Easter Rebellion of 1916 (Schafer et al. 2006).

Without mentioning Lucian Pye's Socialization Paradigm (Pye 1972, 1991), Stephen Walker adopted his own version, placing causal links between concepts, thereby formalizing propositions (Figure 5.1): (1) Socialization experiences cultivate a need pattern before children have coherent political beliefs. (2) Later in life, individuals adopt beliefs (an operational code) to fulfill their pattern of psychological needs. (3) When event stimuli prompt leaders to respond, they utilize their operational codes as the lens for filtering information about the situation and then identifying options. (4) Resulting decisions, therefore, reflect their psychological needs.

In 1984, Walker and a collaborator, political scientist Lawrence Falkowski, diagrammed more detail by locating the decision-maker's personality calculations between stages 4 (decision stimulus) and 5 (decision output) in Figure 5.1 (Walker and Falkowski 1984a: Figure 1). Later, Walker (1990: 415) hypothesized that anomalies discovered in previous studies constituted evidence of personality needs rather than cognitive perceptions or misperceptions of decision targets. His hypothesis was that a decision-maker's ego-defense and superego (self–other) relations always filter target perceptions.

Accordingly, Walker redefined "operational code" as "a set of alternative 'states of mind'." Drawing upon cognitive psychology (Hermann

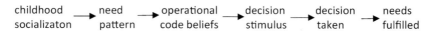

Figure 5.1 Socialization Paradigm of Operational Code Formation (*Source* Walker 1983)

1988; Larson 1994), he advanced the view that leaders compartmentalize (have different operational codes for different issue-areas or decision targets). For example, Tony Blair and Bill Clinton held positive views about democracies and negative opinions concerning nondemocracies—and slanted their perceptions accordingly (Schafer and Walker 2006). In addition, decision-makers sometimes receive contradictory information, often disagree with their advisers, and display small or large learning curves after coming to power (Walker and Schafer 2006b: 237).

Walker and Falkowski (1984a, b) established contact with biographers and colleagues of seven decision-makers, posing questions in the reformulated Holsti typology. What they found was incongruity—"hybrid" types: Decision-makers were not logically consistent, instead falling into two or more belief categories. In other words, no strict self-enforcement mechanism in individual operational codes was evident. Cognitive consistency was no longer to be assumed as a fundamental characteristic of operational codes but instead might be a recipe for decision-making blunders.

At this point, many operational code studies began to emerge within political psychology journals. For example, measures of needs for achievement, affiliation, and power were integrated into studies of several political leaders (Walker and Falkowski 1984b; Walker 1995).

Originally, operational code research was concerned with the Cold War. When the Berlin Wall tumbled, the approach waned. Military-strategic concerns had lower priority than new international issues, ranging from democracy expansion, environmental problems, ethnic and race relations, government apologies for past errors, human rights, informal diplomacy, regional cooperation, to UN peacekeeping (Haas 1997). Stephen Walker and his political psychologist colleague Mark Schafer (2006a: 140–143) then transformed Leites' approach into a set of axioms and theorems, presumed self-evident, instead of hypotheses or propositions for testing.

The post-Cold War focus, more scholarly than policy-oriented (Walker and Schafer 2006a: 4), asked three major questions: Why do some decision-makers rely on rigid operational codes, while others appear inconsistent with what might appear to be their micro-codes? If one reason is that initially they are members of ideological groups (and their meso-codes), why did they join one group rather than another? And if they adapt their personal (micro) codes to actual situations when they rise to power, what is the real reason for cognitive consistency or inconsistency?

Efforts to link cognitive with psychological elements have been problematic (Lepgold and Lamborn 2001). Walker (2002, 2003, 2004) drew four major conclusions: (1) Operational codes are unimportant under ideal conditions (substantive rationality) of the Rational Choice Paradigm—namely, when decision-maker X correctly determines power relations, institutional constraints, and shared norms vis-à-vis decision target Y. (2) Operational codes play a definitive role when there is lack of clarity in power relations, institutional constraints, and shared norms. (3) Bounded rationality exists when an operational code is internally consistent and applied calculatingly. (4) But if an operational code is inconsistent, then psychological factors prevail.

Regarding George's tenfold scheme, Walker and Schafer (2010: 5498) claimed that "the diagnostic function of philosophical beliefs and the prescriptive function of instrumental beliefs can interact to constrain and even specify behavior without being internally consistent or interdependent with one another." But such a loose set of beliefs might not necessarily qualify as an operational code.

Returning to Holsti's idea of "master beliefs," Walker and two colleagues (Walker, Schafer, Young 2003: 231–235; cf. Walker and Schafer 2006a, b, 2010: 5492, 5504–5505) identified three concepts as central to the operational codes of decision-makers: (1) cognitive image of the hostility or friendliness of other countries, (2) preference for incremental decisions or fundamental policy changes, while navigating between old beliefs and new realities, and (3) learning capabilities, as reflected in adjustments in behavior to achieve political goals.

The belief triad was labeled mirroring (image-oriented), steering (means-oriented), and learning (strategy-oriented). All three elements would be present in rational decision-making. The cognitive image was one of George's philosophical components, and the action belief came from George's instrumental components, so learning was added as a new component. They also noted that decision-makers often apply "analogical reasoning"—an understanding of past history achieved through socialization as a "shortcut" to deal with (frame) present situations (Walker and Schafer 2010: 5506). What thus emerged was advocacy of a Socialization Paradigm (Figure 5.2), albeit unacknowledged.

Indeed, several studies have identified operational codes consistent with the Socialization Paradigm: In one study over time, the experience of joining intergovernmental organizations has served to change

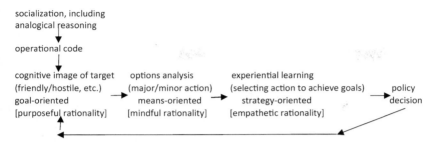

Figure 5.2 Cognitive Decision-Making Map of Walker, Schafer, and Young (*Source* Walker et al. 2003)

the attitudes of Chinese leaders toward the world, though not fundamental beliefs about strategy (He and Feng 2015). Positing socialization as a three-stage process, another study identified China as moving to the *adaptation stage* at the end of the Cold War, subsequently advanced to the *superficial socialization stage*, but has not moved to the *fundamental socialization stage* (Checkel 2005). Political scientists Cameron Thies and Marijke Breuning (2012) have argued that operational codes change as countries perceive new roles in the international community. However, attitude change involves an unlearning process before new roles are adopted (Clark 2009). The intellectual history of the operational code thereby advanced to encompass role theory.

Role Theory

In recent years, Walker and associates have celebrated role theory as a comprehensive way to understand how leaders behave when they are suddenly thrust into the position of decision-makers (Walker, Malici, Shafer 2011: ch14). Among new concepts put forward are role competition, conception, conflict, demands, enactment, expectations, interaction, location, and role strain. Yet classic role theory (Mead 1934; Merton 1940; Parsons 1951; Holsti 1970; Erikson 1980) is a variant within the larger Socialization Paradigm.

Efforts to employ role theory, however, have been judged to lack "theoretical innovation and methodological rigor" (Malici and Walker 2017: 57). By focusing on role theory, Walker began to divert attention away from operational codes, which are located at an early level in decision processes (Figure 5.2). When he began to re-focus on a tool of the Rational Choice Paradigm—game theory strategy—at the endpoints (Hoagland and Walker 1979: 134; Marfleet and Walker 2006; Walker, Malici, Schafer 2011: ch14), relevance to the Cold War was obvious.

In one study, a 2 × 2 matrix was constructed of operational code themes, almost identical to the one Holsti (1977) might have designed three decades earlier (cf. Snyder and Diesing 1977). Process tracing, as recommended by Alexander George (1979), returned within comprehensive studies on blunders in American and British foreign policy (Walker and Malici 2011; Walker 2013; Malici and Walker 2017), which used extensive diagrams to depict episodes in terms of game theory diagrams, all descriptive rather than tests of propositions to determine why blunders occur. Meanwhile, the term "operational code" almost entirely disappeared within the indexes of the latter three volumes, though reappearing in *Operational Code Analysis and Foreign Policy Roles* (Schafer and Walker 2022).

The game theory focus actually shifted to the Triumphalist variant of Social Darwinism in strategic thinking: The aim was to determine losers and winners and, using the Deterrence Paradigm, to avoid losses. The quest was to improve hitherto underdeveloped role theory into a "theory of everything" (Walker 2013: 188)—that is, the long-sought but elusive Cognitive Decision-Making Paradigm. But the focus remained on how to navigate a nonexistent Cold War.

Yet much micro-operational code research continues without invoking role theory and game theory. Despite being nestled into a routine, operational code research remains saddled with several unresolved methodological problems needing attention, which are addressed next.

METHODOLOGICAL PROBLEMS

In a review of research on operational codes in 1998, Stephen Walker and his colleagues Mark Schafer and Michael Young concluded that operational code research had "languished" because qualitative studies had been insufficiently objective (Walker, Schafer, Young 1998: 176). But their efforts at quantitative analyses have encountered problems, as noted next:

Some scholars have constructed very different operational codes for the same decision-maker (e.g., Malone 1971 versus Walker and Falkowski

5 DEVELOPMENTS AND PROBLEMS IN OPERATIONAL CODE ... 117

1984a, b). Yet few attempts have been made to validate the verbal foundations for constructing operational codes in qualitative studies ever since Nathan Leites tried to do so. As Walker and Schafer (2010: 5495) noted, qualitative content analysis involves either the direct method (quoting statements of principles) or the indirect method (inferring principles from texts). Using the indirect method, Leites (1951, 1953) knew how the Politburo deviated from Russian national culture, but he also used the direct method by quoting statements.

Leites was aware that his Bolshevism Code failed the internal (logical) validity test because the principles were internally inconsistent. But his operational code formulation passed the external (outcome) validity test because he demonstrated how the principles were indeed applied to actual decisions.

Later, internal validity of an operational code was established in a study that derived similar results from both a quantitative and a qualitative content analysis (Stuart and Starr 1981/1982). External validity was established in a study of Henry Kissinger's operational code, based on qualitative content analysis of words, by demonstrating that he took actions consistent with his code regarding the American intervention into Vietnam (Walker 1977). Similar efforts at qualitative validation are rare, however.

Walker and associates have developed quantitative techniques for measuring beliefs, using coding rules based on Alexander George's ten parameters and Ole Holsti's six categories (Walker, Schafer, Young 1998: 178–182). Known as the Verbs-in-Context (VICs) system, a seven-point scale represents verbs on both cooperative/positive and conflictual/negative continua (Schafer and Walker 2006). The procedure locates and scales verbs within texts, identifying the object (self or other) and intensity of transitive verbs (Young 2001). The method, now on www.profilerplus.org, has been applied to some recent studies of decision-makers (e.g., Malici 2006).

Walker and Schafer (2010: 5493, 5503) celebrated quantification as a transformation of operational code research into a realm of more coherence. But two important questions remain—(1) whether verbs chosen are in fact are reliable or valid measures of beliefs and (2) whether 10 or 16 beliefs are empirically distinct or collinear.

Proceeding with an analysis of verbs articulated by President Jimmy Carter during each year of his administration (Walker et al. 2003: 237–240), the statistical plot of belief frequencies yielded stability for the first three years but a shift after the Soviet Union entered Afghanistan and the Vietnamese army chased the Khmer Rouge out of Cambodia. Thus, Carter's originally-determined operational code appeared to fall apart when he was socialized by new information (events) that shattered a component of his original code; because of "experiential learning," he broke out of his former consistency, as explained in more detail in Chapter 7 of the present volume.

Results of quantitative content analysis have been similar to more conventional qualitative studies (Rosati 1987; Skidmore 1993/1994), giving external validity to the quantitative exercise. But the obvious question is whether Carter had a more complex operational code all along, with some beliefs contingent on experience—a question that quantitative analysis has not answered.

Since the quantitative study about Carter yielded little not already found qualitatively, the question was why bother to use quantitative analysis in the first place? The answer was that any decision-maker can be evaluated within a few minutes by inputting statements into a computer file for quantitative processing. But that meant that operational code analysis had been reduced to a quantitative exercise, a basis for "instant theses," contrary to the qualitative (process tracing) analyses that political scientists Alexander George and Andrew Bennett (2004) have trumpeted. Besides, a superficial count of word frequencies can hardly be equivalent to a belief that usually takes themes and sentences to delineate.

Further tests tried to demonstrate the utility of the quantitative approach. About 100 such exercises have been conducted of leaders, often seeking to find either rigidity or fluidity in belief systems—notably, such leaders as Tony Blair (Schafer and Walker 2006), George W. Bush (Marfleet and Miller 2005), Fidel Castro (Malici and Malici 2005a, b), Jacques Chirac (Marfleet and Miller 2005), Lyndon Johnson (Walker and Schafer 2000), Kim Jong-Il (Malici and Malici 2005a, b), Xi Jinping (He and Feng 2013) , Shimon Peres (Crichlow 1998), Vladimir Putin (Dyson 2001), Yitzhak Rabin (Crichlow 1998), and Mao Zedong (Feng 2005). And many more.

Although Akan Malici (2017) has claimed that recent studies have validated the quantitative measures, external and internal validity tests have rarely been run. In one study, an effort was made to validate a quantification of beliefs with a count of events (Schafer and Walker 2006). In another study, the quantitative exercise was validated by a qualitative historical analysis (Schafer, Robison, Aldrich 2006). The conclusion appears to be that qualitative narratives are no better or worse than quantitative studies, though they cross-validate (cf. Gaddis 1992/1993).

Several studies demonstrate that prepared statements are sometimes far more cautious than spontaneous remarks; public statements also differ from private comments (Dille 2000; Schafer and Crichlow 2002; Renshon 2009; Dyson and Raleigh 2014). In other words, studies that combine both sources lack internal validity unless there is a separate analysis of prepared, spontaneous, public, and private statements. Few operational code studies have thus far sought to correct that validity problem.

Nevertheless, the most significant assumption in operational code research is whether Alexander George correctly identified two empirically distinct components for any foreign policy operational code, with five subcomponents each (Table 4.2). He identified the first parameter in each column as the basic belief; he claimed that the other four parameters were "derived" from that belief. A simple factor analysis could determine whether there are two distinct factors (bidimensionality), and the relative importance of each of the five components on each factor. But no such exercise has ever been undertaken.

Instead, when Walker, Schafer, Young (2003) qualitatively tried to identify key components of decision-making, they arrived at tridimensionality—the three concepts of cognition, action, and learning. All three were embedded in Holsti's formulation (Figure 4.1).

Yet another problem is reliability. For qualitative studies to be judged reliable, at least two different researchers (or the same scholar at two different times) must examine the same case and derive nearly identical findings. One example is Table 3.2 in the present volume. Although reliability checks have been rare (cf. Shimko 1992; Hartz 1996: 945), quantitative counting by computer programs definitely ensures reliability (cf. Schafer and Walker 2006) albeit not validity.

In short, quantitative methodological advances have not been paralleled with a solution to the problem of validity, though reliability has been solved through computerized analysis. George's operational code bidimensionality (instrumental, philosophical) remains an unsettled assumption, inconsistent with Walker's conceptual tridimensionality (cognition, action, and learning). Meanwhile, the terms used in quantitative content analysis recall the Cold War, placing priority on how decision-makers view the world in terms of conflict.

120   M. HAAS

In the future, artificial intelligence might be a better way to discern operational codes, using thematic content analysis. Development of the new methodology is expected soon (Grimmer, Roberts, Stewart 2022).

THEORETICAL CONFUSION

Most operational code research consists of a series of descriptive case studies on individual decision-makers without systematic testing of theoretical propositions or explanations. Conclusions from one study have not cumulated to inform the next study, whereupon a mass of findings could be summarized as a correction to a theory. One reason is that scholars have used the term "theory," which has many possible meanings (Rapoport 1958), without a postpositivist paradigmatic understanding of the term.

Stephen Walker and Mark Schafer (2010: 5492), for example, have disputed that "operational code theory" exists while also incoherently defining that "theory" as an "alliance of attribution and schema theories from psychology and game theory from economics applied to the domain of politics." They also have agreed with Akan Malici (2017) that realism, liberalism, and constructivism are "grand theories" (Walker 2004, 2011a, b, c, d, e; Walker and Schafer 2006a, b: 240; 2010: 5503, 5509), but in fact all three are ideological dogmas that advance apriori axioms without ever testing them.

Indeed, when realism has been unpacked into testable propositions within the Power Balancing Paradigm (Morgenthau 1948), results have refuted the axioms (Bueno de Mesquita 1981, 1985; Niou, Ordeshook, Rose 1989; Niou and Ordeshook 1990; Haas 2018; cf. Kupchan 1994). Efforts to integrate operational code research into the various ideologies have been a waste of time, with no accumulation in knowledge of the sort that results from a paradigm-based aggregate of results of proposition testing. Paradigmatic confusion has particularly clouded the discussion about the need of "operational code theory" to abandon "cognitive consistency theory" (Walker and Schafer 2010: 5497).

To clarify, exponents of "operational code theory" do not agree on what that theory is. Instead, operational code is a *concept* hypothesized to play a specific middle role within the multifaceted decision-making process. And cognitive consistency is not a theory but instead a *concept* referring to whether decision-makers rigidly self-enforce their codes. Decision-making maps could be the basis for theories (Figures 5.1 and

5 DEVELOPMENTS AND PROBLEMS IN OPERATIONAL CODE ...

5.2) if the concepts ("constructs," in Walker's terminology) were operationalized at each stage of the decision-making process, something that could have been done but has inexplicably been absent.

Moreover, if theories have viable precision, at least one concept must be identified as the dependent variable. The most common concepts suggested as endpoints in foreign policy studies are whether a decision involves the use of force or is a blunder. In other words, operational code research has primarily focused on intermediate processes and has failed to generate wisdom regarding how to avoid unnecessary violence or miscalculations (cf. Schafer, Robison, Aldrich 2006). Although recent studies have applied operational code analysis to studies of foolish decisions (Walker and Malici 2011; Walker 2013; Maliciand Walker 2017), conclusions are specific to each event rather than building on previous studies to expand broader paradigmatic knowledge.

A mid-level (meso) empirical theory exists when a puzzle has been identified, linked concepts are hypothesized to solve the puzzle, and empirical indicators of concepts determine whether hypothesized correlations in fact explain the puzzle. Paradigms operate at the macro-level, positing a causal understanding of systemic phenomena; they incorporate several mid-level theories that apply at various levels of analysis, based on concepts that are functionally equivalent at all levels. Mid-level theories provide explanations of specific phenomena, whereas paradigms provide comprehensive understanding of phenomena at multiple levels of analysis (cf. Lepgold and Lamborn 2001: 4).

Most of the operational code literature refers to one paradigm out of many possible—the Rational Choice Paradigm, which claims that humans generally make rational decisions. The paradigm is alleged to apply at many levels—families, neighborhood community organizations, political parties, city councils, national legislatures, foreign policy decision-makers, as well as governing bodies of international governmental and nongovernmental organizations. The Rational Choice Paradigm, as developed over the past two centuries, includes several variants— Cost–Benefit, Deterrence, Social Darwinism, Pressure Group Theory, Hegemonism, Balance-of-Power, Selectorate, Resource Mobilization, and Social Exchange (cf. Haas 2017a, b). David Easton (1991) once identified the Rational Choice Paradigm as dominant within political science, though some economists have recently claimed to have refuted the paradigm's claims about human behavior (Banarjee and Duflo 2019).

Nevertheless, operational code analysis has not been conducted as a tool to prove or disprove the Rational Choice Paradigm as applied to foreign policy. Solving the puzzle why some decision-makers make mistakes, while others are rationally clever, has been a major goal in exploring the crucial role of operational codes within the decision-making process. One hypothesis has been that internally consistent operational codes allow decisionmakers to make rational decisions—rational, that is, within the boundaries of a consistent code (e.g., Dulles). When the code is inconsistent, bounded rationality might apply, though the resulting decision might be rational in achieving a desired objective (e.g., Kennedy in the Cuban Missiles Crisis). Although the Rational Choice Paradigm appears to have been rejected in operational code research, a possible replacement—a Cognitive Decision-Making Paradigm—remains undeveloped for foreign policy studies (Haas 2017a: 153–162).

As noted above, Walker later accessed the Socialization Paradigm, without so noting, to explain that operational codes are a function of psychological need patterns (Figure 5.1). He also specified that the decision-making process (from stimulus to response) involves exposure to friends and foes and perhaps also recollections of events (Figure 5.2). The Socialization Paradigm, in which role occupancy is a source of beliefs, has gained considerable support (Walker, Malici, Schafer 2011: ch14–15; Thies and Breuning 2012; He and Feng 2015), albeit without reference to the extensive Socialization Paradigm literature that has flourished since first developed by George Herbert Mead (1934), with notable applications since the 1940s (Lazarsfeld, Berelson, Gaudet 1944) and criticisms in the present (Connell 1987; Höppner 2017; Saint Martin 2017). With Stephen Walker an important exception, most international studies scholars shun social science paradigms, refusing to read a literature of extreme relevance while instead clumsily re-inventing theoretical wheels.

Some scholars pretend that role theory has replaced operational code theory, since roles generate codes. However, individuals craft their own codes before they become decision-makers. The focus on roles is a subset within theories that deal with operational codes.

Paradigms that deal with democratic goals are generally ignored within the elitist bent of operational code analysis. The Mass Society Paradigm, once considered the dominant paradigm in sociology (Bell 1961), examines how civil society and public opinion impact group, governmental, and global forces to work for or against the needs of the public in governmental decisions. The Mass Society Paradigm was originally developed by

Émile Durkheim (1893) and others (Kornhauser 1959; Habermas 1981) as an alternative to the Marxian Paradigm. The latter made many predictions about the inevitable obsolescence of capitalism which have not yet come true (Marx and Engels 1848).

The Community Building Paradigm, another democratic perspective at the foundation of the discipline of international studies (Haas 2017a: ch6; 2017b: ch8), initially made predictions about how to achieve greater intergovernmental cooperation in Europe (Haas 1964). Studies of decision-making focusing on operational codes, however, have increasingly focused on individuals rather than the major goal that began the discipline of international relation after World War I—namely, how to bring about a more peaceful world. In a recent qualitative study, for example, multinational task forces within alliances provide interaction (and thereby socialization) opportunities that build mutual trust (Hatzakis and Searle 2006). In other words, the Socialization Paradigm parallels the policy-relevant Community Building Paradigm. Cultural macro-code research also feeds into the Community Building Paradigm (Haas 2017a, b).

Conclusion

Rather than subscribing to just one paradigm, however, wise advisers to decision-makers have opinions on many paradigms, believing that some are more important than others in governing. Operational code research has operated primarily at a pre-theoretical level, assuming that dilemmas of the Cold War persist into the present. Using wordcounting to determine beliefs is clearly invalid; beliefs are complex ideas, worthy of theme content analysis, not just simple quantitative constellations of words.

Accordingly, Part III provides a new way to define the operational code of a government leader—the degree to which an individual subscribes to all possible relevant paradigms. Such an approach transforms operational code analysis into a tool of applied science.

References

Banarjee, Abhijit, and Esther Duflo. 2019. *Good Economics for Hard Times*. New York: Hatchett.

Bell, Daniel A. 1961. *The End of Ideology: On the Exhaustion of Political Ideas in the 1950s*. New York: Collier.

124 M. HAAS

Bueno de Mesquita, Bruce. 1981. *The War Trap*. New Haven, CT: Yale University Press.

Bueno de Mesquita, Bruce. 1985. The War Trap Revisited: A Revised Expected Utility Model. *American Political Science Review* 79 (1): 156–177.

Checkel, Jeffrey T. 2005. International Institutions and Socialization in Europe: Introduction and Framework. *International Organization* 59 (4): 801–826.

Clark, Richard E. 2009. Resistance to Change: Unconscious Knowledge and the Challenge of Unlearning. In *Fostering Change in Institutions, Environments, and People*, eds. David C. Berliner and Haggai Kupermintz, Chap. 5. New York: Routledge.

Connell, R.W. 1987. Why the 'Political Socialization' Paradigm Failed and What Should Replace It. *International Political Science Review* 8 (3): 215–233.

Crichlow, Scott. 1998. Idealism or Pragmatism: An Operational Code Analysis of Yitzhak Rabin and Shimon Peres. *Political Psychology* 19 (4): 683–706.

Dille, Brian. 2000. The Prepared and Spontaneous Remarks of Presidents Reagan and Bush: A Validity Comparison for At-a-Distance Measurements. *Political Psychology* 21 (3): 573–585.

Dollard, John, Neal Miller, Leonard Doob, Orville H. Mowrer, and Robert Sears. 1939. *Frustration and Aggression*. New Haven, CT: Yale University Press.

Durkheim, Émile. 1893. *The Division of Labor in Society*. New York: Free Press, 1997.

Dyson, Stephen Benedict. 2001. Drawing Policy Implications from the 'Operational Code' of a 'New' Political Actor: Russian President Vladimir Putin. *Policy Sciences* 34 (3–4): 329–346.

Dyson, Stephen Benedict, and Alexandra L. Raleigh. 2014. Public and Private Beliefs of Political Leaders: Saddam Hussein in Front of a Crowd and Behind Closed Doors. *Research and Politics* 1 (1): 1–7.

Easton, David. 1991. Political Science in the United States: Past and Present. In *The Development of Political Science*, eds. David Easton, John G. Gunnell, and Luigi Graziani, Chapter 12. New York: Routledge.

Erikson, Erik H. 1980. *Identity and the Life Cycle*. New York: Norton.

Feng, Huiyun. 2005. The Operational Code of Mao Zedong: Defensive or Offensive Realist? *Security Studies* 14 (4): 637–662.

Gaddis, John Lewis. 1992/1993. International Relations Theory and the End of the Cold War. *International Security* 17 (3): 5–58.

George, Alexander L. 1979. The Causal Nexus Between Cognitive Beliefs and Decision-Making Behavior: The 'Operational Code'. In *Psychological Models in International Politics*, ed. Lawrence S. Falkowski, 95–124. Boulder, CO: Westview.

George, Alexander L., and Andrew Bennett. 2004. *Case Studies and Theory Development in the Social Sciences*. Cambridge: MIT Press.

Grimmer, Justin, Margaret E. Roberts, and Brandon M. Stewart. 2022. *Text as Data: A New Framework for Machine Learning and the Social Sciences.* Princeton, NJ: Princeton University Press.

Haas, Ernst B. 1964. *Beyond the Nation State: Functionalism and International Organization.* Stanford, CA: Stanford University Press.

Haas, Michael. 1992. *Polity and Society: Philosophical Underpinnings of Social Science Paradigms.* New York: Praeger.

Haas, Michael. 1997. International Communitarianism: The New Agenda of World Politics. In *Deconstructing International Relations Theory,* ed. Michael Haas, 102–126. New York: Norton.

Haas, Michael. 2017a. *International Relations Theory: Competing Empirical Paradigms.* Lanham, MD: Lexington.

Haas, Michael. 2017b. *Political Science Revitalized: Filling the Jigsaw Puzzle with Metatheory.* Lanham, MD: Lexington.

Haas, Michael. 2018. *American Diplomacy with North Korea and Vietnam: Explaining Failure and Success.* New York: Peter Lang.

Habermas, Jürgen. 1965. *The Theory of Communication Action.* Boston: Beacon, 1981.

Hartz, Charles A. 1996. Ideology, Pragmatism, and Ronald Reagan's World View: Full of Sound and Fury, Signifying … ? *Presidential Studies Quarterly* 26 (4): 942–949.

Hatzakis, Tally, and Rosalind Searle. 2006. Grounding Trust in Inter-Organizational Alliances: An Exploration of Trust Evolution. *Management Revue* 17 (1): 72–89.

He, Kai, and Huiyun Feng. 2013. Xi Jinping's Operational Code Beliefs and China's Foreign Policy. *Chinese Journal of International Politics* 6 (3): 209–231.

He, Kai, and Huiyun Feng. 2015. Transcending Rationalism and Constructivism: Chinese Leaders' Operational Codes, Socialization Processes, and Multilateralism After the Cold War. *European Political Science Review* 7 (3): 401–426.

Hermann, Margaret G. 1988. The Empirical Challenge of the Cognitive Revolution. *International Studies Quarterly* 32 (1): 175–204.

Hoagland, Steve W., and Stephen G. Walker. 1979. Operational Codes and Crisis Outcomes. In *Psychological Models in International Politics,* ed. Lawrence F. Falkowski, 125–167. Boulder, CO: Westview.

Holsti, Kalevi J. 1970. National Role Conceptions in the Study of Foreign Policy. *International Studies Quarterly* 14 (3): 233–309.

Holsti, Ole R. 1977. A Typology of 'Operational Code' Belief Systems. In *Decision-Making Research: Some Recent Developments,* eds. Daniel Heradstveit and Ove Narvesen, 31–131. Oslo: Norsk Utenrikspolitisk Institutt.

126   M. HAAS

Höppner, Grit. 2017. Rethinking Socialization Research Through the Lens of New Materialism. *Frontiers in Sociology* 2 (13). www.frontiersin.org/articles/10.3389/fsoc.2017.00013/full.

Kornhauser, William. 1959. *The Mass Society Theory of Politics*. New York: Free Press.

Kupchan, Charles. 1994. *The Vulnerability of Empire*. Ithaca, NY: Cornell University Press.

Larson, Deborah Welch. 1994. The Role of Belief Systems and Schemas in Foreign Policy Decision Making. *Political Psychology* 15 (1): 17–33.

Lazarsfeld, Paul F., Bernard Berelson, and Helen Gaudet. 1944. *The People's Choice: How the Voter Makes Up His Mind in a Presidential Campaign*. New York: Duell, Sloan, Pearce.

Leites, Nathan. 1951. *The Operational Code of the Politburo*. New York: McGraw Hill.

Leites, Nathan. 1953. *A Study of Bolshevism*. Glencoe, IL: Free Press.

Lepgold, Joseph, and Alan C. Lamborn. 2001. Locating Bridges: Connecting Research Agendas on Cognition and Strategic Choice. *International Studies Review* 3 (3): 3–29.

Malici, Akan. 2006. Germans as Venutians: The Culture of German Foreign Policy Behavior. *Foreign Policy Analysis* 2 (1): 37–62.

Malici, Akan. 2017. Foreign Policy Belief Systems and Operational Code Analysis. In *Oxford Research Encyclopedia of World Politics*. New York: Oxford University Press.

Malici, Akan, and Johnna Malici. 2005a. The Operational Codes of Fidel Castro and Kim Il Sung: The Last Cold Warriors? *Political Psychology* 26 (3): 387–412.

Malici, Akan, and Johnna Malici. 2005b. When Will They Ever Learn? An Examination of Fidel Castro and Kim Jong-Il's Operational Code Beliefs. *Psicología Política* 31 (1): 7–22.

Malici, Akan, and Stephen G. Walker. 2017. *Role Theory and Role Conflict in U.S.-Iran Relations: Enemies of Our Own Making*. New York: Routledge.

Malone, Craig S. 1971. The Operational Code of Lyndon Baines Johnson. Mimeo, Stanford, CA, July.

Marfleet, B. Gregory, and Colleen Miller. 2005. Failure After 1441: Bush and Chirac in the UN Security Council. *Foreign Policy Analysis* 1 (3): 333–360.

Marfleet, B. Gregory, and Stephen G. Walker. 2006. A World of Beliefs: Modeling Interactions Among Agents with Different Operational Codes. In *Beliefs and Leadership in World Politics: Methods and Applications of Operational Code Analysis*, eds. Mark Schafer and Stephen G. Walker, 53–73. New York: Palgrave Macmillan.

5 DEVELOPMENTS AND PROBLEMS IN OPERATIONAL CODE ... 127

Marx, Karl, and Friedrich Engels. 1848. Manifesto of the Communist Party. In *The Marx-Engels Reader*, ed. Robert C. Tucker, 335–362. New York: Norton, 1972.

Mead, George H. 1934. *Mind, Self, and Society*. Chicago: University of Chicago Press.

Merton, Robert K. 1940. Bureaucratic Structure and Personality. *Social Forces* 18 (4): 560–568.

Morgenthau, Hans J. 1948. *Politics Among Nations: The Struggle for Power and Peace*. New York: Knopf.

Niou, Emerson, and Peter Ordeshook. 1990. Stability in Anarchic International Systems. *American Political Science Review* 84 (4): 1207–1234.

Niou, Emerson, Peter Ordeshook, and Gregory Rose. 1989. *The Balance of Power*. New York: Cambridge University Press.

Parsons, Talcott. 1951. *The Social System*. Glencoe, IL: Free Press.

Pye, Lucian W. 1972. Culture and Political Science: Problems in the Evaluation of the Concept of Political Culture. *Social Science Quarterly* 53 (2): 285–296.

Pye, Lucian W. 1991. Political Culture Revisited. *Political Psychology* 12 (3): 487–508.

Rapoport, Anatoli. 1958. Various Meanings of 'Theory.' *American Political Science Review* 52 (4): 972–988.

Renshon, Jonathan. 2009. When Public Statements Reveal Private Beliefs: Assessing Operational Codes at a Distance. *Political Psychology* 30 (4): 649–661.

Rosati, Jerel A. 1987. *The Carter Administration's Quest for Global Community: Beliefs and Their Impact on Behavior*. Columbia: University of South Carolina Press.

Saint Martin, Jenna. 2017. *Socialization: The Politics and History of a Psychological Concept, 1900–1970*. M.A. Thesis, Wesleyan University, Middletown, CT.

Schafer, Mark, and Scott Crichlow. 2002. The Process-Outcome Connection in Foreign Policy Decision Making: A Quantitative Study Building on Groupthink. *International Studies Quarterly* 46 (1): 45–68.

Schafer, Mark, and Stephen G. Walker. 2006. Democratic Leaders and the Democratic Peace: The Operational Codes of Tony Blair and Bill Clinton. *International Studies Quarterly* 50 (3): 561–583.

Schafer, Mark, and Stephen G. Walker, eds. 2022. *Operational Code Analysis and Foreign Policy Roles: Crossing Simon's Bridge*. New York: Routledge.

Schafer, Mark, Sam Robison, and Bradley Aldrich. 2006. Operational Codes and the 1916 Easter Rising in Ireland: A Test of the Frustration-Aggression Hypothesis. *Foreign Policy Analysis* 2 (1): 63–82.

Shimko, Keith L. 1992. Reagan on the Soviet Union and the Nature of International Conflict. *Political Psychology* 13 (3): 353–377.

128 M. HAAS

Skidmore, David. 1993/1994. Carter and the Failure of Foreign Policy Reform. *Political Science Quarterly* 108 (4): 699–729.

Snyder, Glenn Herald, and Paul Diesing. 1977. *Conflict Among Nations: Bargaining, Decision Making and System Structure in International Crises.* Princeton, NJ: Princeton University Press.

Stuart, Douglas, and Harvey Starr. 1981/1982. The 'Inherent Bad Faith' Model: Dulles, Kennedy, and Kissinger. *Political Psychology* 3 (1): 1–33.

Thies, Cameron G., and Marijke Breuning. 2012. Integrating Foreign Policy Analysis and International Relations Through Role Theory. *Foreign Policy Analysis* 8 (1): 1–4.

Walker, Stephen G. 1977. The Interface Between Beliefs and Behavior: Henry Kissinger's Operational Code and the Vietnam War. *Journal of Conflict Resolution* 21 (1): 129–168.

Walker, Stephen G. 1983. The Motivational Foundation of Belief Systems: A Re-Analysis of the Operational Code Construct. *International Studies Quarterly* 27 (1): 179–201.

Walker, Stephen G. 1990. The Evolution of Operational Code Analysis. *Political Psychology* 11 (2): 403–418.

Walker, Stephen G. 1995. Psychodynamic Processes and Framing Effects in Foreign Policy Decision-Making: Woodrow Wilson's Operational Code. *Political Psychology* 16 (4): 697–717.

Walker, Stephen G. 2002. Beliefs and Foreign Policy Analysis in the New Millennium. In *Millennial Reflections on International Studies*, eds. Michael Brecher and Frank P. Harvey, 502–513. Ann Arbor: University of Michigan Press.

Walker, Stephen G. 2003. Operational Code Analysis as a Scientific Research Program: A Cautionary Tale. In *Progress in International Relations Theory: Appraising the Field*, eds. Colum Elman and Miriam Fendius Elman, 245–276. Cambridge, MA: MIT Press.

Walker, Stephen G. 2004. Role Identities and the Operational Codes of Political Leaders. *Advances in Political Psychology* 1 (1): 71–106.

Walker, Stephen G. 2011a. Foreign Policy Analysis and Behavioral International Relations. In *Rethinking Foreign Policy Analysis: States, Leaders, and the Microfoundations of Behavioral International Relations*, eds. Stephen G. Walker, Akan Malici, and Mark Schafer, 3–20. New York: Routledge.

Walker, Stephen G. 2011b. The Integration of Foreign Policy Analysis and International Relations. In *Rethinking Foreign Policy Analysis: States, Leaders, and the Microfoundations of Behavioral International Relations*, eds. Stephen G. Walker, Akan Malici, and Mark Schafer, Chapter 15. New York: Routledge.

Walker, Stephen G. 2011c. Macropolitics and Foreign Policy Decisions: The Billiard Ball Model of International Relations. In *Rethinking Foreign Policy Analysis: States, Leaders, and the Microfoundations of Behavioral International*

Relations, eds. Stephen G. Walker, Akan Malici, and Mark Schafer, Chapter 2. New York: Routledge.

Walker, Stephen G. 2011d. Micropolitics and Foreign Policy Decisions: The Behavioral Model of International Relations. In *Rethinking Foreign Policy Analysis: States, Leaders, and the Microfoundations of Behavioral International Relations*, eds. Stephen G. Walker, Akan Malici, and Mark Schafer, Chapter 3. New York: Routledge.

Walker, Stephen G. 2011e. Quantum Politics and Operational Code Analysis: Theories and Methods. In *Rethinking Foreign Policy Analysis: States, Leaders, and the Microfoundations of Behavioral International Relations*, eds. Stephen G. Walker, Akan Malici, and Mark Schafer, Chapter 4. New York: Routledge.

Walker, Stephen G. 2013. *Role Theory and the Cognitive Architecture of British Appeasement Decisions*. New York: Routledge.

Walker, Stephen G., and Lawrence S. Falkowski. 1984a. The Operational Codes of U.S. Presidents and Secretaries of State: Motivational Foundations and Behavioral Consequences. *Political Psychology* 5 (2): 237–266.

Walker, Stephen G., and Lawrence S. Falkowski. 1984b. The Belief Systems and Crisis Behavior of U.S. Foreign Policy Leaders. Paper presented at the annual convention of the International Society of Political Psychology.

Walker, Stephen G., and Akan Malici. 2011. *U.S. Presidents and Foreign Policy Mistakes*. Stanford, CA: Stanford University Press.

Walker, Stephen G., and Timothy G. Murphy. 1981. The Utility of the Operational Code in Political Forecasting. *Political Psychology* 3 (1/2): 24–60.

Walker, Stephen G., and Mark Schafer. 2000. The Political Universe of Lyndon B. Johnson and His Advisors: Diagnostic and Strategic Propensities in Their Operational Codes. *Political Psychology* 21 (3): 529–543.

Walker, Stephen G., and Mark Schafer. 2006a. Belief Systems as Causal Mechanisms in World Politics: An Overview of Operational Code Analysis. In *Beliefs and Leadership in World Politics: Methods and Applications of Operational Code Analysis*, eds. Mark Schafer and Stephen G. Walker, Chapter 1. New York: Palgrave Macmillan.

Walker, Stephen G., and Mark Schafer. 2006b. Structural International Relations Theories and the Future of Operational Code Analysis. In *Beliefs and Leadership in World Politics: Methods and Applications of Operational Code Analysis*, eds. Mark Schafer and Stephen G. Walker, Chapter 12. New York: Palgrave Macmillan.

Walker, Stephen G., and Mark Schafer. 2010. Operational Code Theory: Beliefs and Foreign Policy Decisions. In *The International Studies Encyclopedia*, ed. Robert A. Denemark, Vol. VIII, 5942–5514. West Sussex, UK: Wiley Blackwell. Reprinted online in Robert A. Denemark and

Renée Marlin-Bennett, eds. 2017. *The International Studies Encyclopedia*. https://www.oxfordreference.com/view/10.1093/acref/978019184 2665.001.0001/acref-9780191842665-e-0291?rskey=hOcAMZ&result=329

Walker, Stephen G., Mark Schafer, and Michael D. Young. 1998. Operational Codes and Role Identities: Measuring and Modeling Jimmy Carter's Operational Code. *International Studies Quarterly* 42 (1): 175–189.

Walker, Stephen G., Mark Schafer, and Michael D. Young. 2003. Profiling the Operational Codes of Political Leaders. In *The Profiling the Operational Codes of Political Leaders: With Profiles of Saddam Hussein and Bill Clinton*, ed. Jerrold Post, Chapter 9. Ann Arbor: University of Michigan Press.

Walker, Stephen G., Akan Malici, and Mark Schafer, eds. 2011. *Rethinking Foreign Policy Analysis*. New York: Routledge.

Young, Michael D. 2001. Building Worldviews with Profiler+. In *Progress in Communications Sciences: Applications of Computer Content Analysis*, ed. Mark D. West, Vol. XVII, 17–32. Westport, CT: Ablex.

PART III

Professionalization Through Options Analysis

In Part I, an analysis of concepts from pre-theories of foreign policy analysis yielded the important finding that violence tends to occur between culturally dissimilar countries. In Part II, the quest was to determine cultural elements of decision-making by focusing on the study of operational codes.

Part III focuses on Options Analysis, using "preference ranking" and "value maximization," which are at the heart of the Rational Actor Paradigm, yet involves other paradigms. Decision-makers choose among options developed at several organizational layers, which often make competing value assessments of foreign policy alternatives but ultimately are constrained by the person who will choose among options in accordance within a multilayered operational code. Options Analysis is developed below by utilizing several paradigmatic perspectives to transform operational code research. The result is a comprehensive explanation why decisions are often much less rational than decision-makers would prefer.

Thanks to paradigmatic perspectives on operational codes, foreign policy analysis can now advance to the level of applied theory—the goal of theoretical critic Larry Laudan (1981). Political scientist David Braybrooke and economist Charles Lindblom (1963: ch4) once spelled out what they called the "synoptic conception" of decision-making: They proposed first laying out all available options, and then they would measure how each option accomplished their values (goals). In so doing they were recalling the options analysis of Jeremy Bentham (1790).

132   PART III: PROFESSIONALIZATION THROUGH OPTIONS ...

Most foreign policy decision-makers today are presented with problems and options by their subordinates, who have a variety of perspectives and talents—but with extremely few options. For example, Henry Kissinger always presented only three options to Richard Nixon, one of which was deliberately foolish (Prentice 2016). Donald Trump was once presented with options about how to respond to Iranian aggression and accepted the one that military advisers considered least acceptable—the assassination of Qasem Soleimani (Lee and Kube 2020). President Joe Biden was presented two options, with pros and cons for each, to deal with the Taliban's capture of U.S.-made helicopters (Wagner 2021).

Advisers to presidents should consider more than just two or three options. As the following chapters argue, evaluations should begin with a dozen or more options before whittling them down into the very best. To do so, each option should be evaluated based on multiple criteria or goals sought—namely, considerations of power, economics, prestige, and the extent to which an option is feasible. Accordingly, Chapter 6 provides a comprehensive listing of criteria that all foreign policy decision-makers must use in choosing between options.

Chapters 7 and 8 analyze the source of two major foreign policy blunders by the United States—regarding Cambodia and North Korea. Among many options to be revealed, the administrations of Jimmy Carter and Ronald Reagan chose the option of secretly funding the Khmer Rouge, thereby making the United States an outlier in efforts to bring peace to Cambodia until the scheme was exposed during the presidency of George H.W. Bush (Haas 1991, 2020). Later, despite efforts of North Korea to comply with a roadmap of reciprocated actions leading to denuclearization and normalization of relations, Barack Obama decided to shut down progress, preferring the option of "strategic patience," which is now also followed by Joe Biden.

Chapter 9 presents an analysis of how President Joe Biden coped with the Ukraine War. After initially adopting several measures, he embraced many options as the situation evolved.

What the analysis of three decision-making situations proves is that Options Analysis, conceived in terms of operational code analysis, can improve foreign policy decision-making. The metric provided for Options Analysis can be employed in any situation in which choices must be made between competing actions. Prospects for more professionalism in decision-making are advanced thereby.

REFERENCES

Bentham, Jeremy. (1780). *An Introduction to the Principles of Morals and Legislation*. Oxford, UK: Clarendon Press, 1907. See *utilitarianism/jeremybentham/#4*.

Braybrooke, David, and Charles E. Lindblom. (1963). *A Strategy of Decision*. New York: Free Press.

Haas, Michael. (1991). *Cambodia, Pol Pot, and the United States: The Faustian Pact*. New York: Praeger.

Haas, Michael. (2020). *Cambodia, Pol Pot, and the United States: The Faustian Pact*, 2nd ed. Los Angeles: Publishinghouse for Scholars.

Laudan, Larry. (1981). *Science and Hypothesis: Historical Essays on Scientific Methodology*. London: Reidel.

Lee, Carole E., and Courtney Kube. (2020). Trump Authorized Soleimani's Killing 7 Months Ago, with Conditions. January 13. https://www.nbcnews.com/politics/national-security/trump-authorized-soleimani-s-killing-7-months-ago-conditions-n1113271. Accessed August 22, 2021.

Prentice, David L. (2016). Choosing "the Long Road": Henry Kissinger, Melvin Laird, Vietnamization, and the War over Nixon's Vietnam Strategy. *Diplomatic History* 40 (3): 445–474.

Wagner, John. (2021). Taliban Capture of U.S.-Made Helicopters Highlights Difficult Choices Biden Had on Afghanistan, Sullivan Says. *Washington Post*, August 13.

Wikipedia. (2023). Foreign Policy Analysis. https://en.wikipedia.org/wiki/Foreign_policy_analysis. Accessed February 6, 2023.

CHAPTER 6

Parameters of Decision-Making and Options Analysis

During the history of foreign policy analysis, efforts to explain why decisions are made politically, psychologically, and sociologically have bypassed the question of how to do so more professionally. Previous operational code analysis has been of little help in improving how decision-makers choose among various options. However, a new way of defining an operational code is to specify an individual's relative weights on basic criteria during policy deliberations. The current chapter, accordingly, provides the tools for professional foreign policy decision-making.

BASIC CRITERIA

When decisions are made, there are two basic components—alternative policy choices (options) and criteria for evaluating options (Table 6.1). Options are usually not difficult to enumerate, though rating each option by a criterion can sometimes be very difficult. The conventional criterion, "national interest," can be defined in terms of four basic criteria for all foreign policy decisions as Power/Security, Economics/Wealth, Ethics/ Prestige, and Feasibility (Table 6.2).

Each category, in turn, consists of subcategories that span most paradigms of international relations theory (Haas 2017a). The term "paradigm" is used rather than "theory" because paradigms are theories that apply at several levels of analysis; theories only apply to one. For

© The Author(s), under exclusive license to Springer Nature Switzerland AG 2023
M. Haas, *Professionalization of Foreign Policy*,
https://doi.org/10.1007/978-3-031-37152-3_6

135

136   M. HAAS

Table 6.1   Parameters of Decision-Making

Criteria	Weight	Option 1	Option 2	Option 3	...	...	Option N
Criterion 1							
Criterion 2							
Criterion 3							
Criterion 4							
	100%						

Table 6.2   Basic Criteria of Decision-Making

Criteria	Weight	Option 1	Option 2	Option 3	...	...	Option N
Security							
Wealth							
Prestige							
Feasibility							
Total	100%						

Source Haas (1991: Table A-1; 2020: Table A-1)

example, the Legal Engineering Paradigm applies the same propositions to both domestic and international law about compliance with new laws and treaties, postulating that new laws will change human behavior (Haas 2017b: 46–51).

Many paradigms relevant to foreign policy have migrated from elsewhere in social science to political science. Similar to mid-level theories, paradigms generally seek to explain a particular phenomenon as an endpoint in a series of linked conceptual variables. The endpoints in a decision-making situation represent goals. Mid-level theories seek empirical evidence about linkages. Theories about operational codes become applied theory when the criteria are used to assess policy options.

Paradigms explained below constitute a set of criteria, not entirely mutually exclusive, that can be applied to evaluate foreign policy options. Accordingly, the new definition of a decision-maker's operational code, as proposed herein for the first time, consists of the relative weights applied to each of the fundamental criteria, which are explained next.

Security Subcriteria. Making decisions about a country in the international system has an impact on the military power of the country,

6 PARAMETERS OF DECISION-MAKING AND OPTIONS ANALYSIS   137

sometimes positive or negative, or neutral in relation to other countries. Decision-makers sometimes seek to increase their country's power but always want to avoid loss of power. Within the field of international relations, several paradigms highlight different ways of looking at national power:

The *Deterrence Paradigm* focuses on how to deter other countries from attacking and weakening the power position of a decision-maker's country. A country's leader will presumably ask whether a particular decision will make the country more or less vulnerable to foreign attacks. Although research on the paradigm (e.g., Schelling 1960) is insufficient to determine how best to deter other countries, prescient leaders will assess how each decision may impact the vulnerability of the country in relation to an adversary (Jervis 1989). The paradigm has also been applied to measures to deter criminal activity with inconclusive results (Pratt et al. 2017).

The *Balance of Power Paradigm* has a different goal in mind. The aim is to ensure that the existing power balance among great powers is stable (Kaplan 1957). If there is an acceptable stable world order, decision-makers seek to keep that order. If the military balance fluctuates and is unstable, then decision-makers will try to bring the power constellation into stability. Very little evidence exists on how best to achieve a balance of power (Zinnes 1967). One study, for example, finds that unipolar systems are more stable than bipolar and multipolar systems (Haas 1970) but not necessarily more just.

The *Hegemony Paradigm* focuses on how some countries seek to establish international stability by dominating other countries, particularly potential competitors. Historical accounts of hegemonistic (unipolar) international systems have been identified historically (Modelski 1987) but lessons learned on how to achieve and lose hegemony have been qualitative, not systematic. Power transition theory (Organski and Kugler 1980), a variant within the Hegemony Paradigm, focuses on strategies used by two types of countries—those on top trying to maintain dominance and those rising in power to achieve equality or superiority with those on top.

The *Triumphalist Social Darwinist Paradigm* seeks to evaluate whether any foreign policy decision will increase or decrease a country's power regardless of its relationships with other countries (Morgenthau 1948). Social Darwinists believe that the international polity consists of countries continually vying for power advantage, so any increment in power

138   M. HAAS

must be pursued relentlessly to prevent other countries from gaining military advantage. A common strategy is for decision-makers to seek and strengthen allies in order to counter another cluster of allied countries that seek dominance.

Accordingly, the security subcriteria involved in foreign policy decision-making are whether a decision increases deterrence, serves to stabilize the world polity, achieves hegemony, or increases military power. Vague axioms from the realist and neorealist ideologies are likely to be invoked in a decision situation involving violence, but the four paradigms are much more specific in their focus. Indeed, advocates of the Balance of Power Paradigm believe that they have tamed realism/neorealism into specific propositions (Wu 2018). Insofar as decision-makers place different emphases (weights) on the criteria, they will have unique operational codes.

Wealth Subcriteria. Any decision by a country in the international system has an impact on the economic wealth of the country, sometimes positive or negative or neutral, always in relation to other competitive countries. Decision-makers seek to increase their country's economic resources but always want to avoid loss of wealth. After all, funds are always spent on foreign policy. Foreign aid as "soft power" is intermediate in cost between war and diplomacy (Nye 1990, 2004). Within the field of international studies, several paradigms highlight various ways of evaluating national wealth from the standpoint of benefits to businesses, citizens, and the government:

The *Cost–Benefit Paradigm* suggests that all decisions should be viewed in dollars-and-cents terms (Steinbruner 1974). The cost should never exceed the benefits, though some costs can be perceived as an investment in tomorrow's wealth. Prospect theory puts more emphasis on benefits than costs, provided that benefits are very tangible (Kahnemann and Tversky 1979). Those who champion benefits over costs, however, have never been able to predict with accuracy who will benefit or lose. The paradigm, in short, is popular though flawed in practice (DeMartino 2022).

The *Libertarian Social Darwinist Paradigm* focuses on whether government interferes with the economy (Hayek 1944). Political interference is considered destructive of a free economy, so the goal is to reduce domestic and foreign interference in the economy. However, noninterference in the domestic economy can serve to favor aggressive giant corporations, oligarchies, and monopolies, which steer wealth toward the

6 PARAMETERS OF DECISION-MAKING AND OPTIONS ANALYSIS   **139**

rich. One Libertarian perspective is the flawed trickle-down theory of economics (Aghion and Bolton 1997). Similarly, the dependency theory of Andre Gunder Frank (1967) viewed the goal of all economies as removing external controls that stand in the way of national economic advancement. Neoliberal and globalization theory advocates agree with laissez-faire economists (Held and McGrew 2007). Dependency theory and globalization theory are theories, not paradigms, because they apply to only one level of analysis.

The *Economic Development Paradigm* expects wealth to improve through measures that increase capital accumulation and productivity (Rostow 1959, 1960). Accordingly, foreign policy decisions must assess the effects of foreign policy decisions on the economic capabilities and resources of the country's economy. Payoffs can enhance a state's role in the world economy by providing increased prosperity and living standards for citizens.

Accordingly, the wealth subcriteria involved in foreign policy decisions are whether a foreign policy option increases economic benefits over costs, frees the economy from foreign competition and domestic constraints, and how a foreign policy option might build a country's capabilities and resources. Foreign policy options, thus, can be assessed through monetization (cf. Moravcsik 2010).

Prestige Criteria. Foreign policy decision-makers are accountable not just for their power and wealth calculations but also for their relationship with supporters internally and externally as well as ethically and historically, often known as the "Idealist" approach. If they fail to bring prestige to their country, the country may be ignored or reviled. Several paradigms stress how a leader can bring prestige to a country through noneconomic soft power (Nye 1990, 2004), something intangible that is often dismissed by those focusing on power and wealth (Hayden 2012). Instead of coercion or bribery, prestige "soft power" criteria aim at co-opting support from other countries through credibility and legitimacy.

The *Community Building Paradigm*, which was developed as the European Union was being constructed (Haas 1964), views foreign policy through the lens of institutionalizing friendships with countries around the world, with social communications across borders as a building block (Deutsch 1953). As later advanced by Global Governance theory (Hewson and Sinclair 1999), an echo of functionalism (Mitrany 1943), the aim is to reduce conflicts through technical cooperation among all countries. The institutions vary from top-down governance, bottom-up governance, market governance, network governance, side-by-side governance, and complex web governance. However, some foreign policy leaders engage in anti-globalist thinking, preferring national autonomy, and do not want their countries to become dependent on external institutions where other countries have a voice (Stiglitz 2017).

The *Legal Engineering Paradigm* presumes that treaties and other agreements between countries will establish a rules-based international order, thereby identifying boundaries between what is and is not acceptable conduct in international affairs (Robinson 2020). Before leaders act, they might want to know whether they are violating international law, so they consult the epistemic community of legal scholars. Although "international law" is contested, and major powers often act with impunity, political scientist Beth Simmons (2009) has found that after countries ratify human rights treaties, they tend to adopt measures to become in compliance, thereby validating the paradigm. Legal engineering is a technique of peacebuilding. France, for example, places a higher weight on the goal of a liberal international order than most countries (Holland 2023) and therefore tries to sponsor peace agreements.

The *Democracy Building Paradigm* imagines that the world will be more peaceful as democracies increase and thrive (Russett 1993). Although empirical claims of the paradigm have been contested (Haas 2014, 2022), decision-makers in democratic countries have generally demonstrated a desire to promote and support democracies abroad, in part because they advance human rights. During the Cold War, however, the United States backed dictatorships loyal to the Western bloc. After 9/11, the United States tried to justify the war against Afghanistan and Iraq as a quest to change dictatorships into democracies, contrary to international law (Lieberfeld 2005).

Accordingly, the prestige subcriteria involved in foreign policy decision-making are whether a decision strengthens intergovernmental alliances and institutions, advances a world of rule by law, or promotes democracy abroad. All three subcriteria have peacebuilding objectives, involving "soft power."

Feasibility Criteria. Only fools make decisions that are incapable of achieving objectives. But blunders receive considerable attention in the history of world diplomacy and politics. Before making a decision, several standard feasibility criteria must be deliberated.

The *Resource Mobilization Paradigm*, often used to describe how political movements become powerful, focuses on the resources and

6 PARAMETERS OF DECISION-MAKING AND OPTIONS ANALYSIS 141

logistics of accomplishing goals after policy directives have been issued (Tilly 1978). The same question exists in foreign policy (Morin and Paquin 2018: ch2). Decision-makers need to know whether resources exist to implement an option and can actually be brought to the places where actions are required. Resources include the economic, military, and personnel capabilities of a government. Sometimes a decision is made without any prior precedent, so the leader is guessing about the capabilities required for a successful decision. Those commanding resources may not know their capabilities but might falsely claim that they have the situation under control, whereupon the blunder is disparagingly blamed on the decision-maker who trusted subordinates to act competently. Whether logistics will mobilize resources is a matter of unique determination in each foreign policy decision.

The *Mass Society Paradigm* stresses that decision-makers must be sure that they have support for their decisions within civil society—pressure groups, political parties, and the media. As a result, decision-makers often float trial balloons or even threats to determine the level of civil society acceptance of a policy decision (Haass 2002). If they err, political consequences can force them out of office—otherwise known as "audience costs" (Kertzer and Brutger 2016) Research on the paradigm began with a focus on alienated and atomized individuals who lack connections with civil society (Durkheim 1897) but has advanced to explain why democracies can flounder or thrive (Kornhauser 1959; Habermas 1981; Haas 2019).

The *Selectorate Paradigm* is more cynical about support for leaders. According to the paradigm, all leaders depend on a selected group of vital supporters, who will definitely react to trial balloons (Bueno de Mesquita et al. 2003). Before a decision is made, an evaluation occurs of whether options under consideration might antagonize those who financed or promoted the candidacy of the foreign policy leader. Research has supported the theory in some but not all contexts (Kennedy 2009). C. Wright Mills (1958) has identified the dangers of relying on biased supporters.

The *Bounded Rationality Paradigm* focuses on the decision-making process itself (Singer and Hudson 2019). Decisions are viewed as the outcome of deliberations among immediate advisers, who may just tell leaders whatever they want to know in a groupthink context. Much of Alexander George's main interest was in bounded rationality, from which he speculated that leaders differ in how they make decisions based on

142   M. HAAS

their information inputs and philosophical beliefs (George 1979). For an option to satisfy the bounded rationality criterion, a leader must be satisfied that all relevant information has been assembled before making a decision, something that long ago was deemed essential by Harold Lasswell and Daniel Lerner (1951).

The *Psychological Needs Paradigm* is premised on the belief that all humans have mental needs. To live a happy life, they must satisfy the needs embedded in their personalities. For David McClelland (1961), the basic needs are for achievement, affiliation, and power, which occupy differing percentages across individuals. More studies are needed to validate the paradigm despite numerous attempts to blame blunders on psychological defects of leaders. Prospect theory, a variant of the Psychological Needs Paradigm, suggests that decision-makers prefer outcomes that are expected to yield some sort of trophy (Levy 1992, 1997). For example, President Donald Trump was delighted to choose the option of assassinating an Iranian general (Lee and Kube 2020). However, did Presidents Jimmy Carter, Ronald Reagan, and George H. W. Bush express any joy in funding the Khmer Rouge? (The answer appears in the following chapter.)

Accordingly, the feasibility subcriteria involved in foreign policy decision-making are whether a decision can be achieved with existing resources and logistics, if civil society approval is likely, whether vital supporters are pleased with a decision, are satisfied that they have sufficient information on which to base a decision, and whether the leader enjoys the decision psychologically. Poliheuristic theory posits that options must satisfy feasibility criteria before any other options are on the table for discussion (Mintz 2003).

TRANSFORMATION OF OPERATIONAL CODES

Accordingly, "operational code" may be redefined as the relative weights that a decision-maker assigns to basic criteria and subcriteria identified in the major paradigms of international studies. To make the new definition more clear, Table 6.2 can be expanded (Table 6.3) and elaborated (Table 6.4). Professional deliberations will ideally utilize the criteria to evaluate alternative options before decisions are made. Each subcriterion may be based on even smaller sub-subcriteria in the mind of a decision-maker, so ratings are likely to be based on a median basis from all facets of each criterion.

6 PARAMETERS OF DECISION-MAKING AND OPTIONS ANALYSIS 143

Table 6.3 Basic Criteria and Subcriteria of Decision-Making for Options Analysis

Criteria	Subcriteria	Weight	Option 1	Option 2	Option 3	Option N
Security	Deter adversary					
	Balance power					
	Maintain power					
	Increase power					
Wealth	Econ. benefits > costs					
	Free economy					
	Increase prosperity					
Prestige	Build institutions					
	Obey national/ international law					
	Favor democracy					
Feasibility	Resource estimate					
	Satisfy civil society					
	Satisfy selectorate					
	Information adequacy					
	Satisfy psych needs					

Operational codes have to be enforced or they do not exist. Most human codes are enforced by superiors on subordinates. But a foreign policy decision-maker is superior, so the code exists only if self-enforced. An operational code consists of weights on all possible criteria for judging options. The code may tend to fluctuate depending on the issue involved; decision-makers sometimes change their criteria weights due to new information and unpredicted events.

Presidents and prime ministers usually seek advisers with the same operational code. However, advisers may have different codes from their leaders and from one another, so option recommendations presented to a government leader might be based on bureaucratic politics, groupthink, or some other basis that might not be the best set of options. That problem is addressed next.

144 M. HAAS

Table 6.4 Foreign Policy Decision-Making Subcriteria Guidelines

Paradigm	*Subcriterion*	*Appropriate Action*
Deterrence	Deter adversary	Take action to warn an adversary of adverse consequences of aggression
Balance of power	Balance power	Work to keep a balance between major powers to minimize war threats
Hegemony	Maintain power	Take action to ensure that the military power of the country does not fall below a level of dominance
Triumphalism	Increase power	Take action to strengthen the military power of the country
Cost–benefit	Econ. benefits > costs	Ensure that governmental and national benefits from a decision exceed costs
Libertarian	Free economy	Take measures to ensure that the economy is free from interference and control
Economic development	Increase prosperity	Make decisions that economically benefit the country
Community building	Build institutions	Increase the number and strength of international institutions
Legal engineering	Observe national/international law	Take action consistent with domestic and international law
Democracy building	Favor democracies and human rights	Make decisions that increase or strengthen democratic governments and human rights
Resource mobilization	Resource estimate Logistics estimate	Make decisions for which resources and logistics to be committed are deemed adequate to accomplish the goals
Mass society	Satisfy civil society	Make decisions that will be approved by citizens, pressure groups, political parties, and the media

(continued)

6 PARAMETERS OF DECISION-MAKING AND OPTIONS ANALYSIS 145

Table 6.4 (continued)

Paradigm	Subcriterion	Appropriate Action
Selectorate	Satisfy selectorate	Make decisions that will be approved by the most important supporters
Bounded rationality	Information adequacy	Make decisions for which there is ample expert information on the situation
Psychological needs	Satisfy psych needs	Make decisions that meet psychological needs of the decision-maker (for power, affiliation, achievement)

COMPUTERIZATION OF OPTIONS ANALYSIS

To professionalize foreign policy decision-making, advisers to decision-makers must accomplish three tasks. Task #1 is to identify foreign policy options for the situation being addressed (Sylvan and Voss 1998; Houghton 2007).

Task #2 is a specification of each adviser's operational code, which is determined by ratings (High, Medium, or Low) on each of the major paradigms used in foreign policy analysis. Presumably advisers are selected because they mirror the preferences of foreign policy decision-makers, but divergence can be useful. A more precise set of weights would be from U (Unacceptable) to E (Excellent).

Task #3 is to assess how well each option accomplishes the criteria (from U to E), something that involves intelligence regarding the decision-making situation and often amounts to guesswork. There are two ways of determining the ratings of each criterion for each option: Either one might rate one criterion on all options or rate each options separately on each criterion. Then any differences between the two ways will lead to some inner deliberation to reach a final judgment.

Scholars seeking to ascertain why a past decision was excellent or a blunder will have to engage in historical analysis in order to fulfill all three tasks. Activists who want to influence ongoing and future deliberations will do the same.

When all three tasks are performed, as in Table 6.5 for four options, the exercise can be further professionalized with the aid of a computer program. That program is known as Decision Pad.

146   M. HAAS

Table 6.5   Scoring and Ranking of Subcriteria of Decision-Making for Options Analysis

Criteria	Subcriteria	Weight	Option 1	Option 2	Option 3	Option 4
Security	Deter adversary	High	U	P	G	E
	Balance power	High	U	G	G	E
	Maintain power	High	U	F	VG	E
	Increase power	High	U	G	G	VG
Wealth	Econ. benefits > costs	Medium	E	G	E	VG
	Free economy	Medium	F	P	P	P
	Increase prosperity	Medium	F	P	P	P
Prestige	Build institutions	Low	U	E	G	G
	Obey national/ international law	Low	F	F	F	F
	Favor democracy	Low	U	E	E	E
Feasibility	Resource estimate	High	E	E	VG	G
	Satisfy civil society	Low	F	F	F	F
	Satisfy selectorate	Medium	U	G	G	G
	Process adequacy	Medium	F	G	VG	VG
	Satisfy psych needs	Low	U	G	VG	E
Scores			3.3	5.9	6.5	6.95
Ranks			4	3	2	1

Note U = unacceptable, P = poor, F = fair, G = good, VG = very good, E = excellent

The history of Decision Pad is instructive on how to professionalize decision-making: The program was developed in 1987 in San Mateo, California, originally as a tool for group decisions about employment. Traditionally, hiring decisions were made without an explicit set of criteria. With the advent of civil rights legislation and affirmative action, the U.S. Equal Employment Opportunity Commission insisted that criteria had to be specified in writing within employment solicitations and applications.

Before the screening of applicants, the judging criteria were weighted. Then each applicant was rated on how well they satisfied the criteria. Because hiring decisions were then made by groups rather than individual recruiters, several persons might rate alternative candidates with differing assessments on each criterion. Decision Pad could then combine them statistically into a single overall rating, yielding a ranking of applicants across all members of the recruitment group. Because the overall rankings might not correspond to individual rankings, the hiring group was then expected to discuss the computer results in order to reach a consensus on who would be hired.

A similar procedure could be followed in making foreign policy decisions (Table 6.5). Variations in the judgments should use the U→E scale in weighting the criteria. Or assessments could be made with numbers from 1 to 10. Decision Pad is flexible.

Thus far, there has been at least one time when Decision Pad has been used by the American government to make a foreign policy decision: After the Cold War, there was a mandate to eliminate unnecessary military bases. Accordingly, existing bases became the options, which were rated within the Department of Defense on the basis of "national security" criteria, doubtless similar to the fourfold scheme outlined above (USGAO 1993). According to the experience of Joseph Nye, no such procedure has ever been used by the Department of State. Until now.

CONCLUSION

Applied science exists when an empirical theory or paradigm is utilized for practical purposes. The present chapter has applied the concept of operational code to serve as a foundation for professionalized decision-making. Currently, foreign policy decision-makers often make snap decisions because their advisers do not carefully consider options before presenting their biased judgments. With Decision Pad, a more professional approach can be attained for decisions on foreign policy as well as any other decisions on any other matters. Three applications in Chapters 7–9 will clarify how Options Analysis can be applied in specific cases.

REFERENCES

Aghion, Philippe, and Patrick Bolton. 1997. A Theory of Trickle-Down Growth and Development. *Review of Economic Studies* 64 (2): 151–172.

DeMartino, George F. 2022. *The Tragic Science: How Economists Cause Harm (Even as They Aspire to Do Good)*. Chicago: University of Chicago Press.

de Mesquita, Bueno, Alastair Smith Bruce, Randolph M. Siverson, and James D. Morrow. 2003. *The Logic of Political Survival*. Cambridge, MA: MIT Press.

Deutsch, Karl W. 1953. *Nationalism and Social Communication: An Inquiry into the Foundations of Nationality*. New York: Wiley.

148 M. HAAS

Durkheim, Émile. 1897. *Suicide*. Glencoe, IL: Free Press, 1951.

Frank, Andre Gunder. 1967. *Capitalism and Underdevelopment in Latin America: Historical Studies of Chile and Brazil*. New York: Monthly Review Press.

George, Alexander L. 1979. The Causal Nexus Between Cognitive Beliefs and Decision-Making Behavior: The 'Operational Code'. In *Psychological Models in International Politics*, ed. Lawrence S. Falkowski, 95–124. Boulder, CO: Westview.

Haas, Ernst B. 1964. *Beyond the Nation State: Functionalism and International Organizations*. Stanford, CA: Stanford University Press.

Haas, Michael. 1970. International Systems: Stability and Polarity. *American Political Science Review* 69 (1): 98–123.

Haas, Michael. 1991. *Cambodia, Pol Pot, and the United States: The Faustian Pact*. New York: Praeger.

Haas, Michael. 2014. *Deconstructing the "Democratic Peace": How a Research Agenda Boomeranged*. Los Angeles: Publishinghouse for Scholars.

Haas, Michael. 2017a. *International Relations Theory: Competing Empirical Paradigms*. Lanham, MD: Lexington.

Haas, Michael. 2017b. *Revitalizing Political Science: Filling the Jigsaw Puzzle with Metatheory*. Lanham, MD: Lexington.

Haas, Michael. 2019. *Why Democracies Flounder and Fail: Remedying Mass Society Politics*. New York: Palgrave Macmillan.

Haas, Michael. 2020. *Cambodia, Pol Pot, and the United States: The Faustian Pact*. 2nd ed. Los Angeles: Publishinghouse for Scholars.

Haas, Michael. 2022. Building Growth Areas in Asia for Development and Peace. *Jadavpur Journal of International Relations* 26 (1): 1–36.

Haass, Richard N. 2002. Think Tanks and US Foreign Policy: A Policy-Makers Perspective. *US Foreign Policy Agenda* 7 (3): 5–8.

Habermas, Jürgen. 1981. *The Theory of Communicative Action*. Boston: Beacon, 1985.

Hayden, Craig. 2012. *The Rhetoric of Soft Power: Public Diplomacy in Global Contexts*. Lanham, MD: Lexington.

Hayek, Friedrich. 1944. *The Road to Serfdom*. London: Routledge.

Held, David, and Anthony McGrew, eds. 2007. *Globalization Theory: Approaches and Controversies*. Oxford: Polity.

Hewson, Martin, and Timothy J. Sinclair, eds. 1999. *Approaches to Global Governance Theory*. Albany: State University of New York Press.

Holland, Jack. 2023. France and the Anglosphere: Military Intervention, Liberal International Order, and the Coalition of Democracies. Paper presented at the Annual Convention of the International Studies Association, Montréal, March 18.

6 PARAMETERS OF DECISION-MAKING AND OPTIONS ANALYSIS 149

Houghton, David Patrick. 2007. Reinvigorating the Study of Foreign Policy Decision Making: Toward a Constructivist Approach. *Foreign Policy Analysis* 3 (1): 24–45.

Jervis, Robert. 1989. Rational Deterrence: Theory and Evidence. *World Politics* 41 (2): 183–207.

Kahnemann, Daniel, and Amos Tversky. 1979. Prospect Theory: An Analysis of Decision Under Risk. *Econometrica* 47 (2): 263–291.

Kaplan, Morton A. 1957. Balance of Power, Bipolarity and Other Models of International Systems. *American Political Science Review* 51 (3): 684–695.

Kennedy, Ryan. 2009. Survival and Accountability: An Analysis of the Empirical Support for "Selectorate Theory". *International Studies Quarterly* 53 (3): 695–714.

Kertzer, Joshua D., and Ryan Brutger. 2016. Decomposing Audience Costs: Bringing the Audience Back into Audience Cost Theory. *American Journal of Political Science* 60 (1): 234–249.

Kornhauser, William. 1959. *The Politics of Mass Society*. New York: Free Press.

Lasswell, Harold, and Daniel Lerner. 1951. *The Policy Sciences: Recent Developments in Scope and Method*. Stanford, CA: Stanford University Press.

Lee, Carole E., and Courtney Kube. 2020. Trump Authorized Soleimani's Killing 7 Months Ago, with Conditions. January 13. https://www.nbcnews.com/politics/national-security/trump-authorized-soleimani-s-killing-7-months-ago-conditions-n1113271. Accessed August 22, 2021.

Levy, Jack S. 1992. Prospect Theory and International Relations: Theoretical Applications and Analytical Problems. *Political Psychology* 13 (2): 283–310.

Levy, Jack S. 1997. Prospect Theory, Rational Choice, and International Relations. *International Studies Quarterly* 41 (1): 87–112.

Lieberfeld, Daniel. 2005. Theories of Conflict and the Iraq War. *International Journal of Peace Studies* 10 (2): 1–21.

McClelland, David C. 1961. *The Achieving Society*. Princeton, NJ: Princeton University Press.

Mills, C Wright. 1958. *The Causes of World War III*. New York: Simon & Schuster.

Mintz, Alex. 2003. *Integrating Cognitive and Rational Theories of Foreign Policy Decision Making: A Poliheuristic Perspective*. New York: Palgrave Macmillan.

Mitrany, David. 1943. *A Working Peace System: An Argument for the Functional Development of International Organizations*, rev. ed. Chicago: Quadrangle, 1966.

Modelski, George. 1987. *Long Cycles in World Politics*. Seattle: University of Washington Press.

Moravcsik, Andrew. 2010. *Liberal Theories of International Relations: A Primer*. Princeton, NJ: Princeton University Press.

Morin, Jean-Frédéric, and Jonathan Paquin. 2018. *Foreign Policy Analysis: A Toolbox*. New York: Palgrave Macmillan.

Morgenthau, Hans. 1948. *Politics Among Nations: The Struggle for Power and Peace*. New York: Knopf.

Nye, Joseph S., Jr. 1990. Soft Power. *Foreign Policy* 80 (1): 153–171.

Nye, Joseph S., Jr. 2004. *Soft Power: The Means to Success in World Politics*. New York: PublicAffairs.

Organski, A.F.K., and Jacek Kugler. 1980. *The War Ledger*. Chicago, IL: University of Chicago Press.

Pratt, Travis C., Francis T. Cullen, Kristie R. Blevins, Leah E. Daigle, and Tamara D. Madensen. 2017. The Empirical Status of Deterrence Theory: A Meta-Analysis. In *Taking Stock: The Status of Criminological Theory*, eds. Francis D. Cullen, John Paul Wright, and Kristie R. Blevins, 367–395. New York: Routledge.

Robinson, Darryl. 2020. *Justice in Extreme Cases: Criminal Law Theory Meets International Criminal Law*. Cambridge: Cambridge University Press.

Rostow, Walt Whitman. 1959. The Stages of Economic Growth. *Economic History Review* 12 (1): 1–16.

Rostow, Walt Whitman. 1960. *The Stages of Economic Growth: A Non-Communist Manifesto*. New York: Cambridge University Press.

Russett, Bruce M., ed. 1993. *Grasping the Democratic Peace: Principles for a Post-Cold War World*. Princeton, NJ: Princeton University Press.

Schelling, Thomas C. 1960. *The Strategy of Conflict*. Cambridge, MA: Harvard University Press.

Simmons, Beth A. 2009. *Mobilizing for Human Rights: International Law in Domestic Politics*. New York: Cambridge University Press.

Singer, Eric, and Valerie M. Hudson, eds. 2019. *Political Psychology and Foreign Policy*. New York: Routledge.

Steinbruner, John D. 1974. *The Cybernetic Theory of Decision: New Dimensions in Political Analysis*. Princeton, NJ: Princeton University Press.

Stiglitz, Joseph E. 2017. *Globalization and Its Discontents Revisited: Anti-Globalization in the Era of Trump*. New York: Norton.

Sylvan, Donald A., and James F. Voss, eds. 1998. *Problem Representation in Foreign Policy Decision Making*. New York: Cambridge University Press.

Tilly, Charles. 1978. *From Mobilization to Revolution*. Reading, MA: Addison-Wesley.

United States, General Accounting Office. 1993. Analysis of DOD's Recommendations and Selection Process for Closures and Realignments. April 15. https://www.gao.gov/assets/nsiad-93-173.pdf.

Wu, Zhengyu. 2018. Classical Geopolitics, Realism and the Balance of Power Theory. *Journal of Strategic Studies* 41 (6): 786–823.

Zinnes, Dina A. 1967. An Analytical Study of the Balance of Power Theories. *Journal of Peace Research* 4 (3): 270–287.

CHAPTER 7

American Policies Toward Cambodia

Having established a methodology to professionalize foreign policy decision-making in theory, the present chapter does so in practice. The focus is on the secret American policy toward the Khmer Rouge during the period from 1979 to 1989.

CAMBODIA, VIETNAM, AND THE UNITED STATES

In 1863, when the territory of the Kingdom of Cambodia was partly controlled by Thailand, with increasing inroads from Vietnam, France accepted the request of Cambodia's King Norodom to establish a French protectorate over the country. Thailand still maintained suzerainty over two provinces in the western part of the country, but in 1867 recognized the French protectorate. In 1887, Cambodia became part of French Indochina along with French colonies and protectorates in Laos and Vietnam. Thailand ceded back both Cambodian provinces to France in 1907. During World War II, Japan drove the French out of Indochina from 1941 to 1945. After the war, from 1946 to 1953, Paris granted Cambodia self-rule as a protectorate within the French Union. In 1953, Cambodia was granted independence.

When the United States decided to intervene in the Vietnamese Civil War on the side of South Vietnam in 1965, Hanoi utilized a supply route from North Vietnam to rebels in South Vietnam through eastern

© The Author(s), under exclusive license to Springer Nature 151
Switzerland AG 2023
M. Haas, *Professionalization of Foreign Policy*,
https://doi.org/10.1007/978-3-031-37152-3_7

Cambodia. Bombing along that route by Presidents Lyndon Johnson and Richard Nixon was unpopular with Cambodians, some of whom began to form a rebel group known as the Khmer Rouge. In 1970, Prince Norodom Sihanouk was ousted by a military coup supported by the United States, and the Khmer Republic was formed. The Khmer Rouge then gained support in the countryside.

Shortly before the United States withdrew personnel from Vietnam in 1975, the Khmer Rouge came to power in Phnom Penh, the capital of Cambodia. Soon, the Cambodian government of the Khmer Rouge ordered the urban population to go to the provinces and engage in agricultural activities. Those whom the Khmer Rouge executed as enemies in the capital were outnumbered by genocide due to mass starvation in the rural areas (Kiernan 2002).

The Khmer Rouge also began unprovoked attacks on what was once called South Vietnam, arguing that the territory was once a part of the Khmer Empire that had been converted by the French into part of their Vietnamese colony. The noise of the firepower was heard as far away as Saigon, and about 30,000 Vietnamese were killed in subsequent battles from 1975 to 1978 (Lindgren et al. 1989: 6) compared to 58,220 Americans dying in Vietnam from 1965 to 1973 (U.S. Archives 2008). The Army of the Republic of Vietnam, with far more strength than the Khmer Rouge, counterattacked in late 1978, driving the Khmer Rouge out of the country during 1979. Cambodians were eager to oust the Khmer Rouge, but the latter relocated to the border of Thailand in 1979.

Hanoi then presided over the establishment of a new government in Phnom Penh, while Vietnamese troops occupied the countryside. Hun Sen, chosen as foreign minister in 1979, became prime minister in 1985. Meanwhile, Vietnam proceeded to train a new Cambodian army that could take over the defense of the country. Because of so many deaths during the Khmer Rouge rule, personnel for the new Cambodian army were difficult to assemble, and training took nearly a decade. When Hanoi judged that the new army was capable of defending the country, Vietnam announced a departure date of September 30, 1989, whereupon France convened the Cambodian Peace Conference in July 1989.

7 AMERICAN POLICIES TOWARD CAMBODIA 153

Table 7.1 United States Funding of the Khmer Rouge, 1980–1986 (in 2021 dollars)

Fiscal Year	Amount
1980	$128,684,281.45
1981	43,146,388.78
1982	10,780,699.66
1983	5,803,177.50
1984	8,728,356.40
1985	1,981,572.80
1986	141,540.91
Total	$199,266,017.50

Source Winer (1986)

AMERICAN POLICY OPTIONS TOWARD CAMBODIA, 1981–1988

Meanwhile, the U.S. government designed a policy to deal with a situation in which Vietnam's army occupied Cambodia and the only resistance was a group of ill-equipped and poorly-trained Cambodians, mostly under the command of the Khmer Rouge, which had retreated near the border of Thailand. For the period from 1979 to 1989, American policy permitted the Khmer Rouge to continue to occupy the Cambodian seat in the United Nations, while secretly funding and supplying weapons to the Khmer Rouge up to 1986. The policy was relatively stable across both the Jimmy Carter and Ronald Reagan administrations and continued when President George H. W. Bush became president in 1989.

Many scenario options were not revealed to the public, involving as they did the Central Intelligence Agency, and the most peculiar option involved making financial contributions to the Khmer Rouge (Table 7.1). Carter Administration's funding of the Khmer Rouge, as determined by National Security Adviser Zbigniew Brzezinski, was to counter Russia's support for Vietnam, a policy continued by the Reagan Administration (Becker 1986: 440; Haas 1991: 83).

OPERATIONAL CODES

Accordingly, the research question is why President Ronald Reagan decided to continue providing financial support to a force associated with blatant genocide. Step 1 is to identify the operational codes of the Socialist Republic of Vietnam and the Reagan Administration during the 1980s.

154   M. HAAS

Hồ Chí Minh, the leader of Vietnam's struggle for independence, died in 1969. After a brief interim period, Phạm Văn Đồng became prime minister of Vietnam in 1969 and served as head of state (chairing the Council of Ministers from 1980) until 1987. His successors served short terms until Đỗ Mười took over from 1988 to 1991. Because American policy toward Cambodia and Vietnam is analyzed below during the 1980s, Phạm Văn Đồng's operational code is explained next.

Phạm Văn Đồng's first political position was as finance minister in 1945. He became foreign minister in 1954 and is credited with successful negotiations that year at the Geneva Conference, when France conceded independence to what was then called North Vietnam (the Democratic Republic of Vietnam). He maintained a neutral position among the party factions, fought corruption, and thus was praised when he retired in 1987 (Karnow 1983; Frankum 2011).

After repeated attacks by the Khmer Rouge army inside the southern border of Vietnam, he called in vain for United Nations action to stop the genocide and attacks on Vietnam (Burchett 1981: 161; Haas 1991: ch9) and then authorized the People's Army of Vietnam to liberate Cambodia from the Khmer Rouge. Before sending the Vietnamese army into Cambodia, Phạm Văn Đồng evidently was assured by the military intelligence that adequate resources existed—and they met very little resistance. Part of Vietnam's army remained in Cambodia in case of advances by the Khmer Rouge army, while another unit was able to defend a nine-day attack on Vietnam by China in 1979. A new Cambodian government, the People's Republic of Kampuchea (PRK), was installed in Phnom Penh in 1979, composed largely of refugees from the former Cambodian government who had fled to Vietnam during the era of the Khmer Rouge. In order to avoid antagonizing the Cambodian people, Vietnamese occupation forces were located outside cities and towns from 1979 to 1989.

Phạm Văn Đồng's operational code was based on the need to prevent the return of the Khmer Rouge to Cambodia, maintain the People's Army of Vietnam, and rebuild war-torn Vietnam. More specifically, he sought to deter the Khmer Rouge as well as China and thus had to balance army strength on two fronts. Although Washington accused Vietnam of wanting to make Cambodia a satellite and sweep through control of Thailand (Slater 1993), no such option was contemplated in Hanoi. Instead, Phạm Văn Đồng sought to increase military power only to the extent that training of a new Cambodian army would permit the Vietnamese army to leave. In economic matters, maintaining Vietnam's army was costly, with few economic benefits. Hanoi controlled the Cambodian economy as a socialist country, and the goal of Vietnam's prosperity was thereby frustrated by the allocation of resources to Cambodia until after Vietnamese forces withdrew from Cambodia in 1989.

In 1979, Vietnam proposed having the United Nations provide peacekeepers for Cambodia, but the Security Council did not take up the matter (NYT 1979). Vietnam claimed that the aim of liberating Cambodia was humanitarian intervention, a judgment supported by a careful legal analysis by Gary Klintworth (1989); so did Prince Norodom Sihanouk (1980: 64). Hanoi requested mediation from UN Secretary-General Kurt Waldheim in 1980, and made another peace proposal with ASEAN in 1982 (Haas 2012: 135).

As a successful negotiator, Phạm Văn Đồng was doubtless frustrated that Vietnam's peace proposals were rejected, and his decision to liberate Cambodia, therefore, did not satisfy any of his psychological predispositions (Table 7.2). Vietnam unilaterally withdrew from Cambodia in 1989, leaving the country's defense to the army of the Cambodian government. Although the Khmer Rouge tried to retake control after Vietnamese troops departed, the new Cambodian army was able to defend the country.

The Reagan Administration clearly made no effort to understand Phạm Văn Đồng's operational code, which brought peace to a country that had experienced the "killing fields." Options identified herein are primarily based on studies regarding the Reagan Administration's stable policies toward Cambodia during the 1980s, designed primarily by Secretary of State George Schultz (Haas 1991: 83–87, 163–166), while President Ronald Reagan was more consumed with the threat from the Soviet Union (Shimko 1992; Edgar 1993). Accordingly, the relevant operational code is the one applied to the Khmer Rouge, which might not apply to any other of Reagan's compartmentalized foreign policy challenges (Table 7.3).

Reagan believed that there was a zero-sum conflict between the Soviet Union and Western countries. Accordingly, he stressed the need to "deter" (WCPD 1984: 41). Vietnam, then aligned with the Soviet Union, was to be deterred, but by balancing power rather than increasing

156   M. HAAS

Table 7.2 Operational Code of Phạm Văn Đồng

Criteria	Subcriteria	Weight
Power	Deter adversary	High
	Balance power	High
	Maintain power	High
	Increase power	Medium
Wealth	Benefits > costs	Low
	Free economy	Low
	Increase prosperity	Low
Prestige	Build institutions	High
	Observe national/international law	High
	Favor democracies	Low
Feasibility	Resource estimate	High
	Satisfy civil society	Medium
	Satisfy selectorate	High
	Information adequacy	High
	Satisfy psych needs	Low

Table 7.3 Operational Code of the Reagan Administration Toward the Khmer Rouge

Criteria	Subcriteria	Weight
Power	Deter adversary	High
	Balance power	High
	Maintain power	High
	Increase power	Medium
Wealth	Benefits > costs	Low
	Free economy	High
	Increase prosperity	Low
Prestige	Build institutions	Low
	Observe national/international law	Low
	Favor democracies	High
Feasibility	Resource estimate	Medium
	Satisfy civil society	Low
	Satisfy selectorate	Low
	Information adequacy	Medium
	Satisfy psych needs	Low

power. According to Reagan, "We do have common interests and foremost among them is to avoid war and reduce the level of arms" (ibid.). Balancing power was to be achieved by maintaining the current level:

"[L]et it be clear we maintain this strength in the hope it will never be used" (WCPD 1982: 769). Support for the Khmer Rouge was aimed at maintaining a stalemate with Vietnam. On economic matters, Reagan believed that the cost of launching war exceeded benefits, and he warned that "wars begin when governments believe the price of aggression is cheap" (WCPD 1984: 41). He made clear that the struggle was between capitalism and communism, and he felt that a freer world economy would bring peace. His policy was not designed to increase American prosperity; in fact, there was a "Reagan recession" in 1982 (Miner 1989). An end to the conflict with the Soviet Union and its allies was calculated to ultimately deliver increased prosperity. Meanwhile, forcing Hanoi to remain in Cambodia was a strategy to support China's efforts to "bleed Vietnam" (Chang 1983) and thereby continue to divide China from an alliance with Vietnam's ally, the Soviet Union. Reagan gave low marks to institutions such as the United Nations, and intervention by ASEAN was rejected, though he supported the Olympic Games was as a way to unite peoples (Israel 1987: 186). His pronouncements about the desirability of democracy and human rights demonstrate why constructing an operational code on public statements can be flawed: He did want more democracies in the world yet he supported the Khmer Rouge (WCPD 1985: 865; 1987: 58). He was not concerned that support for rebels in a civil war constitutes a war crime, according to the Convention on Duties and Rights of States in the Event of Civil War (1928, Article 1). That the United States supported the Khmer Rouge as the occupant of the Cambodian seat in the United States without controlling the territory of the country was almost unprecedented. Secret funding also contradicted the norm that Congress must approve any support for foreign violence. That the aid to Pol Pot's Khmer Rouge forces was secret demonstrated that his support for the "will of the American people" (WCPD 1986: 129) was hollow. He was confident that he had the resources to continue funding the Khmer Rouge, and he even cut the amounts, evidently based on information about the continuing stalemate. There is no evidence that he sought wide support from Republican Party leaders, his selectorate, though members of Select Intelligence Committees in the House and Senate were doubtless briefed on the secret funding. Reagan conducted the Cold War with religious fervor, but never demonstrated that he was also satisfying psychological needs (Scott 1996). The ratings provided herein differ slightly from my previous exercise (Haas 2020: Table 3.3).

158 M. HAAS

OPTIONS ANALYSIS

The Reagan Administration continued to support the Khmer Rouge but placed more emphasis than the Carter Administration on uniting opposition to Vietnam's occupation of Cambodia between the Khmer Rouge and non-Communist factions. The list of options below also includes some that might have been considered if decision-making had been under public scrutiny (Table 7.4). Each option, in turn, is a summary of a scenario. More details about the scenarios are provided in an Appendix to the chapter below. Most options involved different approaches to the four competing factions—the Khmer Rouge, the People's Republic of Kampuchea (PRK) established in Phnom Penh under Vietnamese occupation, the faction supporting former leader Prince Norodom Sihanouk, and the non-Communist democratic resistance faction constructed by Son Sann, a devout Buddhist politician.

Weights assigned to the criteria (High, Medium, or Low) constitute the operational code of the Reagan Administration. Next, scoring

Table 7.4 Policy Options of the United States Toward Cambodia and Pol Pot, 1981–1988

Option	Content of Option
1	Secretly assist Pol Pot's Khmer Rouge
2	Legitimize the Phnom Penh government (PRK) of Hun Sen
3	Assist the PRK in becoming a democracy
4	Bring Prince Sihanouk back to power
5	Divide Cambodia into 4 zones controlled by each faction
6	Pay little attention to Cambodia
7	Divide Cambodia into 2 zones (Khmer Rouge, PRK)
8	Forge a 4-party coalition government
9	Empower the non-Communist resistance to win
10	Forge a 3-party coalition (without the PRK)
11	Forge a 3-party coalition (without the Khmer Rouge)
12	Forge a 4-party interim government, then hold elections
13	Have the UN take over the country, transitional to elections
14	Resolve all conflicts in the region (a "grand design")
15	Aid the PRK and let time resolve conflict with others
16	A neutralized PRK with no role for Khmer Rouge
17	Let ASEAN negotiate peace for Cambodia
18	Send U.S. military to overthrow the PRK

Source Haas (2020: 160–161)

7 AMERICAN POLICIES TOWARD CAMBODIA   159

is based on how much each option would accomplish each subcriterion (Excellent, Very Good, Good, Fair, Poor, or Unacceptable). Decision Pad was used to process ratings. After the matrix was filled, scores were calculated by the program and ranked (Table 7.5). The option best fulfilling the criteria was given a rank of #1.

Of course, the weights and assessments provided herein could be challenged. Accordingly, James Scott, author of a definitive book on the Reagan Administration (Scott 1996), was asked what weights he would assign. Although Scott's weights differed somewhat, there were a few differences in the outcome matrix. Differences between the present matrix and the one previously offered (Haas 2020: Table 3.2) indicate a reliability coefficient of 97%.

Empower the Non-Communist Resistance (Option 9) had the very top rank. Secretly Assist the Khmer Rouge (Option 1) ranked second. Not far from Option 1 were two options that in retrospect should have been seriously considered because they eventually were selected by countries outside the United States: In third place was the decision to bring back Sihanouk as leader of the Cambodian government (Option 4), and in fourth place was having the United Nations maintain the peace and establish a new regime with elections (Option 13). Sending American troops to drive the Vietnamese army out of Cambodia (Option 18) was in fifth place, Options 4, 13, and 18 were evidently not proposed to President Reagan. Concern that Vietnam might sweep control of all of Southeast Asia far outweighed any consideration of the perilous condition of how millions of Cambodians were desperately trying to recover from the "killing fields."

Reagan's Vice President, George H. W. Bush, continued the same hostile policy when he became president in 1989, though secret funding had already stopped. But his advisers evidently failed to inform him of information about the increasing legitimacy of the Hun Sen government and Vietnam's pleas for United Nations intervention. The Khmer Rouge continued to occupy the Cambodian seat in the United Nations General Assembly when Bush was inaugurated and continued to do so until the rigid Vietphobic American position was discredited before the world in 1989, as noted next.

Table 7.5   Matrix of Subcriteria of Cambodia Decision-Making with Options Assessments

Criteria	Subcriteria	Weight	1	2	3	4	5	6	7	8	9
Power	Deter adversary	High	E	U	U	P	P	U	U	P	E
	Balance power	High	VG	U	U	F	F	U	U	F	VG
	Maintain power	High	G	U	U	F	P	U	U	P	V
	Increase power	Medium	F	U	U	U	P	U	P	P	F
Wealth	Benefits > costs	Low	P	U	U	F	P	P	P	P	F
	Free economy	Medium	P	U	U	F	P	U	U	P	P
	Increase prosperity	Low	P	P	P	P	P	P	P	P	P
Prestige	Build institutions	Medium	U	U	U	F	F	U	F	F	F
	Observe national/international law	Low	U	P	F	G	F	E	P	F	P
	Favor democracies	High	U	U	P	F	P	U	U	U	P
Feasibility	Resource estimate	Medium	G	U	F	P	P	E	P	P	G
	Satisfy civil society	Low	U	U	U	F	P	P	P	P	G
	Satisfy selectorate	Low	P	U	U	U	P	U	U	P	G
	Information adequacy	Medium	P	P	P	F	P	E	P	P	F
	Satisfy psych needs	Low	U	U	U	F	P	P	P	P	F
Score			3.4	0.3	0.9	3.2	2.4	2.3	1.1	2.2	4.4
Rank			2	18	16	3	9	10	15	11	1

Criteria	Subcriteria	Weight	10	11	12	13	14	15	16	17	18
Power	Deter adversary	High	U	U	P	P	P	U	U	P	VG
	Balance power	High	U	U	F	P	E	U	U	P	VG
	Maintain power	High	U	U	P	P	P	U	U	P	VG
	Increase power	Medium	U	U	P	P	P	U	U	P	P
Wealth	Benefits > costs	Low	P	P	P	F	U	U	P	P	U
	Free economy	High	P	P	P	P	P	P	U	P	P
	Increase prosperity	Low	P	P	P	P	P	P	P	P	U
Prestige	Build institutions	Low	F	F	F	E	P	P	P	F	P
	Observe national/international law	Low	F	F	F	E	P	U	G	G	U
	Favor democracies	High	P	P	F	F	U	U	U	P	P
Feasibility	Resource estimate	Medium	P	P	P	U	U	P	P	P	U
	Satisfy civil society	Low	U	P	F	G	G	F	U	F	U
	Satisfy selectorate	Low	P	U	P	P	P	U	P	P	P
	Information adequacy	Medium	P	P	P	U	P	P	U	F	U
	Satisfy psych needs	Low	P	P	P	P	P	P	P	P	P
Score			1.4	1.4	2.6	2.9	2.5	0.8	0.9	2.5	2.7
Rank			12	12	6	4	7	18	16	7	5

Cambodian Peace Agreement

In 1979, General Võ Nguyên Giáp announced that the People's Army of Vietnam would be withdrawn from Cambodia by the end of 1990. In 1983, the withdrawal date was moved up to 1988, when half of Vietnam's troops evacuated. Early in 1989, an exact date was fixed as September 26, 1989 (Haas 2012: 13–36).

France then organized a peace conference in July 1989 to legitimate a new government in Cambodia. Although most countries voted for Option 13, the administration of President George H. W. Bush insisted that there should be a four-party government including the Hun Sen government, the Sihanouk faction, the non-Communist faction, and the Khmer Rouge (Option 8). But such a ridiculous proposal was rejected by American allies, who were shocked at American intransigence at the Paris Conference. As a result, the conference lack consensus and failed. The United States was then sidelined while a peace process continued after the conference (ibid.: ch3). Vietnamese troops left Cambodia on schedule, and fighting resumed at the border, but the Cambodian army held back the forces of the Khmer Rouge and the non-Communist resistance.

In 1990, Australia, France, and Indonesia diligently worked on a draft agreement similar to Option 13. When France reconvened the Paris Conference on Cambodia in 1991, the United States supported the settlement.

United Nations personnel and U.S. embassy staff arrived in Cambodia in January 1992. The task of the UN Transitional Authority for Cambodia was to achieve a cease-fire and to organize democratic elections. The Hun Sen government was left in place, and the UN only monitored the cease-fire and the election (ibid.: ch4). In 1993, after free and fair elections were held, the UN departed, and a new democratically elected Cambodian government gained control (ibid.: ch5).

After the elections in 1993, the new Cambodian government restored Norodom Sihanouk to the position of king, but he had little power under the constitution approved by the new parliament. He abdicated in 2004, and his son Norodom Sihamoni became the new king.

Although the vote in 1993 was divided between Prime Minister Hun Sen and a rival, a coup in 1997 firmly established Hun Sen's rule. Hun Sen agreed to step down in 2023 when his son Hun Manet was scheduled to become the new prime minister.

CURRENT RELATIONS WITH THE UNITED STATES

Ever since 1993, the United States has played little role in the modernization of the country after so many years of devastation, refusing to atone for past blunders (Haas 2020: ch8). Although China also supported the Khmer Rouge, Beijing has outspent the United States in assisting the war-torn country, notably since 2010, when Cambodia and China signed a "comprehensive strategic partnership." China has financed a considerable portion of Cambodia's infrastructure, has brought more than 100 new businesses to the country, has leased lands resulting in the eviction of 770,000 Cambodians, and brought 250,000 Chinese to live in the country. An Options Analysis conducted elsewhere (Haas 2021), indicates that the principal American interest today is to support the growth of civil society and cultural events. Meanwhile, Beijing controls so much of the Cambodian economy that Phnom Penh has become a reliable ally.

APPENDIX: AMERICAN POLICY OPTIONS FOR CAMBODIA, 1981–1988

Scenario 1: *Secretly assist Pol Pot's Khmer Rouge*. The aim was to prevent the People's Army of Vietnam (PAVN) from conquering Thailand and forcing Vietnam to direct resources to the possibility of a Khmer Rouge resurgence. With additional support, the Khmer Rouge might defeat the non-Communist resistance (NCR). The probability of attaining scenario 1 was low, as it conflicted with the minimum goals of the Cambodian government, which could count on the Socialist Republic of Vietnam (SRV) and Soviet military aid. The probability fell when Vietnamese forces first trounced the Khmer Rouge in combat during 1978 and 1979 and then crushed their base in 1985.

Scenario 2: *Legitimize the People's Republic of Kampuchea Government (PRK) of Hun Sen*. The scenario was advanced by the PRK, the Soviet Union, and Vietnam. To eliminate the three rival factions, all external powers had to walk away from Cambodia, believing that Cambodian resistance lacked credibility. Since the Khmer Rouge was the only effective resistance force, advocates of this view pointed out that Son Sann's democratic (KPNLF) and Sihanoukist forces (ANS) were junior partners when the Cambodian Government of Democratic Kampuchea (CGDK) was formed in 1982 with the Khmer

Rouge. The probability of legitimizing the PRK was low since China objected to leaving Vietnam with hegemony over Indochina. But Phnom Penh gained increased respectability by rebuilding Cambodian schools and providing stable rules for rice farmers to return to normalcy. Later, as PAVN departed from Cambodia, CGDK aid collapsed; the former occurred in 1989, though NCR support doubled at the end of that year. Thus, this scenario rose in prominence over time.

Scenario 3: *Assist the PRK in becoming a democracy*. The leader of the government would be Son Sann, who would have to discredit all rival factions. To do so, Sihanouk would have to die, China would have to stop aiding Pol Pot, the United States would need to bankroll Son Sann exclusively, and the PRK would have to lose SRV—Soviet support. As Son Sann's group was internally divided between civilian and political factions, the probability of this scenario was pitifully low, although the U.S. government might have preferred this scenario.

Scenario 4: *Bring Prince Sihanouk back to power*. Prince Norodom Sihanouk would possess real power only if all four Cambodian factions laid down their arms after Sihanouk won in internationally supervised elections, which presupposed external disengagement, incarceration of the leadership of the Khmer Rouge, Sihanouk's popularity with the people, a Sino–Soviet détente, an imposed international settlement, and the unpopularity of the PRK. The probability was low on all counts until a peace process emerged.

The next three scenarios aimed to leave the situation so entangled that each actor might get something but fall short of full satisfaction:

Scenario 5: *Divide Cambodia into 4 zones controlled by each faction*. A Balkanization option envisaged an increased level of warfare in which the four factions would occupy and defend their own pieces of Cambodian real estate—a war of each against all. A worst-case scenario, feared by all and proposed by none, would result from a greatly increased supply of defensive and offensive arms to all four factions, followed by more battles and guerrilla warfare. The scenario was possible only in case of an intensification of the Cold War as well as increased Sino–Soviet hostility. Such a prospect was contrary to the interests of all actors, so it had a low probability.

Scenario 6: *Pay little attention to Cambodia*. The "sideshow" option was a continuation of ongoing policies for protracted but stalemated low-level military conflict. This scenario was eloquently identified by William Shawcross (1979) for the 1965–1978 era. The persistence of Sino–Soviet and Russo–American Cold Wars as well as the continued Sino–Vietnamese confrontation guaranteed that this scenario would continue as long as the involved parties preferred not to escalate their conflicts, having checkmated one another. This was the most likely scenario until Soviet party leader Dimitri Gorbachëv decided to urge an end to the Cold War, beginning in 1985.

Scenario 7: *Divide Cambodia into two zones* (Khmer Rouge versus PRK). The Koreanization option envisaged two Cambodias separated indefinitely. A formal agreement would allow a strip of territory inside Cambodia to house the resistance forces, with the PRK being dominant in the rest of the country. The PRK and SRV would have to accept a rival enclave inside Cambodia. Thailand would have to accept a PRK Finlandized to the SRV. More aid was needed to make the CGDK viable, economically and militarily. The probability was close to zero, since Vietnam's troops would be unacceptably close to Bangkok.

The next five scenarios pretended that a coalition solution was possible:

Scenario 8: *Forge a 4-party coalition government*. Based on the Laotian model of the 1960s, a quadripartite Cambodia envisaged that the four factions would stop fighting and start learning to live together. Alternatively phrased, since the four factions were "facts of life," all might have to be included in a settlement. There would have to be national reconciliation and a cessation of outside aid. Because sharp divisions accounted for the conflict in the first place, and external powers had a vested interest in the outcome, what was required was a common threat, such as a famine or plague that would threaten to wipe out the Khmer race. The probability, in short, was zero. Nonetheless, this scenario was advanced by U.S. delegates at the Paris Conference in 1989, thereby blocking an agreement.

166   M. HAAS

Scenario 9: *Empower the non-Communist resistance (NCR) to win.* A non-Communist Cambodia would occur if Sihanouk and Son Sann were to prevail against the other two factions. Son Sann and Sihanouk would have to accept each other and prevail against both the PRK and the Khmer Rouge. There would have to be a withdrawal of aid from Communist countries, an increase in NCR aid, an overwhelming NCR victory in elections, and a disappearance of the Khmer Rouge. The probability was extremely low because the non-Communist resistance factions were divided politically and were not effective fighting forces at any time.

Scenario 10: *Forge a 3-party coalition without the PRK.* A tripartite CGDK solution meant the dissolution of the Phnom Penh government and fraternal cooperation between the Khmer Rouge both non-Communist resistance factions. Necessary conditions were external disengagement, the collapse of PRK legitimacy, and a change of heart by Pol Pot to accept the NCR. The probability was zero since the Khmer Rouge could hardly be expected to fight to regain power and then abandon the struggle. A CGDK victory would likely unravel, leaving Pol Pot in power.

Scenario 11: *Forge a 3-party coalition without the Khmer Rouge.* The idea was of an anti-Khmer Rouge tripartite government in which the Hun Sen, Sihanouk, and Son Sann factions joined forces. Some Indonesian defense ministry officials preferred this solution, which could occur after a defeat of the Khmer Rouge and a détente between the other three factions. A Vietnamese troop withdrawal, Phnom Penh's acceptance of multipartism, and a PRC decision to abandon the Khmer Rouge would have to come first. Since the CGDK refused to accept PRK as an interlocutor during most of the 1980s, this scenario was infeasible until 1988, when the three met together at an initial Jakarta Informal Meeting, which launched negotiations between the warring parties.

Scenario 12: *Forge a 4-party interim government, then hold elections.* Whereas CGDK advanced the idea of an interim quadripartite government, Scenario 12 was Hun Sen's alternative—an interim council to arrange for elections, leaving the Hun Sen government in place. CGDK would have to suffer defeat due to an end to external aid, and massive defections of soldiers would have to benefit the Hun Sen government, whence a strong Hun Sen army would replace PAVN. None of these events materialized. At the Paris Conference in 1989 Hun Sen modified his proposal from a quadripartite to a bipartite council so that Hun Sen government would not have to go on record as accepting responsibility for including the Khmer Rouge.

Clever package deals underlay the next two scenarios.

Scenario 13: *Have the UN take over the country, transitional to elections.* UN bureaucrats might take over the top positions of the Cambodian government until elections determined who would rule in a postwar Cambodia, with UN peacekeepers kept in place to enforce a cease-fire and military demobilization. The Hun Sen government would have to surrender its administrative authority, the Khmer Rouge would have to hibernate, and major powers would have to pay for the costs involved. The conditions required war weariness on all sides. The probability was low, as Vietnam was ready to defend the PRK, and the Khmer Rouge showed no peaceful intentions. Even the UN General Assembly opposed a broad UN solution, demanding instead that Vietnam pull out of Cambodia without UN peacekeepers in place, thereby laying a red carpet for the Khmer Rouge to return to power.

Scenario 14: *Resolve all conflicts in the region.* A Metternichian "grand design" for Indochina or Southeast Asia had some precedence: At the Peace of Westfalia of 1648, territories shifted from one country to another to bring peace. But the rise of nationalism in the nineteenth century reduced the viability of this method of conflict resolution. To keep all parties content, what could be exchanged? In the case of Cambodia, China could drop the Khmer Rouge in exchange for renunciation by Vietnam to all claims to the Paracel and Spratly Islands in the South China Sea. Similar to the détente following the Cuban missile crisis, there might be a recognition of the legitimate security needs of all countries in the region. A "grand design" could be achieved through such measures as an internationally guaranteed neutralization of Cambodia, a reduction of troops at the borders of neighboring countries, and mutual nonaggression pledges. Sino–Vietnamese and U.S.–Vietnamese normalization also could be thrown into the negotiation pot. Although the Nonaligned Movement (NAM) adopted elements of this scenario as its peace plan in 1979, the Cambodian parties most directly involved seemed eager to impose a military solution during most of the 1980s. With the conflict so intensely polarized, diplomacy played a small role at first. There was little incentive for horse trading, so the probability for this scenario was rather low.

Three scenarios expected the Cambodian conflict to obsolesce over the long run:

Scenario 15: *Aid the Hun Sen government and let time resolve conflict with others.* In a Yugoslavianization scenario, Cambodia would become independent of its patrons, and a new generation of leaders would rise to the top in all four factions within 40 years of worldwide détente and increased Japanese and Western development aid to the PRK. Although the short-term probability was low, this scenario was a long-term possibility (cf. Haas 1984).

Scenario 16: *A neutralized Hun Sen government with no role in Khmer Rouge.* This scenario, sometimes called the Austrian model, entailed an international treaty of guarantee, thereby canceling the Cambodia–Vietnam friendship treaty that allowed Hanoi to send troops at the request of Phnom Penh. The Hun Sen government and Vietnam would have to be satisfied that the Khmer Rouge would no longer pose a threat. China would have to stop aid to the Khmer Rouge when convinced that a neutralized Cambodia would not be Finlandized to Vietnam. Since mere legal guarantees were suspect, in light of the erosion of previous political settlements involving Laos and Vietnam, the probability of Austrianization was low.

Scenario 17: *Let ASEAN negotiate peace for Cambodia.* What was sought by foreign ministries in Indonesia and Malaysia was an ASEANization of Cambodia. Under this scenario, the three Indochinese countries would be gradually brought into the framework of the Association of South-East Asian Nations (ASEAN). External countries would have to leave Cambodia alone while Cambodia, Laos, and Vietnam became assimilated to ASEAN's consensus-building norms for decision-making (Haas 1989), whence they could be admitted as members. Acceptance of the scenario by all ASEAN and Indochinese countries had to be coupled with a withdrawal of American and Chinese aid to the Khmer Rouge. However, ASEAN countries allowed the Khmer Rouge to continue to participate in the Colombo Plan and a few other regional organizations, whereupon Vietnam ceased to participate.

7 AMERICAN POLICIES TOWARD CAMBODIA 169

This leaves a final scenario from the realm of fiction. It is from the plot of the famous novel *The Ugly American* (Lederer and Burdick 1958):

Scenario 18: *Send U.S. military to overthrow the PRK.* If this occurred, Vietnam would no longer have a Cambodian government to support, and the Cambodian people might welcome the CGDK resistance coalition. Delegitimization of the Hun Sen government, a required condition, would occur due to developments such as exposure of government corruption, excessive repression, economic mismanagement, and efforts at Vietnamese colonization of Cambodia. But as time went on, Hun Sen rebuilt a normal government in Cambodia over the ruins of the Khmer Rouge. The probability of scenario 18 was low, and it declined over time.

REFERENCES

Becker, Elizabeth. 1986. *After the War Was Over: The Voices of Cambodia's Revolution and Its People*. New York: Simon & Schuster.

Burchett, Wilfred. 1981. *The China Cambodia Vietnam Triangle*. Chicago: Vanguard.

Chang, C.Y. 1983. The Sino-Vietnam Rift: Political Impact on China's Relations with Southeast Asia. *Contemporary Southeast Asia* 4 (4): 538–564.

Edgar, Tracey. 1993. *Operational Code Beliefs of Ronald Reagan: The Nature of the International Environment and Image of the Soviet Union*. Master of Arts Thesis, University of British Columbia.

Frankum, Ronald B., Jr. 2011. *Historical Dictionary of the War in Vietnam*. Lanham, MD: Scarecrow Press.

Haas, Michael. 1984. The Indo-China Tangle. *The Nonaligned World* 2 (1): 79–96.

Haas, Michael. 1989. *The Asian Way to Peace: A Story of Regional Cooperation*. Westport, CT: Praeger.

Haas, Michael. 1991. *Cambodia, Pol Pot, and the United States: The Faustian Pact*, 1st ed. Westport, CT: Praeger.

Haas, Michael. 2012. *Modern Cambodia's Emergence from the Killing Fields: What Happened in the Critical Years?* Los Angeles: Publishinghouse for Scholars.

Haas, Michael. 2020. *Cambodia, Pol Pot, and the United States: The Faustian Pact*, 2nd ed. Los Angeles: Publishinghouse for Scholars.

Haas, Michael. 2021. Options Analysis: How Foreign Policy Decisions Are Made with an Explanation Why the United States Bankrolled the Khmer Rouge. Paper presented at the Annual Convention of the International Studies Association, Western Branch, Pasadena, CA, September.

Israel, Fred L. 1987. *Ronald Reagan's Weekly Radio Addresses*, Vol. I. Delaware: Scholarly Resources.

Karnow, Stanley. 1983. *Vietnam: A History*. New York: Viking.

Kiernan, Ben. 2002. *The Pol Pot Regime: Race, Power, and Genocide in Cambodia Under the Khmer Rouge, 1975–79*. New Haven, CT: Yale University Press.

Klintworth, Gary. 1989. *Vietnam's Intervention in Cambodia in International Law*. Canberra: Australian Government Publishing Service.

Lederer, William J., and Eugene Burdick. 1958. *The Ugly American*. New York: Norton.

Lindgren, Goren, G. Kenneth Wilson, and Peter Wallensteen. 1989. Armed Conflicts over Government and Territory. In *States in Armed Conflict 1988*, ed. Peter Wallensteen, 35–72. Uppsala: Department of Peace and Conflict Research, University of Uppsala.

Miner, Jerry. 1989. The Reagan Deficit. *Public Budgeting & Finance* 9 (1): 15–32.

New York Times. 1979. Vietnamese Says Army Will Stay in Cambodia Till Regime Is Firm. *New York Times*, November 7.

Scott, James M. 1996. *Deciding to Intervene: The Reagan Doctrine and American Foreign Policy*. Durham. NC: Duke University Press.

Shawcross, William. 1979. *Sideshow: Nixon, Kissinger and the Destruction of Cambodia*. New York: Simon & Schuster.

Shimko, Keith L. 1992. Reagan on the Soviet Union and the Nature of International Conflict. *Political Psychology* 13 (3): 353–375.

Sihanouk, Norodom. 1980. *War and Hope: The Case for Cambodia*. New York: Pantheon.

Slater, Jerome. 1993. The Domino Theory and International Politics: The Case of Vietnam. *Security Studies* 3 (2): 186–224.

United States Archives. 2008. Vietnam War U.S. Military Fatal Casualty Statistics. April 29. https://www.archives.gov/research/military/vietnam-war/casualty-statistics.

Weekly Compilation of Presidential Documents. 1981–1988. Washington, DC: Government Printing Office.

Winer, Jonathan. 1986. Letter from Jonathan Winer, Counsel to Senator John Kerry, to Larry Chartienes, Vietnam Veterans of America, October 22.

CHAPTER 8

American Policies Toward North Korea

North Korea provides another example of a strategic decision toward an adversary in terms of operational codes and Options Analysis. Korea was a unified monarchy until Japan seized control and governed the peninsula as a colony during the years 1910 to 1945. Then came World War II. After Japan's defeat, the Soviet Union and the United States agreed to share the northern and southern half on a trusteeship basis until a new Korean government could be established. Elections held by the United Nations in 1948, however, were boycotted throughout the peninsula. Instead, the Republic of Korea was established that year in the south, prompting the declaration of the Democratic People's Republic of Korea (DPRK) in the North. Ever since, the two halves of Korea have never been reunited. The major reason is that American foreign policy decision-makers have repeatedly chosen the wrong options, and North Korea has become a nuclear power as a result.

NORTH KOREA, SOUTH KOREA, AND THE UNITED STATES

After North Korea attacked South Korea in 1950, the United States sought to defend South Korea and gained UN Security Council's permission to establish the UN Command. Due to mutual exhaustion, the Armistice Agreement ended the war in 1953. Ever since, the United States has tried to isolate North Korea, otherwise known as

© The Author(s), under exclusive license to Springer Nature   171
Switzerland AG 2023
M. Haas, *Professionalization of Foreign Policy*,
https://doi.org/10.1007/978-3-031-37152-3_8

the Democratic People's Republic of Korea while the latter has sought normalization and a peace agreement (Myung-Lim 2021).

Annual American military exercises with South Korean forces, which began in 1955, have been perceived in Pyongyang as a dress rehearsal for an imminent military takeover of North Korea. In effect, they have been wargames planning to conquer North Korea. Even more threatening, the United States located nuclear weapons for the first time in South Korea in 1958 (Selden and So 2004: 77–80), thereby violating the Armistice Agreement.

Any country under nuclear threat has the right of self-defense under the Treaty on the Non-Proliferation of Nuclear Weapons (NPT). With the aid of the Soviet Union, North Korea built a nuclear power plant in 1965 and soon began to develop missiles that might carry conventional weapons. In 1974, Pyongyang first proposed a peace treaty but found no interlocutors (Wilson 1974). In 1983, Pyongyang offered to abandon its nuclear power plant if Washington agreed to normalize relations (cf. Tucker 2001: 429–431). Again, there was no response from the United States.

When the Cold War ended, North Korea was left without a strong alliance partner. China and Russia were steering their own courses, and the United States had the capability, nuclear and otherwise, of winning in a showdown war, though China and Russia might again defend North Korea. In 1991, North and South Korea signed a denuclearization pledge (Lee 2009). Contrary to that pledge, the United States deployed Patriot missiles to South Korea in 1994. North Korea considered the action, another violation of the Armistice Agreement of 1953, as an imminent threat. Pyongyang realized that only possession of a nuclear deterrent would maintain its sovereignty but only had a couple of nuclear power plants.

In 1994, North Korean leader Kim Il-Sung invited former president Jimmy Carter to seek a dialog with the United States, thanks to prior diplomacy by Secretary of State Madeleine Albright. As a result, Washington learned that Pyongyang was willing to suspend operations of a 50-megawatt plutonium reactor in exchange for energy aid, including heating oil and a light-water reactor to replace the graphic nuclear reactor. Negotiations proceeded, and in October 1994 a deal was formalized by the administration of Bill Clinton as the *Agreed Framework* (1994), involving a "road map" that would involve several reciprocated steps.

Under the agreement, North Korea promised (1) abandonment of work on its sole nuclear reactor, (2) remain in the NPT, (3) allow full inspection of its nuclear facilities, (4) store all spent nuclear fuel, (5) can all spent fuel rods and rod fragments, (6) freeze all nuclear activity, (7) upon receipt of the light-water reactors, admit past violations to International Atomic Energy Agency (IAEA), and then (8) dismantle the nuclear program and (9) expel all spent rods from the country. In exchange, the United States promised (1) to supply light-water reactors to the DPRK, (2) never to use nuclear weapons against North Korea, (3) to supply heavy fuel oil to North Korea for electricity after all spent fuel was stored, (4) to normalize relations with the DPRK after successful inspections, storage of all spent nuclear fuel, and canning of all spent fuel rods and rod fragments. Although not in the agreement, the United States canceled joint military exercises with South Korea in 1994 and 1995 and removed North Korea from the list of "rogue states" in 1996, when separate talks began to halt North Korean missile development, including missile sales. Eight rounds of missile talks proceeded until 2000.

But in 1996 bilateral wargames resumed, dooming missile talks. Meanwhile, North Korea awaited heavy fuel oil shipments, which repeatedly arrived late (Manyin and Niktin 2014).

A light-water reactor was the key to the agreement, but Congress would not supply funds. American diplomats had to seek funding elsewhere, and Japan and South Korea agreed to assist. No contract was signed until 2000, and a construction site was not selected until 2001.

After becoming president in 2001, George W. Bush reviewed relations with North Korea. In 2002, allegations from some persons in his administration were made that Pyongyang was secretly developing nuclear weapons. Although North Korea denied the accusation, and little evidence was presented to back up the allegations (Jackson 2018), Bush's Axis of Evil Speech in 2002 blasted Iran, Iraq—and North Korea.

Pyongyang then asked Japan to intervene (Kaseda 2003: 125). As a result, Bush suggested new talks (Slevin 2002). Assistant Secretary of State James Kelly flew to Pyongyang to offer a "bold initiative"—if North Korea would abandon nuclear power facilities, the United States would commit $95 million to build the light-water reactor (Samore 2004: 11–12; BBC 2002). Thus, the Bush Administration was ignoring the prior promise to proceed toward the normalization of relations with North Korea. Oil shipments were then blocked in November 2002, and the Bush Administration unilaterally withdrew from the *Agreed Framework*

(Pollack 2003). No light-water reactor ever reached North Korea more than eight years after the signing of the *Agreed Framework*.

Accordingly, North Korea announced the resumption of its nuclear program in 2003, hoping thereby to provoke the United States into further negotiations, including normalization talks (Samore 2004). In response, Washington insisted on full denuclearization before normalization talks (Litwak and Daily 2016). Yet another chance to denuclearize was lost.

Next, China intervened by setting up Six-Party Talks, which included China, Japan, both Koreas, Russia, and the United States, starting in August 2003. In the fourth round, held in September 2005, there was agreement to revive parts of the *Agreed Framework*. The *Joint Statement* of 2005 involved the following actions promised by North Korea: (1) dismantling of its nuclear program, (2) re-joining the NPT, and (3) accepting IAEA inspections. The United States, in turn, pledged (1) never to attack or invade North Korea, (2) to sign a security agreement with the DPRK, (3) to resume heavy fuel oil shipments, (4) to supply a light-water reactor, and (5) to normalize relations with North Korea.

A "road map" to implement the *Joint Statement* was drawn up in 2007 by political scientist Bruce Bueno de Mesquita. In Stage 1, North Korea would receive 50,000 tons of fuel oil and in return would shut down and seal the nuclear facility at Yongbyon as well as allow IAEA inspections. In Stage 2, North Korea would disable all plutonium facilities, while keeping its peaceful nuclear facility in operation, and provide a complete accounting of its nuclear program. In response, the DPRK would receive another shipment of 50,000 tons of fuel oil. Washington would then lift economic sanctions and remove North Korea from the list of states supporting terrorism, which would then lift restrictions on foreign assistance and exports of dual use items (USDOS 2021). In Stage 3, North Korea would discuss ending its nuclear programs and missile sales, while the United States would begin normalization talks. Progress on the former was to be calibrated with the latter.

By May 2007, North Korea had shut down the Yongbyon reactor (Kaku 2012), and IAEA inspectors had verified the closure. Stage 1 had been completed. Details of Stage 2 were then agreed upon: (1) Three key nuclear facilities at Yongbyon were to be disabled in a series of eleven steps. (2) North Korea would give a complete accounting of its nuclear program. (3) Fuel oil shipments were to be increased to 1 million tons. (4) IAEA inspectors were to be admitted.

8 AMERICAN POLICIES TOWARD NORTH KOREA   175

In Stage 3, Pyongyang would (1) shut down Pyongyang completely, and (2) sign a denuclearization agreement. In response, Washington pledged (1) to offer humanitarian aid, (2) to send more fuel oil, and (3) to begin bilateral normalization talks (Scanlon 2007).

Stage 2 progress was jeopardized when the United States disputed North Korea's accounting of its nuclear program; secret nuclear sites were suspected. Nevertheless, Pyongyang gained approval when the report was expanded, including details about the dismantling of Yongbyon. Pyongyang also pledged never to proliferate nuclear technology.

Consistent with Stage 2, IAEA inspectors were admitted (Guardian 2008). After North Korea renounced prior terrorist acts, some American sanctions were lifted. The New York Philharmonic performed in Pyongyang in February 2008. American relations with North Korea were definitely improving when Barack Obama entered the White House in January 2009.

OPERATIONAL CODES

Kim Il-Sung, who is considered the founder of North Korea, died in July 1994. The *Agreed Framework* was signed by his successor, Kim Jong-Il, in October 1994, and he lived until 2011. Consequently, he is the only North Korean leader who dealt with the United States to cover the years described above.

As a dictator in a totalitarian state, he was responsible for taking measures to ensure that the United States would be deterred from attacking his country (Table 8.1). To do so, he went beyond balancing and maintaining power to actively increasing missile and nuclear capabilities in what is perhaps the most militarized country on the planet. Although many parts of the Communist bloc countries loosened state control of their economies at the end of the Cold War, the DPRK economy was "eroded" to the extent that some corruption existed as efforts were undertaken to bring prosperity to the country (Scobell 2014: 38, 44–48). Because of sanctions, monetary activity must ensure that the country does not become bankrupt. His desire for normal relations clearly illustrated that he wanted more prosperity for his country. Many negotiations with the United States occurred at the United Nations, which both Koreas joined in 1991. Under his leadership North Korea began to join about 60 intergovernmental organizations (Wikipedia 2023) and signed and observed many agreements with South Korea. His charming

176   M. HAAS

personality caught the attention of former Secretary of State Madelene Albright, who reported he was "knowledgeable, good humored, and relatively normal" (Scobell 2014: 7). Nevertheless, sanctions were first imposed by the United Nations Security Council in 2006, when North Korea first tested ballistic missiles (Davenport 2022); four more UN sanctions were adopted under his successor, Kim Jong-Un. Although the DPRK has violated the sanctions, dozens of other countries have done so as well (Albright 2020). Kim Jong-Il has been called a "micromanager" (Scobell 2014: 9), thus relying heavily on intelligence information. He organized rallies to support his rule, and members of the DPRK parliament sycophantically saluted him. Because he appeared to need praise, he rarely heard intelligence information that displeased him, so he relied on "informers" (Oh and Hassig 2000: 98). He was judged to be a very rational decision-maker albeit quite ruthless in domestic matters to counter possible disloyalty (Martin 2006: 684).

Barack Obama's unique operational code was initially formed outside the continental United States. Although he lived a few years in Indonesia, he was born in the land of Aloha, where he acculturated to living with many persons of diverse racial backgrounds; half of the children born in Hawai'i today have parents of different races (Haas 2010: Chapter 9). His father was from Kenya, but did not live with him; instead, he lived

Table 8.1 Operational Code of Kim Jong-Il

Criteria	Subcriteria	Weight
Power	Deter adversary	High
	Balance power	High
	Maintain power	High
	Increase power	High
Wealth	Benefits > costs	High
	Free economy	Low
	Increase prosperity	High
Prestige	Build institutions	High
	Observe natl/internatl law	Low
	Favor democracies	Low
Feasibility	Resource estimate	High
	Satisfy civil society	Low
	Satisfy selectorate	Medium
	Information adequacy	Medium
	Satisfy psych needs	High

with a White mother and White grandparents. At the age of 18, he began college at Occidental College, located in a quiet suburban enclave in Los Angeles. From that time forward, he experienced racial discrimination—a shock much greater than someone of the same age coming out as gay or lesbian. Although identified as a "Black president," he was biracial and always drew on his multiracial experience. In accordance with the operational code in the Islands (Haas 2011), he was accustomed to listening humbly to persons of differing views, provided that they expressed themselves respectfully, and he tried to find ways to fulfill objectives that would draw from their diverse experiences and wisdom, thereby taking much time to decide. He tried to bring Aloha to Washington, where politics was too polarized to understand his main goal of human reconciliation. However, he succeeded in having Congress adopt Hawai'i's medical insurance, the "employer mandate," in use while he was a boy, now known as Obamacare.

As president, Obama compartmentalized foreign policies, treating each situation on its own (Lizza 2012: 445), so any statement of his operational code on one subject will not necessarily apply to North Korea. Despite Russia's intervention in Georgia in 2008, he sought greater cooperation with Russia (Deyermond 2013), not deterrence, a ploy that failed to restrain Russia's seizure of eastern parts of Ukraine in 2014, though some military aid went to the Kyiv government to counterbalance the Russian occupation. He was influenced by Defense Secretary Robert Gates, a holdover from the administration of George W. Bush, to balance and contain China, rejecting the diplomacy option of Richard Holbrooke (Lizza 2012: 436, 438). His withdrawal of American forces from Iraq and reduction in forces in Afghanistan after an unsuccessful short-term surge were signs that he wanted to maintain rather than overextend power, but the effect was to reduce the global role of the United States at a time when the world power structure was becoming more multipolar (Skidmore 2012; Dolan 2018: 2, 5). Because Obama had to give priority to coping with the Great Recession upon entering the White House, many initial decisions involved reduced funding (Dolan 2018: Chapter 2; Lizza 2012: 439). Increasing sanctions on North Korea, a cost-free policy for the United States except for the financial impact of enforcement, were aimed at increasing economic instability in North Korea (ibidem.). Although Obama sought to rebuild the reputation of the United States after the "bad" Iraq War, he accused members of the North Atlantic Treaty Organization of being "free riders," not burden sharers

178   M. HAAS

(ibid., p. 433; Dolan 2018: 2). Despite pursuing a denuclearization agreement with Iran, he abandoned one with North Korea. Nevertheless, he succeeded in fostering a worldwide agreement on climate change. As a law student, he greatly impressed Professor Laurence Tribe (2012), who hired him as his principal research assistant at Harvard University School of Law. Crimes against humanity by terrorists and Syria's use of chemical weapons greatly angered Obama (Forsythe 2011; Power 2019: 365); Beauregard 2022). He verbally supported democracy around the world, notably during the Arab Spring, but normalized relations with undemocratic Cuba (Bouchet 2013). Although he wanted to end American involvement in Iraq as too costly, he increased troops by 17,000 in the "good" Afghan War but insisted on a time limit for the "surge," so he was quite attentive to resource feasibility. Due to polarized politics, he enjoyed more success with Democrats than Republicans in foreign affairs, though his speeches boosted overall confidence in his capabilities (Eichenberg 2009); one reason appears to be that he supported his "realist" policies with "idealist" rhetoric (David 2016). Nevertheless, journalists complained that he sought to muzzle officials so that they would not leak policy deliberations (Downie and Rafsky 2013). Meanwhile, no Korean public interest organizations in the United States have ever demonstrated any interest in forging peace with North Korea (Haas 2018: 126). One key indicator of his desire to satisfy his selectorate within the Democratic Party was his appointment of Hillary Clinton as Secretary of State (Lizza 2012: 432), though his deference to Defense Secretary Gates was evidence of his bipartisan outreach (Marsh 2014: 279). Probably no other American president has demonstrated such a compulsion to achieve information adequacy (ibid., p. 429; Tutar 2022: Table 3), resulting in decisions that were sometimes delayed as long as a month (Marsh 2014: 266). Regarding his psychological needs, in general, he has been described as having "monkish" discipline (Rhodes 2019: 298–299), though Bashar al-Assad's use of chemical weapons provoked anger and outrage and a determination to punish the Syrian government (Power 2019: 365). He had high needs for achievement and affiliation (Tutar 2022: Table 4). In sum, contradictions plague any attempt to intuit his operational code (Table 8.2).

8 AMERICAN POLICIES TOWARD NORTH KOREA   179

Table 8.2 Operational Code of Barack Obama

Criteria	Subcriteria	Weight
Power	Deter adversary	Low
	Balance power	Medium
	Maintain power	Medium
	Increase power	Low
Wealth	Benefits > costs	High
	Free economy	Medium
	Increase prosperity	Low
Prestige	Build institutions	Medium
	Observe natl/internatl law	High
	Favor democracies	Medium
Feasibility	Resource estimate	High
	Satisfy civil society	High
	Satisfy selectorate	High
	Information adequacy	High
	Satisfy psych needs	Medium

OPTIONS ANALYSIS

From 1998 to 2008, South Korea maintained a "sunshine policy," in which the two Koreas cooperated at low levels—cultural exchanges, family reunification sessions, South Korean factories in the North, sports cooperation, and tourism—as a way to build confidence toward an eventual reunification (Hogarth 2012). Both the Bush and Obama administrations provided little support for the "sunshine policy," and a new political party was elected in South Korea during 2008 with much less interest in the policy.

By the time of the Seventh Round of Six-Party Talks in December 2008, North Korea had completed 8 of the 11 dismantlement steps, though plutonium remained weaponized (Niktin 2009: 12). But the latest fuel oil shipment had not arrived, and normalization talks were not scheduled, which Pyongyang correctly believed to be clear violations of the *Joint Statement*, Stage 2. North Korea then announced that its nuclear program would re-start, and IAEA inspectors were not allowed into the country, seeking thereby to apply pressure on the incoming Obama Administration to live up to the *Joint Statement*.

While campaigning for president in 2008, Barack Obama promised to meet North Korean leader Kim Jong-Il. After becoming president, however, he took no steps to carry out his promise.

In April 2009, Pyongyang for the first time launched a communications satellite, a move not covered by the *Joint Statement* and thus not a violation of the agreement to suspend missile tests. The Obama Administration, nevertheless, interpreted the launch as a violation of the spirit of the agreement, though later failed missile tests proved that the technology to launch a satellite was not the same thing as having offensive missile capability (Kim and Tong-Hyung 2023). The United States then stopped the flow of food aid, imposed sanctions, refused to engage in further talks (George 2019), and asked the UN Security Council to adopt sanctions (Aljazeera 2009). Having thereby snubbed Pyongyang, yet another opportunity for negotiations was lost. In December 2009, Obama in vain tried to revive the Six-Party Talks (CNN 2009; Dale 2019). Seven years later, China complained that Washington was still not trying to resume negotiations (Choe 2016).

However, the proposed "Leap Day" deal in February 2012 would have sent American food aid to North Korea if Pyongyang suspended nuclear testing, long-range missile testing, and uranium enrichment, but talks ended two months later. In 2013, as in the past, Kim issued threats to attract negotiations. Obama's extraordinary response, clearly drawn from the respectfulness norm in Hawai'i's operational code (Haas 2011: ch1), equated Kim's personality with the behavior of a brat, commenting "You don't get to bang your spoon on the table and somehow you get your way" (Dale 2019).

Obama instead adopted the policy of "strategic patience" aiming at bringing Pyongyang to the bargaining table by sanctioning North Korea's economy, hoping that the regime would collapse (Choi 2015). The same policy had been briefly adopted by the previous administration, and continued through the rest of the Obama Administration. Despite a brief rapprochement during the Trump Administration, the policy resumed under the Biden Administration.

Trade restrictions between the United States and North Korea were based on the Trading with the Enemy Act of 1917 from 1950 to 2008, when they were superseded by provisions of the International Emergency Economic Powers Act of 1977. In February 2016, Congress adopted the North Korea Sanctions and Policy Enhancement Act, which requires the president to sanction entities contributing to the DPRK's arms trade, human rights abuses, mineral or metal trade, nuclear program, or other illegal activities, including cybersecurity abuse, and money laundering (Fifield 2016).

8 AMERICAN POLICIES TOWARD NORTH KOREA 181

The policy of "strategic patience" was chosen as a "do nothing" option, awaiting unilateral Pyongyang to take steps toward denuclearization while the United States continued wargames and reviewed other responses in case of an attack from North Korea. Unfortunately, the record does not indicate whether any other serious options were considered during the Obama Administration to appeal to Pyongyang (Table 8.3). Nevertheless, other administrations doubtless considered war on North Korea, since that was the content of annual war games between South Korea and the United States. Both Jimmy Carter and Donald Trump threatened to withdraw troops from South Korea but later relented.

The *Agreed Framework*, the *Joint Statement*, and the later *Singapore Declaration* of 2018 adopted by President Donald Trump and Kim Jong-Un of North Korea had one option in common—a road map involving simultaneous steps toward denuclearization of North Korea and normalization of DPRK relations with the United States. Although South Korea had abandoned the "sunshine policy" during the Obama Administration, the United States could have expressed support and adopted a DPRK-USA sunshine policy following up the New York Philharmonic Orchestra's performance in Pyongyang in 2008. A minimal proposal, which North Korea repeatedly advocated, was to replace the Armistice Agreement of 1953 with a peace agreement, thus ending the war once and for all. Another option was for Washington to ask Beijing and Moscow to apply pressure on North Korea to denuclearize, though

Table 8.3 Policy Options of the United States Toward North Korea, 2009–2016

Option	Content of Option
1	Resume the Six-Party Talks
2	"Strategic patience," awaiting unilateral denuclearization
3	American pursuit of war on North Korea
4	American military withdrawal from South Korea
5	Denuclearization + normalization road map
6	Support "sunshine policy"
7	Peace agreement
8	Ask China and Russia to apply pressure on North Korea
9	Economic sanctions on North Korea
10	Negotiations without preconditions

182   M. HAAS

neither country showed any interest in enforcing UN Security Council sanctions against North Korea. More details on scenarios for each option appear in the chapter's appendix.

The highest priorities, again with 97% reliability, were "strategic patience" and sanctions, both far above any other options (Table 8.4). Support of the "sunshine policy" and resumption of the Six-Party Talks came next, but considerably below the top two options. Then came the proposal to have China and Russia intervene, though China's response has long been for the DPRK and the United States to return to the negotiating table, while Russia has been trying to advance economically. Resumption of negotiations ranked even father below. Two unacceptable options were a war on North Korea, which was always "on the table," and the withdrawal of American troops from South Korea.

CURRENT RELATIONS

Soon after Donald Trump became president, Secretary of State Rex Tillerson declared an end to the policy of "strategic patience"; denuclearization before normalization talks was the apparent default policy (Gearan and Fifield 2017). Although there was serious consideration of a "nosebleed" strike on North Korea, some foreign policy advisers objected (Shin 2021: 184). Pyongyang then tried to get attention by missile tests, cyberattacks, and arresting Americans on tour in North Korea (Haas 2018: 91). The American response was an American missile launched into the Pacific, negotiations to gain the release of Americans held in Pyongyang, and more sanctions. Acerbic words were also exchanged, including a Trump threat to nuke North Korea followed by a statement by Tillerson and several military officials that no such option was on the table (McManus 2017). According to Chinese and Russian sources, Kim Jong-Un hoped that talks would begin; he promised to freeze its nuclear program if the United States would cancel its war games with South Korea (Buncombe 2017). The only response came from Washington was a resumption of war games, including South Korea's first test of a missile (Smith-Spark et al. 2017), whereupon more North Korean missiles were launched, a nuclear bomb was tested, more nasty words were exchanged on both sides, and even scolding of Washington came from Beijing and Moscow. In December 2017, Tillerson promised negotiations without preconditions but relented when a White House statement insisted that

8 AMERICAN POLICIES TOWARD NORTH KOREA — 183

Table 8.4 Matrix of Subcriteria of North Korea Decision-Making with Options

Criteria	Subcriteria	Weight	1	2	3	4	5	6	7	8	9	10
Power	Deter adversary	Low	F	P	U	U	F	P	F	P	VG	F
	Balance power	Medium	F	P	U	U	P	P	P	P	G	P
	Maintain power	Medium	F	F	U	U	P	P	P	P	G	P
	Increase power	Low	P	P	U	U	P	P	P	P	F	P
Wealth	Benefits > costs	Medium	P	E	U	P	P	F	F	P	G	P
	Free economy	Medium	P	P	U	U	U	P	U	U	U	F
	Increase prosperity	High	P	P	U	P	P	P	P	P	P	P
Prestige	Build institutions	Medium	F	P	U	U	F	F	F	F	P	P
	Observe national/ International law	High	F	F	U	P	F	F	F	F	G	F
	Favor democracies	High	U	U	U	U	U	U	U	U	U	P
Feasibility	Resource estimate	High	F	E	U	E	P	F	P	G	F	U
	Satisfy civil society	High	F	P	U	U	P	F	F	P	P	P
	Satisfy selectorate	High	P	G	U	U	P	F	P	P	G	P
	Information adequacy	High	P	E	U	VG	P	F	P	F	F	P
	Satisfy psych needs	Medium	F	F	U	U	F	F	G	P	F	P
Score			2.9	4.3	0	1.9	2.2	3.0	2.0	2.5	3.9	2.2
Rank			4	1	10	9	7.5	3	5	6	2	7.5

denuclearization would have to occur before negotiations (Spetalnick and Brunnstrom 2017).

The election in 2017 of South Korean President Moon Jae-In, an advocate of the "sunshine policy," changed the situation. He proposed talks with North Korea, which accepted the invitation in January 2018, ostensively because Winter Olympics were scheduled for Korea later that year. After Kim and Moon met in February, American diplomacy became more respectful, and "love letters" from Kim to Trump paved the way, occasionally quite rockily (Haas 2018: 98), for a summit in Singapore, held on June 12, 2018. The *Singapore Declaration* consisted of a mutual

184   M. HAAS

promise to pursue a simultaneous "road map" toward denuclearization and normalization.

Preparations then ensued for a summit to be held in Hanoi in 2019. Tillerson's successor, Mike Pompeo, then appointed Stephen Biegun to draw up plans for the summit. Aware that Trump was interested in a tourist resort along a North Korean beach, Biegun and his North Korean counterpart began to draw up a "road map" similar to the *Agreed Framework* and *Joint Statement*. However, no agreement occurred before or during the summit on what percentage of American sanctions would be lifted in response to DPRK's efforts to shut down some of its nuclear capabilities (Shin 2021: 314–315).

Before the Hanoi Summit, Washington was then teeming with concern that Trump would give up too much as negotiations proceeded. Even before the Singapore Summit, National Security Adviser John Bolton, later echoed by Vice President Mike Pence, stated that he favored denuclearization before talks, a policy that he was aware had worked in regard to Libya (Davenport and Atlas 2018). In response, Kim called Pence a "dummy" (Choe 2018). But when the Hanoi Summit began, Pompeo sat alongside Bolton at the table opposite their North Korean counterparts, with Biegun seated behind the table. When Bolton again stated his "denuclearization first" policy as the American position, the conference ended (Brennan 2019). Once again, North Koreans were rebuffed. Trump allowed one adviser, a relic of the Cold War, to prevail over another.

During the rest of the Trump Administration, the policy of "strategic deterrence" resumed. The Biden Administration continued the policy of "strategic patience," including war games with South Korea but now including Japan. North Korea launched more missile tests in 2022 than in all previous years (DuBois 2022), as usual in response to the war games. The Biden Administration then objected to the tests but appeared oblivious that the war games posed a much bigger threat to North Korea. Although officials in the United States often say that they are open to talks without preconditions, Washington indicates that the subject of the talks will be denuclearization without normalization, a condition entirely unacceptable to North Korea.

CONCLUSION

Pyongyang clearly realizes that a long history of American diplomatic betrayal, misconduct, and reversals will continue indefinitely. Whenever North Korea launches a missile, they are reacting to something negative from the United States, and thereby suggesting talks to smooth the situation. But Washington then decodes the invitation to negotiate as a "threat" and maintains diplomatic deafness—a clear case of the type of metacommunication failure that prompted Nathan Leites to develop operational code research. Despite a recent plea to change course, expressed by an expert at the U.S. Institute of Peace who participated in previous negotiations with North Korea (Aum 2022), the Biden Administration is focused instead on the Ukraine War, the subject of the following chapter.

APPENDIX: AMERICAN POLICY OPTIONS FOR NORTH KOREA, 2009–2018

Scenario 1: *Resume the Six-Party Talks*. The Obama Administration reacted to North Korea's launch of a communication satellite as a violation of the letter of the *Joint Statement*. To continue progress, Washington would have to conclude that the launch was not a violation in discussions with Pyongyang and maintain trust with North Korea, which would then continue to achieve the rest of the agreement, working toward denuclearization. The Obama Administration would have had to review previous agreements, approve the ongoing progress, and send new personnel to participate in the Six-Party Talks. China was ready to serve as a host.

Scenario 2: *"Strategic patience," awaiting unilateral denuclearization*. The United States would continue to isolate North Korea, impose sanctions, maintain a military presence in the South, conduct annual "war games," have the UN Security Council impose sanctions, and refrain from negotiations except to reclaim American hostages. Meanwhile, North Korea would continue to increase its own nuclear deterrent. Washington hoped that Pyongyang would become so economically desperate or unable to constrain a rebel movement that self-denuclearization would emerge. Doing nothing in diplomacy always has a high likelihood.

Scenario 3: *American war on North Korea*. After a "false flag" complaint, American military could carefully wipe out all offensive capabilities from North Korea, followed by carpet bombing. Troops would enter the country from all sides. The government in Pyongyang would be overthrown. South Korea would be involved from Day One and achieve reunification. The United States would then become known for hegemony-seeking and would lose support around the world. China would either seize Taiwan during the operation or defend North Korea— or both. Russia might then advance militarily in the Baltics and Eastern Europe. The likelihood was zero.

Scenario 4: *American military withdrawal from South Korea*. Although an American nuclear deterrent would remain in the air and sea, North Korea would be pleased that Washington would finally be granting its repeated request to remove troops from the Korean peninsula. There would be no more "war games" on land simulating an attack on the North, so Pyongyang would not automatically engage in countermoves. South Korea would then develop its own nuclear deterrent with funding from the United States in defiance of the Nonproliferation Agreement. With China increasingly posing a military threat, Washington was unlikely to remove troops from the region.

Scenario 5: *Denuclearization + normalization road map*. Negotiations would ensue to restore the *Joint Statement* of 2005 so that both sides will take calibrated, step-by-step actions so that North Korea will denuclearize while relations with the United States will gradually normalize. The United States will establish a diplomatic office in Pyongyang, and North Korea will have a similar office in Washington. Cultural and economic relations would gradually expand. Because the Obama Administration stopped progress being undertaken by North Korea, prospects evaporated.

Scenario 6: *Support "sunshine policy."* An optimistic Obama Administration would hope that a South Korean government committed to the "sunshine policy" would be elected in the future. Families divided by the border would then meet. Tourism in the north would resume. South Korean businesses would be re-established in the north. Gradual demilitarization of adjacent territories would begin and expand. There would be no more attacks on naval vessels that might stray across the border. The future administration of Moon Jae-In (2017–2022) demonstrated how such progress can proceed, but the Obama Administration had no support from South Korea to do so.

Scenario 7: *Peace agreement*. After the armistice in 1918, there was a peace agreement in 1919, but no parallel exists regarding the Korean War. North Korea has repeatedly asked for a peace agreement without preconditions. The agreement would abolish the need for United Nations supervision, which is ongoing today. The two Koreas, which already have agreed in principle on a peace agreement, have already prepared such a text (Park 2021). South Korea might invite the United States to sign on and provide security guarantees, though North Korea would retain nuclear capabilities until later negotiations begin on a road map for the complete normalization of relations along with denuclearization. Mutual distrust made the option unlikely.

Scenario 8: *Ask China and Russia to apply pressure on North Korea*. American relations with China and Russia would have to improve considerably before requests to apply pressure would have any chance of success. North Korea would also have to become more dependent on both countries to succumb to their pressure. The likelihood has been zero for some time.

Scenario 9: *Economic sanctions on North Korea*. North Korea is a country with considerable marketable minerals, so the aim of sanctions would be to prevent the country from achieving wealth through international trade. North Korean ships were to be seized. In addition, any recipient of trade from North Korea would also be subject to sanctions. In due course, the country was expected to be so isolated from the rest of the world and so poor that the people of North Korea would rise up to achieve regime change. China and Russia do not approve of North Korean bluster and therefore have sometimes voted for sanctions, but they have not implemented sanctions.

Scenario 10: *Negotiations without preconditions*. The only thing required for negotiations is to propose talks, set up a time and place, and meet. But some unilateral reciprocated signs of goodwill would be needed before the option would occur. The most obvious location would be the United Nations headquarters in New York. At such a meeting, each side would have to act respectfully, setting agendas for further discussion. The option differed from previous invitations for negotiations where one side required that the other must stop something before talks would ensue. Secret talks are very likely if something extraordinary occurs, such as damage inflicted on an American ship at sea by the North Korean navy, but Pyongyang has no interest in being lectured about denuclearization before normalization.

REFERENCES

Agreed Framework. 1994, October 21. Agreed Framework Between the United States of America and the Democratic People's Republic of Korea. https://www.atomicarchive.com/resources/documents/deterrence/agreed-framework.html.

Albright, David, Sarah Burkhard, and Spencer Faragasso. 2020, July 1. Alleged Sanctions Violations of UNSC Resolutions on North Korea for 2019/2020: The Number Is Increasing. https://isis-online.org/isis-reports/detail/alleged-north-korea-sanctions-violations-2020.

Aljazeera. 2009, April 8. North Korea Defends Rocket Launch. https://www.aljazeera.com/news/2009/4/8/north-korea-defends-rocket-launch.

Aum, Frank. 2022, December 22. Don't Isolate North Korea: Why Another Pressure Campaign Would Be a Mistake. https://www.foreignaffairs.com/north-korea/dont-isolate-north-korea?utm_medium=newsletters&utm_source=fatoday&utm_campaign=Open%20Secrets&utm_content=20221222&utm_term=FA%20Today%20-%20112017.

Beauregard, Philippe. 2022. The Current Analysis Resolving Conflicting Emotions: Obama's Quandaries on the Red Line and the Fight Against ISIS. *Foreign Policy Analysis* 18 (4): orac016. https://doi.org/10.1093/fpa/orac016.

Bouchet, Nicolas. 2013. The Democracy Tradition in US Foreign Policy and the Obama Presidency. *International Affairs* 89 (1): 31–51.

Brennan, David. 2019, September 20. John Bolton Was a "Troublemaker" and Trump Was "Wise" to Remove Him, North Korean Nuclear Negotiator Says. https://www.newsweek.com/john-bolton-was-troublemaker-trump-was-wise-remove-him-north-korean-nuclear-negotiator-says-1460368.

British Broadcasting Corporation. 2002, April 3. US Grants N Korea Nuclear Funds. http://news.bbc.co.uk/2/hi/asia-pacific/1908571.stm.

Buncombe, Andrew. 2017, October 23. North Korea's Nuclear Threat is Now at a "Critical and Imminent Level," Says Japan. www.independent.co.uk/news/world/americas/us-politics/north-korea-latest-us-threat-trump-kim-jong-un-japan-critical-imminent-level-a8015511.html.

Cable News Network. 2009, December 16. Obama Wrote Letter to N. Korean Leader, Official Says. http://www.cnn.com/2009/POLITICS/12/16/obama.nkorea.letter/index.html.

Choe, Sang-Hun. 2016, January 21. U.S. Weighs Tighter Sanctions on North Korea If China Fails to Act. *New York Times*.

Choe, Sang-Hun. 2018, May 27. North Korea Willing to Talk About "Complete Denuclearization". *New York Times*.

Choi, Jong Kun. 2015. The Perils of Strategic Patience with North Korea. *Washington Quarterly* 38 (4): 57–72.

8 AMERICAN POLICIES TOWARD NORTH KOREA 189

Dale, Daniel. 2019, July 1. Obama Never "Begged" for a Meeting with Kim Jong Un. https://www.cnn.com/2019/07/01/politics/fact-check-obama-never-begged-to-meet-with-kim-jong-un/index.html.

Davenport, Kelsey. 2022, January. UN Security Council Resolutions on North Korea. https://www.armscontrol.org/factsheets/UN-Security-Council-Resolutions-on-North-Korea.

Davenport, Kelsey, and Terry Atlas. 2018. "Libya Model" Upsets Summit Planning. *Arms Control Today* 48 (5): 22–23.

David, Steven. 2016. Obama: The Reluctant Realist. In *US Foreign Policy and Global Standing in the 21st Century: Realities and Perceptions*, eds. Efraim Inbar and Jonathan Rynhold, Chapter 3. New York: Routledge.

Deyermond, Ruth. 2013. Assessing the Reset: Successes and Failures in the Obama Administration's Russia Policy, 2009–2012. *European Security* 22 (4): 500–523.

Dolan, Chris J. 2018. *Obama and the Emergence of a Multipolar World Order: Redefining US Foreign Policy*. Lanham, MD: Rowman & Littlefield.

Downie, Leonard J., Jr., and Sara Rafsky. 2013. *The Obama Administration and the Press*. New York: Committee to Protect Journalists.

DuBois, Megan. 2022, December 21. A Year in Brinkmanship on the Korean Peninsula. https://foreignpolicy.com/2022/12/21/north-korea-2022-nuclear-missile-brinkmanship-kim-jong-un/.

Eichenberg, Richard C. 2009. Public Opinion and Foreign Policy in the Obama Era. *Politique Américaine* 2 (14): 11–24.

Fifield, Anna. 2016, February 22. Punishing North Korea: A Rundown on Current Sanctions. *Washington Post*.

Forsythe, David P. 2011. US Foreign Policy and Human Rights: Situating Obama. *Human Rights Quarterly* 33 (3): 767–789.

Gearan, Anne, and Anna Fifield. 2017, March 17. Tillerson Says "All Options Are on the Table" When It Comes to North Korea. *Washington Post*.

George, Kavitha. 2019, February 24. Obama's Approach to North Korea Was Worlds Apart from Trump's Strategy. https://www.bustle.com/p/what-did-obama-do-about-north-korea-trumps-approach-is-worlds-apart-16003666.

Guardian. 2008, October 11. US Removes North Korea from Terrorism Blacklist. https://www.theguardian.com/world/2008/oct/11/korea-usa-terrorism-blacklist.

Haas, Michael. 2010. *Looking for the Aloha Spirit: Promoting Racial Harmony*. Los Angeles: Publishinghouse for Scholars.

Haas, Michael, ed. 2011. *Barack Obama, the Aloha Zen President: How a Son of the 50th State May Revitalize American Based on 12 Multicultural Principles*. Santa Barbara, CA: Praeger.

Haas, Michael. 2018. *American Diplomacy with North Korea and Vietnam: Explaining Failure and Success*. New York: Peter Lang.

190   M. HAAS

Hogarth, Hyun-key Kim. 2012. South Korea's Sunshine Policy, Reciprocity and Nationhood. *Perspectives on Global Development and Technology* 11 (1): 99–111.

Jackson, Van. 2018. Threat Consensus and Rapprochement Failure: Revisiting the Collapse of US-North Korean Relations, 1994–2002. *Foreign Policy Analysis* 14 (2): 235–253.

Joint Statement of the Fourth Round of the Six-Party Talks Beijing. 2005, September 19. https://2001-2009.state.gov/r/pa/prs/ps/2005/53490.htm.

Kaku, Michio. 2012, June 10. Images of North Korean Reactor Hit at Progress of Talks. *International Herald Tribune.*

Kaseda, Youshinori. 2003. Japan and the Korean Peace Process. In *The Korean Peace Process and the Four Powers*, eds. Tae-Hwan Kwak and Seung Ho Joo, Chapter 7. Aldershot, UK: Ashgate.

Kim, Hyung-Jin, and Kim Tong-Yung. 2023, June 1. Spy Satellite Launch Failure Deals Setback to Kim. *Los Angeles Times.*

Lee, Jae-Bong. 2009. US Deployment of Nuclear Weapons in 1950s South Korea & North Korea's Nuclear Development: Toward Denuclearization of the Korean Peninsula. *Asia-Pacific Journal* 8 (1): 3–09.

Litwak, Robert, and Robert Daly. 2016, May 6. How to Freeze N. Korea's Nukes. *Los Angeles Times.*

Lizza, Ryan. 2012. Obama: The Consequentialist. In *The Domestic Sources of Foreign Policy: Insights and Evidence*, ed. James M. McCormick, 6th edition., Chapter 24. Lanham, MD: Rowman & Littlefield.

Manyin, Mark K. and Mary Beth D. Niktin. 2014, April 2. "Foreign Assistance in North Korea," *Congressional Research Service*, Washington, DC.

Marsh, Kevin. 2014. Obama's Surge: A Bureaucratic Politics Analysis of the Decision to Order a Troop Surge in the Afghanistan War. *Foreign Policy Analysis* 10 (3): 265–288.

Martin, Bradley K. 2006. *Under the Loving Care of the Fatherly Leader.* New York: St. Martin's Griffin.

McManus, Doyle. 2017, August 16. They Pulled the U.S. Back from the Nuclear Brink. *Los Angeles Times.*

Niktin, May Beth. 2009, July 1. North Korea's Nuclear Weapons: Technical Issues. https://www.everycrsreport.com/files/20090701_RL34256_fc98336 5999257e1edf9c81b11af7f890ca2b73b.pdf.

Oh, Kongdan, and Ralph C. Hassig. 2000. *North Korea Through the Looking Glass.* Washington, DC: Brookings.

Myung-Lim, Park. 2021. The Korean Peace Agreement and the Korean Peace Regime: A Concrete Draft for Perpetual Peace in Practice. *Korea Observer* 52 (2): 313–341.

Pollack, Jonathan D. 2003. The United States, North Korea, and the End of the Agreed Framework. *Naval War College Review* 56 (3): 10–50.

Power, Samantha. 2019. *The Education of an Idealist: A Memoir*. New York: Dey Street Books.

Rhodes, Ben. 2019. *The World as It Is: A Memoir of the Obama White House*. New York: Random House.

Samore, Gary S. 2004. The Korean Nuclear Crisis. *Survival* 45 (1): 7–24.

Scanlon, Charles. 2007, February 13. The End of a Long Confrontation? http://news.bbc.co.uk/2/hi/asia-pacific/6357853.stm.

Scobell, Andrew. 2014. *Kim Jong Il and North Korea: The Leader and the System*. Scotts Valley, CA: CreateSpace.

Selden, Mark, and Alvin Y. So. 2004. *War and State Terrorism: The United States, Japan, and the Asia-Pacific in the Long Twentieth Century*. Lanham, MD: Rowman & Littlefield.

Shin, David W. 2021. *Kim Jong-Un's Strategy for Survival: A Method to Madness*. Lanham, MD: Lexington.

Singapore Declaration. (2018, June 12). Joint Statement of President Donald J. Trump of the United States of America and Chairman Kim Jong Un of the Democratic People's Republic of Korea at the Singapore Summit. https://kls.law.columbia.edu/sites/default/files/content/docs/Panmunjom%20Monitor/2.%20Singapore%20Summit%20Joint%20Statement%20(2018.06.12).pdf.

Skidmore, David. 2012. The Obama Presidency and US Foreign Policy: Where's the Multilateralism? *International Studies Perspectives* 13 (1): 43–64.

Slevin, Peter. 2002, May 1. N. Korea and U.S. to Meet. *Washington Post*.

Smith-Park, Laura, Taehoon Lee, and Catherine Treyz. 2017, September 2. U.S., South Korea Set to Revise Bilateral Missile Treaty. https://www.abc57.com/news/us-south-korea-set-to-revise-bilateral-missile-treaty.

Spetalnick, David, and David Brunnstrom. 2017, December 13. Despite Tillerson Overture, White House Says Not Right Time for North Korea Talks. https://www.reuters.com/article/us-northkorea-missiles-usa-diplomacy-idUSKBN1E72HW.

Tribe, Laurence. 2012, June 12. Frontline Interview. https://www.pbs.org/wgbh/pages/frontline/government-elections-politics/choice-2012/the-frontline-interview-laurence-tribe/.

Tucker, Nancy Bernkopf, ed. 2001. *China Confidential: American Diplomats and Sino-American Relations, 1945–1996*. New York: Columbia University Press.

Tutar, F. Necmiye. 2022. Re-Assessing Leaders and Foreign Policy Characteristics in the USA: A Case of George W. Bush and Barack Obama. *International Journal of Humanities* 6 (1): 78–102.

United States, Department of State. 2021. State Sponsors of Terrorism. https://www.state.gov/state-sponsors-of-terrorism/. Accessed October 26, 2021.

Wikipedia. 2023. Foreign Relations of North Korea. https://en.wikipedia. org/wiki/Foreign_relationsof_North_Korea#International_organizations. Accessed February 17, 2023.

Wilson Center. 1974, May 13. Letter from Government of North Korea. https://digitalarchive.wilsoncenter.org/document/114199.pdf?v=a44 2459c1736595237e1e8f62780a1bb.

CHAPTER 9

American Policies Toward Ukraine

American policy toward Ukraine is considerably more complicated than the cases of Cambodia, Vietnam, and North Korea. Moreover, a wealth of information about Ukraine has been widely disseminated. Discovering the operational codes of Hanoi and Pyongyang seemed less important to American foreign policy decision-makers because both countries had little power to contest any options. In the case of the Ukraine War, Russia is the aggressor—a country with a population of 140 million that has a large stockpile of nuclear weapons, while Ukraine is a nonnuclear country with a population of about 41 million. The American response to the Ukraine War has been a series of decisions over time rather than just the maintenance of one steadfast option, as will be explained below.

UKRAINE AS AN INDEPENDENT COUNTRY

The territory now identified as Ukraine has been a staging ground for wars over centuries. What has united the people who consider themselves Ukrainians is a common language and a common history of domination by Austria, Germany, Lithuania, the Mongols, Poland, Russia, and the Soviet Union. According to the Helsinki Agreement of 1975, European countries (including the Soviet Union) agreed that existing borders of countries should be respected. In 1991, after the collapse of the Soviet Union, Ukraine declared itself independent. Several Eastern European

© The Author(s), under exclusive license to Springer Nature Switzerland AG 2023
M. Haas, *Professionalization of Foreign Policy*,
https://doi.org/10.1007/978-3-031-37152-3_9

193

countries then joined the North Atlantic Treaty Organization (NATO) to guard themselves from being reconquered by Russia. But Ukraine, with initial governments friendly to Russia, did not join NATO.

Upon independence, Ukraine held a large number of nuclear weapons that Moscow had stationed in its territory. Because Ukraine did not want them, the Budapest Memorandum was drawn up in 1994, and Kyiv also agreed to join the Treaty on the Non-Proliferation of Nuclear Weapons (Similar agreements applied to Belarus and Kazakhstan). Under the terms of the Budapest Memorandum, signed in Paris, Ukraine's nuclear weapons were sent to the Russian Federation to be decommissioned. Signatories Britain, Russia, and the United States promised that they would respect Ukraine's sovereignty without a specific pledge on how to do so (Borda 2022). Political scientist John Mearsheimer (1993) then predicted that without a nuclear deterrent, Russia would inevitably go to war with neighboring Ukraine.

Mearsheimer (2022a) also warned that the expansion of NATO to countries closer to Russia was unacceptable to Russian President Vladimir Putin, who viewed the new constellation of forces as a threat. Any attempt to bolster Ukraine's defenses, according to Mearsheimer, might be perceived in the Kremlin as a pretext for war.

As long as Ukraine was led by an ally of Russia, Putin was satisfied. In 2014, the ouster of President Victor Yanukovych, who fled to Russia, prompted a Russian invasion that carved out Crimea as a new part of Russia while Russian military forces took control of parts of two easternmost provinces, which then claimed to be independent republics. France and Germany next mediated between Russia and Ukraine to formulate the Minsk Agreement of 2014, followed by a revised Minsk II in 2015.

The Minsk framework provided for a ceasefire, withdrawal of heavy weapons from the front line, and an exchange of prisoners of war. Ukraine agreed to grant self-government to areas in the east known as Donbas. But Russia never honored the provision allowing Ukraine to control its borders, and low-level fighting continued thereafter in Donbas.

Although Congress appropriated funds to support Ukraine in 2014, President Donald Trump tried to block their release. Nevertheless, $2 billion in American aid was spent for military trainingand security protection from 2014 to 2022, albeit nothing for crucial weapons to reverse Russian advances (Beliakova and Metz 2023). Putin was aware that American supplies assisted Ukraine, though somewhat routinely by Washington.

9 AMERICAN POLICIES TOWARD UKRAINE 195

When Joe Biden became president, more funds were released to Ukraine. Determining American options toward the Ukraine War evidently involved the Biden Administration in assessing the operational codes of the leader of Russia and well as the current president of Ukraine.

VLADIMIR PUTIN'S OPERATIONAL CODE

The operational code of Vladimir Putin is quite obvious (Table 9.1), since he has made several public statements about his aims, notably his *On the Historical Unity of Russians and Ukrainians* (Putin 2021). As most of his analysts have agreed, including British scholar Mark Galeotti (2022), his highest priority has focused on a need to build an institution—restore the Russian Empire to the days when tsars were successful in expanding the territory of the country. Because Ukraine was once part of Russia and the Soviet Union, he wants to restore history (Kalb 2015; Hill and Stent 2022).

Despite the rise of Russia from Mongol subjugation during 1220–1450 (Halperin 1987), he does not understand that the barbaric age of imperialism is long past. Respect for national sovereignty was accepted under international law in the Peace of Westfalia of 1648 (Stanovaya 2022). His interest in reuniting Russians outside Russia mirrors Hitler's quest to

Table 9.1 Operational Code of Vladimir Putin

Criteria	Subcriteria	Weight
Power	Deter adversary	Low
	Balance power	Low
	Maintain power	High
	Increase power	HIgh
Wealth	Benefits > costs	Low
	Free economy	Low
	Increase prosperity	Medium
Prestige	Build institutions	High
	Obey natl/intnatl law	Low
	Favor democracies	Low
Feasibility	Resource estimate	Medium
	Satisfy civil society	Low
	Satisfy selectorate	High
	Information adequacy	Low
	Satisfy psych needs	High

expand Germany (*Lebensraum*) to include more Germans (cf. Michlin-Shapir 2021), though Putin claimed that he would "de-Nazify" Ukraine. He regards the West as morally bankrupt, seeking a hegemonic "new world order," a phrase once used by former President George H.W. Bush.

In 2008, President George W. Bush promised Ukraine eventual NATO membership (Kaplan 2023: 21). Ukraine, meanwhile, was serving as a buffer to NATO while Ukrainian leaders were friendly to Russia. But Putin's friend, Ukrainian President Viktor Yanukovych, was ousted by a revolution in 2014, whereupon Putin evidently panicked, fearing that Ukraine would join NATO. Russian troops were soon dispatched to take over Crimea and parts of the Donbas region close to the Russian border. In response, Western leaders sent munitions to support the Ukrainian national army, which was then primarily located in the Donbas areas. When Russia threatened to stop gas deliveries to Ukraine after the 2014 invasion, Putin was surprised that neighboring countries filled the gap (Biden and Carpenter 2018: 51). He was aware that the Obama Administration's support for Ukraine was limited, and the Trump Administration was friendly to Putin, but the election of Joe Biden as president in 2020 was viewed with alarm in the Kremlin.

In early 2021, Putin decided to take control of Ukraine militarily. His plans were drawn up by his defense minister, the chief of the military's general staff, and a few members of the intelligence agency, the Federal Security Service (Knight 2023: 33)—in other words, a small number of persons who held their positions by saying whatever Putin wanted to hear. The threat was on full display while Russian troops gathered along a wide perimeter on the northern border of Ukraine from Belarus to Russia in 2021.

Putin's Make Russia Great Again goal is not just to maintain Russian power but to extend territory by annexing Ukraine as a likeminded country. Power balancing and deterrence of possible American and Western support for Ukraine were not given much weight in his deliberations. Fearing a threat from NATO, Putin did not explain why he wanted to expand Russian borders even closer to NATO countries than before. He was willing to devote whatever resources he thought would accomplish his objective, but the cost–benefit analysis was not a consideration. After all, much of Europe depended on Russian gas and oil. He believed that the addition of Ukraine, once called the "breadbasket of Europe," would strengthen Russian economic resources. However, military control of Ukraine was more important to him than the economic cost.

European countries had been importing Russian fossil fuels, so Putin did not anticipate that they would support Ukraine. Sanctions later imposed by NATO countries weakened the Russian economy, but not yet severely, partly because Moscow prepared for them before the war (Harrell 2023; Kimmage and Lipman 2023; Mehrotra 2023). Nevertheless, oil sales were cut in half, and international businesses left the country; the ruble at first plunged to the lowest level ever, but temporarily recovered (Whalen and Belton 2023; Kantchev and Gershkovich 2023). Similar to the current military standoff, sanctions have become a war of attrition with more yet to unfold, including secondary sanctions (Standard & Poors 2023). Russian frozen bank assets, amounting to $300 billion, and properties held by Russians overseas can still be seized on the grounds that the Kremlin's war violates international law; later, Russian assets could be used to pay Ukraine reparations for the damage inflicted on the country (Summers et al. 2023). Meanwhile, Russian unemployment is at 10 percent, with a decline in income and consumption (Fishman 2023). The resulting G-7 cap on Russian oil prices produced a 60 percent decline in revenue, but the Russian economy did not collapse (cf. McFaul 2023; Motyl 2023; Mehrotra 2023; Fishman 2023).

As the war unfolded, the Russian army committed at least 80,000 war crimes, most notably by bombing civilian targets (Freking 2023). Putin clearly wanted to end Ukrainian democracy. However, the selectorate that keeps him in power consists of his fellow intelligence officers, not the military (Galeotti 2022), and he may have jeopardized their support by replacing the military commanders in January and August 2023 (McFaul 2023). He believed that military resources were initially adequate, but his military feasibility (troops and weapons) and process feasibility (logistics) estimates were flawed. Evidently, the military was supplying him with incorrect information. He thought that he would command Ukrainian public support the way he controls Russian media, but he underestimated public opposition, especially when so many young Russian men defected rather than joining his later partial mobilization call-up for "reserves" while a brain drain of 500,000 young professionals left in droves as Russia's economy spluttered, causing a labor shortage (Harrell 2023; Kantchev and Gershkovich 2023). Nevertheless, he avoided full mobilization (total war) and overmilitarization, thereby easing some pressure on the public (Soldatov and Borogan 2023), though conscription requirements were tightened in mid-April 2023 (Dixon 2023). Putin's approval ratings had surged in capturing Crimea, so he evidently thought that

198   M. HAAS

he needed a win in Ukraine to impress his selectorate to run again in the 2024 Russian presidential election (Knight 2023: 34). Nevertheless, Russian propaganda has caused many ordinary Russians, who prefer to remain indifferent to the war, to accept the idea that the survival of their country is at stake (Yaffa 2023). Highest priority of all is Putin's psychological need to have history remember him as the greatest Russian ruler of all time. But the clock is ticking, and he has rumored to be receiving chemotherapy for cancer (Postma 2023).

Putin (2021) has argued that Ukrainians, sometimes known as "Little Russians," were merely an ethnic group that historically was part of the Russian Empire. Putin did not explain why his logic did not also involve absorbing Belarus, often called "White Russia," but Belarus's leader has been extremely friendly. When the war began, Putin was to learn that Ukrainians would show defiant willingness to defend their own identity and country. When Putin's initial assault on Ukraine proved to be a blunder, he resisted reformulating his operational code but altered his options assessment: The nature of the war changed from one of a quick takeover of "little Russians" into a terroristic effort to obliterate Ukrainian identity, with the objective of eventual Russification, a characteristic of what has been called "new wars" that involve the "clash of civilizations" (Kaldor 2005; Huntington 2000). A similar campaign in North America once went by the slogan "manifest destiny."

OPERATIONAL CODE OF VOLODYMYR ZELENSKY

American intelligence information indicated that Russian resources and logistics were sufficient to win a war with Ukraine in a few days. But neither Biden nor Putin understood the operational code of Ukraine's President Volodymyr Zelensky (Table 9.2), and therefore both miscalculated.

One reason for underestimating Zelensky was the superficial view that he was a mere comedian. But the ability to formulate jokes as well as make them up on the spot requires top-level intelligence (Greengrass et al. 2012). Indeed, Zelensky's oratorical skills have been compared to Winston Churchill's (Marr 2022). Another misperception was the determination and strength of the Ukrainian army, which had been actively engaged in combat from 2014 to 2021, learning how to fight Russians in the Donbas region, while most of the Russian army was in the barracks.

9 AMERICAN POLICIES TOWARD UKRAINE 199

Table 9.2 Operational Code of Volodymyr Zelensky

Criteria	Subcriteria	Weight
Power	Deter adversary	High
	Balance power	Low
	Maintain power	High
	Increase power	High
Wealth	Benefits > costs	Low
	Free economy	Low
	Increase prosperity	Low
Prestige	Build institutions	High
	Obey natl/intnatl law	High
	Favor democracies	High
Feasibility	Resource estimate	High
	Satisfy civil society	High
	Satisfy selectorate	High
	Information adequacy	Low
	Satisfy psych needs	Medium

Volodymyr Zelensky's operational code gave the highest priority to defeating Russia and regaining territories occupied by Russian troops. He wanted to increase the military power of Ukrainian forces and not only chase Russians forces out of Ukraine but deter any future aggression even though his forces would never balance the combined mobilized strength of the Russian air force, army, and navy. He was willing to sacrifice the Ukrainian economy to preserve the country's sovereignty. To win, he realized that he would need support from Western countries, hoping for years to join the European Union and NATO. He repeatedly asked for more and higher quality weapons (Keaten 2023a).

His army followed Geneva Convention protocols so that he would be ready to pounce on any Russian war crimes, since the world already knew how Russian military activities in Syria were violations of international law (Mello 2023). He permitted the first war crimes trials in Ukraine to be held in May 2022 (WSJ 2022a).

As a democratically elected leader, Zelensky acted to assure that civil society, including the Ukraine media, were fully behind him, thereby assuring that Ukrainian troops would be energized to fight vigorously. Due to his level of concern over the resources to win the war, he repeatedly requested more military aid, and he capitalized on the logistics of support from countries that backed Ukraine. American intelligence

200   M. HAAS

sources so deeply infiltrated the Russian military that Ukraine could determine the strength of future attacks (Harris and Lamothe 2023), while his own information sources were excellent about battlefield realities.

When audiences cheer and laugh at whatever comedians say, they tend to have strong egos; the same is true of politicians who win elections. Zelensky, while appearing humble, clearly has enjoyed his role as a charismatic leader of a country fighting a formidable enemy (Baer 2022). The Ukrainian people are united in defense of their country (Ash 2023).

Biden's Operational Code

Joseph Robinette Biden, Junior, is possibly the most qualified president in American history. While serving many years in the Senate and as vice president, his views have been developed with considerable sophistication. He met foreign leaders on many occasions before becoming president. He has often stated his opinions and is well known for advancing alliance building, bipartisanship, and support for democracy (Gearan 2021).

In 2017, President Donald Trump said that there were "good people" on the side of "Jews will not replace us" marchers in Charlottesville, Virginia. That extraordinary spectacle prompted Biden to decide to run for president, later explaining that he wanted to save the "soul of America" (Washpost 2020). He then authored an essay "How to Stand Up to the Kremlin" in the first issue of *Foreign Affairs* of 2018 along with Michael Carpenter, Senior Director of the Penn Biden Center for Diplomacy and Global Engagement (Biden and Carpenter 2018). The essay, subtitled "Defending Democracy Against Its Enemies," stated several principles that he later applied to Ukraine (Table 9.3).

Perhaps the most basic principle has been his commitment to democracy. He was pleased that most countries formerly within the Soviet bloc became democracies after the fall of the Soviet Union. But he is disappointed that the people of Russia continue to live in an undemocratic country that has weaponized economic, informational, military, political, and technological resources to attack Western democracies (ibid., p. 45). Directly contrary to the Trump Administration, one significant goal was advanced by Biden: "[T]he United States must lead its democratic allies and partners in increasing their resilience, expanding their capabilities to defend against Russian subversion, and rooting out the Kremlin's network of malign influence" (pp. 45–46).

Table 9.3 Operational Code of Joe Biden

Criteria	Subcriteria	Weight
Power	Deter adversary	High
	Balance power	High
	Maintain power	Medium
	Increase power	Low
Wealth	Benefits > costs	Medium
	Free economy	Low
	Increase prosperity	High
Prestige	Build institutions	High
	Oey natl/intnatl law	High
	Favor democracies	High
Feasibility	Resource estimate	High
	Satisfy civil society	Low
	Satisfy selectorate	Medium
	Information adequacy	High
	Satisfy psych needs	Medium

Biden and Carpenter judged that Russia was weak in several respects beyond lack of grassroots public support. They noted that Russian life expectancy was 153rd in the world, and population was likely to decrease 20 percent by 2050 (p. 47). With an economy dependent on the sale of gas and oil, the country's prosperity would rise and fall with world market prices. Biden and Carpenter interpreted Putin's aggression in Ukraine as "a desire to protect its wealth and power" as well as "a message to other governments in the region that pursuing Western-backed democratic reform will bring dire consequences" (p. 45). They argued that the Kremlin, though appearing strong, lacked public support from the Russian people, so one purpose of fighting against the West appeared to be to divert public attention from kleptocratic corruption, political suppression, and socioeconomic malaise at home.

Biden was vice president when Russia annexed Crimea and the eastern part of Ukraine in 2014. In response, the Obama Administration imposed about 950 sanctions (Castellum 2023), sending Biden as a skilled diplomat to unite members of the North Atlantic Treaty Organization in the event of more aggression. Obama successfully asked Congress for funds to assist the new democratic Ukraine government while mobilizing NATO countries to confront the problem (Obama 2014). In effect, his 2018 essay was a declaration that he favored strengthening capabilities in NATO countries to deter further Russian aggression, both military and cyber, as well as intelligence and law enforcement crackdowns on cyber-crimes and secret funding of political campaigns to undermine democracy (Biden and Carpenter 2018: 53–54).

In a public seminar later in January 2018 (CFR 2018), Biden claimed that NATO stabilized Eastern Europe after the fall of the Soviet Union. And he even suggested that steps should be taken to encourage the Russian people to oppose Putin. Nevertheless, he was concerned over corruption in Ukraine, so he was pleased when the deputy defense minister resigned in 2023 for embezzling payments for food supplies to Ukrainian troops (Beliakova and Metz 2023).

While a candidate for president in 2020, Biden revealed more of his foreign policy agenda in another essay published in *Foreign Affairs*, entitled "America Must Lead Again" (Biden 2020). Running against incumbent President Donald Trump, he stressed the need for the United States to have credibility again, increase the ability to contend with adversaries, renew alliances, and stress democratic values (ibid., pp. 64–65). He also identified democracy as the foundation for economic prosperity and sought to have the United States cement the rules of international trade with new trade agreements that promote freer trade without corruption. Among his proposed reforms, later fulfilled as president, was a world-wide Summit for Democracy that would include civil society (p. 67). He promised to "mobilize collective action on global threats" (p. 71). Stating that possession of military might is not enough to influence the world order, he urged the use of diplomacy as "the first instrument of American power" (p. 72). While assuring that he would use force when necessary, as a last resort, he stressed the need to revive NATO through more military spending by Europeans to deter "Russian aggression" (p. 73).

The first attempt to codify the "Biden operational code" was by an Israeli (Masoudi 2021). Written in Hebrew, he summarized his thesis in English as follows:

> Biden's foreign policy perceptions are strategically based on cooperation with American allies, democratic alliance-building against American rivals and restoring American rule-based global leadership. In terms of tactical issues, the finding shows that Biden's foreign policy is likely to frame in terms of step-by-step approach, preference of diplomacy with all sides involved and importance of American public support in foreign policy area.

Russia's move to surround Ukraine with fully armed military troops, starting in the spring of 2021, prompted Biden to apply his operational code. When Biden and Putin had a summit meeting on June 16, 2021, Putin defended the military buildup and declared that he encountered no hostility from Biden (Chance and McGee 2021). Although they then agreed to work toward a new Minsk-type agreement, there was no follow-up (Tass 2021).

Six weeks later, evidently in response to the latest Putin essay, Biden rushed $60 million of "largely defensive" weapons to Ukraine. He hoped that the move would deter but not be viewed as provocative by the Kremlin. Putin may have interpreted the new military strength of Ukraine forces as yet another reason for him to attack Ukraine on a larger scale.

AMERICAN RESPONSE TO RUSSIA'S THREATENED INVASION

Thanks to an account provided by five journalists, Biden Administration deliberations are now a matter of public record (Harris et al. 2022). Their narrative begins with a meeting of top officials during October 2021, when large-scale encampments of Russian troops began to increase in Belarus on Ukraine's northern border.

Biden's first question was about the accuracy of the intelligence about Russian intentions toward Ukraine since 190,000 to 250,000 Russian troops reportedly were poised for action on Ukraine's north (Adu 2022; Knight 2023: 33). He was informed that a large-scale invasion would occur, but nobody knew when the war would start. An initial decision was to dispatch two emissaries: (1) CIA Director William Burns flew to Moscow to warn that there would be "consequences" if Putin launched a war. (2) Director of National Intelligence Avril Haines went to NATO headquarters to share intelligence about the likelihood of war. From a policy standpoint, with the rules-based international order in mind, Biden eventually made the decision to help Ukraine defend itself while limiting the scope inside Ukraine to avoid a direct American confrontation with Russia. The initial intelligence consensus was that Ukraine would lose without outside assistance (Cohen 2023).

Just before Burns and Haines left Washington, Biden shared intelligence with Britain, France, and Germany at the G-20 Summit in Rome. In addition, Secretary of State Antony Blinken chatted with Ukraine's President Volodymyr Zelensky on the sidelines of the international summit on climate change in Glasgow, Scotland. The aim was to inform Zelensky that intelligence predicted inevitable war. To the apparent chagrin of Zelensky, Blinken evidently promised nothing more in support.

Biden telephoned Putin about the troop buildup on December 7, 2021, offering to negotiate a solution to Russia's objections to the location of NATO troops and weapons on Russia's borders within the Baltic states, Bulgaria, Poland, and Romania while giving assurance that Ukraine would stay out of NATO. He also warned Putin of "significant and severe economic harm" in the event of an attack (Talcott 2021). Two days later, Biden called Zelensky to assure him that the United States would respect Ukraine's sovereignty and try to bring a peaceful settlement to the Russian threat on its northern border, where Russian military encampments seemed poised for action (Williams and Zinets 2021).

As an intelligence leak later indicated, Washington had an asset in the Kremlin, relaying plans for the war (Reuters 2023). At the end of 2021, the United States decided to release more information about the Russian troop buildup along with scenarios of "false flag" operations that Russians might use to justify the invasion of Ukraine. However, the release of the "secret" information, aimed at deterring Putin, did not stop the war.

Despite Russia's objections to existing NATO capabilities close to its borders, the weapons supplied to NATO countries and Ukraine during 2021 were calibrated in Washington to be non-provocative to Russia. Meanwhile, Ukrainian officials in 2021 feared that high-level preparations for defense might provoke panic, thereby adversely impacting their economy. Modest American shipments of military support were to be part of a "non-provocation strategy," but they proved insufficient to deter Russia.

Next, Russia prepared treaties regarding NATO deployments to present to Deputy Secretary of State Wendy Sherman, who headed a delegation to meet with Russians in Geneva on January 10, 2022. Sherman rejected the treaty offers but agreed to negotiate a relocation of troops and weapons. The Russians were disappointed and did not agree to Sherman's counterproposal. The Biden Administration then sent more military forces to all six NATO countries bordering Russia as well as Hungary. While assuring Russia that no American troops would be deployed in Ukraine, a direct communication line was established between the Ukrainian military and the U.S. European Command, and Biden authorized another shipment of weapons, worth $200 million, to Ukraine (AP 2022d).

9 AMERICAN POLICIES TOWARD UKRAINE   205

Burns met Zelensky in Kyiv on January 12, 2022, warning that Russians wanted to seize the capital, had a plan to do so, and wanted to capture Zelensky personally. That was evidently the moment when Zelensky disclosed that Ukraine was determined to fight back. Hitherto, his plan had been to downplay the possibility of attack, thereby avoiding panic that might result in the chaos of a refugee outflux, while the Ukraine military quietly prepared.

On January 19, Blinken was in Kyiv telling Zelensky and his Defense Secretary, "We will support you whatever you want to do," evidently still believing that Zelensky might move the capital eastward. Based on inadequate intelligence about Ukrainian military capabilities, the Biden Administration predicted that Russia would achieve a quick victory. Fearing that the United States would make a deal with Russia after conquering Ukraine, Zelensky was determined to prepare for the role of commander-in-chief. Instead of all the posturing over the past months, Zelensky wanted a real deterrent—Ukraine's admission to the European Union and NATO. After all, Russia and Ukraine had been at war since 2014, and Zelensky had been asking for more military power for years (Ward and Forgey 2022).

That same day in January, Biden held a press conference, again issuing the warning that a major attack on Ukraine would result in "severe costs to the Russian economy" (Egan 2022). But he annoyed Zelensky when he said that the cost would be less in case of a smaller attack, hinting that NATO was not yet united on what to do.

On January 21, Blinken met Russian Foreign Minister Sergei Lavrov in Geneva. Blinken once again offered to discuss Russian security concerns in the region. Blinken reiterated that crippling sanctions would be applied very quickly if Ukraine were attacked, and massive NATO military support for Ukraine would then begin. Lavrov did not respond, giving the impression that war was indeed imminent.

British Defense Minister Ben Wallace went to Moscow on February 11 to ask his opposite number, Sergei Shoigu, whether Russia was willing to accept the diplomacy option. The answer was "No." Shoigu even lied, saying that no invasion was planned. On February 12, Biden telephoned Putin again, reiterating previous statements.

Dmitry Kozak, Putin's deputy chief of staff, meanwhile, tried to hammer out an agreement with Ukraine to avoid war. Although Ukraine had agreed to never join NATO, Putin wanted more concessions and scuttled the deal (Farberov 2022).

Six days later, the annual Munich Security Conference (February 18–20) convened virtually, with about 70 democratic countries in attendance. Biden's speech stressed that "American is back" as a friendly partner with countries around the world (Duclos 2021). He urged democracies to unite in response to challenges from China and Russia. At the end of the meeting, Biden privately telephoned leaders of several NATO countries, confiding that war was imminent in Ukraine.

Soon afterward, French President Emmanuel Macron called Putin, asking for a meeting that might resolve Russian concerns about NATO. Putin rebuffed Macron, saying casually that he would consult his advisers.

After the Munich conference, Ukraine's Foreign Minister Dmytro Kuleba flew to Washington, where he finally received definitive intelligence about Russia's plans to capture Kyiv. Ukraine then continued preparing for an attack with much better information. The first clue about a major war came on February 21, when the two easternmost provinces of Ukraine, mostly occupied by Russian forces, were declared independent countries by Vladimir Putin as the Donetsk People's Republic and the Luhansk People's Republic.

Russia Attacks Ukraine

At about 4 a.m. on February 24 (or 23, depending on the time zone), 2022, Russian troops entered the northern part of Ukraine, with one column headed for the capital city, Kyiv (Knight 2023: 33) and another headed from the Donbas toward Crimea (Gatopoulos and Fraser 2022). Prior to the attack, Russia controlled 7 percent of Ukraine's territory in the Donbas region (O'Hanlon et al. 2023). The aim was 100 percent control, arrest of the "Nazis," and installation of a puppet ruler. But instead of a quick victory, the initial attack was only the first of several phases of the war (cf. Harding 2023; cf. Knight 2023).

Phase One

Few Russian commanders on the ground were aware of the plan to capture Ukraine until only a few hours before the orders were issued, so their planning was hurried (Knight 2023: 33). When the war began, Putin's imperfect justification included such disinformation as that his "special military operation" was preemptive, since he claimed the United

States planned to attack Russia (Levin-Banchik 2022). Ukraine's continuing attempt to retake the Russian-occupied Donbas territories in eastern Ukraine provided another justification for Putin's attack on February 23/24. He discounted American military aid previously sent to Ukraine.

On February 27, Putin warned that nuclear weapons would be used if NATO "entered the war" and put them on "highest alert" (Meyer 2022). That prospect, which still bothers political scientist John Mearsheimer (2022b), appeared to vary from the Russian military doctrine, which has long specified that nuclear weapons would only be used in defense of the homeland, Russia's allies, and the nuclear stockpile (Buck 2022). On March 4, Russia took control of Ukraine's largest nuclear power plant (Gatopoulos and Fraser 2022).

Initially, Russia sent 150,000 troops (Agencias 2022), while the Ukrainian army had 200,000. The attack increased defense forces to 700,000, according to President Zelensky (2022). By mid-March, Russia controlled 22 percent of Ukraine (Ledur 2022).

Meanwhile, anti-war demonstrations emerged in 47 cities throughout Russia, though they were all brutally suppressed (Dixon 2022a). Russia alleged that the Central Intelligence Agency and NATO were responsible for the unrest (Stewart and Haigh 2022).

Even though Ukraine initially called for a "no-fly zone" over the country (Hughes 2022), Biden opposed Poland's offer to send military units and fighter jets to Ukraine as "too provocative" (DeLuce 2022). Biden presumed that such escalation would be a NATO threat to Russia. However, Turkey sent drones in March to assist Ukraine (Yackley 2022). Russia never achieved air dominance (VOA 2022). Ukrainian defensive capabilities proved adequate.

Nevertheless, Biden rushed 17,000 anti-tank weapons to Ukraine in a week (Sanger et al. 2022a). In the first month, a total of $3 billion in weapons went to Ukraine, causing panic among Russian soldiers (Debusmann 2022).

The United States also responded with sanctions, otherwise known as economic warfare. Soon after the February attack, major efforts were undertaken to bleed the Russian economy, nearly returning to the days in the Cold War when the Soviet Union was largely frozen out of the world economy (USITA 2022). In addition, tariffs on Russian aluminum increased by 200 percent (Harrell 2023). The United States soon began rounding up support for sanctions from NATO countries and allies elsewhere (Skrypchenko 2022). Sanctions did not hurt Putin personally, but

208   M. HAAS

initial sanctions banned most banking with Russia, trade with companies in nearly every economic sector, and personal sanctions were increasingly placed on political and business elites (Nakashima and Somnez 2022), reducing support from his selectorate of oligarchs (Knight 2023: 34). Although sanctions did not stop Russia's aggression, as Biden had hoped (Kantchev and Gershkovich 2023), they did mean that Russia had less cash to buy weapons abroad. Some American companies announced plans to leave Russia, and 211 did so, but 1,228 stayed, including Procter and Gamble (LRO 2023); fewer than 9 percent of European countries and G-7 countries withdrew (USG 2023). Sanctions did not disrupt the lives of most Russians, who could receive replacements for McDonald's and Starbucks to get hamburgers and coffee from other local merchants.

Although one American sanction was to cease sales of electronics to Russia, several economists later pointed out that the products of several technology companies could still be used. They recommended that the phones and operating systems should be shut off, in part because Russians were still using Android devices on the battlefield to communicate and coordinate attacks (Fedyk et al. 2022). Nevertheless, Ukraine was being assisted with far more advanced technology (Ignatius 2022a), thereby penetrating and exposing Russian military secrets (Zegart 2023).

Zelensky also urged the United States to designate Russia as a "state sponsor of terrorism," which would mean even stiffer sanctions. Moscow responded to Zelensky's plea by threatening to end diplomatic relations with Washington (Simon and Hanna 2022). Biden refused Zelensky's request (Cherner 2022; McCarthy 2022).

In March 2022, Ukrainian refugees began fleeing portions of the country under attack. Soon, about 8 million were internally displaced, and 6 million went to neighboring countries. One year later only 5.4 million were internally displaced, but 8 million had gone abroad, though some returned (Rodriguez and Batalova 2022; O'Hanlon et al. 2023; Sullivan 2023). The Biden Administration opened the door to admit a possible 100,000 as refugees, but the actual number accepted was close to 300,000 (Ainsley 2023; Sullivan 2023).

Phase Two

Within a few weeks, American and Russian prior intelligence was proved wrong (Menon 2023). Instead of a blitzkrieg for a quick surrender, the road to Kyiv was blocked when Ukrainian forces disrupted parts of the route, blowing up bridges and other access points. Meanwhile, Russian forces lacked the logistics to cope with the situation. Ukrainian troops, fighting for their country, have consistently outperformed much less enthusiastic Russian troops, even elite Russian forces (cf. Ju 2022; Horton 2023). Although not well understood at the time, guerrilla forces in Belarus also disrupted the northern supply route into Ukraine (AP 2023a).

The second phase involved a withdrawal of Russian troops from the north and redeployment into western and southern Ukraine, seeking to build a "land bridge" from Russia to Crimea (Atlamazoglou 2021). They soon seized about twice the territory captured in 2014. Although a Ukrainian missile destroyed the Black Sea flagship of the Russian fleet in mid-April (Lamothe et al. 2022), Russian forces won control of Ukraine's Black Sea port of Mariupol in May.

In response, President Volodymyr Zelensky declared that he was determined to fight back to reclaim sovereignty in the name of democracy. Biden then broadcast the aim of promoting democratic values, thereby countering the nihilistic propaganda war waged by the Kremlin about the Russian goal of "de-Nazification" of Ukraine (Snyder 2022). With bipartisan support, the Biden Administration then gradually began to escalate the supply of weapons to Ukraine, each time providing training for the Ukrainian military to use increasingly sophisticated weapons (DeYoung et al. 2022; AP 2023k; Lamothe 2023b).

In phase two, Biden's aim changed from initial ambiguity to providing only enough resources for Ukraine to defend itself; the goal of defeating Russia came in the next phase of the war. Biden once suggested that Putin should no longer rule Russia, though as a hope rather than a policy (Megerian 2022).

Soon after Ukraine recaptured a suburb of Kyiv, extensive evidence of war crimes emerged from the rubble (Hudson et al. 2022). Biden pinned the label "war criminal" on Putin within his call to mobilize worldwide support for Ukraine (Kelly and Gangitano 2022). American personnel were then assigned to document war crimes (Biesecker and Kinetz 2022; Hathaway 2023).

Phase Three

After Russia's seizure of southeastern Ukraine, thereby controlling 17 percent of the country (Ledur 2022), Ukraine began to take the offensive to recapture territories occupied by Russia during phase two (Vergun 2022; Arhirova and Karmanau 2022; Ritter and Kozlowska 2022; Cohen 2023). The Ukraine army utilized newly supplied weapons, including medium-range rocket systems, even attacking Crimea (Taylor et al. 2023).

As territories were recaptured, more war crimes were found. So many homes had been destroyed that refugees had no homes to reoccupy (Adler 2022).

A new American strategy emerged at the end of April 2022, when Defense Secretary Lloyd Austin said, "We want to see Russia weakened to the degree that it can't do the kinds of things that it has done in invading Ukraine" (Bertrand et al. 2022). Rather than a status quo ante, the policy changed to one of supporting total victory for Ukraine. Finland and Sweden then applied for NATO membership in mid-May.

Putin evidently took Austin's remark quite seriously, confirming his suspicion that NATO was using the Ukraine conflict to advance the ultimate aim of destroying Russia. Then on June 2, Putin released a six-page document detailing conditions under which he would use nuclear weapons (Putin 2022). For Putin, the expansion of NATO was evidently a red line that the West had already crossed (Carbonaro 2022). His concept of "deterrence" appeared to justify the initial preemptive strike and possible more in the future.

Public opinion was increasingly favorable to Ukraine around the world (Gramlich 2023). Tangible support came in the form of enforcing sanctions and in some cases supplying weapons.

In July, due to Russian control of the Black Sea, Ukrainian wheat was unable to be shipped to relieve hunger in Africa and elsewhere. UN Secretary-General Antonio Guterres soon raised an alarm. Turkey then mediated an agreement between Russia and Ukraine to allow grain shipments in July (WSJ 2022b). Both Russian and Ukrainian grain were included in the deal, which was at first extended in 2023 for another year but later stopped (AP 2023e).

Meanwhile, other elements of the Ukrainian economy were being damaged by the Russian embargo. Washington responded by spending billions to help the Ukraine government to pay monthly bills (Summers et al. 2023).

By mid-August 2022, more than $10 billion in American weapons had been sent to Ukraine (Mitchell 2022). American naval vessels had entered the Black Sea.

Nevertheless, after six months of fighting, Zelensky hinted that he would accept neutralization of Ukraine (Visser 2022). Russia was uninterested (Freedman 2022).

In August, the Ukrainian army advanced toward recapturing the country's largest nuclear power plant, which had been seized by Russian troops. Concern emerged about whether there would be an explosion by stray bullets (Gatopoulos and Fraser 2022). UN Secretary-General António Guterres and officials from the International Atomic Energy Agency then visited the site, urging demilitarization (Arhirova 2022). The United States agreed. But Russia was determined to hold onto the site, which was not generating power, and installed multiple rocket launchers and "protective structures" (Reuters 2022; Castillo 2022). China and Russia blocked a UN Security Council resolution to neutralize the site.

Turkey's Prime Minister Tayyip Erdogan had tried to start peace negotiations in March, but now Guterres and Turkey served as mediators. As a bargaining chip, Turkey offered to rebuild Ukraine's infrastructure. Zelensky asked Guterres to recall Ukrainians deported to Russia during the war as well as to release Ukrainians captured by Russian forces. When Secretary of State Blinken announced in mid-2022 that he was seeking an exchange of prisoners held in both countries unrelated to Ukraine, his counterpart Lavrov protested that negotiations should involve quiet diplomacy (DeYoung 2022).

Although European countries were initially slow to provide economic aid (Stein 2022; O'Hanlon et al. 2023), weapons were then being supplied by every European country except for Albania, Austria, Bosnia, Hungary, Ireland, Kosovo, and Moldova (Castellum 2023). Meanwhile, Egypt, Israel, and South Korea were initially reluctant to do so despite their receipt of billions of dollars in American military assistance (Bulow et al. 2023).

In addition, Australia, the European Union, Japan, South Korea, Switzerland, and Taiwan supported a total of about 9,500 economic sanctions on Russia. The total sanctions imposed by the United States was 1,948 (Al Jazeera 2022; Arhirova 2023b; Statistica 2023b; Castellum 2023).

Prominent countries that have not sided with Ukraine include Brazil, China, India, Saudi Arabia, and South Africa. The issue was too remote

212   M. HAAS

for African, Latin American, and Southeast Asian countries to sign on. Russian messaging has evidently worked there in portraying the conflict as NATO aggression (Harrell 2023).

Phase Four

Starting in September, Russia tried to consolidate victories, holding "plebiscites" in Donetsk and Luhansk, two regions previously occupied, as well as Kherson and Zaporizhia, two more recently Russian-controlled provinces in southeastern Ukraine (Dixon 2022b). After the "vote" favored annexation with Russia, Putin proceeded to annex the areas as part of Russia (Arhirova et al. 2022). In October 2022, the UN General Assembly rejected Russia's recent "referenda" to annex four territories of Ukraine, then occupied by Russian forces, by a vote of 143-5-35.

Putin also called up 300,000 "reservists" and retired soldiers to fight, provoking widespread domestic protests (Dixon 2022c), which stopped after police crackdowns and promises not to use new recruits at the battlefront (Ilyushina 2022a). Despite the Kremlin's propaganda effort to declare victory, some Russians remained firmly opposed.

On the same day as Putin's "reserve" call-up announcement, Saudi Arabian and Turkish efforts at mediation were announced. Russia released several prisoners, including two American volunteers (Ritter 2022), which one Russian officer identified as "sabotage" (AP 2022c). In exchange, Ukraine returned Russian prisoners.

Another war crime, however, was not mentioned in public discussions: Putin authorized a mercenary group known as the Wagner Group to assist the Russian army, contributing about 10,000 troops (BBC 2023b), contrary to the International Convention against the Recruitment, Use, Financing and Training of Mercenaries of 1989.

Russia's extension of its border to include four Ukrainian provinces plus Crimea meant that any further Ukrainian military action would be against "Russian territory," where he soon declared martial law. Then on September 21, Putin again threatened weapons of mass destruction, including biological, chemical, and nuclear weapons. Although he was trying to deter the West (Dixon et al. 2022), Western countries considered them bluffs, and Washington imposed more sanctions, warning that more were likely (Borger et al. 2022; Abutaleb 2022). China and India firmly opposed any use of nuclear weapons by Russia (India Today 2023). New Russian recruits were not immediately deployed because they had to endure training while Russian commanders planned how to use them.

Aware of Moscow's declining position, North Korea sold artillery shells from its stockpile, and Egypt once secretly planned to manufacture and ship rockets to Russia (AP 2022b; Hill et al. 2023). Russian recruiters went to Afghanistan in order to recruit American-trained Afghan soldiers, more than 20,000 of whom live precariously due to their roles in the war against the Taliban (Condon 2022). Iran provided drones (Warrick et al. 2022). China, despite condemning NATO actions, continued to maintain neutrality (Appel 2022; Mehrotra 2023).

Whether the influx of new troops would make any difference sparked skepticism, as problems of poor command capabilities, logistics, troop morale, war clothing, and weapons supply were likely to continue (Beevor 2022; Freedman 2022). Of the 250,000 troops deployed by Moscow during 2022 (Adu 2022), constituting 97 percent of the Russian army (Khurshudyan et al. 2023), some 200,000 casualties (dead and wounded) were estimated, whereas Ukrainian casualties were about 120,000 and civilian deaths amounted to 30,000 (France24 2023; Ilyushina 2023; Khurshudyan et al. 2023).

Putin's public actions, therefore, contradicted the propaganda that Russia was winning the war. In response to his partial draft, cars lined up driving out of the country, and a torrent of flights were booked for foreign destinations. An estimated 250,000 departed for adjacent countries in the new two weeks (i24 2022; Kolesnikov 2022) and at least 500,000 by the end of the year (Ebel and Ilyushina 2023).

One reason for Ukraine's success is the way Zelensky mobilized a nation to fight with gusto. Ever since 2014, American personnel stationed at NATO bases in Germany had been training Ukrainian soldiers on how to use new weapons as well as how to conduct guerrilla war against parts of Ukraine already seized by Russia (Garamone 2022). Another factor, less well understood, is that the war for democracy attracted hundreds of thousands of volunteers from other countries (Judah 2023). Although some Americans volunteers were captured, no Russian escalation resulted (Hallam and Regan 2022). A new Ukrainian nonprofit, the Come Back Alive Foundation, provided $163.5 military equipment and services directly to the Ukrainian army during the first year of the war, bypassing the defense bureaucracy in Kyiv (Beliakova and Metz 2023).

In September, Washington agreed to send Abrams tanks, six months earlier than previously planned (Lamothe et al. 2022c; Lamothe 2023c),

214   M. HAAS

though Biden still refused to respond to Zelensky's request for long-range missiles, fearing that Russia would regard the move as unacceptable NATO escalation (Sanger et al. 2022b). But Baltic countries and Poland disagreed, awaiting approval from Washington to send considerably more military assistance (Blann 2023c). Yet if Biden approved, sending those weapons might be viewed in the Kremlin as a provocative NATO-level decision; allowing the Baltics and Poland to do so on their own might not.

However, Republicans in the House of Representatives after the November 2022 elections appeared reluctant to appropriate funds for what might become another "endless war." Biden then urged Zelensky to make headline gains (Abultaleb and Hudson 2023).

Battles revealed that the Russian army was far less eager to fight, had poor logistics, and out-of-date military supplies that were likely to run out at some point (Arkin 2022). Russia's top-down strategic military left little opportunity for tactical adjustments on the war front. Some Russian troops even tried to sell their weapons on the black market (Power 2023: 24). Russia lacked competent noncommissioned officers and much more, so Ukrainian forces blitzkrieged to overtake unsuspecting Russian forces (Khurshudyan et al. 2022).

Ukrainian forces reclaimed the Black Sea port town of Kharkiv in September (Lamothe et al. 2022b). And they were advancing to retake the northern city of Kherson in November (Ledur 2022).

Phase Five

The fifth phase began in October. Ukraine was progressing toward possible complete victory due to higher morale in the army and more precise weaponry (Zagorodnyuk 2022). More than one-third of the Russian territory gained in previous attacks was recovered (O'Hanlon et al. 2023).

After an explosion on the Crimea bridge, Russia dramatically launched attacks on Ukrainian cities, hospitals, power stations, and residences as if carrying out a genocidal goal of extermination that would return the country's economy to agriculture (Ryan et al. 2022). The aim was to make the country bankrupt and uninhabitable as winter approached. Putin possibly hoped that more refugees would leave Ukraine. Nevertheless, he finally indicated that no nuclear weapons would be used in Ukraine (AP 2022a).

9 AMERICAN POLICIES TOWARD UKRAINE 215

Regardless of Putin's attempt to terrorize the country, 70 percent of Ukrainians in an October poll wanted to continue fighting until Russians are kicked out of the country, and 94 percent were confident that their armed forces could do so (Sands and Jeong 2022). Support lagged in the east and south, accounting for the 26 percent who preferred a peace agreement to stop the war.

Then Putin made a surprise announcement on October 20 that he had no desire to use nuclear weapons in Ukraine, though he would do so to defend Russia itself (AP 2022a). Having declared that five provinces, including Crimea, are now part of Russia, his remarks were unclear whether his "defense of Russia" included the five provinces annexed from Ukraine. His announcement was timed with the departure of British Prime Minister Liz Truss, whom he accused of being eager to use nuclear weapons, again claiming that the West sought global supremacy. Putin also said that he was open to diplomacy (Ignatius 2022b).

In November, Chief of Staff General Mark Milley declared that a continual ground war would repeat the carnage of World War I; he said that peace talks were needed (Zubok 2022). Whether Russia would negotiate peace while losing due to Ukrainian advances remained a puzzle (Posen 2023). Putin's message at the end of 2022 was that he, not Zelensky, favored peace negotiations, but of course on his own terms (Gans 2022).

In early December, Ukraine launched missile attacks inside Russia with no strong backlash from Russia (Stein et al. 2022). Washington then finally decided to send expensive Patriot Missiles that might reach inside Russia (AP 2023c). Although the Defense Department predicted that training to use the weapons would take several months, Ukrainians proved to be fast learners and were soon operating the missiles (Lamothe et al. 2022a; AP 2023i; Cohen 2023).

Ukraine's president Zelensky promised to continue fighting until recovering all territory lost in 2014 and earlier in 2022; his occasion for the announcement was a personal address to Congress in late December 2022 (Wilkinson et al. 2022). His main goals in flying to Washington were to answer American critics of aid as well as to encourage increased shipments of more up-to-date armaments (DeYoung et al. 2022), including tanks and missiles.

As winter 2023 approached, Putin threatened to cut off supplies of gas and grains to Europe (Ilyushina 2022b). The European Union instead organized an energy plan, including increased use of renewables, to

216   M. HAAS

become entirely independent of Russian sources (Cooban 2022; BBC 2023b). During all 2022, Ukraine received $113 billion in economic, humanitarian, and military assistance (Freking 2023).

Phase Six

Russian winter weather stopped Napoléon and Hitler, so winter 2023 was expected to slow down the war. But the winter was mild. Russia was caught in a winter stalemate, while Ukraine had the advantage of fighting on home turf (Beevor 2022). Russian forces were concentrated in the southeastern part of the country, with 320,000 Russian troops opposing 200,000 active Ukrainian forces along a 600-mile front (Ledur et al. 2023; Statistica 2023a).

When 2023 began, Putin replaced the commander of Russian forces in Ukraine, General Sergei Surovikin, who previously commanded Russian forces in Syria (Knight 2023: 34). Clearly, he was upset that his plans for annexation had been foiled (AP 2023j).

Biden's limit on offensive weapons lessened in January 2023, when longer-range missiles and tanks were first pledged (Jakes and Erlanger 2023; Jordans and Grieshaber 2023; AP 2023k). But shipments arrived very slowly (O'Grady et al. 2023). Ukraine still wanted long-range missiles and jet fighter planes, which Washington considered as too escalatory during 2022. However, the option remains that F-16 jets would be sent for a long-term war, particularly if China were to send military aid to Russia (Karanth 2023).

Another surge of Russian aerial attacks occurred in February (AP 2023d). But Ukrainians shot down most drones and missiles and restored power stations while also relying on donations of generators and transformers (King 2023).

Attacks on Crimea continued right up to the first anniversary of the war and beyond (Taylor et al. 2023). Ukraine's apparent strategy was to recover the Russian occupation territories beyond Donbas, thereby letting Crimea fall like an apple from a loaded tree.

In February, the United Arab Emirates mediated a swap that returned 63 Russian soldiers and presumably a similar number of Ukrainians (AP 2023f). As usual, most of those exchanged were suffering from serious illnesses.

In late February, Biden bravely visited Zelensky in Kyiv and then went to Poland to make an address, celebrating NATO's efforts to support

Ukraine. The next day he met the Bucharest 9 (Bulgaria, the Czech Republic, Estonia, Hungary, Latvia, Lithuania, Poland, Romania and Slovakia), which impressed him with the need to take a much harder line and supply maximum possible weapons to Ukraine. Formed after Russia's annexation of Crimea, the Bucharest 9 expressed determination and increased readiness to defend countries bordering on Russia (TVP 2023).

Meanwhile, Putin decided to announce that Russia was suspending cooperation but not compliance with the New Strategic Arms Reduction (START) Treaty, and was prepared to deploy a newly developed nuclear missile (RS-28 Sarmat) to defend Russia, which he believed was already under attack (Falconbridge 2023). His "suspension," interpreted as a bluff, was condemned by Biden (Wilkinson 2023). Meanwhile, Ukrainian drones were hitting targets inside Russia, even forcing a closure of the air space over St. Petersburg (Blann 2023a), but made a point that no American weapons were launched at Russia.

On the first anniversary of the war, protests emerged again in Russia (Ilyushina et al. 2023; Knight 2023: 34–35). Later in March, Putin appeared to copycat Biden by helicoptering to the port city of Mariupol at night to declare victory in a two-day tour of the previously carved-out territory between Donbas and Crimea (Ilyushina 2023).

Also on the anniversary of the start of the war, China proposed a peace plan, though Zelensky also had a plan of his own, and Biden reacted that Beijing's plan was tilted toward Russia (Dutton 2023). Although China sent thousands of M16s as "hunting rifles" as a token gift to Moscow (First Post 2023), the balance of power was clearly in Beijing, which could assist Russia massively and turn the tide of the war. Russian exports of crude oil to China increased by 44 percent and natural gas doubled during the first year of the war, while Chinese exports to Russia increased by almost 13 percent (Ebel and Kuom 2023).

Thanks to the mobilization of support for Ukraine, the UN General Assembly passed a resolution on February 23, 2023, calling for an immediate end to the war and the withdrawal of Russian forces from Crimea (UNGA 2023). The vote was 141 in favor, 7 against (Belarus, Eritrea, Mali, Nicaragua, North Korea, Russia, Syria) and 32 abstentions (including China, India, Pakistan). The resolution also called for the prosecution of war crimes and empowered the General Secretary to pursue the impact of the war on such matters as energy, the environment, finance, food security, as well as nuclear security and safety. Secretary-General

António Guterres identified a lot of human rights violations that had been compiled by the UN Human Rights Council (Keaten 2023b).

In March 2023, the International Criminal Court issued an arrest warrant for Putin, holding him personally responsible for "attacks on civilians and energy-related infrastructure, willful killings, unlawful confinement, torture, rape and other sexual violence, as well as unlawful transfers and deportations of children." At least 1,400 Ukrainian children had been kidnapped from their parents and sent to Russia for "re-education" (Picheta and Said-Moorhouse 2023; Freking 2023). Maria Lvova-Belova was also indicted for her role in managing the relocation program for children.

Russian troops tried to claim towns along the 160-mile arc from Donbas to Crimea but stalled in trying to capture Avdiivka, Bakhmut, Kupiansk, Lyman, and Soledar during winter months (Meldrum 2023; Kullab and Karmanau 2023; Blann 2023b; Santora et al. 2023). Ukrainian forces had decided to dig in to deprive Putin of any possible success.

Finland became a member of NATO in March 2023, evidently prompting Putin to announce that he would locate nuclear weapons in Belarus (Masih et al. 2023; Ritter 2023). Another pretext was Britain's decision to provide Ukraine with ammunition capable of piercing armor that had amounts of depleted uranium. Putin may also have reacted to damage inflicted by a Ukrainian drone on a residential building 110 miles south of Moscow. Zelensky then asked the UN Security Council to discuss the nuclear threat, though Moscow justified the move as similar to American bases with nuclear weapons in Germany and Turkey.

Fortunately, when a Russian warplane downed an American spy drone in the international airspace over the Black Sea, the matter was resolved quickly in March (AP 2023j). An earlier American drone had been intercepted the previous month, and a British spy aircraft was nearly shot down by a Russian missile in September 2022, though kept secret until a document leak (Lamothe 2023a).

By the end of winter, Ukraine had engaged in 300 shellings inside Russia by artillery and missiles as well as 27 drone attacks (Chen and Ilyushina 2023). One such attack killed about 300 Russians in a military base (Knight 2023: 35). Moscow was again caught bluffing, failing to carry out the threat to unleash weapons of mass destruction. Phase six, in short, was a period of relative stalemate (Khurshudyan et al. 2023).

9 AMERICAN POLICIES TOWARD UKRAINE 219

Phase Seven

The seventh phase had yet to unravel. After a wet April, with temperatures about the same as New York, springtime offensives were presumably planned by both sides to begin in the second week of May (AP 2023l; Menon 2023; Posen 2023), but the uncertainty was on full display. The question was which side had the most military power to prevail. Lacking sufficient air support, Ukraine was to face considerable challenge while facing landmines and trenches that would block any advance.

Ukraine was determined to push forward with 1,550 armed tanks and 30,000 troops Responding to depletion of Ukrainian ammunition and weapons of warfare, the United States sent air defense weapons, anti-tank weapons, howitzers, High Mobility Artillery Rock Systems (HIMARS), as well as infantry vehicles and tanks, bringing the total then allocated to $33 billion (Knight 2023: 33). Patriot missiles, which cost $4 million per missile, finally arrived (AP 2023c). NATO was supplying more advanced technology than Moscow's army (Massicot 2023, AP 2023h). But pessimism arose because Ukrainian troops, only a few of whom had prior combat experience, were hoping to receive sufficient replacements of artillery shells and mortar bombs (Khurshudyan et al. 2023). The Czech Republic, Poland, and Slovakia decided to send about a dozen MiG-29 fighter jets despite having been previously discouraged by Biden to do so (AP 2023g; Ritter and Hazell 2023). Russia, having trained new recruits, decided to return to bombing of Ukraine cities after an interval of two months, but still had no unified command over various paramilitary units (Rose et al. 2023).

Because NATO countries share military intelligence and ship weapons to Ukraine (Ritter and Hazell 2023), Putin realized that he was actually confronting NATO and therefore sought support from China. But after Chinese leader Xi Jinping visited Moscow in April, Beijing pledged not to do so (AP 2023b). After the first communication between Zelensky and Xi Jinping on April 26, China decided to play a constructive intermediate role (Khurshudyan and Shepherd 2023).

While Russia continued to bomb infrastructure, Ukrainians had been quickly restoring electricity grids damaged by Russian attacks. By mid-April 2023, Ukraine amazingly resumed the export of electricity (Kullab 2023).

When evidence emerged in mid-April that a 21-year-old National Guard technician posted secret information on the Internet, there was apprehension whether Russia would learn detailed assessments of Ukrainian military units, including their weaponry and deployment. With information about where Ukraine was positioning tanks, Russians could design countermeasures. But by then the information was outdated (McManus 2023). What was most damaging from the leaked documents was the pessimism of the Biden Administration over prospects for Ukraine's "spring offensive," an observation that might discourage other countries from providing support. In due course, as Ukraine discovered how Russian troops had solidified their lines, the "spring offensive" became a protracted summer offensive.

American public support for Ukraine also declined (McManus 2023). Following Trump, more Republicans were claiming that the defense of Ukraine was not in the American national interest (Haltiwanger 2023). By midsummer 2023, $43 billion had been sent in military aid, with an additional $17 billion in nonmilitary assistance (Mellen and Galocha 2023).

Both Russia and Ukraine took time to celebrate Easter Sunday. In observance, there was a prisoner swap involving 130 Ukrainians and presumably the same number of Russians (Arhirova 2023a, 2023c).

The conflict appeared to be a war of attrition that could last a decade, giving rise to calls for diplomacy (Haass and Kupchan 2023). At the end of April, Pope Francis unveiled a peace mission, with a priority on returning children forcibly removed from Ukraine (Winfield 2023).

Yet both Russia and Ukraine were not yet exhausted, believing that their victory was inevitable. In such cases, the war ends when one or both sides are exhausted. Dramatic possibilities exist for the second year and beyond. But the next task herein is to assess which policy options the Biden Administration chose and why.

Options Assessment

Whether the Ukraine situation will head toward escalation or a negotiated settlement is currently unfathomable. What can be done is to summarize policy options considered by the Biden Administration as of May 1, 2023, when both armies were hoping for a successful spring offensive (Table 9.4). More details on each option appear in an appendix to the chapter.

9 AMERICAN POLICIES TOWARD UKRAINE   221

Table 9.4   Policy Options of the United States Toward Ukraine in 2023

Option	Content of Option
1	Stop aiding Ukraine
2	Support Ukraine's request to join NATO
3	Support Ukraine with intelligence about Russia
4	Support Ukraine with more defensive military weapons
5	Support Ukraine with jet airplanes and long-range missiles
6	Support Ukraine with U.S. naval vessels in the Black Sea
7	Send American combat troops to fight for Ukraine
8	Train Ukraine troops outside of Ukraine
9	Apply heavy economic sanctions on Russia gradually
10	Threaten to permanently weaken Russian power
11	Seek to undermine Putin
12	Take measures to encourage Russians to revolt
13	Encourage NATO allies and other countries to support Ukraine
14	Accept Ukrainian refugees as immigrants
15	Demand war crimes trial of Putin and Russian soldiers
16	Support diplomacy to end the war
17	Agree to an end to the war that establishes a status quo ante
18	Support Ukraine to achieve total victory
19	Support neutralization of the large Ukrainian nuclear power plant
20	Designate Russia as a "state sponsor of terrorism"

Unlike previous presidents, Joe Biden has maintained high-level control of American foreign policy goals, consigning his National Security Adviser and Secretary of State to subordinate roles. According to Joe Biden's operational code, prestige elements almost outflank his pursuit of power for the United States in the world, provided that measures taken are feasible bureaucratically, economically, and militarily. His lesser concern for economic elements risked electoral disaster in 2022 due to inflation, which was in part a result of his policy toward Ukraine (Caldara et al. 2022). His strong moral views about the "soul of America" are a centerpiece of his operational code, resulting in firm support for Ukraine. Nevertheless, the most cautious element among his options was that the level of weaponry sent to Ukraine was chosen to avoid escalating the conflict, thereby frustrating Zelensky. However, whenever Russia escalated, such as by massive bombing of civilian targets, Biden increased the level of weapons sent to Ukraine.

Biden's operational code is identified by weights on the criteria in Tables 9.3 and 9.5 (High, Medium, or Low). Judgments appearing in the other columns in Table 9.5 represent the degrees to which Biden appears to rate each option on the criteria (Excellent, Very Good, Good, Fair, Poor, Unacceptable).

Applying his weights, High priority is assigned to deterrence, power balancing, upholding the American economy, building international institutions, abiding by international law, strengthening democracy, and ensuring that objectives match resources. Low priorities are increasing American power, achieving a freer domestic and world economy, and paying attention to civil society (pressure groups, political parties, and media). All other criteria have Medium weights.

Based on assessments of how well each option fulfills the 15 subcriteria of power, wealth, prestige, and feasibility (Table 9.5), the top choice appears as Option 13 (Encouraging NATO allies and other countries to support Ukraine), evidently because the only cost was diplomatic. The second most popular option is the unfulfilled goal of neutralizing Ukraine's large nuclear plant from the war (#19). Next comes sending defensive military weapons to Ukraine (Option #4), followed by the promise to support Ukraine's goal of total victory (Option #18). Yet the cost of American military support for Ukraine is only 5 percent of the Pentagon's budget (Kaplan 2023: 22).

The fifth choice, in accordance with Biden's operational code, may be surprising—the decision to admit Ukraine to NATO (#2). Ukraine formally applied for NATO membership at the end of September 2022 (Balmforth 2022), and NATO's Secretary General now openly says that Ukraine will eventually join (Sabbagh and Rankin 2023). However, Biden's support for Ukraine has been so substantial that Ukraine became a de facto member of NATO in 2022. The next priority is the demand for war crimes trials of Putin and Russian soldiers (#15).

The two following options were tied: Applying heavy economic sanctions on Russia (#9), and training Ukrainian troops outside the country (#8). Next came American naval vessels in the Black Sea, a symbolic move to counter Russia's blockade of Ukrainian harbors (#6).

Tied for positions 9 and 10 were two quite different options: One was to supply American intelligence to the Ukrainian army (#3), which ended up having more on-the-ground intelligence in close proximity to Russian armed forces. Sending American jets (#5), however, was a tantalizing option; but when Putin threatened nuclear retaliation, Biden did not proceed. Jets were approved after the spring and summer stalemates frustrated Ukrainian progress.

Table 9.5 Matrix of Criteria and Subcriteria of Ukraine Decision-Making with Options Assessments

Criteria	Subcriteria	Weight	1	2	3	4	5	6	7	8	9	10
Power	Deter adversary	High	U	P	F	V	F	G	V	P	V	P
	Balance power	High	U	G	F	E	V	V	G	P	V	P
	Maintain power	Medium	P	F	F	V	G	G	G	F	V	F
	Increase power	Low	P	G	F	V	V	G	G	P	V	P
Wealth	Benefits > costs	Medium	F	G	V	V	V	F	P	G	G	G
	Free economy	Low	P	P	P	P	P	P	P	P	P	P
	Increase prosperity	High	P	P	P	P	P	P	P	P	P	P
Prestige	Build institutions	High	U	V	F	F	F	F	G	P	F	P
	Obey natl/intnatl law	High	G	F	G	G	F	G	P	P	F	P
	Favor democracies	High	U	E	E	E	E	E	E	G	V	G
Feasibility	Resource estimate	High	E	E	V	G	G	V	G	V	V	V
	Satisfy civil society	Low	F	G	P	F	E	P	U	P	P	P
	Satisfy selectorate	Medium	U	V	V	G	F	G	F	V	G	V
	Information adequacy	High	E	G	G	G	G	V	P	G	G	G
	Satisfy psych needs	Medium	U	E	E	V	G	G	U	V	E	V
Score			2.7	6.1	5.5	6.5	5.5	5.7	4.3	6	6	4.1
Rank			18	5	9.5	3	9.5	8	16	6.5	6.5	17

(continued)

Table 9.5 (continued)

Criteria	Subcriteria	Weight	11	12	13	14	15	16	17	18	19	20
Power	Deter adversary	High	F	G	E	P	G	F	P	E	E	U
	Balance power	High	G	V	V	P	G	F	G	E	V	E
	Maintain power	Medium	G	G	V	P	G	G	F	V	F	V
	Increase power	Low	F	G	V	P	V	E	P	V	F	G
Wealth	Benefits > costs	Medium	F	G	E	G	C	F	G	F	E	U
	Free economy	Low	P	P	P	P	P	P	P	P	P	U
	Increase prosperity	Low	P	P	P	F	P	P	G	P	P	P
Prestige	Build institutions	High	P	P	V	G	V	V	F	V	E	U
	Obey natl/internatl law	High	P	P	G	V	V	V	G	F	E	F
	Favor democracies	High	E	E	E	V	V	V	G	E	E	P
Feasibility	Resource estimate	High	P	P	G	G	F	F	F	G	F	F
	Satisfy civil society	Low	F	P	F	P	G	G	G	P	F	V
	Satisfy selectorate	Medium	G	V	V	F	G	V	G	G	G	P
	Information adequacy	High	P	P	G	P	P	P	P	F	F	F
	Satisfy psych needs	Medium	E	E	E	V	E	E	F	V	G	G
Score			4.4	4.9	7.1	4.4	6	5.4	4.5	6.3	6.9	3.7
Rank			14.5	12	1	14.5	6	11	13	4	2	17

The least desirable policies were to stop aiding Ukraine (Option #1) and declaring Russia a "state sponsor of terrorism" (#20). Also unacceptable were the options of seeking to undermine Putin domestically and sending American troops to Ukraine (Options #10 and #7). Ratings may shift later during 2023, however.

The nuclear option is not included among the options because most observers believe that the option would never emerge despite Putin's repeated threats (Talmadge 2022). Should Russia's partial mobilization fail, Putin is determined to win in what he considers a war against Western efforts to demote his country's international status (Stanovaya 2022). Were Russia to use nuclear weapons, one of Biden's likely responses would be to ask American and NATO troops to enter the war, ultimately dooming Putin's goals and tenure in office (Zagorodnyuk 2022). Zelensky's request for a no-fly zone might finally be honored if a Russian "dirty bomb" or tactical nuclear weapon were unleashed, but Ukraine has enough land-to-air missiles that Russia no longer has air superiority.

Nevertheless, the war has gone through several phases, so the matrix changed over time. During Phase One, Option #1 had a very high score because judgments regarding power subcriteria were considerably higher. In Phase Two, feasibility judgments increased. Biden increased his emphasis on democracy and war crimes during Phase Three. During Phase Four, Biden increased judgments regarding the dispatch of much heavier weapons. Problems of domestic support for the war emerged in Phase Five. Table 9.5 represents Phases Six and Seven.

CONCLUSION

Other options are possible. For example, to end the war, after consulting with Vladimir Putin, one proposed peace agreement contains the following: (1) Redo elections of annexed regions under UN supervision. (2) Keep Crimea formally part of Russia. (3) Assure water supply to Crimea. (4) Neutralization of Ukraine (Boot 2022). None were deemed feasible by October 1, 2022, when Ukraine was liberating areas formerly occupied by Russian troops. The proposal came from Elon Musk, who is not taken seriously in Washington.

The chapter has applied the concept of operational code to a set of decision options, presuming to reflect the internal decision-making of President Joe Biden. If his foreign policy advisers had been allowed to use Decision Pad before he finalized his primary decision to back Ukraine,

226   M. HAAS

then the selectorate subcriterion weight might have been High rather than Medium. When such a change was performed, however, only four options were affected: Jet planes dropped by two ranks; threats to weaken Russian power and support for diplomacy decreased by one rank; and acceptance of Ukrainian refugees increased by one rank. In other words, his advisers appeared more cautious about sending jet planes, more skeptical of diplomacy and idle threats to weaken Russia, but more accepting of Ukrainian refugees. A similar exercise in autumn 2023 might find different Biden weights on the criteria. Wisdom always emerges after the fact.

APPENDIX: AMERICAN POLICY OPTIONS FOR UKRAINE

Scenario 1: *Stop aiding Ukraine.* When Russia initially posted troops along the northern border of Ukraine, the United States tried diplomacy to prevent war and threatened only sanctions, not military support. One option was to allow Russia to win if Ukraine could not defend itself. That option always remains, though now very unlikely, since Biden lauds Ukraine as a democracy.

Scenario 2: *Support Ukraine's request and join NATO.* Ukrainian President Zelensky frequently expressed a desire to join the European Union and NATO. Believing that such a move was provocative, the United States indicated that the option was open but did not take positive steps in that direction. However, the option remains a possible bargaining chip to end the war.

Scenario 3: *Support Ukraine with intelligence about Russia.* Initially, the United States did not share much intelligence with Ukraine, fearing that Soviet moles would get hold of the information. Just before the Russian attack, the intel was widely shared with Ukraine and would likely continue as long as the war proceeded.

Scenario 4: *Support Ukraine with more defensive military weapons.* Congress voted some military weapons, and Biden had some gradually shipped after Russia began a military buildup north of Ukraine. Zelensky kept asking for more weapons before and after the attack on February 24. However, Biden denied Zelensky's request for high-level weaponry until Russia escalated destruction. Republicans gained control of the House of Representatives after the November 2022 elections, and they might vote to withhold more funding for expensive weapons, so the future of the scenario is uncertain.

Scenario 5: *Support Ukraine with jet airplanes and long-range missiles.* Ukraine's leader has complained that he wants more weapons to defeat Russia and retake lost territories. The United States has been sending high-quality weapons, but during the first year opposed jet aircraft and long-range missiles as escalatory. In response, Russia threatened tactical nuclear weapons. But adjacent countries decided to do so outside of a NATO consensus.

Scenario 6: *Support Ukraine with U.S. naval vessels in the Black Sea.* American naval ships were not in the Black Sea before the war began, giving Russia an opportunity to attack southern Ukraine. To the chagrin of Putin, some ships of the American Sixth Fleet returned in November 2021 to "international waters," but American naval ships will inevitably cross the paths of the Russian Navy, leading to a possible escalation. Nevertheless, Russia gave Ukraine an opportunity to ship wheat from Odessa due to UN pressure. Ukraine captured Snake Island in the Black Sea, frustrating Putin. The probability of American seapower to enter the conflict is as low as airpower and landpower.

Scenario 7: *Send American combat troops to fight for Ukraine.* Biden has repeatedly said that no American troop units would be sent to Ukraine. Russia would consider such a move to be an escalation, justifying a nuclear response. Nevertheless, American volunteers are present in Ukraine, and two American volunteers reportedly were captured by Russian-backed separatists in Donetsk in June 2022. The probability of sending entire units is low.

Scenario 8: *Train Ukraine troops outside of Ukraine.* Sophisticated weapons sent by Washington and its allies can only be operated by Ukrainian troops after training. The United States has sent trainers to Germany for that purpose and will continue to do so. The probability is high.

Scenario 9: *Apply heavy economic sanctions on Russia gradually.* As Biden warned before February 24, sanctions were applied on Russian personnel and the Russian economy after the attack. They were imposed slowly so that the effects would creep up, but the aim was to uncouple Russia from the world economy, causing inflation inside Russia. Getting Western Europe, particularly Germany, to join an embargo on Russian gas and oil was difficult at first but succeeded (BBB 2023a). World food and gas prices increased, resulting in inflation. Although the Republican Party was eager to use inflation as a campaign issue in the 2022 midterm elections, gas prices decreased slowly throughout the summer and fall. Most Republicans voted to support Biden's Ukraine policy, so maintaining sanctions is highly likely until the war ends.

Scenario 10: *Threaten to permanently weaken Russian power.* When war becomes a stalemate between both sides, the eventual loser is the one that runs out of ammunition or the will to fight. In midsummer 2022, Defense Secretary Lloyd Austin announced that the West has the capability of bleeding Russian strength by supporting Ukraine to the point that Putin's imperialist vision would no longer be feasible. However, such a goal appeared to be an existential threat to Russia that would reinvigorate Putin's goal of restoring the Russian Empire. Austin's policy option appeared to be a bluff. Russia's future is based on a large population, lots of oil and gas, and newly fertile agricultural lands due to global warming. A verbal threat, however, costs nothing.

Scenario 11: *Seek to undermine Putin.* Biden's offhand account that he would rather see Putin out of power is a clue of the policy option, though Biden soon assured that he was not advocating regime change in Russia. Travel sanctions have been carefully designed to punish those close to Putin so that they might decide to retain their resources by working to get him out of office, since rumors suggest that he has few years of life left due to his cancer problem. The probability of undermining clever Vladimir Putin is low.

Scenario 12: *Take measures to encourage Russians to revolt.* Economic sanctions, including the closure of McDonalds in Moscow, were aimed at provoking civilian unrest as prices skyrocketed inside Russia. Nevertheless, Putin controls messaging in Russia and has had protesters arrested, though his support lagged when he called up 300,000 soldiers to fight in Ukraine. The Central Intelligence Agency may have increased operations inside Russia to support a revolt, but Russian organized groups in civil society lack the resources to conduct a coup or civil war.

Scenario 13: *Encourage NATO allies and other countries to support Ukraine.* Early visits by Biden Administration officials to Europe were aimed at rounding up support. Since Russia could easily block energy shipments to Germany, much attention was directed to Berlin, which agreed when Washington promised to fill the energy gap. Biden evidently won over European leaders by warning that Ukraine was only the beginning target in Putin's desire to re-establish control over Eastern Europe. In short, the policy was successful.

Scenario 14: *Accept Ukrainian refugees.* While millions fled to neighboring countries and beyond, the Biden Administration had to reverse restrictive Trump Administration policies by increasing the annual cap on refugees. Little specific opposition emerged, though Republicans could use the issue to win in future elections. The process of granting special status for Ukrainians has now been completed.

Scenario 15: *Demand war crimes trial of Putin and Russian soldiers.* News of Russian bombing of civilian targets prompted Biden to accuse Putin of being a war criminal, though the immediate aim was to marshal support for Ukraine. When Biden repeated the same charge after evidence emerged from territory recaptured by Ukraine, his order was to have government officials document specific war crimes; the task will be a lengthy process, clearly indicating that he would press the case after the war to make Putin a pariah. He prefers to involve the International Criminal Court, though the United States is not a member.

Scenario 16: *Support diplomacy to end the war.* Although Biden and other members of his administration contacted Putin and Russian officials, hoping to prevent the attack on February 24, 2022, they were unsuccessful. The reason for quiet diplomacy was that Russia's relocation of troops on the borders surrounding northern Ukraine constituted a threat of potential war. But rather than unifying the world to an impending war, public and private diplomacy was unsuccessful. Turkey's leader and the UN Secretary-General have sought to mediate between Russia and Ukraine, with no diplomatic role so far for the United States. American diplomacy may support the efforts of Turkey and the UN, provided that Ukraine does not object to what they propose.

Scenario 17: *Agree to an end to the war that establishes a status quo ante.* One possible proposal is for the United States to demand that Russia withdraw to territories occupied before February 24, leaving Russian forces in control of land seized from Ukraine in 2014. The United States would then withdraw all military support and rescind sanctions imposed on Russia. Ukraine will resist the option as long as American military support continues.

Scenario 18: *Support Ukraine to achieve total victory.* Ukraine appears committed to recapture all Russian-annexed territories, including Crimea and southeastern Ukraine, even if combat continues for years. The United States now appears to support Ukraine's current objectives. A verbal commitment is inexpensive, but indefinite lethal or nonlethal aid may dwindle if the situation becomes a costly stalemate.

Scenario 19: *Support neutralization of the large Ukrainian nuclear power plant.* Ukraine is trying to take back the Zaporizhzhia nuclear

230 M. HAAS

plant, which was seized by Russia early in the war. The International Atomic Energy Agency wants the facility neutralized before a possible catastrophe. Putin does not want to give up control. Any proposed UN Security Council resolution to do so will be vetoed by Russia.

Scenario 20: *Declare Russia as a "state sponsor of terrorism."* Although President Zelensky has asked for such a declaration, the effect would be to allow lawsuits against Russia for damages that could be taken out of currently seized Russian assets in American banks. In addition, the law would ban direct and third-country trade with Russia. Some members of Congress might pass a resolution to do so, but Biden opposes the move, aware that Russia may consider such an action to begin World War III.

REFERENCES

Abutaleb, Yasmeen. 2022, September 30. U.S. Imposes New Sanctions Over Russia's Illegal Annexation. *Washington Post.*

Abutaleb, Yasmeen, and John Hudson. 2023, February 13. U.S. Warns Ukraine it Faces a Pivotal Moment in War. *Washington Post.*

Adler, Nils. 2022, October 16. The Bleak Ukraine Landscape Russian Forces Leave Behind. *Los Angeles Times.*

Adu, Aletha. 2022, February 10. 250,000 Russian and Local Troops Gather on Ukraine's Borders in "Dangerous Moment". https://www.mirror.co.uk/news/world-news/250000-russian-local-troops-gather-26199688.

Agencias. 2022, February 26. How Many Troops Has Russia Sent into Invasion of Ukraine? https://en.as.com/en/2022/02/24/latest_news/1645729870_894320.html.

Ainsley, Julia. 2023, February 24. U.S. Has Admitted 271,000 Ukrainian Refugees Since Russian Invasion, Far Above Biden's Goal of 100,000. https://www.nbcnews.com/politics/immigration/us-admits-271000-ukrainian-refugees-russia-invasion-biden-rcna72177.

Al Jazeera. 2022, June 5. Weapons to Ukraine: Which Countries Have Sent What? https://www.aljazeera.com/news/2022/6/5/weapons-to-ukraine-which-countries-sent-what.

Appel, Hilary. 2022, September 24. Roundtable Remarks at the Annual Convention of the International Studies Association, Western Branch, Pasadena, CA.

Arhirova, Hanna. 2022, September 7. Nuclear Safety Zone in Ukraine Urged. *Los Angeles Times.*

Arhirova, Hanna. 2023a, April 17. More Than 100 Ukrainian POWs Freed in Swap. *Los Angeles Times.*

Arhirova, Hanna. 2023b, January 15. U.K. to Supply Tanks to Ukraine; Attacks Escalate. *Los Angeles Times*.

Arhirova, Hanna. 2023c, April 11. Ukraine and Russia Send Home Troops in a Swap. *Los Angeles Times*.

Arhirova, Hanna, and Yuras Karmanau. 2022, September 10. Ukraine Reclaims Territory in Kharkiv Region. *Los Angeles Times*.

Arhirova, Hanna, Yuras Karmanau, and Sabra Ayres. 2022, October 20. Putin Decrees Martial Law in Ukraine Areas. *Los Angeles Times*.

Arkin, William M. 2022, March 1. Shocking Lessons U.S. Military Leaders Learned by Watching Putin's Invasion. https://www.newsweek.com/shocking-lessons-us-military-leaders-learned-watching-putins-invasion-1683625.

Ash, Timothy Garton. 2023. Ukraine in Our Future. *New York Review of Books* 70 (8): 39–42.

Associated Press. 2022a, October 27. Putin Says "No Need" for Using Nuclear Weapons in Ukraine. https://www.pbs.org/newshour/world/vladimir-putin-rules-out-using-nuclear-weapons-in-ukraine.

Associated Press. 2022b, November 4. Pyongyang Arming Russia, U.S. Says. *Los Angeles Times*.

Associated Press. 2022c, September 22. Ukraine Rebels Release U.S. Pair, 8 Others. *Los Angeles Times*.

Associated Press. 2022d, January 19. The U.S. Will Provide $200 Million in Military Aid to Ukraine Amid Crisis. https://www.npr.org/2022c/01/19/1074020018/the-u-s-will-provide-200-million-in-military-aid-to-ukraine-amid-crisis.

Associated Press. 2023a, March 13. Belarus Saboteurs Disrupt Russia War Effort. *Los Angeles Times*.

Associated Press. 2023b, April 15. China Vows to Not Sell Arms to Parties in Ukraine War. *Los Angeles Times*.

Associated Press. 2023c, April 20. Patriot Missiles Join Kyiv's Arsenal. *Los Angeles Times*.

Associated Press. 2023d, February 11. Russia Picks Up Pace of Air Bombardments in Ukraine. *Los Angeles Times*.

Associated Press. 2023e, March 19. Russia, Ukraine Extend Grain Shipping Deal. *Los Angeles Times*.

Associated Press. 2023f, February 5. Russia, Ukraine Swap Scores of POWs. *Los Angeles Times*.

Associated Press. 2023g, April 19. Slovakia Sends MiGs to Ukraine. *Los Angeles Times*.

Associated Press. 2023h, April 28. Ukraine Weighs Plan for Counteroffensive. *Los Angeles Times*.

Associated Press. 2023i, January 11. Ukrainians to Train on Patriot System in U.S. *Los Angeles Times*.

Associated Press. 2023j, March 16. U.S., Russia Defense Chiefs Discuss Reaper Drone Crash. *Los Angeles Times.*

Associated Press. 2023k, February 3. U.S. Ultimately Agrees to Send Kyiv Longer-Range Missiles. *Los Angeles Times.*

Associated Press. 2023l, March 24. Zelensky Visits Front as Kyiv Hints at New Phase in War. *Los Angeles Times.*

Atlamazoglou, Constantine. 2021, November 16. US Warships Went on Another Mission to a European Hotspot, and Putin Says They're in Russia's "Crosshairs". https://www.businessinsider.com/us-navy-warships-in-black-sea-amid-nato-russia-tensions-2021-11.

Baer, Daniel. 2022, August 5. When Politics Returns to Kyiv: How Ukrainian Democracy Will Be Tested After the War. https://www.foreignaffairs.com/ukraine/when-politics-returns-kyiv.

Balmforth, Tom. 2022, September 30. Ukraine Applies for NATO Membership, Rules Out Putin Talks. https://www.reuters.com/world/europe/zelenskiy-says-ukraine-applying-nato-membership-2022-09-30/.

Beevor, Antony. 2022, December 29. Russia's New Winter War: Could Putin Go the Way of Napoleon and Hitler? https://www.foreignaffairs.com/russian-federation/russias-new-winter-war?utm_medium=newsletters&utm_source=fatoday&utm_campaign=Russia%E2%80%99s%20New%20Winter%20War&utm_content=20221229&utm_term=FA%20Today%20-%2011 2017.

Beliakova, Polina, and Rachel Tecott Metz. 2023, March 17. The Surprising Success of U.S. Military Aid to Ukraine: Kyiv's Determination Has Improved Washington's Spotty Track Record. https://sites.tufts.edu/fletcherrussia/the-surprising-success-of-u-s-military-aid-to-ukraine/.

Bertrand, Natasha, Kylie Atwood, Kevin Liptak, and Alex Marquardt. 2022, April 26. Austin's Assertion that US Wants to "Weaken" Russia Underlines Biden Strategy Shift. https://www.cnn.com/2022/04/25/politics/biden-administration-russia-strategy/index.html.

Biden, Joseph R., Jr. 2020. Why America Must Lead Again: Rescuing U.S. Foreign Policy After Trump. *Foreign Affairs* 99 (2): 64–76.

Biden, Joseph R., Jr., and Michael Carpenter. 2018. How to Stand Up to the Kremlin: Defending Democracy Against its Enemies. *Foreign Affairs* 97 (1): 44–57.

Biesecker, Michael, and Erika Kinetz. 2022, December 31. Evidence of Russian War Crimes Mounting. *Los Angeles Times.*

Blann, Susie. 2023a, February 28. Putin Orders Ukraine Border Tightening as Drones Hit Russia. https://www.aol.com/news/flurry-drone-strikes-hits-russia-152301636.html.

Blann, Susie. 2023b, February 16. Russia Claims Some Minor Progress in Ukraine's East. *Los Angeles Times.*

9 AMERICAN POLICIES TOWARD UKRAINE 233

Blann, Susie. 2023c, February 1. "Ukraine Needs Fighter Jets, Missiles…We Need to Act". *Los Angeles Times.*

Boot, Max. 2022, October 3. Sorry, Elon Musk. You Don't Have the Formula to End the Ukraine War. *Washington Post.*

Borda, Aldo Zammit. 2022, March 2. Ukraine War: What Is the Budapest Memorandum and Why Has Russia's Invasion Torn It Up? https://theconversation.com/ukraine-war-what-is-the-budapest-memora ndum-and-why-has-russias-invasion-torn-it-up-178184.

Borger, Julian, Pippa Crerar, and Pjotr Sauer. 2022, September 21. Biden Denounces Putin's Nuclear Threats as "Reckless" in UN Address. https://www.theguardian.com/us-news/2022/sep/21/joe-biden-putin-nuclear-weapons-ukraine-un-general-assembly.

British Broadcasting Corporation. 2023a, January 18. Germany Says It Is No Longer Reliant on Russian Energy. https://www.bbc.com/news/business-64312400.

British Broadcasting Corporation. 2023b, January 23. What Is Russia's Wagner Group of Mercenaries in Ukraine? https://www.bbc.com/news/world-609 47877.

Buck, Kate. 2022, March 28. Russia Outlines Four Reasons It Would Use Nuclear Weapons. https://www.yahoo.com/news/russia-outlines-4-reasons-it-would-use-nuclear-weapons-160825581.html?fr=yhssrp_catchall.

Bulow, Nabih, Terry Castleman, and Tracy Wilkinson. 2023, April 16. 3 U.S. Allies Balked Over Ukraine, Leak Reveals. *Los Angeles Times.*

Caldera, Dario, Sarah Conlisk, Matteo Iacoviello, and Maddie Pen. 2022, May 27. The Effect of the War in Ukraine on Global Activity and Inflation. https://www.federalreserve.gov/econres/notes/feds-notes/the-eff ect-of-the-war-in-ukraine-on-global-activity-and-inflation-20220527.html.

Carbonaro, Giulia. 2022, May 10. Russia Says They Will Use Nuclear Weapons on These Conditions. https://www.msn.com/en-us/news/world/russia-says-they-will-use-nuclear-weapons-on-these-conditions/ar-AAX6nPF.

Castellum. 2023, February 24. Russian Sanctions Dashboard. https://www.castellum.ai/russia-sanctions-dashboard?utm_campaign=wp_the_daily_202& utm_medium=email&utm_source=newsletter&wpisrc=nl_daily202.

Castillo, E. Eduardo. 2022, December 9. Ukraine Says Russia Arming Nuclear Plant. *Los Angeles Times.*

Chance, Matthew, and Luke McGee. 2021, June 17. Putin Got Exactly What He Wanted from Biden in Geneva. https://www.cnn.com/2021/06/16/eur ope/vladimir-putin-met-joe-biden-and-got-what-he-wanted-intl-cmd/index. html.

Chen, Janice Kai, and Mary Ilyushina. 2023, March 20. Drone Strikes, Sabotage, Shelling: Russia's War on Ukraine Comes to Russia. *Washington Post.*

Cherner, Julia. 2022, March 20. Durbin Defends Biden Administration Decision on Fighter Jet Deliveries to Ukraine. https://abcnews.go.com/Politics/dur bin-defends-decision-fighter-jet-deliveries-ukraine/story?id=83552583.

Cohen, Eliot A. 2023, February 22. Move Fast and Win Things: What the War in Ukraine Has Revealed About Statecraft. https://www.foreignaffairs.com/ ukraine/move-fast-and-win-things-statecraft?utm_medium=newsletters&utm_ source=fatoday&utm_campaign=Xi%20the%20Survivor&utm_content=202 30222&utm_term=FA%20Today%20-%2011 2017.

Condon, Bernard. 2022, November 2. U.S.-Trained Afghans Being Recruited by Russia. *Los Angeles Times.*

Cooban, Anna. 2022, May 18. Europe Plans to Spend $221 Billion to Ditch Russia's Energy. https://www.cnn.com/2022/05/18/energy/europe-repower-plan-russian-energy/index.html.

Council on Foreign Relations. 2018, January 23. Foreign Affairs Issue Launch with Former Vice President Joe Biden Tuesday. https://www.cfr.org/event/ foreign-affairs-issue-launch-former-vice-president-joe-biden.

De Luce, Dan, and Mosheh Gains. 2022, March 9. Biden Admin Rules Out Transfer of Polish Fighter Jets to Ukraine. https://www.nbcnews.com/pol itics/national-security/biden-admin-rules-transfer-polish-fighter-jets-ukraine-rcna19398.

Debusman, Bernt, Jr. 2022, April 21. What Weapons Has the US Given Ukraine—and How Much Do They Help? https://www.bbc.com/news/ world-us-canada-60774098.

DeYoung, Karen. 2022, July 29. Blinken, Lavrov Discussed Potential Prisoner Exchange for Griner, Whelan. *Washington Post.*

DeYoung, Karen, Dan Lamothe, and Isabelle Khurshudyan. 2022, December 23. Inside the Monumental, Stop-Start Effort to Arm Ukraine. *Washington Post.*

Dixon, Robyn. 2022a, February 24. Attack on Ukraine Brings Rare Sight in Russia: Protests in Cities Against Putin and Invasion. *Washington Post.*

Dixon, Robyn. 2022b, September 20. Russia Moves Toward Annexing Ukraine Regions in a Major Escalation. *Washington Post.*

Dixon, Robyn. 2022c, September 7. Russians Back War in Ukraine, But Report Finds Notable Opposition: Most Russians Are Still Sure They Are Not on the "Bad Side" in the War Against Ukraine. *Washington Post.*

Dixon, Robyn. 2023, April 11. Russia Moves to Tighten Conscription Law, Pressing More Men to Fight. *Washington Post.*

Dixon, Robyn, Catherine Belton, and Mary Ilyushina. 2022, September 21. Putin Drafts up to 300,000 Reservists, Backs Annexation Amid War Losses. *Washington Post.*

Duclos, Michel. 2021, February 24. The Munich Security Conference 2021— America Is Back, But What About the Europeans? https://www.institutm ontaigne.org/en/blog/munich-security-conference-2021-america-back-what-about-europeans.

Dutton, Jack. 2023, February 27. Russia Responds to China's Peace Plan for Ukraine. https://www.newsweek.com/russia-responds-china-ukraine-peace-plan-1783975.

Ebel, Francesca, and Mary Ilyushina. 2023, February 13. Russians Abandon Wartime Russia in Historic Exodus. *Washington Post.*

Ebel, Francesca, and Lily Kuom. 2023, March 20. Xi and Putin Hold Talks in Russia, Trading Compliments, Amid War in Ukraine. *Washington Post.*

Egan, Matt. 2022, January 21. Gas Prices Could Soar If Russia Invades Ukraine. https://www.cnn.com/2022/01/20/business/gas-prices-russia-ukraine-putin/index.html#:~:text=President%20Biden%20warned%20Wednesday%20of%20imposing%20%E2%80%9Csevere%20costs,relies%20on%20its%20oil-and-gas%20exports%20for%20its%20economy.

Faberov, Snejana. 2022, September 14. Putin Rejected Ukraine Peace Deal Struck by Aide as War Began: Report. https://nypost.com/2022/09/14/putin-rejected-ukraine-peace-deal-struck-by-aide-as-war-began/.

Falconbridge, Guy. 2023, February 23. Putin Says Russia to Deploy Sarmat Nuclear Missiles. https://www.aol.com/news/putin-russia-pay-increased-attention-114656618.html.

Fedyk, Anastasia, Yurly Gorodnichencko, and James Hodson. 2022, December 21. Stop Russia from Using Western Technology Against Ukraine. *Los Angeles Times.*

First Post. 2023, March 17. China Takes US for a Ride, Sends Copies of Famed American M16s as "Hunting Rifles" to Russia in Thousands. https://www.firstpost.com/world/china-takes-us-for-a-ride-sends-copies-of-famed-american-m16s-as-hunting-rifles-to-russia-in-thousands-12307912.html.

Fishman, Edward. 2023, February 23. A Tool of Attrition: What the War in Ukraine Has Revealed About Economic Sanctions. https://www.foreignaffairs.com/ukraine/tool-attrition?utm_medium=newsletters&utm_source=fatoday&utm_campaign=The%20Quiescent%20Russians&utm_content=20230223&utm_term=FA%20Today%20-%20112017.

France24. 2023, January 22. Russia Taken 180,000 Dead or Wounded in Ukraine: Norwegian Army. https://www.france24.com/en/live-news/20230122-russia-taken-180-000-dead-or-wounded-in-ukraine-norwegian-army.

Freedman, Lawrence. 2022, September 23. All the Tsar's Men: Why Mobilization Can't Save Putin's War. https://www.foreignaffairs.com/ukraine/all-tsars-men?utm_medium=newsletters&utm_source=fatoday&utm_campaign=All%20the%20Tsar%E2%80%99s%20Men&utm_content=20220923&utm_term=FA%20Today%20-%20112017.

Freking, Kevin. 2023, April 20. Congress Is Told of Atrocities in Ukraine. *Los Angeles Times.*

Galeotti, Mark. 2022. *Putin's Wars: From Chechnya to Ukraine.* Oxford, UK: Osprey.

Gans, Jared. 2022, December 25. Putin Says He Is Ready to Negotiate "with Everyone Involved" Over Ukraine. https://www.msn.com/en-us/news/world/putin-says-he-is-ready-to-negotiate-with-everyone-involved-over-ukraine/ar-AA15EJlj.

Garamone, Jim. 2022, April 29. U.S. Troops Train Ukrainians in Germany. https://www.defense.gov/News/News-Stories/Article/Article/3015610/us-troops-train-ukrainians-in-germany/.

Gatopoulos, Derek, and Susan Fraser. 2022, August 19. Erdogan Visits Ukraine, Acting as Go-Between in War. *Los Angeles Times*.

Gearan, Anne. 2021, April 26. In Foreign Policy, Biden Adopts Elements from Former Boss Obama—and from Former Rival Trump. *Washington Post*.

Gramlich, John. 2023, February 23. What Public Opinion Surveys Found in the First Year of the War in Ukraine. https://www.pewresearch.org/fact-tank/2023/02/23/what-public-opinion-surveys-found-in-the-first-year-of-the-war-in-ukraine/.

Greengross, Gil, Rod A. Martin, and Geoffrey Miller. 2012. Personality Traits, Intelligence, Humor Styles, and Humor Production Ability of Professional Stand-Up Comedians Compared to College Students. *Psychology of Aesthetics, Creativity, and the Arts* 6 (1): 74–82.

Haass, Richard, and Charles Kupchan. 2023, April 13. The West Needs a New Strategy in Ukraine: A Plan for Getting from the Battlefield to the Negotiating Table. https://www.foreignaffairs.com/ukraine/russia-richard-haass-west-battlefield-negotiations.

Hallam, Jonny, and Helen Regan. 2022, June 20. Captured American Fighters Purportedly Held by Russian-Backed Separatists in Donetsk. https://www.cnn.com/2022/06/20/world/americans-missing-ukraine-donetsk-intl-hnk/index.html.

Halperin, Charles. 1987. *Russia and the Golden Horde: The Mongol Impact on Medieval Russian History*. Bloomington: Indiana University Press.

Haltiwanger, John. 2023, April 12. Trump Is Trying to Win More GOP Voters with Bizarre Takes on the Ukraine War and Praise for Putin. https://www.businessinsider.com/trump-offers-false-takes-on-ukraine-praises-putin-tucker-interview-2023-4.

Harding, Luke. 2023. *Invasion: The Inside Story of Russia's Bloody War and Ukraine's Fight for Survival*. New York: Vintage.

Harrell, Peter. 2023, March 27. The Limits of Economic Warfare: What Sanctions on Russia Can and Cannot Achieve. https://www.foreignaffairs.com/united-states/limits-economic-warfare?utm_medium=newsletters&utm_source=fatoday&utm_campaign=The%20Limits%20of%20Economic%20Warfare&utm_content=20230327&utm_term=FA%20Today%20-%20112017.

Harris, Shane, Karen DeYoung, Isabelle Khurshudyan, Ashley Parker, and Liz Sly. 2022, August 16. Road to War: U.S. Struggled to Convince Allies, and Zelensky, of Risk of Invasion. *Washington Post.*

Harris, Shane, and Dan Lamothe. 2023, April 8. Intelligence Leak Exposes U.S. Spying on Adversaries and Allies. *Washington Post.*

Hathaway, Oona A. 2023, January 17. Russia's Crime and Punishment: How to Prosecute the Illegal War in Ukraine. https://www.foreignaffairs.com/ukr aine/russia-crime-and-punishment-illegal-war-in-ukraine?utm_medium=new sletters&utm_source=fatoday&utm_campaign=America%E2%80%99s%20C hina%20Policy%20Is%20Not%20Working&utm_content=20230126&utm_ term=FA%20Today%20-%20112017.

Hill, Evan, Missy Ryan, Siobhán O'Grady, and Samuel Oakford. 2023, April 11. Egypt Secretly Planned to Supply Rockets to Russia, Leaked U.S. Document Says. *Washington Post.*

Hill, Fiona, and Angela Stent. 2022. The World Putin Wants: How Distortions About the Past Feed Delusions About the Future. *Foreign Affairs* 101 (5): 108–122.

Holland, Steve, and Idrees Ali. 2023, August 18. US Approves Sending F-16s to Ukraine from Denmark and Netherlands. https://www.reuters.com/world/ us-approves-sending-f-16s-ukraine-denmark-netherlands-2023-08-17/.

Horton, Alex. 2023, April 14. Russia's Commando Units Gutted by Ukraine War, U.S. Leak Shows. *Washington Post.*

Hudson, John, David L. Stern, Felicia Sonmez, and Brittany Shammas. 2022, April 4. Biden Says Bucha Killings a "War Crime," Seeks New Russia Sanctions. *Washington Post.*

Hughes, Siobhan. 2022, March 17. Zelensky Asks U.S. Again for No-Fly Zone. *Wall Street Journal.*

Huntington, Samuel P. 2000. *The Clash of Civilizations?* New York: Palgrave Macmillan.

i24. 2022, September 26. Over 250,000 Men Left Russia to Avoid Mobilization. https://www.i24news.tv/en/news/ukraine-conflict/1664202371-over-250- 000-men-left-russia-to-avoid-mobilization#:~:text=to%20avoid%20mobiliz ation-,Over%20250%2C000%20men%20left%20Russia%20to%20avoid%20m obilization,-i24NEWS.

Ignatius, David. 2022a, December 19. How the Algorithm Tipped the Balance in Ukraine. *Washington Post.*

Ignatius, David. 2022b, October 27. Putin Demands We Listen to Him. The U.S. Should Take Him Up on It. *Washington Post.*

Ilyushina, Mary. 2022a, September 21. As Mobilization Begins in Russia, Sold-Out Flights, Protests and Arrests. *Washington Post.*

Ilyushina, Mary. 2022b, September 7. Putin, in Defiant Speech, Threatens Western Gas and Grain Supplies. *Washington Post.*

Ilyushina, Mary. 2023, March 19. Putin Visits Occupied Mariupol, Staking Claim to Invaded Ukrainian Lands. *Washington Post*.

Ilyushina, Mary, Robyn Dixon, Adela Suliman, and Francesca Ebel. 2023, February 24. Protests in Russia Denounce Ukraine Invasion; Antiwar Rallies Held Worldwide. *Boston Globe*.

India Today. 2023, February 25. India, China May Have Prevented Russia from Nuking Ukraine, Says US. https://www.indiatoday.in/world/story/india-china-prevented-russia-from-nuking-ukraine-says-us-2339412-2023-02-25.

Jakes, Lara, and Steven Erlanger. 2023, January 12. Western Tanks Appear Headed for Ukraine, Breaking Another Taboo. *New York Times*.

Johnson, Loch K. 1989. Covert Action and Accountability: Decision-Making for America's Secret Foreign Policy. *International Studies Quarterly* 33 (1): 81–109.

Jordans, Frank, and Kirsten Grieshaber. 2023, January 26. U.S., Germany to Send Tanks to Ukraine. *Los Angeles Times*.

Ju, Changwook. 2022, March 30. Do Conscripts Fight More Poorly Than Volunteers? Theory and Evidence from Modern Battles. Paper presented at the annual convention of the International Studies Association, Nashville, TN.

Judah, Tim. 2023. Ukraine's Volunteers. *New York Review of Books* 70 (1): 22–24.

Kalb, Marvin. 2015. *Imperial Gamble: Putin, Ukraine, and the New Cold War*. Washington, DC: Brookings Institution Press.

Kaldor, Mary. 2005. Old Wars, Cold Wars, New Wars, and the War on Terror. *International Politics* 42 (4): 491–498.

Kantchev, Georgia, and Evan Gershkovich. 2023, March 28. Russia's Economy Is Starting to Come Undone. *Wall Street Journal*.

Kaplan, Fred. 2023. Putin's Miscalculation. *New York Review of Books* 70 (1): 21–22.

Karanth, Sanjana. 2023, February 26. White House Defends Not Sending F-16 Jets to Ukraine. https://www.huffpost.com/entry/white-house-jake-sullivan-ukraine-f16-jets_n_63fba60ae4b0db7a1f665c2b?yptr=yahoo.

Keaten, Jamey. 2023a, January 19. "Tyranny Is Outpacing Democracy". *Los Angeles Times*.

Keaten, Jamey. 2023b, February 28. U.N. Chief Recaps Russia's Rights Violations. *Los Angeles Times*.

Kelly, Laura, and Alex Gangitano. 2022, March 17. Biden Raises Stakes with Allegations of Russian War Crimes. https://thehill.com/policy/international/598690-biden-raises-stakes-with-allegations-of-russian-war-crimes/.

Khurshudyan, Isabelle, and Christian Shepherd. 2023, April 26. Ukrainian President Zelensky Held "Meaningful" Call with China's Xi Jinping. *Washington Post*.

Khurshudyan, Isabelle, Paul Sonne, and Karen DeYoung. 2023, March 13. Ukrainian Casualties Are Estimated at Up to 120,000, and According to the United Nations, More Than 8,000 Ukrainian Civilians Have Been Killed. *Washington Post*.

Khurshudyan, Isabelle, Paul Sonne, Serhiy Morgunov, and Kamila Hrabchuk. 2022, December 29. Inside the Ukrainian Counteroffensive That Shocked Putin and Reshaped the War. *Washington Post*.

Kimmage, Michael, and Maria Lipman. 2023, January 13. Wartime Putinism: What the Disaster in Ukraine Has Done to the Kremlin—and to Russia. https://www.foreignaffairs.com/ukraine/wartime-putinism.

King, Laura. 2023, February 23. Ukraine Saves Power Grid, Keeping Darkness at Bay. *Los Angeles Times*.

Knight, Amy. 2023. Putin's Folly. *New York Review of Books* 70 (6): 33–35.

Kolesnikov, Andrei. 2022, September 30. Putin's Roulette: Sacrificing His Core Supporters in a Race Against Defeat. https://www.foreignaffairs.com/russian-federation/putin-roulette-sacrificing-supporters-race-against-defeat?utm_medium=newsletters&utm_source=fatoday&utm_campaign=Putin%E2%80%99s%20Roulette&utm_content=20220930&utm_term=FA%20Today%20-%20112017.

Kullab, Samya. 2023, April 12. Ukraine Resumes Exports of Electricity. *Los Angeles Times*.

Kullab, Samya, and Yuras Karmanau. 2023, February 14. Battles Rage Near Strategic East Ukrainian City. *Los Angeles Times*.

Lamothe, Dan. 2023a, April 9. Russia Nearly Shot Down British Spy Plane Near Ukraine, Leaked Document Says. *Washington Post*.

Lamothe, Dan. 2023b, January 15. U.S. Begins Expanded Training of Ukrainian Forces for Large-Scale Combat. *Washington Post*.

Lamothe, Dan. 2023c, March 21. U.S. Will Speed Transfer of Abrams Tanks to Ukraine, Pentagon Says. *Washington Post*.

Lamothe, Dan, Karen DeYoung, and Alex Horton. 2022a, December 13. Pentagon Preparing to Send Patriot Missile System to Ukraine. *Washington Post*.

Lamothe, Dan, Claire Parker, Andrew Jeong, Reis Thebault, and Maite Fernández Simon. 2022b, April 14. Russia Says Flagship Missile Cruiser Has Sunk After Explosion Off Coast of Ukraine. *Washington Post*.

Lamothe, Dan, Liz Sly, Alex Horton, Missy Ryan, and Michael E. Miller. 2022c, November 10. Russian Retreat from Kherson City Sets Stage for More Hard Combat. *Washington Post*.

Leave Russia Organizations. 2023. Stop Doing Business with Russia. https://leave-russia.org/?utm_campaign=wp_the_daily_202&utm_medium=email&utm_source=newsletter&wpisrc=nl_daily202. Accessed April 20, 2023.

Ledur, Júlia. 2022, November 21. What Russia Has Gained and Lost So Far in Ukraine, Visualized. *Washington Post*.

Ledur, Júlia, Laris Karklis, Ruby Mellen, Chris Alcantara, Aaron Steckelberg, and Lauren Tierney. 2023, February 21. Follow the 600-Mile Front Line Between Ukrainian and Russian Forces. *Washington Post*.

Levin-Banchik, Luba. 2022, September 24. Roundtable Remarks at the Annual Convention of the International Studies Association, Western Branch, Pasadena, CA.

Marr, Andrew. 2022, March 23. Zelensky Doesn't Know the End of His Story. Churchill Didn't Either. *New York Times*.

Massicot, Dara. 2023. What Got Wrong: Can Moscow Learn from Its Failures in Ukraine?". *Foreign Affairs* 102 (2): 78–93.

Masih, Niha, Ellen Francis, Miriam Berger, Mikhail Klimentov, and Sammy Westfall. 2023, April 6. Ukraine Live Briefing: Macron Urges Xi to Help End War; U.S. Demands Access to Reporter Jailed in Russia. *Washington Post*.

Masoudi, Heidarali. 2021. Joe Biden's Operational Codes in Foreign Policy. *Political and International Approaches* 12 (2): 95–122. https://doi.org/10.29252/piaj.2021.214997.

McCarthy, Charlies. 2022, September 6. Biden's Final Decision: Russia Not State Sponsor of Terrorism. https://www.newsmax.com/newsfront/joe-biden-russia-state-sponsor/2022/09/06/id/1086244/.

McFaul, Michael. 2023, January 24. Are We Seeing the Beginning of the End of Putinism? https://www.washingtonpost.com/opinions/2023/01/24/putin-ukraine-war-legitimacy-support/?utm_campaign=wp_post_most&utm_medium=email&utm_source=newsletter&wpisrc=nl_most&carta-url=https%3A%2F%2Fs2.washingtonpost.com%2Fcar-ln-tr%2F38f1ab6%2F63d162561b79c61f87646fe0%2F596d3a3eade4e24119dee3ad%2F17%2F72%2F63d162561b79c61f87646fe0&wp_cu=3fe4fbcdb8fb29cce66ed047dd764612%7C857c8380-c3fa-11df-bd09-12313b066011.

McManus, Doyle. 2023, April 16. Leaks Increase Stakes for Ukraine's Spring Offensive. *Los Angeles Times*.

Meansheimer, John J. 1993. The Case for a Ukrainian Nuclear Deterrent. *Foreign Affairs* 72 (3): 50–66.

Mearsheimer, John J. 2022a, June 23. The Causes and Consequences of the Ukraine War. https://www.russiamatters.org/analysis/causes-and-consequences-ukraine-war.

Mearsheimer, John J. 2022b, August 17. Playing with Fire in Ukraine: The Underappreciated Risks of Catastrophic Escalation. *Foreign Affairs*. https://www.foreignaffairs.com/ukraine/playing-fire-ukraine?utm_medium=newsletters&utm_source=fatoday&utm_campaign=Playing%20With%20Fire%20in%20Ukraine&utm_content=20220817&utm_term=FA%20Today%20-%2011112017.

9 AMERICAN POLICIES TOWARD UKRAINE 241

Megerian, Chris. 2022, March 28. Biden Says No One Believes U.S. Wants to "Take Down Putin". https://www.pbs.org/newshour/politics/watch-biden-says-no-one-believes-u-s-wants-to-take-down-putin.

Mehrotra, Karishma. 2023, February 23. Yellen at G-20 Says Oil Price Cap Is Working and Denting Russian Revenue. *Washington Post.*

Meldrum, Andrew. 2023, January 14. Ukraine Denies Russia Has Captured Town in the East. *Los Angeles Times.*

Mellen, Ruby, and Artur Galocha. 2023, August 10. A Look at the Amount of U.S. Spending Powering Ukraine's Defense. *Washington Post.*

Mello, Brian. 2023, April 8. Old Wars, New Wars: The Problem of Russia's War in Ukraine. Paper Presented at the Annual Convention of the Western Political Science Association, San Francisco.

Menon, Rajan. 2023, April 12. Ukraine's Best Chance: A Successful Offensive Could End the War with Russia. https://www.foreignaffairs.com/ukraine/ukraines-best-chance?utm_medium=newsletters&utm_source=twofa&utm_campaign=The%20West%20Needs%20a%20New%20Strategy%20in%20Ukraine&utm_content=20230414&utm_term=FA%20This%20Week%20-%2011201712017.

Meyer, David. 2022, February 28. Putin Put His Nuclear Forces on the Highest Alert. Would He Really Press the Button? https://fortune.com/2022/02/28/how-likely-putin-trigger-nukes-nuclear-weapons/.

Michlin-Shapir, Vera. 2021. *Fluid Russia: Between the Global and the National in the Post-Soviet Era.* Dekalb: Northern Illinois University Press.

Mitchell, Ellen. 2022, August 19. Pentagon Announces Extra $775M in Weapons to Ukraine. https://thehill.com/policy/defense/3608169-pentagon-announces-extra-775m-in-weapons-to-ukraine/.

Moytl, Alexander J. 2023, February 21. How Long Will Russians Tolerate Putin's Costly War in Ukraine. *Los Angeles Times.*

Nakashima, Ellen, and Felicia Somnez. 2022, February 24. U.S. Targets Major Russian Banks and Tech Sector with Sweeping Sanctions and Export Controls Following Ukraine Invasion. *Washington Post.*

O'Grady, Siobhán, Alex Horton, Isabelle Khurshudyan, and Anastacia Galouchka. 2023, March 23. Ukraine, Pumped Up by Western Weapons, Is Held Back by Slow Deliveries. *Washington Post.*

O'Hanlon, Michael, Constanze Stelzenmüller, and David Wesse. 2023, February 21. These Charts Suggest Peace Isn't Coming to Ukraine Anytime Soon. *Washington Post.*

Obama, Barack. 2014, March 20. Statement by the President on Ukraine. https://obamawhitehouse.archives.gov/the-press-office/2014/03/20/statement-president-ukraine.

Picheta, Rob, and Lauren Said-Moorehouse. 2023, March 17. ICC Issues War Crimes Arrest Warrant for Putin for Alleged Deportation of

Ukrainian Children. https://www.cnn.com/2023/03/17/europe/icc-russia-war-crimes-charges-intl/index.html.

Posen, Barry R. 2023, January 4. Russia's Rebound: How Moscow Has Partly Recovered from Its Military Setbacks. https://www.foreignaffairs.com/ukr aine/russia-rebound-moscow-recovered-military-setbacks?utm_medium=new sletters&utm_source=twofa&utm_campaign=The%20Case%20for%20Taking% 20Crimea&utm_content=20230106&utm_term=FA%20This%20Week%20-% 20112017.

Postma, Ali. 2023, April 13. Vladimir Putin: Leaked Documents Claim He Is Receiving Treatment for His Health Condition. https://www.msn.com/en-us/health/other/vladimir-putin-leaked-documents-claim-he-is-receiving-tre atment-for-his-health-condition/ar-AA19Os57?li=BBnba9O.

Power, Samantha. 2023. How Democracy Can Win: The Right Way to Counter Autocracy. *Foreign Affairs* 102 (2): 38–52.

Putin, Vladimir. 2021, July 12. On the Historical Unity Between Russians and Ukrainians. http://en.kremlin.ru/events/president/news/66181.

Putin, Vladimir. 2022, June 2. Basic Principles of the Russian Federation's State Policy in the Domain of Nuclear Deterrence. https://www.globalsecurity. org/wmd/library/news/russia/2020/russia-200608-russia-mfa01.htm#:~: text=State%20policy%20on%20Nuclear%20Deterrence%20is%20defensive% 20by,aggression%20against%20the%20Russian%20Federation%20and%2For% 20its%20allies.

Reuters. 2022, September 3. Russia Says It Foiled Ukrainian Attempt to Seize Nuclear Plant. https://www.usnews.com/news/world/articles/2022-09-03/russia-says-it-foiled-ukrainian-attempt-to-seize-nuclear-plant.

Reuters. 2023, April 10. Kremlin, Asked If Russia Behind U.S. Intelligence Leaks, Says Moscow Is Always Blamed for Everything. https://www.reuters. com/world/europe/kremlin-asked-if-russia-behind-us-intelligence-leaks-says-moscow-is-always-2023-04-10/.

Ritter, Karl. 2022, September 22. Ukraine's Mariupol Defenders, Putin Ally in Prisoner Swap. https://apnews.com/article/russia-ukraine-putin-kyiv-mid dle-east-e4e75f0af5dad49e2acf764981e1c85c.

Ritter, Karl. 2023, March 27. Ukraine Seeks Emergency U.N. Talks Over Nuclear Plan. *Los Angeles Times*.

Ritter, Karl, and Dino Hazel. 2023, March 17. Video Said to Show Intercept of U.S. Drone. *Los Angeles Times*.

Ritter, Karl, and Joanna Kozlowska. 2022, September 11. Russia Announces Retreat from 2 Areas. *Los Angeles Times*.

Rodriguez, Joshua, and Jeanne Batalova. 2022, June 22. Ukrainian Immi-grants in the United States. https://www.migrationpolicy.org/article/ukrain ian-immigrants-united-states.

9 AMERICAN POLICIES TOWARD UKRAINE 243

Rose, Andrea, Hanna Arhirova, and David Rising. 2023, April 29. Russian Missile, Drone Strikes Kill 23 in Ukraine. *Los Angeles Times*.

Ryan, Missy, Isabelle Khurshudyan, and Mary Ilyushina. 2022, October 10. Russia Strikes Kyiv and Cities Across Ukraine After Crimea Bridge Attack. *Washington Post*.

Sabbagh, Dan, and Jennifer Rankin. 2023, April 21. All Nato Members Have Agreed Ukraine Will Eventually Join, Says Stoltenberg. https://www.theguardian.com/world/2023/apr/21/all-nato-members-have-agreed-ukraine-will-eventually-join-says-stoltenberg.

Sands, Leo, and Andrew Jeong. 2022, October 18. Most Ukrainians Want to Keep Fighting Until Russia Is Driven Out, Poll Finds. *Washington Post*.

Sanger, David E., Eric Schmitt, Helene Cooper, Julian E. Barnes, and Kenneth P. Vogel. 2022a, March 6. Arming Ukraine: 17,000 Anti-Tank Weapons in 6 Days and a Clandestine Cybercorps. *New York Times*.

Sanger, David E., Anton Troianovski, Julian E. Barnes, and Eric Schmitt. 2022b, September 17. Ukraine Wants the U.S. to Send More Powerful Weapons. Biden Is Not So Sure. *New York Times*.

Santora, Marc, Matthew Mpoke Bigg, and Richard Pérez-Peña. 2023, March 14. Russian Attacks Yield Little But Casualties in Wide Arc of Ukraine. *New York Times*.

Simon, Delaney, and Michael Wahid Hanna. 2022, August 4. Why the U.S. Should Not Designate Russia as a State Sponsor of Terrorism. https://www.crisisgroup.org/united-states/why-us-should-not-designate-russia-state-sponsor-terrorism.

Skrypchenko, Tetyana. 2022, June 20. World's Support to Ukraine: Which Countries Support Providing Weapons to Ukraine and Sanctions Against Russia. https://www.eurointegration.com.ua/eng/articles/2022/06/20/7141506/.

Snyder, Timothy. 2022. Ukraine Holds the Future: The War Between Democracy and Nihilism. *Foreign Affairs* 101 (5): 124–141.

Soldatov, Andrei, and Irina Borogan. 2023, March 6. Russia's Halfway to Hell Strategy: Why Putin Has Not Yet Launched a Total War in Ukraine. https://www.foreignaffairs.com/ukraine/russias-halfway-hell-strategy?utm_medium=newsletters&utm_source=fatoday&utm_campaign=Russia%E2%80%99s%20Halfway%20to%20Hell%20Strategy&utm_content=20230306&utm_term=FA%20Today%20-%20112017.

Standard and Poors. 2023, February 27. Sanctions Against Russia: A Timeline. https://www.spglobal.com/marketintelligence/en/news-insights/latest-news-headlines/sanctions-against-russia-8211-a-timeline-69602559#:~:text=Adopts%20a%20ninth%20package%20of%20sanctions%20on%20Russia,Mir%2C%20Rossiya%201%2C%20REN%20TV%20and%20Pervyi%20Kanal.

244   M. HAAS

Stanovaya, Tatiana. 2022, October 6. Putin's Apocalyptic End Game in Ukraine: Annexation and Mobilization Make Nuclear War More Likely. foreignaffairs.com.

Statistica. 2023a, February 8. Comparison of the Military Capabilities of Russia and Ukraine as of 2023. https://www.statista.com/statistics/1296573/russia-ukraine-military-comparison/#:~:text=Ukraine%27s%20Army%20counted%20approximately%20500%20thousand%20military%20personnel,soldiers%20were%20part%20of%20the%20country%27s%20reserve%20forces. Accessed February 23, 2023a.

Statistica. 2023b, February. Total Bilateral Aid Commitments to Ukraine Between January 24, 2022 and January 15, 2023b, by Type and Country or Organization. https://www.statista.com/statistics/1303432/total-bilateral-aid-to-ukraine/. Accessed February 23, 2023b.

Stein, Jeff. 2022, October 15. U.S. Grows Frustrated Over Europe's Delayed Economic Aid to Ukraine. *Washington Post.*

Stein, Jeff, Annabelle Timsit, Rachel Pannett, Emily Rauhala, Claire Parker, Alex Horton, and Maham Javaid. 2022, December 5. Ukraine Live Briefing: Kremlin Says Ukrainian Drones Attacked Bases Deep in Russia; Missile Strikes Cause Power Outages in Ukraine. *Washington Post.*

Stewart, Will, and Elizabeth Haigh. 2022, December 25. "CIA Is Behind Spate of Explosions in Russia": US Army Special Ops Veteran Claims Intelligence Agency and NATO Ally Are Conducting Sabotage Missions. https://www.dailymail.co.uk/news/article-11572881/CIA-spate-explosions-Russia-veteran-claims-CIA-NATO-ally-sabotage.html.

Sullivan, Eileen. 2023, March 14. Many Ukrainians in U.S. Get a Reprieve. *New York Times.*

Summers, Lawrence H., Philip D. Zelikow, and Robert B. Zoellick. 2023, March 20. The Moral and Legal Case for Sending Russia's Frozen $300 Billion to Ukraine. *Washington Post.*

Talcott, Shelby. 2021, December 7. Biden to Threaten Putin with "Significant and Severe Economic Harm" If Russia Invades Ukraine. https://dailycaller.com/2021/12/07/joe-biden-russian-vladimir-putin-ukraine-economic-harm-sanctions/.

Talmadge, Caitlin. 2022, September 21. Why Russia's Mobilization May Lower the Risk of Nuclear War—For Now. *Washington Post.*

Tass. 2021, June 17. Biden's Support of Minsk Accords During Geneva Summit Seen as Russia's Success—Expert. https://tass.com/world/1303871.

Taylor, Adam, Júlia Ledur, Francesca Ebel, and Mary Ilyushina. 2023, April 3. A Web of Trenches Shows Russia Fears Losing Crimea. *Washington Post.*

TVP. 2023, February 22. Bucharest Nine Leaders, U.S. President, NATO SecGen Sign Joint Declaration. https://tvpworld.com/66508719/bucharest-nine-leaders-us-president-nato-secgen-sign-joint-declaration.

United Nations General Assembly. 2023, February 23. UN General Assembly Calls for Immediate End to War in Ukraine. https://news.un.org/en/story/2023/02/1133847.

United States, International Trade Administration. 2022, July 21. Sanctions Framework. https://www.trade.gov/country-commercial-guides/russia-sanctions-framework.

University of Saint Gallen. 2023, January 19. War in Ukraine: Many Firms Continue to Operate in Russia. https://www.unisg.ch/en/newsdetail/news/war-in-ukraine-many-firms-continue-to-operate-in-russia/?utm_campaign=wp_the_daily_202&utm_medium=email&utm_source=newsletter&wpisrc=nl_daily202.

Vergun, David. 2022, August 12. Ukrainian Forces Make Some Gains in North, South. https://www.defense.gov/News/News-Stories/Article/Article/3126704/ukrainian-forces-make-some-gains-in-north-south/.

Visser, Nick. 2022, March 28. Volodymyr Zelenskyy Open to Ukraine Adopting Neutral Stance to Secure Russian Peace Deal. https://www.huffpost.com/entry/zelesnkyy-ukraine-neutral-stance-peace_n_62411f73e4b0e340f6a5476f.

Voice of America. 2022, November 7. UK Defense Ministry: Russia's Lack of Air Superiority Exacerbated Due to Poor Training. https://www.voanews.com/a/uk-defense-ministry-russia-s-lack-of-air-superiority-exacerbated-due-to-poor-training/6823338.html.

Wall Street Journal. 2022a, May 31. Two Russian Soldiers Convicted in Second Ukrainian War-Crimes Trial. *Wall Street Journal*.

Wall Street Journal. 2022b, July 22. Ukraine, Russia Agree on Safe Corridor for Wheat Exports. *Wall Street Journal*.

Ward, Alexander, and Quint Forgey. 2022, July 20. Western Fighter Jets Heading to Ukraine? https://www.politico.com/newsletters/national-security-daily/2022/07/20/western-fighter-jets-heading-to-ukraine-00046854.

Warrick, Joby, Souad Mekhennet, and Ellen Nakashima. 2022, November 19. Iran Will Help Russia Build Drones for Ukraine War, Western Officials Say. *Washington Post*.

Washington Post. 2020, August 20. Biden on Charlottesville: "For Me, a Call to Action". *Washington Post*.

Whalen, Jeanne, and Catherine Belton. 2023, February 15. Sanctions Haven't Stopped Russia, But a New Oil Ban Could Cut Deeper. *Washington Post*.

Wilkinson, Tracy. 2023, February 23. Putin's Exit from Treaty Sends West a Nuclear Reminder. *Los Angeles Times*.

Wilkinson, Tracy, Courtney Subramanian, and Nolan D. McCaskill. 2022, December 22. Zelensky Tells Congress: Aid "Is Not Charity". *Los Angeles Times*.

Williams, Matthias, and Natalia Zinets. 2021, December 9. Biden Assures Zelenskiy That NATO Membership in Ukraine's Hands, Kyiv Says. https://www.reuters.com/world/europe/ukrainian-president-zelenskiy-holding-talks-with-biden-adviser-says-2021-12-09/.

Winfield, Nicole. 2023, April 30. Pope Speaks of Secret Peace "Mission," Help for Ukraine Kids. *Washington Post*.

Yackley, Ayla Jean Yackley. 2022, March 11. Ukraine Army Hails Turkish Drones But Ankara Plays Down Weapons Sales. https://www.washingtonpost.com/world/2022/11/21/russia-territory-gains-ukraine-war/.

Yaffa, Joshua. 2023, February 23. The Quiescent Russians: What the War in Ukraine Has Revealed About Putin's Public. https://www.foreignaffairs.com/ukraine/quiescent-russians?utm_medium=newsletters&utm_source=fatoday&utm_campaign=The%20Quiescent%20Russians&utm_content=20230223&utm_term=FA%20Today%20-%2011 2017.

Zagorodnyuk, Andriy. 2022, October 12. Ukraine's Path to Victory: How the Country Can Take Back All Its Territory. https://www.foreignaffairs.com/ukraine/ukraines-path-victory?utm_medium=newsletters&utm_source=fatoday&utm_campaign=Ukraine%E2%80%99s%20Path%20to%20Victory&utm_content=20221012&utm_term=FA%20Today%20-%2011 2017.

Zegart, Amy. 2023, January/February. Open Secrets: Ukraine and the Next Intelligence Revolution. https://www.foreignaffairs.com/world/open-secrets-ukraine-intelligence-revolution-amy-zegart?utm_medium=newsletters&utm_source=twofa&utm_campaign=Putin%E2%80%99s%20Last%20Stand&utm_content=20221223&utm_term=FA%20This%20Week%20-%2011 2017.

Zelensky, Volodymyr. 2022, May 21. Ukraine Has 700,000 Soldiers Fighting the Russian Army – Zelensky. https://news.yahoo.com/ukraine-700-000-soldiers-fighting-123200688.html?fr=yhssrp_catchall.

Zubok, Vladislav. 2022, December 21. No One Would Win a Long War in Ukraine: The West Must Avoid the Mistakes of World War I. https://www.foreignaffairs.com/ukraine/no-one-would-win-long-war-ukraine?utm_medium=newsletters&utm_source=fatoday&utm_campaign=A%20Free%20World%2C%20If%20You%20Can%20Keep%20It&utm_content=20221221&utm_term=FA%20Today%20-%2011 2017.

CHAPTER 10

Implications for Foreign Policy Research

The main puzzle posed herein is why there are so many foreign policy blunders. Yet foreign policy analysis within the discipline of international studies has involved more research on the past than advice for the future. What has been presented above can correct the problem.

As indicated in Part I, there was an early concern over rational and irrational decision-making followed by a desire to rebuild the international arena with institutions and laws to increase chances for peace. Then came behavioral foreign policy analysis, which identified causes of blunders in specific situations without developing broader theories to integrate findings. In Chapter 3, concepts developed by various pre-theories were pooled to find major statistical dimensions. A causal analysis determined that dangerous foreign policy decisions are most likely when adversaries are culturally dissimilar.

With culture thus identified as a crucial element accounting for foreign policy catastrophes, the focus in Part II shifted to discovering cultural influences on decision-makers, in particular through research on operational codes. Initially, as described in Chapter 4, the study of operational codes was mainly descriptive. Efforts to turn operational code analysis into a predictive theory, as critiqued in Chapter 5, have been unsuccessful, largely because the focus was only on a few words rather than the fact that beliefs can be quite complex.

© The Author(s), under exclusive license to Springer Nature Switzerland AG 2023
M. Haas, *Professionalization of Foreign Policy*,
https://doi.org/10.1007/978-3-031-37152-3_10

247

248   M. HAAS

Part III posed the task of how to utilize operational codes in an entirely new way—by reformulating the content of operational codes to serve as parameters of Options Analysis. Chapter 6 identified the four basic criteria that all foreign policy decision-makers should use in appraising alternative policy options—power, economics, prestige, and feasibility. Subcriteria, in turn, were rooted in several social science paradigms. A foreign policy leader's operational code was defined as the set of weights applied to the various subcriteria when options are being deliberated. After assigning weights to the criteria, Options Analysis involves determining how well policies rate along the dimensions of an operational code. Examples were American foreign policy decisions regarding Cambodia, North Korea, and Ukraine. Using a computer program known as Decision Pad, the criteria weights and option judgments can be used to determine a ranking of the options for advisers to present to a foreign policy leader. The matrix of options provided herein was the first to provide criteria for supporting options since almost 2,500 years earlier, following the tradition of Jeremy Bentham (1780).

OPTIONS ANALYSIS

The present volume proposes Options Analysis as a new tool in academic research as well as a way to professionalize decision-making in actual situations—to overcome unprofessional behavior by foreign policy advisers who push their own agendas. One benefit of Options Analysis is retrospective—to improve how to study why decision-makers in the past have chosen some policies rather than others by identifying their criteria and how they score each alternative policy choice on each criterion. The second benefit of Options Analysis is prospective—to provide a model of how to professionalize future foreign policy decision-making.

Regarding retrospective foreign policy analysis, Options Analysis rises above many theories of foreign policy decision-making that have been developed over the years in competition with one another. Until now, few have been linked within larger paradigms. Options Analysis incorporates all previous foreign policy theories at the paradigmatic level by identifying the criteria used to assess policy options.

The retrospective lessons presented herein point out the continuing impact of blunders in relation to Cambodia and North Korea. Based on Reagan's operational code, which prioritized secret funding of the Khmer Rouge, one option that had a high score was eventually accepted due to external pressure—having the UN transition the country from a threat of war to a condition of peace. Far too much emphasis was placed on bleeding Vietnam than on concern for the condition of the decent people of Cambodia who deserved to exist in a state of normality. Because Reagan was more focused on ending the Cold War, subordinates evidently prevailed in imposing hawkish Cold War thinking on Vietnam, something that a truly professional Options Analysis could have avoided. Although the United States later normalized relations with Vietnam (Haas 2018: ch3), Washington still neglects Cambodia.

In regard to North Korea, the United States has consistently ignored Pyongyang's pleas for normalization, preferring to maintain warlike relations. Obama's operational code prioritized hostility in the form of cutting off negotiations and applying sanctions, though the third highest option was to continue a "sunshine policy." North Korea twice took positive steps to follow roadmaps toward denuclearization, anticipating normalization (Haas 2018: ch4), yet was betrayed both times. Then President Donald Trump reopened a period of mutual reciprocal tension reduction, only for him to cave into the views of hawkish advisers, once again proving that a professional Decision Pad exercise would have brought positive denuclearization and normalization. The result is that North Korea is now a formidable nuclear power.

The present analysis of American policy toward Kyiv and Moscow has also discovered some peculiarities. Despite Biden's operational code, which now fully supports the defense and even offense of Ukraine, poor intelligence in the beginning favored almost a do-nothing response to the threat of Russian aggression. Today, several options have high scores yet remain unfulfilled. Admission of Ukraine to the North Atlantic Treaty Organization (NATO) has the fifth-highest rating. Sending American combat troops to Ukraine has the sixteenth score, lower than sending offensive weapons. One might question the accuracy of ratings in Table 9.5, but such any counterargument would have to be accompanied by either a change in Biden's operational code weights or the judgments on how well each option fulfills all 15 subcriteria. Implementing both options would clearly be viewed by the Kremlin as unacceptable escalation, so that is why the Biden Administration has been cautious. But Ukraine is already a de facto member of NATO, and American soldiers training the Ukrainian army on how to use new weapons may already be inside the country. Biden's greater experience than his subordinates

250   M. HAAS

and his propensity to seek consensus clearly give the impression that his Ukraine policy is being crafted in a professional manner.

Regarding prospective foreign policy analysis, what Options Analysis does is to rise above the familiar dichotomy between rational and irrational modes of decision-making. Policy advisers rating options separately and secretly from one another are much less likely to engage in bureaucratic or organizational struggles, crisis modes, cultural bias, groupthink, messaging bias, misperceptions, muddling through, a prospect theory blunder, satisficing, and similar monotheoretical routes to irrationality. What Options Analysis does is to fulfill Alexander George's "multiple advocacy" suggestion (George 1972). Options Analysis can also transform the image of poliheuristic decision-making, which portrays rejection of options as a dismissive decision (Mintz 2003), by professionalizing the evaluation of all possible options.

In addition, Options Analysis refocuses operational code research by ascending beyond Ole Holsti's focus on beliefs, as measured by word counts. He was interested in general ideas about how images and values mediate between events (information inputs) and decisions (Holsti 1962) rather than on how both elements serve to prioritize specific options. Whereas he posited that images and values would be of less significance when rationality prevailed, how else can decisions emerge without criteria and options assessments? After Alexander George (1969) differentiated between several types of beliefs, Holsti accepted only the dichotomy between conflictual versus harmonious orientations (Holsti 1977), which George indicated would be the basis for a selection of "goals." George's other beliefs (optimism/pessimism, future predictability, confidence in the option selected, and whether the decision-maker felt that chance played a role in history) were posited to guide the selection of "means." Such analyses can be useful in explaining why decision-makers differ psychologically, thereby illuminating biographical and historical analysis, but their approaches did not have an applied science application regarding how to improve actual decisions. And they were mainly derived from Cold War thinking.

Options Analysis also encourages consideration of Joseph Nye's concept of "soft power," expanding traditional concerns over the use of military and monetary resources over the need to attract prestige— playing an exemplary role in the international system (Nye 1990, 2004). In contrast with foolish decisions regarding Cambodia and North Korea, Joe Biden clearly has given high priority to soft power elements in his foreign policy toward Russia's invasion of Ukraine. Yet Biden's broadening of foreign policy criteria has yet to be applied to correct past mistakes involving Cambodia and North Korea, which have now been chased into the orbit of the People's Republic of China.

Options Analysis also encourages more development of paradigms and concepts that link propositions within with paradigms—in effect, revitalizing international relations research, as Richard Ned Lebow (1981) once suggested when he found flaws in the Deterrence Paradigm. Judgments about how well Option X achieves deterrence should be based on evidence derived from more research rather than guesswork. After all, decision-makers cannot await for more knowledge about how to deter adversaries; they must decide on the spot, so they need advice from advisers who consult accumulated knowledge in foreign policy research.

For another example, decision-makers must rely on a careful assessment of whether sufficient resources exist to carry out alternative foreign policy options, utilizing the Resource Mobilization Paradigm. One tool in studying resource mobilization is simulation. Recently, the Center for Strategic and International Studies completed 24 wargames to determine how the United States might counter China's possible invasion of Taiwan, finding that the cost would be considerable and concluding that the United States needs to strengthen existing resources (Cancian et al. 2023).

Thus, more research on paradigms will broaden both knowledge and improve judgments regarding alternative foreign policy options. Instead of foreign policy analysis as a never-ending work in progress, a much higher level of professionalism can now emerge, turning foreign policy analysis into an applied science. Meanwhile, instead of seeking a single theory, the field can now pursue multiple paradigms as alternative explanations for foreign policy puzzles.

Decision-Making Implications

Utilization of Options Analysis by actual decision-makers will ensure that foreign policy advisers will assess future policy alternatives for their impact on the military power, economy, and prestige of a country as well as an assessment of the feasibility of each option. Decision Pad is a statistical program that ranks options on the basis of how well their scenarios accomplish the main foreign policy criteria. Joseph Nye (2022), once an important advisor in several roles of American foreign policy, has

252   M. HAAS

informed me that he knows of no use of Decision Pad in the United States Department of State. Not yet, that is.

Clearly, the same methodology can be used in any situation where there are policy options, criteria for evaluating options, and weights applied to the criteria. Rather than presenting just a few options based on biases of those making decisions, Options Analysis opens the door to more professionalism in curriculum development, employment decisions, legislative alternatives, medical policy, and many other aspects of public policy through the use of Decision Pad. Indeed, Options Analysis enables a president or prime minister to have greater supervision of advisers by insisting that they assess each option on the basis of the four main criteria applied to foreign policy decisions.

Options Analysis may also be used by teams of scholars outside government to make recommendations to presidents and prime ministers while a decision-making process is ongoing. Based on Options Analysis, foreign policy scholars can then write op-eds and make Twitter recommendations for decision-makers to consider.

As a result of Options Analysis, more democratic outcomes may emerge in foreign policy—provided that important information is shared by the government with the public. Scholars with differing operational codes may agree on policies that foreign policy leaders might not otherwise hear from their advisers. Therein lies prospects for not only professionalization of foreign policy but also democratization.

REFERENCES

Bentham, Jeremy. 1780. *An Introduction to the Principles of Morals and Legislation*. Oxford, UK: Clarendon Press, 1907. See *utilitarianism/jeremy-bentham/#4*.

Cancian, Mark F., Matthew Cancian, and Eric Heginbotham. 2023, January 9. The First Battle of the Next War: Wargaming a Chinese Invasion of Taiwan. https://www.csis.org/analysis/first-battle-next-war-wargaming-chinese-invasion-taiwan.

George, Alexander L. 1969. The "Operational Code": A Neglected Approach to the Study of Political Leaders and Decision-Making. *International Studies Quarterly* 13 (4): 190–222.

George, Alexander L. 1972. The Case for Multiple Advocacy in Making Foreign Policy. *American Political Science Review* 66 (3): 751–785.

Haas, Michael. 2018. *United States Diplomacy with North Korea and Vietnam: Explaining Failure and Success*. New York: Peter Lang.

Holsti, Ole R. 1962. The Belief System and National Images: A Case Study. *Journal of Conflict Resolution* 6 (3): 244–252.

Holsti, Ole R. 1977. A Typology of "Operational Code" Belief Systems. In *Decision-Making Research: Some Recent Developments*, eds. Daniel Heradstveit and Ove Narvesen, 31–131. Oslo: Norsk Utenrikspolitisk Institutt.

Lebow, Richard Ned. 1981. *Between Peace and War: The Nature of International Crisis*. Baltimore: Johns Hopkins Press.

Mintz, Alex. 2003. *Integrating Cognitive and Rational Theories of Foreign Policy Decision Making: A Poliheuristic Perspective*. New York: Palgrave Macmillan.

Nye, Joseph S., Jr. 1990. Soft Power. *Foreign Policy* 80 (1): 153–171.

Nye, Joseph S., Jr. 2004. *Soft Power: The Means to Success in World Politics*. New York: PublicAffairs.

Nye, Joseph R., Jr. 2022, January 16. Personal Communication.

Afterword

So whither next for Options Analysis?? I can see several directions suggested by the work of Michael Haas:

Expansion of Operational Code Analysis

Michael Haas expands Options Analysis by incorporating operational code analysis as developed by Nathan Leites (1951, 1953) for the USSR. Haas views the durability of operational codes as a feature of long-lasting political cultures, hard for outsiders to comprehend easily, but definitely worthy of systematic study, all the more because, in Haas' judgment, cultural clashes bear a high responsibility for the geneses of wars.

The cultural roots of war have been independently studied and documented by Lewis Fry Richardson, in his magnum opus, *Statistics of Deadly Quarrels* (1960): In sum, cultural similarities are pacific in their effects. Mutual misunderstanding of culturally rooted operational codes may reasonably then be scrutinized in the outbreaks of wars, especially those outbreaks which seem to defy rational analysis.

© The Editor(s) (if applicable) and The Author(s), under exclusive license to Springer Nature Switzerland AG 2023
M. Haas, *Professionalization of Foreign Policy*,
https://doi.org/10.1007/978-3-031-37152-3

EXTENSION OF BLUNDER ANALYSIS TO A MULTINATIONAL AND THEORETICAL LEVEL

The Soviet placement and later withdrawal of nuclear weapons in the Cuban Missile Crisis of 1962, dogged by cultural clashes and unpleasant surprises, which could be, and sometimes was represented as victorious, may be usefully compared with Vladimir Putin's military staff's apparent conviction that Russia's invasion of Ukraine in February 2022 would surely produce a short victorious war.

An interesting version of blunder analysis might inspect the failed invasions of Russia by Charles XII of Sweden, Napoleon Bonaparte, and Adolf Hitler. None of these disasters could be treated as anything but what they were. Were there involved in the lead-in to each option disastrously chosen perhaps some common belief, for instance a reiterated belief that, underlying a Russian elite with an operational code of resilience and resistance that could be easily skimmed off, there would be found a very different Russian popular-cultural operational code of obedient suffering and enduring submissiveness? And perhaps also the examples of the conquests of Russia by Vikings, Mongols, and even 1918 Germany with the dictated Treaty of Brest-Litovsk?

MODES OF EXPERIENCE IN OPTIONS ANALYSIS

In his philosophical classic *Experience and Its Modes* (1933), Michael Oakeshott examined the experiential modes of History, Science, and Practice. The subject of foreign policy decision-making can be pursued in all three modes of discourse and understanding, most urgently in the case of gross blunders made at the highest levels of state power. I would suggest that the world of practical discourse in any such blunder as the U.S.-sponsored 1961 exile invasion of Fidel Castro's Cuba (Bay of Pigs crisis) focus on the options the foreign policy practitioners saw as open to their choices and the responses they anticipated from the elite and non-elite actors in Cuba can be studied as options were selected and analyses updated. Later, the world of historical discourse can be consulted for ex post facto investigation of the differences between the expectations of the practitioners and the actual consequences of their actions. And as the body of such discourse expands, the scientific mode of discourse can and should seek patterns of failure, and ask such questions as do patterns

AFTERWORD 257

of failure (and of course success) correlate with, and even result from, culture-specific operational codes?

In such work, it must be recognized, not only national cultural operational codes exist: Herbert Spencer (1881a, 1881b) distinguished "militant" and "industrial" types of society; Tom Paine (1791/1792) contrasted "society" with "the state"; Joseph Schumpeter (1919) distinguished between atavistic class ways of thinking and those specific to the rise of capitalist social strata; E. H. Carr (1939) contrasted "Utopian" and "Realist" styles of thought about international relations. Operational code analysis would seem to have a long and durable future, and accordingly Options Analysis likewise.

In sum, it seems to me that there is a lot to be learned from the historical and scientific examination of great blunders in foreign policy and the mindsets that led to them and that Options Analysis augmented with operational code analysis provides a useful set of tools for structuring such study.

This is the right moment, I think, to pass the buck to the reader: You have seen Michael Haas's detailed case for the value of an expanded Options Analysis; and now—Judge for yourself!

David O. Wilkinson

REFERENCES

Carr, Edward Hallett. 1939. *The Twenty Years Crisis, 1919–1939: An Introduction to the Study of International Relations*. London: Macmillan.

Leites, Nathan. 1951. *The Operational Code of the Politburo*. New York: McGraw Hill.

Leites, Nathan. 1953. *A Study of Bolshevism*. Glencoe, IL: Free Press.

Oakeshott, Michael. 1933. *Experience and Its Modes*. Cambridge, UK: Cambridge University Press.

Paine, Thomas. 1791/1792. *Rights of Man*. New York: Grove Press, 2008.

Richardson, Lewis Fry. 1960. *Statistics of Deadly Quarrels*. Chicago: Quadrangle.

Schumpeter, Joseph A. 1919. *Imperialism and Social Classes: Two Essays*. Eastford, CT: Martino, 2014.

Spencer, Herbert. 1881a. The Industrial Type of Society. *The Contemporary Review* 40: 507–533.

Spencer, Herbert. 1881b. The Militant Type of Society. *The Contemporary Review* 40: 337–360.

INDEX

A
Abel, Theodore, 18, 29, 52, 53, 74
academic source, 62
Adams, James Truslow, 14
affective aspects, 52, 53, 55, 58
Afghanistan, 24, 118, 140, 177, 213
Afghan soldiers, 213
Afghan War, 178
Africa, 13, 210
agglutination, 28
aggressiveness, 16, 71
aggressor, 30, 193
Agreed Framework (1994), 172, 174, 175, 181, 184
al-Assad, Bashar, 178
Albania, 211
Albright, Madeleine, 172, 176
Algeria, 7, 12
alienation, 13
alignment status, 53, 61
Allied Powers (World War I), 15, 76
allies, 138, 157, 162, 200, 202, 207, 222, 227

Allison, Graham, 31–34, 40, 55, 56, 71, 74
Aloha, 176, 177
Aloha State. *See* Hawai'i
ambassadors, 52, 73
"America Must Lead Again" (2020), 202
American embassies, 34, 36
American foreign policy, 88, 171, 193, 221, 251
American Revolution, 9
analogical reasoning, 114
anarchy, 7
Angell, Norman, 14
annexation, 16, 212, 216, 217
anomie, 102
anthropologists, 26, 86, 88, 96, 102
Aquinas, Thomas, 8, 13
Arab Spring, 178
Arctic Council, 104
Aristotle, 6
Armageddon, 85
armaments, 15, 18, 215
armies, 10, 220

© The Editor(s) (if applicable) and The Author(s), under exclusive license to Springer Nature Switzerland AG 2023
M. Haas, *Professionalization of Foreign Policy*,
https://doi.org/10.1007/978-3-031-37152-3

260 INDEX

armistice, 15, 24, 40, 53, 55, 171, 172, 181, 187
army morale, 214
arrest, 218
arrest warrant, 218
ASEANization, 168
Association of South East Asian Nations (ASEAN), 155, 157, 168
Athens, 6, 10
atomic bombs, 58
atomization, 141
attacks on civilians, 218
attacks on energy-related infrastructure, 218
Augustine, Bishop of Hippo, 7, 8
Austin, Lloyd, 210, 228
Australia, 162, 211
Austria, 193, 211
Austria-Hungary, 29
authority contracted, 61
Axis of Evil Speech (2002), 173

B
Bacon, Francis, 8
Balance-of-Power Paradigm, 121
Baltic Sea countries, 214
bankruptcy, 175, 196, 214
bargaining, 28, 31, 33, 34, 39, 180, 211, 226
Bateson, Gregory, 26, 56, 87, 96
battlefield, 12, 56, 200, 208
Behavioral research, 35, 36
Belarus, 194, 196, 198, 203, 209, 217, 218
belief system, 92–94, 98, 118
Bentham, Jeremy, 8, 10, 12, 18, 248
Bernoulli, Daniel, 34
Biden Administration, 180, 184, 195, 203–205, 208, 209, 220, 228, 249
Biden, Joseph, Jr., 200

Biegun, Stephen, 184
biological weapons, 212
bipartisanship, 71, 88, 200
biracial ancestry, 177
Bismarck, Otto von, 11–13
"black box", 26, 27, 93
black market, 214
Black Sea, 209–211, 214, 218, 221, 222
Blair, Tony, 113, 118
"bleed Vietnam" policy, 157
Blinken, Antony, 203–205, 211
blitzkrieg, 208, 214
blockades, 222
blunders, 30, 31, 73, 86, 88, 92, 100, 113, 116, 140, 142, 163, 247, 248
Bohlen, Charles "Chip", 73
Bolshevik Revolution, 16, 57–59, 89
Bolshevik Russia, 15
Bolshevism code. *See* Politburo code
Bolton, John, 139, 184
bombs, 58, 219
Bonaparte, Napoléon, 9
Bosnia, 211
Bounded Rationality Paradigm, 141
Brady, Linda, 29
brainwashing, 59
Brandeis, Louis, 14
Brazil, 211
"breadbasket of Europe", 196. *See also* Ukraine
Brecher, Michael, 35
Britain, 15, 52, 74, 75, 194, 203, 218
London, 75
British Commonwealth of Nations, 15
Brody, David, 30
Brown, Jerry, 24
Brummer, Klaus, 40
Brzezinski, Zbigniew, 153
Budapest Memorandum (1994), 194
Buddhists, 158

Bueno de Mesquita, Bruce, 34, 120, 141, 174
Bulgaria, 204, 217
bureaucracy, 33, 213
bureaucratic politics theory, 31
bureaucrats, 33, 86, 101, 167
Burke, Edmund, 7
Burn, C. Delisle, 16
Burns, William, 203
Bush, George H.W., 24, 118, 142, 153, 159, 162, 173, 177, 179, 196

C

Calculations, 5, 9, 25. *See also* rational decisions
California, Los Angeles, 177
Cambodia, 118, 151–155, 157–160, 162–169, 193, 248, 250
  Kingdom of, 151
Cambodian Peace Conference (1989), 152
Cambodian-Vietnamese War, 155, 159
cancer, 198, 228
capital accumulation, 10, 12, 139
capitalism, 8, 11, 12, 16, 123, 157
Carpenter, Michael, 196, 200–202
Carr, E.H., 18, 23
Carter, Jimmy, 34, 117, 118, 142, 153, 158, 172, 181
Castro, Fidel, 32, 118
Catholic Church, 13
Causal analysis, 93, 247
ceasefire, 194
Center for Advanced Study in the Behavioral Sciences, Stanford, 25
Center for Strategic and International Studies, 251
Central Commission for the Navigation of the Rhine, 12
charisma, 200

checks and balances, 7
chemical weapons, 178
chemotherapy, 198
chess, 28
Chicago Haymarket Square, 54, 55, 58, 77
Chicago police, 54, 55, 58
child training, 6
China, 9, 55, 101, 115, 154, 157, 163, 164, 167, 168, 172, 174, 177, 180, 182, 185–187, 206, 211, 213, 216, 217, 219, 251
  Beijing, 163, 181, 182, 217, 219
Churchill, Winston, 198
civilian killings, 197, 213, 221, 228
civilization, 17
civil rights legislation, 146
civil society, 37, 39, 54, 57, 102, 122, 141–144, 146, 156, 163, 199, 202, 222
civil wars, 33, 35, 75, 157, 228
"clash of civilizations, The", 37, 198
class struggle, 26, 90, 94
Clausewitz, Karl von, 12, 18
Clinton, Bill, 113, 172
Clinton, Hillary, 178
code, 89, 90, 94, 96, 98, 100, 117
  macro-level, 87, 88, 121
  meso-level, 90, 96
  micro-level, 87, 90
Code of Hammurabi, 100
coding manual, 93
cognitive aspects, 52, 54, 55, 58
cognitive balance, 95
cognitive complexity, 55
cognitive consistency, 34, 113, 120
cognitive decisions, 99, 116, 122
cognitive map, 96
"cognitive revolution", 99
Cold War, 24–26, 35, 36, 59, 60, 85, 88, 92, 94, 98–100, 103, 113, 115, 116, 119, 123, 140, 147,

262 INDEX

157, 164, 165, 175, 207, 249, 250
Colombo plan, 168
Come Back Alive Foundation, 213
comedians, 200
communication reduction, 61
communications satellite, 180
Community building paradigm, 23, 87, 90, 101, 123, 139
commutation, 54
comparative politics, 88
compartmentalization, 113, 155, 177
"comprehensive strategic partnership", 163
compromise, 10, 32, 33, 56, 75
computer programs, 119
concepts, 27, 29, 31, 33, 37, 51, 60, 63, 88, 93, 101, 112, 115, 119, 121, 251
Concert of Europe, 10, 12
Condorcet, Marquis de, 8
conflict, 7, 25, 29, 37, 71, 93, 95, 103, 115, 119, 155, 165, 167, 168, 210, 212, 220, 221, 227
Congress of Vienna, 9, 10
conscription, 197
conservatism, 7
constructivism, 37–39, 120
constructs. *See* concepts
Contending Theories of International Relations, 32
content analysis, 24–26, 29, 90, 94, 112, 117–120, 123
continuousness, 62
control over events, 53, 61
Convention on Duties and Rights of States in the Event of Civil War (1928), 157
correct intelligence, 61
Correlates of War Project, 30
correlations, Pearsonian, 63, 72

corruption, 14, 154, 169, 175, 201, 202
Cost–Benefit Paradigm, 138
cost effectiveness, 26
Council on Foreign Relations, 15, 24
crisis, 25, 29, 34, 63, 99, 167, 250
crisis decisions, 29, 63
Crisis model, 72
criteria, 15, 25, 27, 30–32, 35, 63, 105, 135, 136, 138–140, 142, 143, 145–147, 158, 221, 222, 226, 248, 250–252
cross testing. *See* theory testing
cruciality, 54, 63, 71
Cuba, 32, 52, 53, 59, 71, 73
Bay of Pigs, 32, 57, 75
Cuban, 32, 40, 56, 75, 167
Cuban Missiles Crisis, 32, 40, 55, 56, 122
cultural anthropology, 86
cultural change, 18
cultural code, 86, 87, 89
Cultural exchange model, 72
cultural exchanges, 179
cultural patterns, 17
cultural similarity, 54, 63, 71
culture, 37, 85, 87, 90, 97, 102, 247
cumulativity, 62
cyberattacks, 182
cybernetic, 33, 38
Czech Republic, 217, 219
Czech troops, 75

D
Dahl, Robert, 28, 33
Darwin, Charles, 11, 12
databases, 27, 60
death sentence, 54, 59
decision latitude, 57, 61
decision-making, 7–9, 16–18, 25, 26, 28–32, 34, 35, 39, 40, 51–54,

56, 59, 60, 62, 63, 70, 71, 86, 89, 92, 94, 96, 97, 99, 111, 113, 114, 119, 120, 122, 123, 136, 141, 145–147, 158, 168, 225, 247, 248, 250, 252
decision-making body, size of, 57
decision-making cycle, 51
decision-making stages, 26, 99, 121
Decision Pad, 145–147, 159, 225, 248, 249, 251, 252
decision target, 112, 114
decision time, 55, 61
decoding, 23, 24, 54, 56
"Defending Democracy Against Its Enemies" (2018), 200
demilitarization, 186, 211
democracy, 6, 15, 37, 98, 113, 140, 157, 178, 197, 200, 202, 209, 222, 225, 226
Democracy Building, 144
Democratic Party, 178
Democratic People's Republic of Korea (DPRK). *See* North Korea
Democratic Republic of Vietnam. *See* North Vietnam
democratization, 252
demographics, 30
"de-Nazification", 209
Deng Xiaoping, 103
denuclearization, 172, 174, 175, 178, 181, 182, 184, 185, 187, 249
"denuclearization first" policy, 184
dependency theory, 139
deportations, 218
desires for achievement, 61
desires for affiliation, 61
desires for power, 63
détente, 95, 164, 166–168
deterrence, 29, 99, 116, 138, 196, 210, 222, 251
Deterrence Paradigm, 29, 35, 99, 137
Dewey, John, 16

dictators, 140
Diderot, Denis, 8
Diesing, Paul, 34, 116
diplomacy, 10, 55, 99, 100, 113, 138, 140, 168, 172, 177, 183, 185, 202, 205, 211, 215, 220, 221, 226
"dirty bomb", 225
disequilibrium, 18
diversionary theory, 16
Dobbs v Jackson (2022), 101
Đỗ Mười, 154
Donetsk People's Republic, 206
"doublethink", 86
Dougherty, James, 9, 16, 32
drones, 207, 213, 216, 217
Dr. Strangelove, 30
Dulles, Allen, 92
Dulles, John Foster, 75, 92, 95
Dunant, Henry, 12, 13
Durkheim, Émile, 13, 87, 123, 141
dynamic equilibrium, 87
dynastic states, 17

E
Eagleton, Clyde, 16
East Coast scholars, 24
Eastern Europe, 24, 186, 202, 228
Easter Rebellion (1916), 112
Economic development, 144
economic sanctions, 174, 211, 222
economists, 26, 121, 139, 208
Egypt, 57, 58, 75, 211, 213
  Aswan Dam, 57, 58
Eisenhower Administration, 75
Eisenhower, Dwight, 24, 73, 92
election (1993), Cambodia, 162
election (2024), Russia, 198
electricity, 13, 173, 219
elite political culture, 96
elites, 6, 16, 208

264 INDEX

embargo, 210, 227
emotional decisions, 9
emotional ties, 17
empirical theories, 40
"employer mandate", 177
enemies, 103, 152
Engels, Friedrich, 11, 123
England. *See* Britain
Enlightenment, 8, 9, 28
entrepreneurs, 9, 26
Epistemic communities, 104
Erdogan, Tayyip, 211
Erikson, Erik H., 38, 115
Eritrea, 217
escalation, 28, 29, 31, 60, 207, 213, 214, 220, 227, 249
Essence of Decision, 31
Estonia, 217
Europe, 9–11, 18, 76, 123, 215, 228
European Commission of the Danube, 12
European Union, 139, 199, 205, 211, 215, 226
Evaluative Aspects, 53, 54, 56, 59
events data, 28
exploitation, 11
extent of documentation, 60, 62

F
factor analysis, 60, 62, 63, 71, 119
factories, 10, 13, 179
Falkowski, Lawrence S., 112, 113, 116
"false flag", 186, 204
feasibility, 33, 35, 38, 140, 142, 178, 197, 222, 225, 248, 251
feudalism, 12
fighter jets, 207, 219
Fine, John S., 59, 76
Finland, 210
Finlandization, 165, 168

First Amendment Liberalism, 102
foreign aid, 138
foreign policy analysis, 5, 6, 17, 23, 27, 28, 34, 36, 37, 39, 87, 135, 145, 247, 248, 250, 251
foreign policy decision-making, 28, 63, 99, 103, 135, 138, 140, 142, 145, 151, 248
foreign policy decisions, 7, 9, 29, 59, 60, 100, 135, 139, 147, 247, 248, 252
foreign policy doctrine, 100
foreign stimulus, 54
formality, 62, 63
fossil fuels, 197
Fourteen Points, 15
framing, 33
France, 9, 12, 14, 15, 29, 75, 140, 151, 152, 154, 162, 194, 203
Frank, Andre Gunder, 139
"free riders", 177
free trade, 12, 15, 104
French Indochina, 151
French revolution, 9
French Union, 151
Freud, Sigmund, 17
frustration, 16, 17, 63, 71, 72, 112
frustration perceptions, 61
Fukuyama, Francis, 37
Full Employment Act (1946), 58, 74
functional theory, 23
Fundamental Nature of the Political Universe, 93
Fundamental Sources of Conflict, 93

G
G-7 meeting, 208
Gaddis, John Lewis, 103, 119
Galeotti, Mark, 195, 197
game theory, 28, 30, 116
Gandhi, Mohandas, 17

INDEX

Garden of Eden, 7
Gates, Robert, 177, 178
Geneva Conference (1954), 154
Geneva Convention for the
   Amelioration of the Condition of
   the Wounded in Armies in the
   Field, 13
genocide, 152–154
geopolitical codes, 102
George, Alexander, 33, 89, 95, 97,
   111, 116–119, 141, 250
Georgia (country), 177
German colonies, 14
Germany, 11, 14, 15, 29, 54, 75,
   193, 194, 196, 203, 213, 218,
   227, 228
   Berlin Wall, 36, 113
   Nazi, 18, 24, 76
global environment, 102
global governance, 23, 37, 104, 139
globalization theory, 37, 139
"Golden Age", 7
Gorbachëv, Dimitri, 165
Gorer, Geoffrey, 89
governmental politics model. *See*
   bureaucratic politics theory
government leader, 86, 123, 143
"grand design", 167
"great departure", 52
great powers, 137
Great Recession (2008–2009), 177
Greece, 6, 10
Greek international system, 6
Greenfield, Kent Roberts, 60
groupthink, 32, 33, 86, 141, 143,
   250
guerrilla forces, 209
Guetzkow, Harold, 28
guidance, 24, 58
Guterres, António, 210, 211, 218

H

Haas, Ernst, 23
Haines, Avril, 203
Hanoi Summit (2018), 184
Harvard University, 178
Hawai'i, 176, 180
Habermas, Jürgen, 123, 141
Hebrew, 202
hegemonism, 121
Hegemony Paradigm, 137
Helsinki Agreement (1975), 193
Helvétius, Claude, 8
Hermann, Charles, 29
Hermann, Margaret, 32, 100
hierarchical resolution, 57
hierarchy, 59
Hiroshima. *See* Japan
historians, 16, 58
History of the Peloponnesian War, The,
   6
Hitler, Adolf, 52, 53, 55–59, 75, 195,
   216
Hobbes, Thomas, 7
Holbrooke, Richard, 177
Holsti, Ole, 30, 31, 38, 51, 92–95,
   97–100, 111, 113–117, 119, 250
horse trading, 168
hospitals, 214
hostility perceptions, 31
Houghton, David, 40, 145
House, Colonel Edward, 14, 95
"How to Stand Up to the Kremlin"
   (2018), 200
humanitarian intervention, 102, 155
human rights, 37, 95, 98, 102, 113,
   140, 157, 180, 218
Hume, David, 7
Hungary, 204, 211, 217
Hun Manet, 162
Hun Sen, 152, 159, 162, 163,
   166–169
"hunting rifles", 217

266 INDEX

Huntington, Samuel, 37, 198
hypotheses, 96, 113

I
idealism, 18, 24
ideological, 27
ideology, 25, 36, 103
immigrants, 229
imperial rule, 10
implementation speed, 58, 62
India, 9, 17, 211, 217
Indonesia, 162, 168, 176
Industrial Revolution, 11
    Second, 13
inertia, 33
inflation, 221, 227
input/output ratio, 56
input intensity, 56, 71
input load, 55, 71
Input range, 56
Inquiry, The, 15
institutions
    political, 18
    social, 18
instrumental parameters of
    decision-making, 98
intelligence estimates, 52
inter-branch process model, 39
intergovernmental organizations, 30,
    40, 104, 114, 175
International Atomic Energy Agency
    (IAEA), 173–175, 179, 211, 230
International Convention against the
    Recruitment, Use, Financing and
    Training of Mercenaries (1989),
    212
International Criminal Court, 218,
    229
international investment, 102
international law, 10, 16, 101, 102,
    104, 136, 140, 195, 197, 199,
    222

international order, liberal, 16, 23,
    103, 140
International Politics, 16
international relations, 15, 16, 27,
    251
international relations textbooks, 39
International Studies Association
    (ISA), 27
international system
    bipolar, 137
    multipolar, 137
    unipolar, 137
international trade, 9, 187, 202
international waters, 227
internment camps, 56, 77
intraorganizational consonance, 57,
    71
*Introduction to the Study of
    International Organization*, 16
"invisible hand", 8
Iran, 173, 178, 213
Iran, Tehran, 34
Iraq, 24, 140, 173, 177, 178
Iraq War, 177
Ireland, 211
Irish Americans, 95
Islam, 9
isms, 39
Israel, 9, 157, 211
Italian War of Independence, 12
Italy, 12, 15
    Solferino, 12

J
Jakarta Informal Meeting, 166
Janis, Irving, 32, 33, 86
Japan, 14, 53, 74, 76, 151, 171, 173,
    174, 184, 211
    Hiroshima, 53, 58, 74, 76
    Nagasaki, 58
Japanese Americans, 77

INDEX

Japanese Peace Treaty, 56, 74
Jervis, Robert, 31, 73, 137
"Jews will not replace us", 200
jigsaw puzzle, 39
jihad, 9
Johnson, Lyndon, 33, 111, 118, 152
Joint Statement (2005), 174, 186
judicial activism, 101
just war, 8

K

Kaarbo, Juliet, 38
Kahn, Herman, 30
Kant, Immanuel, 8
Kaplan, Abraham, 25, 28
Kazakhstan, 194
Kellerman, Barbara, 32
Kelman, Herbert, 16, 25
Kennedy Administration, 32, 52, 53, 56, 57, 73, 75, 76
Kennedy, John F., 32
Kenya, 176
Khmer Empire, 152
Khmer Rouge, 118, 142, 151–155, 157–159, 162–169, 248
kidnapping, 218
"killing fields", 155
Kim Il-Sung, 172, 175
Kim Jong-Il, 118, 175, 176, 179
Kim Jong-Un, 176, 181, 182
Kissinger, Henry, 111, 117
kleptocracy, 201
Klintworth, Gary, 155
Kluckholm, Clyde, 90
Koiso, Kuniaki, 74
Korea, Kaeson, 58, 76
Koreanization, 165
Korean War (1950–1953), 53, 54, 59, 76
Korea, Panmunjom, 57, 58, 76
Kosovo, 211

Kozak, Dmitry, 205
Kuleba, Dmytro, 206

L

Laos, 57, 75, 151, 168
Lasswell, Harold, 23–26, 28, 90, 142
Latin America, 212
Latvia, 217
Lavrov, Sergei, 205, 211
Lazarsfeld, Paul, 29, 122
League of Nations, 15
Leap Day deal, proposed (2012), 180
learning, 98, 113, 114, 119, 165, 198
learning rate, 56, 70
Lebow, Richard Ned, 34, 251
Legal Engineering Paradigm, 136, 140
legitimization, 32, 164
Leites, Nathan, 25, 26, 89–92, 94–100, 105, 113, 117
length of description, 60
Lenin, Vladimir, 15, 26, 53, 75, 89
Lerner, Daniel, 25, 142
level of analysis, 54, 93, 139
level of problem, 61
Levy, Jack, 34, 142
Liberalism, 37, 93, 120
Libya, 184
Lieber Code, 13
Lieber, Francis, 13
Lindblom, Charles, 25, 27, 28
Lippmann, Walter, 14
Lithuania, 193, 217
"Little Russia", 198
Lloyd George, David, 15
Locke, John, 7
logistics, 31, 141, 142, 197–199, 209, 213, 214
"love letters", 183
Lowell, A. Lawrence, 14
Luhansk People's Republic, 206

268 INDEX

Lundberg, Craig, 31
lust for conquest, 7
Lvova-Belova, Maria, 218

M
MacArthur, Douglas, 54, 55, 57, 76
Macron, Emmanuel, 206
Madison, James, 7
Majak, Roger, 31
malaise, 201
Malenkov, Gregori, 90
Mali, 217
Malici, Akan, 98, 115–118, 120–122
mandates, 15
"manifest destiny", 198
Mao Zedong, 103, 118
marriage, 12, 101
martial law, 212
Marxian Paradigm, 26, 90, 123
Marx, Karl, 11, 13, 14, 90, 123
Mass Society, 144
Mass Society Paradigm, 102, 122, 141
master beliefs, 93, 114
Maurice A., East, 28
maximizing, 27, 38, 63, 71
McClelland, Charles, 27, 28
McClelland, David, 28, 142
McDonalds, 228
Mead, George Herbert, 38, 115, 122
Mearsheimer, John, 37, 194, 207
media, 102, 141, 144, 197, 199, 222
mediation, 155, 212
Merton, Robert K., 86, 100, 101, 115
metacommunication, 26, 56
metaconcepts, 51
Metternich, Klemens von, 9, 10
México, 14
micromanagement, 176
microtheories, 40
Middle Ages, 13

military bases, 147
military conquest, 9
military draft, 58
military secrets, 208
military training, 75, 194
Milley, Mark, 215
Mill, John Stuart, 11
Mills, C. Wright, 24
"mindguards", 86
Minsk Agreement (2014), 194
Minsk Agreement II (2015), 194
Mintz, Alex, 38, 142, 250
mirroring, 114
miscalculations, 5, 16, 121
misperceptions, 16, 31, 56, 73, 112, 250
missiles, 59, 71, 73, 172, 176, 182, 184, 214–216, 218, 219, 225, 227
missile testing, 180
Mitrany, David, 23, 37, 104, 139
mokusatsu, 54
Moldova, 211
monarchs, 6
Mongols, 193
monopolies, 11, 138
Monroney, Mike, 74
Moon Jae-In, 183, 186
Morgenstern, Oscar, 30
Morgenthau, Hans, 24, 35, 103, 120, 137
Moser, Sheila, 35
Mueller, John, 33
multidimensionality, 39, 100
multi-issue problem, 61
multilevel analysis, 39
multiparty system, 166
multiple advocacy, 33, 250
Munich Security Conference (2022), 206
Murray, Henry, 28
Murray, James E., 74

Musk, Elon, 225
myth systems, 100

N
Napoléon III, 12
national culture, 26, 32, 96, 97, 117
national identity, 10
nationalism, 10, 16, 167
national security, 102, 147, 153, 184, 221
needs for achievement, 55, 70, 113, 178
needs for affiliation, 55
needs for power, 55, 95
neofunctional theory, 23
neoliberal theory, 37
neorealism, 36, 37
Neumann, John von, 30
neutralism, 75
neutrality, 13, 213
neutralization, 167, 211
"new wars", 198
"new world order", 37, 196
New York City, 187
New York Philharmonic Orchestra, 181
New York Public Library, 14
Nicaragua, 217
Nietzsche, Friedrich, 7
1984 (1949), 86
Nixon, Richard, 152
"no-fly zone" (proposed), 207, 225
noise level, 54, 61
Nonaligned Movement (NAM), 167
non-Communist Cambodian resistance, 163
normalization of relations, 173, 187
Norodom, King, 151
North America, 198
North Atlantic Treaty Organization (NATO), 194, 196, 197, 199, 201–207, 210, 212–214, 219

Secretary General, 222
North Korea
Pyongyang, 76, 172, 173, 175, 180–182, 185–187, 193, 249
Yongbyon, 174, 175
North, Robert, 27, 29–31
North Vietnam, 151, 154
Norway, 52, 54, 74
"nosebleed" strike, proposed, 182
nuclear power, 88, 171–173, 207, 249
nuclear stockpile, 207
nuclear testing, 180
nuclear weapons, 25, 172, 173, 193, 194, 207, 210, 212, 214, 215, 218, 225, 227
Nye, Joseph, 37, 138, 139, 147, 250, 251

O
Obama administration, 179–181, 185, 186, 196, 201
Obama, Barack, 175, 176, 179
Obamacare, 177
Oblique rotation, 63
Occidental College, 177
officiality, 57, 63
Oglesby, Richard, 59, 77
oligarchies, 138
Olympic Games, 157
ongoing violence, 53, 70
open agreements, 15
Operational Code Analysis and Foreign Policy Roles (2022), 116
operational codes, 26, 39, 87–89, 93, 95–97, 99, 102, 105, 111–116, 120, 122, 123, 136, 138, 153, 171, 193, 195, 247, 248, 252
opinions, 86, 105, 113, 123, 200
Options Analysis, 145–147, 158, 163, 171, 248, 250–252
organizational process theory, 32

270 INDEX

Orwell, George, 86

P

Pakistan, 217
Paracel Islands, 167
paradigms, 35, 36, 40, 121–123,
135–139, 142, 145, 248, 251
Paris Peace Conference (1919), 15
participant observation, 86–89, 96
Pathet Lao, 75
peace, 10, 14, 15, 17, 18, 23, 29, 30,
37, 74, 75, 140, 155, 157, 159,
162, 164, 167, 172, 178, 181,
187, 211, 215, 217, 220, 225,
247, 249
peace agreement, 17, 140, 172, 181,
187, 215, 225
peacebuilding, 140
Peace of Westfalia 1648, 167, 195
peace talks, 215
Pearl Harbor, 18, 56, 58, 74, 77
Pence, Mike, 184
penetration, 59
Pennsylvania, 59, 76
People's Republic of Kampuchea
(PRK), 154, 158
Peres, Shimon, 118
Perfectibility Theory, 8
personality needs, 112. *See also* needs
for achievement; needs for
affiliation; needs for power
pessimism, 8, 219, 220, 250
Pfaltzgraff, Robert, 9, 16, 32
Phạm Văn Đồng, 154, 155
philanthropy, 8
Philipps, Warren, 36
Philosophical Parameters of
Decision-Making, 98
Plato, 6
plebiscites, 15, 212
plutonium, 172, 174, 179

Poland, 53, 58, 75, 193, 204, 207,
214, 216, 217, 219
police, 10, 54, 77, 103, 212
poliheuristic theory, 38, 142
Politburo Code, 89, 95, 101
political culture, 6, 88–90, 96, 100
political parties, 96, 102, 121, 141,
222
political personality, 100
political process model, 39
political science, 15, 95, 121, 136
political scientists, 27, 34, 35, 115,
118
political suppression, 201
Pol Pot, 157, 164, 166
polyarchy, 28, 57
Pompeo, Mike, 184
Poor Laws, 10
Pope Francis, 220
postbehavioralism, 35
Post, Emily, 87
Potsdam Declaration, 54, 74, 76
Potter, Pitnam, 16
power, 6, 10, 17, 18, 24, 27, 28, 30,
31, 33, 35, 37, 54, 71, 93, 113,
114, 136, 137, 152, 154, 156,
167, 172, 193, 197, 211, 216,
222, 225, 228, 248, 250
Power and Society (1950), 25
power balance, 30, 137
Power Balancing Paradigm, 120
power stations, 214
power superiority, 54
Power transition theory, 137
pragmatism, 70
precedent, 70, 141
precedent invoked, 61
preconditions, 182, 184, 187
predictions, 123
predispositions, 155
preemptive war, 206, 210
presidential nominations, 54

Pressure Group Paradigm, 121
pressure groups, 33, 102, 141, 144, 222
prestige, 35, 139, 140, 221, 222, 248, 250, 251
pre-theory, 29, 62, 91, 92
prices, 11, 76, 197, 201, 227, 228
prime ministers, 12, 15, 143, 252
primitive instincts, 17
prior concern, 52, 63
prior planning, 53
prisoner's dilemma, 30
prisoners of war (POWs), 76, 194
prisoner swap, 220
probability of office-holding, 53
procedurality, 62
process tracing, 99, 116, 118
Procter and Gamble, 208
professionalization, 135, 145, 147, 151, 248, 250, 252
progressive movement, 14
proletariat, 90, 94
promotive, 59, 63
propaganda, 23, 37, 39, 198, 209, 212, 213
prospect theory, 34, 70, 138, 142
prosperity, 139, 155, 157, 175, 201, 202
protesters, 58, 77, 228
Pruitt, Dean, 30
Prussia, 11
psychological needs, 6, 28, 112, 157, 178
Psychological Needs Paradigm, 142
psychologists, 16, 26, 38
psychology, 55, 71, 113, 120
  cognitive, 112
public interest organizations, 178
public opinion, 15, 29, 33, 94, 122, 210
puppet ruler, 206

Putin, Vladimir, 118, 194, 195, 206, 225, 228
Pye, Lucian, 88, 103, 112

Q
Q-Sort Method, 60
quadripartite government, 166
quarantine, 59, 73

R
Rabin, Yitzhak, 118
range of alternatives, 57
rape, 218
Rapoport, David, 30, 120
ratification, 74
Rational Actor Paradigm, 39
Rational Choice Paradigm. See
  Rational Actor Paradigm
rational decisions, 121, 122
Reagan Administration, 153, 155, 158, 159
Reagan recession (1982), 157
Reagan, Ronald, 142, 153, 155
realism, 24, 27, 35–37, 93, 120
Red Cross Convention (1864), 13
"red line", 210
refugees, 75, 154, 208, 210, 214, 226
Reisman, W.Michael, 100–102, 104
reliability, 60, 119, 159, 182
relocation, 204, 218, 229
repatriation, 59, 76
representative government, 9, 10
Republican Party, 15, 157, 227
Republic of Korea. See South Korea
republics, 194
Resource Mobilization Paradigm, 140, 251
respectfulness, 180
reunification, 179, 186
revocability, 58
Ricardo, David, 10

272 INDEX

rice farmers, 164
Richardson, Lewis Fry, 72
Rickman, John, 26, 89
risk propensity, 55
"road map", 172, 174, 184
Robinson, James, 31, 59, 74
Rockefeller Foundation, 24
"rogue states", 173
Role theory, 38, 115, 116, 122
Romania, 204, 217
Roosevelt, Franklin Delano, 56, 58
Rosenau, James, 23, 29, 37, 51, 59, 73, 92, 104
Rourke, Francis, 33
Ruesch, Jürgen, 26
rules-based international order, 13, 15, 23, 103, 140, 203
Russett, Bruce, 29, 36, 37, 140
Russia
  Crimea bridge, 214
  Kremlin, 92, 194, 196, 201, 203, 209, 214, 249
  Moscow, 24, 90, 182, 194, 203, 208, 213, 218, 228
  Murmansk, 56, 75
  Siberia, 54, 57, 75
  Vladivostok, 75
Russian "reservists", 212
Russian culture, 89
Russian Empire, 195, 198, 228
Russian Federal Security Service, 196
Russian Federation. *See* Russia
Russian military doctrine, 207
Russian Navy, 227
Russian Provisional Government, 77

S
"safe for democracy", 14
San Mateo, California, 146
satisficing, 32, 250
Saudi Arabia, 211, 212

Savage, Leonard, 34
Schafer, Mark, 38, 99, 100, 111–122
Schelling, Thomas, 29, 137
Schisms, 87
Schlesinger, Arthur, Jr., 32, 52, 53, 75
Schultz, George, 155
Schuman, Frederick, 16
science
  applied, 123, 147, 250, 251
  empirical, 147
  theoretical, 24
scientific methods, 23
Scottish Americans, 95
Scott, James, 13
scree test, 63
security
  economic, 38
  military, 98
  social, 38
Selective Service Act (1950), 74
Selectorate Paradigm, 141
self-aggrandizement model, 39
self-determination of peoples, 15, 17
self-esteem, 55
self-interest, 7, 10, 11, 38
Serbia, 29
sexual violence, 218
Shawcross, William, 165
Sherman, Wendy, 204
Shoigu, Sergei, 205
Shotwell, James, 14
Sihanouk, Norodom, 152, 155, 158, 159, 162, 164, 166
Simmons, Beth, 140
Simon, Herbert, 27, 32, 97
simulation, 28, 251
sin, 7
Singapore Declaration (2018), 181, 183
Singer J., David, 30, 91, 93
Six-Party Talks (2003–2009), 174, 179, 180, 182, 185

Slovakia, 217, 219
Smith, Adam, 8
Snyder, Glenn, 34
Snyder, Richard, 26, 51, 92
Social and Cultural Dynamics, 17
social class
   educated upper, 5
   lower, 5
   middle class, 10
   working class, 11, 15
social cooperation, 11
Social Darwinism, 11, 12, 116, 121
Social Exchange Paradigm, 121
socialism, 11, 155
Socialist Party, 12
Socialization
   adaptation, 115
   fundamental, 115
   superficial, 115
Socialization paradigm, 38, 39, 103,
      112, 114, 115, 122, 123
sociologists, 26, 88
sociometric change, 58, 70
"soft power", 138, 139
solidarity
   mechanical, 87
   organic, 87
Son Sann, 158, 163, 164, 166
Sorokin, Pitirim, 17, 18, 37
"soul of America", 200, 221
South Africa, 211
South China Sea, 167
Southeast Asia, 159, 167
South Korea, 24, 74, 171–173, 175,
      179, 181, 182, 184, 186, 187,
      211
South Pacific, 14
sovereignty, 172, 194, 195, 199, 204,
      209
Soviet bloc, 200
Soviet Union, 24, 73, 88
   Stalingrad, 55–57, 59, 76

Spanish-American War, 16
Sparta, 6
"special military operation", 206
Spencer, Herbert, 12, 14
sphere of competence, 52
Spinoza, Baruch, 7
sports cooperation, 179
Spratly Islands, 167
Sprout, Harold, 27
Sprout, Margaret, 27
spurious relationships, 63
spy aircraft, 218
stabilizing, 59
Stalin, Josef, 26, 53, 89
standard operating procedures, 32
Stanford University, 25
Starbucks, 208
"state sponsor of terrorism", 225
Statistics of Deadly Quarrels (1960),
      72
steering, 33, 114, 172
Steinbruner, John, 33, 35, 138
stereotypic decoding, 56, 62
stimulus $\rightarrow$ response model, 31
"strategic patience", 180–182
stress, 29, 30, 33, 34, 139
structural aspects, 53, 54, 57, 59
structuralism, 37
structural realism, 99
Structural theory, 7
structuredness, 62
Study of Bolshevism, A (1953), 26, 89
Study of War, A (1942), 18
success, 34, 58, 104, 178, 187, 213,
      218
Suez Canal, 56, 75
Summit for Democracy, 202
summit meeting, 203
"sunshine policy", 181, 182, 186
Sun Tzu, 12, 18
superego, 112
supranational community, 18

274 INDEX

Surovikin, Sergei, 216
surplus value, 11
Suzuki, Baron Kantarō, 53, 74, 76
Sweden, 210
Switzerland, 211
Syria, 178, 199, 216, 217

T

Taiwan, 76, 186, 251
Taliban, 213
talkathons, 56
tanks, 213, 215, 216, 219, 220
tariffs, 207
tension management, 5
Terhune, Kenneth, 32
territorial occupation, 30
terrorism, 174
Teune, Henry, 35
Thailand, 151–154, 163, 165
The Art of War, 12
The Descent of Man in Relation to Sex (1871), 12
Theis, Cameron, 38, 115
The Operational Code of the Politburo (1951), 26, 89
theory building, 34, 38, 250
Theory of International Politics, 36
theory testing, 37
The Policy Sciences, 25
The Ugly American (1958), 169
The War Trap, 34
threat of violence, 55, 71
Thucydides, 6, 24
Tillerson, Rex, 182, 184
time pressure, 53, 63
Tōjō, Hideki, 74
tolerance of ambiguity, 55, 70
top-down rule, 11
torture, 102, 218
totalitarian state, 175
"total war", 197

tourism, 179, 186
Trading with the Enemy Act (1917), 180
transcience, 62
treaties, 10, 12, 13, 136, 140, 204
Treaty of Versailles, 15
Treaty on the Non-Proliferation of Nuclear Weapons (NPT), 172–174
Tribe, Laurence, 178
Triumphalism, 144
troop mobilization, 14, 54, 56, 57, 74, 159
truckers, 76
Truman, Harry, 53, 74, 76
Trump Administration, 180, 184, 196, 200, 229
Trump, Donald, 142, 181, 182, 194, 200, 202, 249
Truss, Liz, 215
trust, 10, 53, 71, 123, 185
Turkey, 207, 210, 211, 218, 229
turning point, 58, 63
Tversky, Amos, 34, 138
Twenty Years Crisis, 18

U

U-Boat, 75
Ukraine
  Avdiivka, 218
  Bakhmut, 218
  Crimea, 194, 196, 201, 209, 212, 214, 216, 217, 225, 229
  Donbas, 194, 196, 198, 206, 207, 216–218
  Donetsk, 206, 212, 227
  Kherson, 212, 214
  Kupiansk, 218
  Kyiv, 177, 194, 205, 206, 208, 209, 213, 216, 249
  Lyman, 218

Mariupol, 209, 217
Odessa, 227
Snake Island, 227
Soledar, 218
Zaporizhzhia, 229
Zaporizhzhia nuclear plant, 230
Ukraine War, 185, 193, 195
Ukrainian cities, 214
uncertainty, 5, 29, 219
United Arab Emirates, 216
United Nations
  General Assembly, 159, 167, 217
  Human Rights Council, 218
  Secretary-General, 155, 210, 211,
    217, 229
  Security Council, 155, 171, 176,
    180, 182, 185, 211, 218
United Nations Charter, 101, 102
United Nations civil service, 101
United Nations Transitional Authority
  for Cambodia (UNTAC), 162
United States
  Central Intelligence Agency, 153
  Chief of Staff, 205
  Congress, 59
  Congress, Select Intelligence
    Committees, 157
  Department of Defense, 147
  Director of National Intelligence,
    203
  Equal Employment Opportunity
    Commission Equal
    Employment Opportunity
    Commission, 146
  European Command, 204
  House of Representatives, 76, 214
  International Development
    Association, 59
  National Security Adviser, 153
  Secretary of State, 75
  Senate, 73, 74
  Supreme Court, 77, 101

United States Institute of Peace, 185
United States Steel Corporation, 76
Universal Postal Union (UPU), 13,
  104
University of Chicago, 95
University of Wales, 16
unlawful confinement, 218
Unwritten constitution, 101
Utilitarianism, 11
Utopia, 18

V
validity, 117–119
variables
  dependent, 52, 53, 55, 58–60, 71,
    121
  independent, 29, 52
Varimax rotation, 63
vassal states, 9
Verbs-in-Context (VICs) system, 117
verstehen, 89, 91, 94
victory, 29, 166, 205, 206, 212, 214,
  217, 220
  total, 210, 222
Viet Cong, 36
Vietminh, 75
Vietnam
  democratic republic of, 154
  Hanoi, 151, 152, 154, 155, 157,
    184, 193
  People's Army of, 154, 162, 163
  republic of, 152, 153, 163
  Saigon, 36, 152
Vietnamese Civil War, 151
violent decision, 72
violent option considered, 62
Virginia, Charlottesville, 200
Võ Nguyên Giáp, 162

W
wages, 15

276 INDEX

Wagner Group, 212
Waldheim, Kurt, 155
Walker, Stephen, 105, 111–113, 116, 120, 122
Wallace, Ben, 205
Waltz, Kenneth, 6, 7, 36, 93
war, 9, 10, 13, 14. *See also* specific wars
  decisions for, 7, 29
  nuclear, 24, 25, 30, 95
war crimes, 13, 197, 199, 209, 210, 217, 222, 225
war crimes trials, 199, 222
"war criminal", 209, 229
warfare, submarine, 14, 75
wargames, 172, 173, 181, 251
warning signs decoded, 61
war of attrition, 197, 220
wealth, 9, 10, 24, 28, 138, 139, 187, 193, 222
wealth, redistribution of, 9
weapons of mass destruction, 212, 218
Weber, Marx, 14, 18
we-feeling. *See* groupthink
welfare state, 9, 12
Wendt, Alexander, 37, 38
West Coast scholars, 27
Western bloc, 25, 36, 140
wheat, 210, 227

White House, 24, 95, 175, 177, 182
Whyte, William H., Jr., 32, 86
Wilhelm, Kaiser, 29
Wilkenfeld, Jonathan, 35
Wilson Administration, 75
Wilson, Woodrow, 14, 17, 52, 53, 75, 95
wordcounting, 123
World War I, 14–17, 23, 29, 123, 215
World War II, 5, 18, 23, 25, 58, 74, 104, 151, 171
World War III, 88, 99, 230
Wright, Quincy, 17, 18, 31

X
Xi Jinping, 118, 219

Y
Yale University, 25
Yanukovych, Victor, 194, 196
Yonai, Mitsumasa, 74

Z
Zelensky, Volodymyr, 198–200, 203–205, 207–209, 211, 213–219, 221, 225, 226, 230
Zimmerman telegram, 14

Printed in the United States
by Baker & Taylor Publisher Services